THE MACMILLAN COMPANY
NEW YORK · BOSTON · CHICAGO · DALLAS
ATLANTA · SAN FRANCISCO

MACMILLAN AND CO., Limited
LONDON · BOMBAY · CALCUTTA · MADRAS
MELBOURNE

THE MACMILLAN COMPANY
OF CANADA, Limited
TORONTO

THE
ROYAL PLAY
OF
Macbeth

KING JAMES VI OF SCOTLAND AND I OF ENGLAND

THE
ROYAL PLAY
OF
Macbeth

When, why, and how it was
written by Shakespeare

BY

HENRY N. PAUL

NEW YORK
THE MACMILLAN COMPANY
1950

I regard the tragedy of "Macbeth," upon the whole, as the greatest treasure of our dramatic literature. . . . In the grandeur of tragedy "Macbeth" has no parallel, till we go back to . . . the Attic stage. . . . In one respect, the tragedy of "Macbeth" always reminds me of Aeschylus's poetry. It has scenes and conceptions absolutely too bold for representation. . . . In like manner, there are parts of "Macbeth" which I delight to read much more than to see in the theatre. . . . Nevertheless, I feel no inconsistency in reverting from these remarks to my first assertion, that, all in all, "Macbeth" is our greatest possession in dramatic poetry.

Thomas Campbell, Life of Mrs. Siddons (1834), Vol. II, pp. 6–9.

The majority of readers, I believe, assign to Macbeth, which seems to have been written about 1606, the pre-eminence among the works of Shakespeare. The great epic drama . . . deserves, in my own judgment, the post it has attained, as being, in the language of Drake, "the greatest effort of our author's genius, the most sublime and impressive drama which the world has ever beheld."

Henry Hallam, Introduction to the Literature of Europe (1854), Vol. III, p. 87.

I think nothing equals Macbeth. It is wonderful. . . .

Abraham Lincoln, Complete Works, Vol. IX, p. 85.

PREFACE

Shakespeare's plays mean what they meant when he wrote them, and that is what we seek to know. To do this it helps to know what ideas were at that time in the minds of the people of England, and much effort has long been expended upon this. But it will help still more to find out what William Shakespeare was doing and thinking about when he wrote. This is more difficult, but is not at all impossible.

This method is applied here to a short but interesting period of Shakespeare's life, in the effort to find out when, why, and how the play of *Macbeth* was written, by looking into the minds both of its author as he wrote the play and of the audience whom he expected to see the play. Such questions are usually briefly discussed in the introduction to the play, but are worthy of more careful examination. The main conclusions reached are dependent upon many independent inferences which corroborate and strengthen each other. I have chosen to make these chapters tedious by setting forth the evidence on which the inferences are based and why I think the evidence reliable, and not by documentary footnotes but by incorporating the evidence in the text so that the reader may, if he wishes, draw his own different conclusions instead of accepting mine. The book, be it understood, can not concern itself with the more far-reaching aesthetic or imaginative appreciation of the play. The attempt here is only to build a proper foundation on which such appreciation should rest. Books which deal with the superstructure already fill many shelves of the *Macbeth* library and will soon fill many more. Excellent short appreciations of the play are those of Professor Thomas M. Parrott and Sir Edmund Chambers in their introductions to their editions of the play.

It is here noted that the chapter of this book entitled "The

Imperial Theme" has already been published in the Adams Memorial volume (New York, 1948) and that the substance of the chapter entitled "Concord, Peace, and Unity" has appeared in an article in the issue of the *Shakespeare Association Bulletin* for October, 1947.

It is no longer possible to specify the predecessors to whom a Shakespearean writer is indebted, for they are usually too numerous and often too indirect. So far as possible the present book does not deal with information, criticism, or interpretation already sufficiently developed in published works. The effort has been to confine the book to the development and elucidation of things which result from new sources of information.

The older editors (prior to 1869) are in their notes on the play of *Macbeth* sometimes not very happy in their interpretations, owing in large part to a difference of environment and lack of sympathy with certain aspects of this play and the wholly changed thought of their times on the subject of witchcraft and concerning the House of Stuart. It is for this reason, I think, that I have found the edition of *Macbeth* by the Clarendon editors (1869) not as helpful as are the others of that series dealing with other Shakespearean plays. But in truth the publication of the *Oxford English Dictionary* has rendered much of the linguistic and exegetical work of the previous editors obsolete or unnecessary.

The New Variorum edition of the play (1873) by Dr. Horace Howard Furness and its later revision (1903) by his son Dr. H. H. Furness, Jr., record most of the criticisms and interpretations found in the older books which are worth preserving, salted down with the inimitable Furness salt. Of the later editors I am much indebted to the Warwick edition of E. K. Chambers, which is particularly informative and accurate. A long step toward attaining a proper perspective by which to interpret this play was taken when Mark H. Liddell published in 1903 his edition of the play in the Elizabethan Shakspere. It is not as well known as it should be, owing perhaps to its rarity and to its eccentric format. Other useful editions are those of A. W. Verity (1901), J. M. Manly (1903), and T. M. Parrott (1904). The Porter and Clarke edition (1903–1904), with many shortcomings, has yet the great advantage of being based on the first folio text, and it exhibits an understanding of the extent of the influence upon the play of King James's interest in the witchcraft of Scotland. Dr. J. Q. Adams published a work on *Macbeth* in 1931, approaching the subject from a somewhat new standpoint and in a new fashion. It is a very helpful book. Still later are the editions of G. L. Kittredge (1939) and J. Dover Wilson (1947), both of which contain important new matter, but both also call for danger signals. Dr. Kittredge treats Macbeth as a victim of fate, and to accomplish this he is compelled to impose upon many lines of the play interpretations which seem to me to be wholly unwarranted. Dr. Dover Wilson's edition unfortunately did not reach me until after my book was practically finished. Along with much that is new and useful, I find that he has been led by certain passages, which admit of a much more easy explanation, to conjecture that our present *Macbeth* is a revised and cut copy of an older *Macbeth* which had been written by William Shakespeare for the entertainment of King James while he was still in Scotland—a very precarious position, as he himself admits with his characteristic frankness. This play was not thus produced by a forging process, but was poured direct from the crucible into the mold and exhibits blow-holes such as always result from this process but which are not found in forgings.

I have frequently printed quotations from the play of *Macbeth* in the text of the first folio; for that text, with its obsolete constructions, so-called "mislineations," and rhetorical punctuation, brings us more nearly in touch with the mind and meaning of William Shakespeare than can any modernized text, however smooth, metrical, and elegant it may be.

Many of my friends of the Philadelphia Shakspere Society have helped me with personal suggestions, as have also the staff of the Folger Shakespeare Library, particularly J. Q. Adams, Giles Dawson, and J. G. McManaway. Professors T. M. Parrott and H. L. Savage of Princeton University and Professor R. M. Smith of Lehigh University have kindly read some of my advance sheets. To all these I here record my sincere thanks. And finally I owe a large debt of thanks to Professors M. W. Black and M. A. Shaaber of the University of Pennsylvania for their generous but acute criticism of parts of my manuscript.

CONTENTS

ILLUSTRATIONS

THE
ROYAL PLAY
OF
Macbeth

THE ROYAL PLAY OF MACBETH

Because Shakespeare's words still mean what they meant when he wrote them with his pen, the first questions that arise in trying to find the meaning of the play of *Macbeth* are: When, why, and how was it written? Search for the answers to these questions produced the chapters of this book, but they were written in quite a different order from that in which they now appear. After they were completed and assembled, there emerged certain very definite, interesting, and partly new propositions which may be thus stated:

1. The play was a royal play specially written for performance before King James. That the play contains lines complimentary to the king has long been recognized; but that the entire play is a royal play for court performance as a compliment to the king, although previously suggested as a possibility, should now be stated as a fact; and it is a fact of the utmost importance to the proper understanding of the play, parts of which take on new meaning when read with this fact in mind.

2. The play was first performed before the king and his brother-in-law King Christian of Denmark on the occasion of the latter's visit to England in the summer of 1606. In the eighteenth century both Capell and Malone announced that the play of *Macbeth* had appeared in the year 1606, and this is the now accepted date. Malone also suggested that it might have been produced before the kings during this visit. Much evidence tending to confirm Malone's conjecture has gradually accumulated and may be found conveniently marshaled in recent editions of the play edited by Cunningham and Adams; but many more proofs have now appeared, and will be found in this book, as a result of which there seems to be

I

no room for doubt as to the correctness of Malone's conjecture. This fact, although of less importance than the first, has considerably influenced the writing of parts of the play and gives much help in their proper interpretation.

3. This first performance of the play was at Hampton Court on the evening of August 7, 1606. This is a new discovery, and the proofs establishing it will be found in the last few chapters of this book. It is of less importance than the others but must be considered as an exceedingly interesting circumstance. Although it has no bearing on why the play was written, it does account for certain things in the play which are otherwise obscure, and helps to account for the unfinished condition of the second scene of the play.

At the outset there should be appreciation of how much light is thrown upon the construction and meaning of the play if it be read as a royal play. It was proper and inevitable in such a play that the author should try to accommodate both his art and his philosophy as embodied in the play to the ideas of the king. Instances of such accommodation in the play of *Macbeth* have long been pointed to, but the sum of these has never yet been adequately determined. This it is now possible to do. It should be done, for many difficult problems concerning the play are solved when it is restored to its rightful position as one of the three or four plays which Shakespeare wrote, not for an audience such as that of the Globe Theater, but for the more highly intelligent audience of the English court.

As a royal play, written for the delectation of two kings, *Macbeth* should be read with the picture in the mind's eye of the great hall at Hampton Court fitted up with a stage and with two royal chairs of state immediately in front of this stage, with accommodation on either side for the English, Danish, and Scottish court. Better and more elaborate stage appointments were there available than at the Globe Theater, and the play needs the help of these things. Most of the scenes of *Macbeth* require a dark stage, which cannot be obtained in an open-to-the-air theater in the afternoon, but was obtainable in the palace of Hampton Court.

This setting was accompanied by the presence of a discriminating and quick-witted audience and of a sympathetic relation between the court and the king's players. The king himself was an interested auditor but would not sit through a long play, a fact which explains the comparative brevity of *Macbeth*. The great necromantic scene with which the play culminates becomes more than a mere spectacle if we see the king sitting in the midst of his court, watching and recognizing his royal progenitors as one by one, in the order of their descent, they slowly cross the stage. Shakespeare was consciously showing the king his "breed," for James was much interested in his ancestors and was directly descended from five characters in the play. The royal presence gave the performance a due decorum often lacking in the public theaters, and this in turn was a stimulus to the actors. They could resort to refinements of delivery and of stage business which in the Globe Theater would have passed unnoticed; and with these helps they might interest these kings in the workings of the minds of two apparently loyal subjects who murdered their king that they might sit on his throne.

King James's impatience with long plays affected the style of the writing of *Macbeth*. When the King's Company gave plays before the king at Whitehall, the players noticed that the king sometimes took a nap and sometimes left before the play was over. The dramatist therefore determined to defer to his king's taste and severely compress his lines. The play contains as much dramatic material as the average play, but a much shorter time of performance is achieved by studied compression of speech. He relied upon the superior perspicacity of the king and his court to catch his meaning.

This compressed style put a heavier burden upon the actors. In no other of Shakespeare's plays is the leading role so dependent upon the creative power of the actor. The brave, imaginative, tempted Macbeth—the craven, con-science-stricken Macbeth—the hardened and hopeless Mac-beth: these changes must be shown even more by the face and bearing of the actor than by the overcompressed lines of the text; and with the eye of imagination we must try to repro-duce the finer touches which the dramatist taught his actors. We may be sure that special instructions were given to Bur-bage as to how to play the leading part. The interest of the king in the workings of the imagination and of the conscience induced the dramatist to develop these psychological themes beyond their development in his other plays; but to do this properly calls for more than ordinary skill and intelligence in the actor. Short sentences and stage business thus acquire an emphasis and meaning which is apt to be lost when the play is given in a public theater. *Macbeth* is essentially a play for the *théâtre intime,* where the facial muscles of the actor can function with greatest effect. The king at Hampton Court sat close to the front of the stage as he watched the face of Burbage picturing the deterioration and ruin of Mac-beth. J. P. Collier, notwithstanding his literary misdeeds, was a very discerning scholar. He published "An Elegy on our late Protean Roscius, Richard Burbage" * containing lines which (whether genuine or not) teach an important truth about this play:

> Tyrant Macbeth, with unwash'd bloody hand,
> We vainly now may hope to understand.

In explanation of which he adds:

> Thy stature small, but every thought and mood
> Might thoroughly from thy face be understood.

This is probably prophecy long after the event, but yet it tells a truth which should be remembered in these days, for the modern actor rarely shows his audience the tyrant Mac-

* *New Particulars,* p. 30.

beth whom Shakespeare drew and Burbage portrayed, and the reader of the play in modern editions may vainly hope to understand him.* To overcome this difficulty, the play must be viewed as the king viewed it in 1606. To understand how Macbeth's guilty conscience works, one must know King James's ideas on the subject of the conscience, for he had written a book in which he had dwelt at length upon this subject, and Shakespeare had read this book. The king was also particularly well versed in the subjects of witchcraft and conjuration. The terror inspired by the witches of Scotland in the time of King James cannot now be re-created, but at least we can learn enough about it to realize the powerful influence it had over the course of the play and the original audience. It is unsafe to try to understand this play and yet to minimize the deeds and influences of the Scotch witches. Modern critics and producers of the play may wish to do so, for modern audiences and readers are not much interested in such things; but the Elizabethans were, and particularly the king and the large number of Scots who surrounded him at court—and the play still really means what it was intended to mean for them. When interpreted in terms of the demonology of its time, the whole play gains immensely both in dramatic force and in moral grandeur.

In examining Shakespeare's plays based upon English history, it is always assumed that his audience knew the main course of that history and that Shakespeare needed not to tell Englishmen such things. If we realize that this play of *Macbeth* was written primarily not for an English but for a Scottish audience, we may make a similar assumption as to the history of Scotland, and this too makes a difference. Scotch people, for example, knew about Scotch witches and particularly about the witches in Forres and their league with

* William Hazlitt in his *Characters of Shakespeare's Plays* (p. 19) is more extreme in his view, stating, "We can conceive no one to play Macbeth properly, or to look like a man who had encountered the Weird Sisters."

the Islesmen against the kings of Scotland. Englishmen did not know of this. Had the play of *Macbeth* been written for an English audience, this must have been explained, but it did not need to be explained to King James.

Dr. A. C. Bradley in his masterly recital of the characteristic marks of the play—darkness, blood, violence, horror—also includes irony, and he gives (*Shakespearean Tragedy*, pp. 338–340) a catalogue of these "Sophoclean ironies" in which characters in the play use words having meanings ominous to an instructed audience though hidden to themselves. To this he appends a note pointing out that some of these would escape an audience ignorant of the story of the play. He finds in this an indication that Shakespeare did not write solely for stage purposes. The more natural explanation is that the play was written for King James and his Scottish friends, who had been since childhood thoroughly familiar with the story of Macbeth, one of the most unforgettable figures in Boece's fabulous history of Scotland.

On May 19, 1603, only a few weeks after James became King of England, he caused the issuance of Royal Letters Patent to William Shakespeare and eight other actors, creating them the "King's Players." They thereafter ranked in the king's household as "Grooms of the Chamber." Their prime function was to play before the king for his "solace and pleasure." Their playing at other times at the public or private theaters was, in theory at least, only to keep themselves in practice for the more important function of entertaining royalty at court.

During the first three years of their service they gave many plays before the king and his court, but so far as we know, they were all plays taken from the company's current repertory. A number of Shakespeare's were among them. But the great dramatist, who as a member of the King's Company had a greater obligation than any other playwright to do so, had not as yet written any play specially designed to honor the

accession of the Scottish king to the English throne. We are
now to inquire when and how and why he fulfilled this obligation by writing the play of *Macbeth*.

The king was not so fond of plays as Queen Elizabeth had
been. He preferred hunting as a diversion. He was apt to
be sleepy in the evening and found it hard to keep awake
through a long play. And yet more plays were given at
court in the early years of his reign than ever before. During
his first winter in London the King's Company gave eight
such performances. Queen Anna had taken the Children of
the Blackfriars under her protection, and they produced at
least three more that same winter; and the Admiral's Company, now attached to Prince Henry, presented five or six
more. But the king found so much drama tiresome and
often failed to attend, leaving the entertainment to the queen
and the prince, who were more fond of such things. The
court plays were usually comedies, topical and satirical, sometimes bordering on farce and burlesque, in which the queen
allowed her player children great liberties. When they hit
off some of the king's foibles, the queen merely laughed, although the older courtiers took offense, contrasting such im-
propriety with the stricter decorum required by the late
queen.

During the following year there was a serious attempt to
produce a play of special interest to the king. It is not known
who wrote it, but it was called *Gowrie* and pictured how four
years earlier, in a friend's house, King James had escaped
death from a treacherous conspiracy. During November,
1604, it was twice rehearsed by the King's Players with some
of the Council present, but it was felt to tread on dangerous
ground and was never played at court. If a murderous attack
by his host upon a King of Scotland is to be shown to James,
it should be upon some other King of Scotland and not upon
James himself. The season saw twelve plays given at court
by the King's Company, three by the queen's, and eight by
the prince's players. But this dramatic season was not a

success. Satirical comedy was much in vogue; some of it honest, much of it frothy. Its tone may be judged by what Calvert wrote on March 28, 1605, to Winwood (*Memorials of Affairs of State,* Vol. II, p. 53):

The Plays do not forbear to present upon their Stage the whole course of this present time, not sparing either King, State or Religion, in so great Absurdity, and with such Liberty, that any would be afraid to hear them.

Shortly after this Ben Jonson wrote in his dedication of *Volpone:*

Now, especially in dramatic, or, as they term it, stage poetry, nothing but ribaldry, profanation, blasphemy, all license of offence to God and man is practised. I dare not deny a great part of this.

"Railing" was the rule. The chief offenders were the Children of the Queen's Revels. A play called *Eastward Ho* had been written for them by a trio of dramatists. It parodied several of Shakespeare's plays, for the children were in sharp rivalry with the King's Players. It ridiculed the Scots and even permitted a boy player to mimic the king's Scottish accent as he called out, "I ken the man weel: he is one of my thirty-pound knights." This displeased the Lord Chamberlain. The boy players played no more that season and the authors of the play went to jail.

In such dramatic surroundings, if William Shakespeare were moved to write a play for his king, what sort of a play would it be? Fortunately we possess an interesting little picture of the dramatist just at this point in his career which answers this question. John Davies of Hereford, a writing master of great proficiency, and a voluminous poetaster, had for some time known Shakespeare. In verses previously published (see Chambers's *William Shakespeare,* Vol. II, pp. 213, 214) he had complained that Fortune had rewarded neither

Shakespeare nor Burbage according to their deserts. In 1610 he published a volume of satirical verses entitled *The Scourge of Folly* (entered in the Stationers' Register October 8, 1610). It contains a collection of epigrams, seemingly written between 1606 and 1609 inclusive, among which is found the following:

> *To our English Terence, Mr. Will: Shake-speare.*
> Some say good *Will* (which I, in sport, do sing)
> Had'st thou not plaid some Kingly parts in sport,
> Thou hadst bin a companion for a *King;*
> And, beene a King among the meaner sort.
> Some others raile; but raile as they think fit,
> Thou hast no rayling, but, a raigning Wit:
> *And* honesty *thou sow'st,* which they do reape;
> *So, to increase their* stocke *which they do keepe.**

Thus do we know that Shakespeare at this time played "kingly parts" in his company; that his was a lofty and not a satirical dramatic art; and that Davies thought if he had not been a professional actor he might have been advanced to some position at court distinctly more honorable than that of a groom of the outer chamber, perhaps even to a place involving some personal contact with his king. His dramas promoted "honesty" and not the ribaldry which Ben Jonson tells us was then in fashion on the stage. *Eastward Ho, The Dutch Courtesan, Volpone, Macbeth,* and *King Lear* all appeared about this time and in the order named. By noting the differing types of these plays, one can form a good idea

* Every one knows what Hamlet had said (Act II, Scene ii) about the "honest method" of writing plays. Davies evidently knew how much profit it had brought the King's Company. John Davies had good opportunity of knowing whereof he spoke, for he had a large acquaintance among the actors, dramatists, and men of letters. Thomas Fuller, in his *Worthies*, calls him "The greatest master of the pen that England in her age beheld." He had been writing master in the families of many of the nobility and at one time had been called upon to improve Prince Henry's penmanship. At the time of writing this epigram he was living in London within hearing of all the current theatrical gossip.

of what was in Davies's mind when he distinguished a dramatist with a "railing wit" from one with a "reigning wit." William Shakespeare was no longer in the mood to write comedies. Never again did he write one. Whatever there had been of his wit that could "rail" died after the writing of *Troilus and Cressida* and *Measure for Measure*. Instead, his "reigning wit" was wholly occupied with high tragedy, and especially with a most ambitious type of play which shows how a man of noble character may permit a bad habit of mind to lead him to his downfall. This had been pressed upon him some five years before while reading Plutarch's *Lives of the Noble Greeks and Romans* preparatory to writing the play of *Julius Caesar,* and from this time on it became the theme of his greatest plays.

Soon after the writing of *Julius Caesar,* the Hamlet theme had fascinated him as, during the last years of the reign of Elizabeth, he wrote and rewrote his *Tragical History of Hamlet, Prince of Denmark*. The noble, philosophic, quickwitted, melancholy prince, with whom Shakespeare fell in love, had developed a fatal defect. He put this thought into the play (*Hamlet,* I, n, 23):

> Oft it chances in particular men,
> That for some vicious mole of nature in them,
> As, in their birth—wherein they are not guilty,
> Since nature cannot choose his origin—
> By the o'ergrowth of some complexion,
> Oft breaking down the pales and forts of reason,
> Or by some habit that too much o'er-leavens
> The form of plausive manners, that these men,—
> Carrying, I say, the stamp of one defect,
> Being nature's livery, or fortune's star,—
> Their virtues else—be they as pure as grace,
> As infinite as man may undergo—
> Shall in the general censure take corruption
> From that particular fault: the dram of eale

Doth all the noble substance of a doubt
To his own scandal.

These interesting lines are found only in the second quarto
of *Hamlet,* printed in 1604–1605; for as the play grew to
greater length the dramatist cut them out as not essential.
As part of the drama of "Hamlet" they are not missed, but
the judgment concerning the defects of human nature that
is here expressed is of the highest value in helping us to
interpret the art of William Shakespeare.   For this reason
these excised lines are worthy of more careful analysis than
is usually accorded them.   Their meaning is obscure because of obsolete terms and unfortunate textual difficulties.
One must be in sympathy with the medieval physiology and
have the Renaissance view of human life as the interplay of
nature's livery, which we now call heredity, and fortune's star,
which we call environment.   One must view an individual as
a complex of humors, that is, a "complexion," and must reflect upon the bad habit which results from the "o'ergrowth
of some complexion" and which produces illness of the mind
and ultimately breaks down the "pales and forts of reason."
One must think of this as a "vicious mole"—a cancerous
growth which will not submit to surgery, but which eats
deeper and deeper into the flesh ("o'er-leavens" is the apt
word used) until it ruins both manners and mind.   Thus all
the "noble substance" of the man is corrupted by this "dram
of eale."

The great thought thus expressed in lines teeming with
pregnant metaphors is Shakespeare's enunciation of his dramatic pattern for tragedy.   Shakespeare's drama "is concerned above all else with the development or deterioration
of a soul" (Spurgeon, *Shakespeare's Imagery,* p. 381).   Liddell
thus defines it: "All of Shakespeare's greatest tragedies present to us the picture of a *mens insana,* a diseased soul whose
powers are out of balance and out of tune through the excess

of some one faculty dominating the others and overthrowing the state of man" (*The Tragedy of Macbeth*, p. xx), by which phrase is meant the coordinated control of man's faculties.*

The *mens insana* thus shown in many of Shakespeare's

---

* The phrase "state of man" likens man's governance of himself to the governance of a kingdom. It is essentially the medieval idea of the microcosm. So Macbeth calls it his *"single* state of man" to distinguish it from the general state of man which is the macrocosm. This "state of man" was much in Shakespeare's thoughts. Read the pregnant lines of Brutus (*Julius Caesar*, II, i, 63):

> Between the acting of a dreadful thing
> And the first motion, all the interim is
> Like a phantasma, or a hideous dream:
> The Genius and the mortal instruments
> Are then in council; and the state of man,
> Like to a little kingdom, suffers then
> The nature of an insurrection.

The same comparison often recurs in *Macbeth* where it is curiously associated with the "state" conferred upon man by the wearing of proper garments or habits. When Macbeth's state of man is shaken by the prophecies (I, iii, 140) so that he yields to his bad habit of being controlled by his imagination, there follows immediately a simile which likens this overthrow of his "state" to the ill wearing of a garment of honor (I, iii, 145). The same connection between man's control of himself and the arrangement of his garments is found in I, vii, 34–36, as is adequately explained in Allen's note quoted in the New Variorum. It may be traced again in II, ii, 37–39, where the balm of hurt minds knits up the raveled sleeve of care. The thought is continued in a speech of Caithness's (V, ii, 15):

> but for certain
> He cannot buckle his distempered cause
> Within the belt of rule.

As Liddell makes clear, "cause" is here the distemper of Macbeth's mind; it is wholly disarranged and out of control. Immediately Angus says "like a giant's robe upon a dwarfish thief." Thus Shakespeare in this play habitually thinks of man's "state" as involving the internal control of his habits and likens this to the external arrangement of his habit. His mind thus equivocally plays with this word "habit." As Miss Spurgeon has pointed out (*Shakespeare's Imagery*, pp. 324–326), this figure of the disarrangement of a garment is a ruling image in *Macbeth*. It is due to the ever present thought of the disarrangement of Macbeth's faculties.

tragedies is not an insane mind as we use the word in these days, but an unhealthy mind. It is the "mind diseased" of the play of *Macbeth*. Shakespeare was fascinated by the attempt to portray in his tragedies how the dram of eale working in different men according to their differing complexions overthrows their native nobility, causing an insurrection in their "state of man."

He first told of such a man in the play of *Hamlet*, the prince whose native resolution was "sicklied o'er with the pale cast of thought." In his recently written play he showed Othello, the noble Moor, maddened and overthrown by his childish credulity. He is now picturing the fate of the irascible and frenzied old King Lear. In the language of Elizabethan psychology these are "distempered" souls, whose single state of man is shaken by an unbalanced temperament. He already has in mind (see *Macbeth*, III, i, 56) similar treatment of more of Plutarch's noble Greeks and Romans, particularly Mark Antony, whose career as told by that author had fascinated him ever since he read it when writing the play of *Julius Caesar*. This theme was to reappear in his subsequently written plays of *Antony and Cleopatra, Coriolanus,* and *Timon of Athens*. The identity of fundamental pattern is unmistakable.

His royal play, therefore, will be a high tragedy and will be built after this same pattern and on a loftier plane and in a more healthy atmosphere than the current plays. It will picture the mind of a noble man distraught and brought to wrack by the corruption of some "habit that too much o'er-leavens the form of plausive manners." Of course this will be superimposed upon a dramatic subject which of itself will suffice to interest the general audience, but for the judicious this insight into the working of a human mind will be the lodestar which will hold their attention.

This is what is found in the play of *Macbeth*. As a drama it has a powerful grip upon the general audience, and our wonder at the depth of the author's knowledge of the mind of man increases each time we read it. Just as Hamlet's too great indulgence in reflection overmasters his power to act, so Macbeth's progressive seduction by his imagination overmasters his conscience. The bad habit which wrought his destruction was the substitution of the imaginary for the real.

SHAKESPEARE AT OXFORD

Shakespeare's connection with Oxford was not academic but social. He was a friend of John Davenant, later mayor of Oxford, and was in the habit of stopping at Oxford to see him as he journeyed to Stratford in the spring and back to London in the fall. John Davenant was a vintner whose wine shop adjoined the inn where Shakespeare lodged. He and three of his sons graduated from the Merchant Taylors' School in London, which enjoyed special relations with St. John's College, Oxford.* We may think it not unlikely that Davenant's tavern at Carfax, not far from St. John's College, was frequented by St. John's men, both graduates and undergraduates.

The story of Shakespeare's intimacy with this family is recorded in the lives of the dramatist Sir William Davenant, who was John Davenant's second son; for Sir William seems to have been more than content to leave unquestioned the gossip that whispered that William Shakespeare was his father. The noticeable thing about these tales, jotted down by three successive Oxford antiquaries, is that the facts which they have recorded for us, and no doubt truthfully, have obviously been selected by scandalmongers because thought to justify an otherwise unfounded suspicion. The facts are these: William Shakespeare was accustomed to visit the Davenant house, where he was much at home; Davenant Senior

---

* St. John's college was founded by Sir Thomas White of London, a master of the Merchant Taylors' Company and a Founder of the Merchant Taylors' School, from which forty-three scholars were assigned by that company to St. John's College, "by continual succession." John Davenant showed his interest in St. John's by donating to it several MSS. His eldest son Robert was a fellow of St. John's. See Boas's *Shakespeare and the University*, p. 44.

was a grave and melancholy man but fond of plays, while his wife was bright and witty and beautiful; this saturnine father had a mercurial son who was named William; and William Shakespeare stood as his godfather at baptism. These facts justify no inference whatever regarding the paternity of Sir William Davenant. We therefore accept the facts and deny the inference. From other sources we know that when John Davenant and his wife died, friends of the Davenant family wrote verses (which may be read in Halliwell-Phillipps's *Outlines*) extolling the marital fidelity of Mistress Davenant, thus recording for posterity their denial of the aspersions which had been cast upon an estimable woman.

But the verdict on this shadowy evidence does not here concern us. For present purposes what we are to note is that the records of St. Martin's Church, Oxford, show that William, son of John and Jane Davenant, was there baptized on March 3, 1606. This should cause us to take notice *that these aspersions could not have come into being,* and that the defensive steps never would have been needed, had not Shakespeare been a visitor at Oxford in the summer of 1605.*

Assuming, therefore, that William Shakespeare spent part of this summer at the inn, later called the Crowne Inn, in Oxford, what did he see and hear? Early in June the city evidenced the great preparations which were being made for the first visit of England's new king to his renowned university. Notices had been sent to the academic body requiring their presence, giving them directions as to the habits to be worn and instructions as to their behavior.

Four stage plays were in rehearsal; one of them, *Ajax Flagellifer,* was a classical tragedy, but the other three, *Alba, Vertumnus,* and *Arcadia Reformed,* were comedies specially

* During the summer of 1605 Shakespeare must have spent some time in Stratford arranging for the purchase by him of an interest in the local tithes. This was concluded by the execution, on July 24, 1605, of an assignment to him of a lease from Raphe Huband. This was not signed by Shakespeare but was witnessed by his solicitor Francis Collins, probably because Shakespeare was then at Oxford.

written for the occasion. Dr. Matthew Gwinn was in charge of the preparations for these plays. He lived in London not far from William Shakespeare, had attended the Merchant Taylors' School, was a fellow of St. John's College and also a Doctor of Medicine, Doctor of Music, and a writer of plays, including *Vertumnus*. For use in these plays the Revels Office in London had sent the necessary costumes and properties to Oxford.

Robert Burton, who had written some part of *Alba*, wrote from Oxford on August 11, 1605, to his brother William:

Here is no news but preparation for the King's coming who will be here on Tuesday come forthenight, Plays, Verses, &c. That part of the play which I made is well liked, especially those scenes of the Magus, and I have had great thanks for my pains of Dr. King our new Dean.

This play was a pastoral comedy and was preserved in MS until 1862, when it was privately printed for the Roxburghe Club. The Latin text of Dr. Gwinn's *Vertumnus* was published by him in 1607, and the English text of Samuel Daniel's play, renamed *The Queen's Arcadia,* is available in his published works; both the latter are light allegorical comedies with much topical satire. Whether, finding William Shakespeare in town, Dr. Gwinn asked his aid, as an experienced playwright and stage manager, in staging these plays is matter of surmise. We know that Inigo Jones was present assisting in some such capacity.

In addition to the four plays to be performed in the great hall of Christ Church, a playlet or "lusiuncula," concerning *Tres Sibyllae,* was written, both in Latin and in English, by Dr. Gwinn for performance by the scholars of St. John's. He published the Latin text of this along with his Latin play of *Vertumnus*. This playlet was to be given before the royal party as they approached the city.

Dr. Gwinn knew how proud was King James of his royal ancestry, traceable far back along many lines of British,

Welsh, Scotch, and English princes. "Ye are come of as honourable predecessours as any Prince living," James had told his son in his *Kingly Gift,* (p. 33). Of one of these predecessors Holinshed in his *Chronicles of Scotland* gave a detailed account, showing how the royal Stuart line of Scotland could be traced back to a certain Thane of Lochabria named Banquo, to whom in the ancient time three women had prophesied that although himself never a king, he should be the father of many kings. To remind him of his descent from Banquo might really interest this king who was so well versed in his genealogy, and therefore Dr. Gwinn founded his playlet upon this ancient legend.

There were also to be ten Latin disputations before the king. To train the disputants was part of the summer's work, and much talk was to be heard in Oxford about the matters to be debated. The questions had been chosen after consultation with persons close to the king, for the list of the "Questions for Disputation at the University of Oxford before the King," which was sent in advance to some of his advisers for approval, is still in the Public Record Office. After revision it was sent to Oxford, where broadside copies were there distributed in advance of the debates. One of these broadsides, with contemporary annotations, is preserved in the Bodleian Library (MS Tanner 75) and is here reproduced. It is worthy the attention of those who wish to look into the mind of this learned king and note what he was thinking about. James had discussed the powers and functions of saints and angels in his theological writings; he had moderated between the puritans and the bishops as to releasing the clergy from visiting parishioners sick with the plague (Canon 67 promulgated by the Convocation of 1604); his views on the tobacco question had been set out in his *Counterblaste* recently published; that a court should give judgment according to the evidence even though contrary to the judge's own knowledge had been ruled in the King's Court of Star Chamber on May 10, 1605 (Hawarde's *Reports of*

QVÆSTIONES, DEO PRO-
PITIO, DISCVTIENDAE
PVBLICE IN COMITIIS

coram Sereniſſimo Rege, menſe Au-
guſt. An. 1605.

Quæſtiones in Theologiâ.

An Sancti & Angeli cognoſcant cogitationes cordium? Neg.
An peſte graſſante teneantur Eccleſiarū paſtores ægros inuiſere? Neg.

Moderator Dr. Abbat Vicecancel.
Reſpondens Dr. Aglionbye.

Opponent. {
Dr. Gordon.   *pro forma.*
Dr. Hollande.   1
Dr. Tomſon.   2
Dr. Fielde.   3
Dr. Riues.   4
Dr. Harding. 5
Dr. Ayrie.   6
}

Quæſtiones in Medicinâ.

beg & more diſputed
after the same
queſtion

An mores nutricum à pueruliſ cum lacte imbibantur? Neg.
An creber ſuffitus Nicotianæ exoticæ ſit ſaniſ ſalutariuſ Neg.

Moderator Dr. Warner.
Reſpondens Dr. Paddy, Eques auratus.

Opponent. {
Dr. Aileworth. 1
Dr. Buſt.   +   *non diſputabit*
Dr. Guinne. 2
Dr. Gifford.   3
Dr. Aſhworth. 4
Dr. Chennell. 5
}

THE OXFORD QUESTIONS

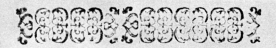

Quæstiones in Iure Civili.

*n iudex in iudicando teneatur sequi legitimas probationes in iudi-
cto deductas, contra veritatem sibi privatim cognitam? Affir.
n Inducia vel fædera sint bonæ fidei, vel strictæ iuris? Sūt bonę fidei.*

Moderator D͡r. Gentilis.
Respondens D͡r. Blincowe.

Opponent.
- D͡r. Weston. 2
- D͡r. Bird. 1
- D͡r. Martin. 3
- D͡r. Husey. 4
- D͡r. Budden. 5
- D͡r. Lloid. 6

Quæstiones in Morali Philosophiâ.

*n tueri fines imperii sit maius quam amplificare? Affirm.
n iustum & iniustum constent lege tantum, non naturâ? Neg.*

Moderator M͡r. Fitzharbert Procurator senior.
Respondens M͡r. Ballowe.

Opponent.
- M͡r. Barkham. 1
- M͡r. Langton. 2
- M͡r. Kinge. 3
- M͡r. Winniffe. 4
- M͡r. Juckes. 5
- M͡r. Thorneton. 6

[handwritten marginalia: they 〈?〉 were disputed after the natural philosophy questions]

Quæstiones in Philosophiâ Naturali.

*n operâ artis possit aurum conflari? Negat.
n imaginatio possit producerē reales effectus? Affirm.*

Moderator M͡r. Porter.
Respondens M͡r. Andrewes.

Opponent.
- M͡r. Lapworth. 1
- M͡r. Baskervile. 2
- M͡r. Clayton. 3
- M͡r. Mocket. 4
- M͡r. Pinke. 5
- M͡r. Boulton. 6

OXON, 1605.

THE OXFORD QUESTIONS

Cases in the Star Chamber, pp. 217 and 218). A king content to guard his frontiers was in the good graces of Jacobus Pacificus; and he had even looked into the problem of transmuting base metal into gold, but had decided that success was unlikely, because otherwise King Solomon would have accomplished it. All these matters were to be debated and they were all known to be of particular interest to King James.

We have five contemporary accounts of the king's visit. Anthony Nixon, a London pamphleteer, came to Oxford to write it up; and his report was immediately published in a forty-five-page pamphlet entitled *Oxford's Triumph,* journalistic in style and rather less reliable than the other accounts which we possess. The college authorities thought so, for in 1607 Isaac Wake, a learned though rather dull Oxonian, in fact the official orator of the university,* published a more detailed account in Latin of the king's sayings and doings, entitled *Rex Platonicus,* with a liberal interlarding of praise for the learning and perspicacity of the king. There is an interesting letter from John Chamberlain to Winwood (published in the *Memorials*) giving his version of what he had seen; and another letter from the Venetian Ambassador, Nicolo Molyno, who was also present, to his Doge and Senate; but most valuable of all is the account of Philip Stringer, who was sent to Oxford from Cambridge to view and report upon all that happened. Cambridge knew its turn would come next, and wished to do even better. Stringer was to point out what had been successful, and also the faults of the Oxford performance which might be amended; and this he did with eyes less prejudiced than those of the Oxonians. His account is of considerable length and after remaining in MS

---

* One of the king's pungent sayings was that "when he was at Oxford one *Wake* made him sleep, but when he was in Cambridge [where he saw *Ignoramus*] one *Sleep* made him wake."

for 170 years was printed among the *Leland Collectanea* (Vol. II, pp. 626–647). Stringer reached Oxford some days before the king arrived, and he tells about the bustle of preparation for the king's visit.

James was to arrive on the afternoon of August 27, 1605, accompanied by his family and a great train of nobility and attendants, entering by the northern road from Woodstock. St. John's College was situated outside the walls of Oxford where this road reaches the north gate. The legend related by Holinshed told that three women "of elder world" met Banquo as he came to a little glade in the woods. Accordingly an arbor of ivy had been erected at the gate of St. John's. "The scholars stood all on one side of the street, and the strangers of all sorts on the other." As the royal procession approached, the king, who was on horseback, accompanied by the Duke of Lennox carrying the king's sword, stopped at this arbor and three students dressed as sibyls (*tres quasi sibyllae*) came forth from the arbor and, speaking in turn, recited Dr. Gwinn's verses. To picture their appearance, look at the woodcut found in the text of Holinshed's *Chronicles* and reproduced on page 22 below, for Gwinn took his account from this book. The first speaker announced that three fate-pronouncing sisters had in the olden time foretold to Banquo, Thane of Lochaber, that, though he should not rule, his immortal descendants should rule an endless empire. The three speakers explained that they were these sisters repeating this prophecy to King James as Banquo's descendant. The first hailed him as King of Scotland, the second as King of England, and the third as King of Ireland. In Wake's account of this performance, which appeared two years later, it is stated that the three sibyls met two Scotch nobles, Macbeth and Banquo. By the time this was written, Shakespeare's play had appeared and reference to Macbeth as accompanying Banquo is perfectly explicable; but *in Dr. Gwinn's playlet Macbeth is not mentioned.*

The playlet is chiefly concerned with the prophecy to Banquo as to the endless empire to be ruled by his descendants and is comprised in thirty neatly turned lines of Latin verse which may be read in Boswell's Malone (Vol. XI, p. 282). There are greetings to the queen and the two princes; the expectation is expressed that the king's empire will equal that of King Canute of old; there is a reference to the founding of St. John's College by Sir Thomas Whyte; and an invitation to the king to visit the university. The verses were repeated in English for the benefit of the queen, who understood no Latin, and written copies available to all were hung on the walls of St. John's. A translation of the first twenty lines of the verses will be found on p. 163 of this volume.

Nixon informs us that *the king did very much applaud this performance,* and this Wake confirms. James knew the Banquo story, for in 1578 his schoolmaster Peter Young, as is recorded in his "Index," had bought for him a copy of Holinshed's *Chronicles* "in tua faire volumes." This was the edition of 1577, with the striking picture of the sibyls meeting Macbeth and Banquo which would have caught the eye of the twelve-year-old king. Likely he had earlier read about this in Boece, as had most educated Scotchmen. Of course he was gratified to find Englishmen acquainted with this old Scottish legend. I have not found the story of Banquo recorded in books published in England prior to 1606 except in Holinshed and in the Dedication to King James by Sir George Buck of the latter's *Daphnis Polystephanos,* published in 1605. It is highly significant that Buck, who was Acting Master of the Revels, was making reference to this legend at this very time, for one would expect him to be consulted by Dr. Gwinn as to suitable subject matter for his lines. The kindly reception by the king of Dr. Gwinn's *Tres Sibyllae* thus gave a clear indication of what sort of dramatic subject would be likely to please the king; Shakespeare's forthcoming play for the king should be connected with Scottish history; it should make reference to the prophecy to Banquo and to the descent from Banquo of the House of Stuart; and it should be short.

But it so happens that there was a corresponding opportunity in the next four days at Oxford to find out what sort of plays did not please the king, for the four plays were duly performed, and Stringer, the observer from Cambridge, tells what the king thought of them.

On the evening of August 27 the play of *Alba* by Robert Burton (who afterward wrote *The Anatomy of Melancholy*) was given with rustical songs and much dancing. The king tried to get away before half the comedy was ended, and would have done so had not the chancellor entreated him to stay.

On August 28 was performed *Ajax Flagellifer,* a Latin version of Sophocles' play. This was notable in that the stage was set with three sets of scenery designed by Inigo Jones after the Italian manner, while the characters were dressed in antique apparel furnished by the Master of the Revels. The king was much wearied by it and "spoke many words of dislike."

The next night was played *Vertumnus* by Dr. Matthew Gwinn, a Latin satirical and allegorical comedy. It was much better than either of the others. Nevertheless the king "distasted it and fell asleep and when he wakened he would have been gone saying I marvel what they think me to be."

On August 30, the last day of the king's visit, was played Samuel Daniel's pastoral comedy in English. But the king had seen too much drama and did not come to the play, visiting instead the library of the university.

Thus much the king's visit to Oxford can teach us as to James's dramatic taste, and thus much and more it could teach William Shakespeare. Whether he was actually present at some of these performances is not very material. The royal comments upon the university plays must have interested both town and gown. *Tres Sibyllae* is the one which is most likely to have been seen by Shakespeare, for every one

he Danes
quithed by
akbeth and
aquho.

To resist these enimies, whiche were alreadie landed, and busie in spoiling the countrey, Makbeth and Banquho were sente with the kings authoritie, who hauing with them a conuenient power, encountred the enimies, slewe parte of them, and chased the other to their shippes. They that escaped and got once to theyr shippes, obtayned of Makbeth for a great summe of golde, that suche of theyr freendes as were slaine at this last bickering might be buried in Saint Colmes Inche. In memorie whereof, many olde Sepultures are yet in the sayde Inche, there to be seene grauen with the armes of the Danes, as

ere buried
S. Colmes
che.

togither without other companie, saue only theselues, passing through the woodes and fieldes, when sodenly in the middes of a laude, there met them .iij. women in straunge & ferly apparell, resembling creatures of an elder worlde, whom when they attentiuely beheld, wondering much at the sight, The first of them spake & sayde: All hayle Makbeth Thane of Glammis (for he had lately entred into that dignitie and office by the death of his father Synel.) The .ij. of them said: Hayle Makbeth Thane of Cawder: but the third sayde: All Hayle Makbeth that hereafter shall be king of Scotland.

The prophesie
of three wome
supposing to
be the weird fi
sters or feiries.

Then Banquho, what maner of women (saith he) are you, that seeme so litle fauourable vnto me, where as to my fellow here, besides highe offices, yee assigne also the kingdome, appointyng fowrth nothing for me at all? Yes sayth the firste of them, wee promise greater benefites vnto thee, than vnto him, for he shall reygne in in deede, but with an vnluckie ende: neyther shall he leaue any issue behinde him to succeede in his place, where contrarily thou in deede shalt not reygne at all, but of thee those shall be borne whiche shall gouerne the Scottishe kingdome by long order of continuall discent. Herewith the foresayde women vanished immediatly out of theyr sight . This was reputed at the first but some vayne fantasticall illusion by Makbeth and Banquho, in so muche that Banquho woulde call Makbeth in ieste kyng of

A thing to
wonder at

D.ij.   Scot=

HOLINSHED'S HISTORY OF SCOTLAND
(Edition of 1577), Page 243

who wished to do so could see it. In Hunter's *New Illustrations* (1845) the author says:

I venture to propound the much higher probability that Shakespeare was at Oxford when the King honoured the university with this visit,—perhaps that he was even present when the youths of Saint John's performed this their brief dramatic entertainment before the King (Vol. II, p. 156).

For this he gives sound reasons; but much more cogent grounds in support of this hypothesis are adducible now than those which led Joseph Hunter to make this statement. The phrase "imperial theme" in the play of *Macbeth* (I, iii, 129) is derived from the phrase "imperium sine fine" in line 2 of Dr. Gwinn's verses. We therefore do not hesitate to follow the lead of editors and critics who have pointed to *Tres Sibyllae* as the *fons et origo* of the play of *Macbeth,* supplying a promising hint as to a good subject related to the king's ancestry at a time when there was a sure feeling in the mind of William Shakespeare that he could meet the king's taste better than any of the four plays which Oxford had produced.* It is true that King Lear was reputed to be an ancestor of King James, but the play he had begun about Lear promised to be too long and the connection was too remote. A shorter Scottish play picturing Banquo as the king's ancestor would evidently be more suitable. Dr. Gwinn's flattering hope expressed in his playlet that King James might resemble King Canute with his fourfold kingdom ("Canutum referas regno quadruplice clarum") may well be matched by the picture of James carrying "two-fold balls and treble sceptres." We can imagine the eagerness

---

* Here, and throughout this book, I assume that William Shakespeare could read Latin. Scholars and critics of his work have been too slow to rid themselves of the baleful influence of Dr. Farmer's charming but fallacious essay. Prof. Baldwin has given it the *coup de grâce* (*William Shakspere's Small Latine and Lesse Greeke,* 1944). The field of investigation of the origins of the ideas of the dramatist is thus enlarged, but as yet the fruits of this enlargement have not been reaped.

with which he looked forward to reading again the account in his Holinshed of the strange prophecy to Banquo in order that he might see whether it could be molded to his purpose.

We must also take account of the considerable probability that George Buck, the acting Master of the Revels, came into contact with William Shakespeare. Buck had been knighted at Whitehall on July 23, 1603, and appointed a gentleman of the king's privy chamber. He must have been at Oxford during the king's visit charged with some oversight of the plays; and it would have been quite in order for Buck to tell the dramatist of the King's Company that since the king did not seem to like the sort of plays he had been shown at Oxford, it would be well for him to write a better play for his king, with suggestions as to subject matter, which sent him to the story of Macbeth as found in Holinshed.

THE WRITING OF THE PLAY

The effort thus far has been to find the urges which brought the dramatist to his task of writing the play of *Macbeth* and which conditioned the sort of a work it was to be. These things reveal *why* William Shakespeare wrote the play, and upon this foundation all that follows must be built. But to know *when and how* the play was written there must be examination of what the people of England and the dramatist and his king and court were doing and thinking about at the time, and of how the language of the play, including several topical allusions, fits into these facts. These interrelationships are partly dependent upon direct evidences and partly upon inferences, and anyone who is asked to accept my conclusions is entitled to know what are the evidences upon which they are based, and what inferences are involved, before the soundness of the conclusions can be weighed. But these inferences sometimes involve tedious and lengthy processes, and sometimes the evidences are extensive. Until the last piece is fitted into a picture puzzle such as this, the demonstration is only tentative. I can only hope that the patient reader before he gets through will be conscious (as I have been) of the click that is audible as the fit of the pieces registers. From the fitting of all these pieces there emerges a picture of when and how the play was produced; and it seems best first to exhibit the picture thus evolved, and afterward, piece by piece, to supply the demonstrations which verify it.

The king left Oxford on Friday, August 30, 1605, late in the afternoon. It had been announced that the four principal dramatic performances which had been given as part of his majesty's entertainment were to be repeated the next week so that those who could not be admitted to the royal showings might yet see the plays. But the Master of the

25

Revels refused to allow his properties to remain so long in Oxford and accordingly the second performances did not occur.

The records of the city of Oxford show that on October 9, 1605, the authorities paid to the King's Players ten shillings, neither the date of performance nor the name of any play being recorded. During the interval of nearly six weeks Shakespeare may have remained in Oxford with the Davenants, or he may have spent some time in Stratford. The theaters in London were closed because of plague from October 5 to December 15, and this may have prolonged his out-of-town stay. But in the autumn of 1605, early or late, probably late, we may think of him in London again at the house of the Mountjoys in Silver Street, where he then lodged, preparing to start work on the play of *Macbeth*. Most assuredly when he began the work he had in his hands a copy of the *Chronicles* of Raphael Holinshed. His own copy (dated 1587) was in three very large unwieldly folios, of which Volume I, containing the history of Macbeth, weighs ten pounds, so he would hardly have been carrying it around with him.

Lines in Act II of the play indicate when the act was written. When Lady Macbeth has rung her little bell, the agreed signal to her husband for the murder, he says:

> Hear it not, Duncan, for it is a knell
> That summons thee to heaven or to hell.

And then his wife:

> Hark! Peace!
> It was the owl that shriek'd, the fatal bell-man,
> Which gives the stern'st good-night.

The source of this superb imagery is unmistakable. The continuator of Stow (1615 ed., p. 862) has entered in his record of things happening in London in May, 1605, the following:

Master Robert Dow of London, Marchant taylor, in his most Christian charity, pitying the miserable or rather desperate Estate of the poor condemned prisoners in Newgate, where very often, and very many of them after judgment of death, and at their very Execution remain most Carelesse of their Soules health jesting, and deriding their imminent daunger and to the judgement of the worlde die reprobate.

Uppon tender Consideration whereof, and good hope of after reformation of such poore prisoners there, as through temptation of Sathan are: and will bee apt to fall into like danger the said Master Dow, hath given competent Maintayance for ever, unto Saint Sepullchers parish for the towling of the great Bell, and for some especial man, by them to bee appoynted to come to the said Prison, the midnight before execution, and then distinctly and solemnly to ring a hand bell: then to pronounce with a loud voice at the prison grate, a godly, and Christian remembrance or exhortation, appointed by the Lorde Bishope, beginning thus:

O Ye Prisoners within condemned, this day to dy, remember your sinnes, call to God for Grace whilst yet you have time.

This was not a bequest but a gift *inter vivos,* for Robert Dow died May 2, 1612, aged ninety-five. Shortly after his death Anthony Nixon wrote a panegyrical tract in praise of him entitled *Londons Dove &c.* (London, 1612), which contains an account of this gift to St. Sepulchre's Church.

Further details of this charity are recorded by Wheatley and Cunningham in their *London Past and Present* (1891, Vol. III, p. 229), whose account is here condensed: There is a tablet in the Church of St. Sepulchre with a list of charitable donations to the church which includes the gift of £50 in the year 1605 by Mr. Robert Dow for ringing the "greatest" bell in this church on the day the condemned prisoners are executed, and for other services forever, concerning such condemned prisoners. It was the custom for the clerk or bell-man of St. Sepulchre's to go under Newgate on the night preceding the execution of a criminal and, ringing his bell, to repeat the following verses:

All you that in the condemned hold do lie,
Prepare you, for tomorrow you shall die.
Watch all and pray, the hour is drawing near,
That you before the Almighty must appear:
Examine well yourselves, in time repent,
That you may not to eternall flames be sent.
And when St. Sepulchre's bell tomorrow tolls
The Lord above have mercy on your souls.
                    Past twelve o'clock!

Similar gifts have been made since. I cannot find that
such a charity had ever before been created. Master Dow's
charity was in full operation during the year 1606, as may be
learned from the account of the execution of Robert Drury
and others at Tyburn, February 26, 1606/7. It is recorded
that the carts carrying the prisoners "stayed before St. Sep-
ulcher's Church, where the most Christian and *charitable
deed of Master Doove at every such time is worthily performed." (A true Report of the Arraignment &c. of Robert
Drury, London, MDCVII)* (Reprinted in *Harleian Miscellany,* Vol. III, pp. 52, 57).

A reference to the "bellman" of the St. Sepulchre charity
is found in Webster's *Duchess of Malfi* (*ca.* 1612) IV, ii, 182.
But a long interval seems to have elapsed before modern
commentators observed the reference to it in Shakespeare's
Macbeth; and during this interval editors often went far
afield in search of what is really near at hand. An "adden-
dum," credited to Professor Hales, describing this gift to St.
Sepulchre's Church is found on page 158 of A. W. Verity's
1930 edition of *Macbeth.*. In *Notes and Queries,* Volume 171,
December, 1936, page 404, occurs a note by Mr. Joseph E.
Morris calling attention to it. G. B. Harrison's *Macbeth*
(1937) in the Penguin Shakespeare (p. 103) has a similar note,
but he has mistaken the date which is fixed by the dated
record on the wall of the church. Kittredge has repeated this
mistake in his edition of the play (1939).

Shakespeare as a wide-awake Londoner may have heard of

this pious gift in May, 1605, as did the continuator Edmond
Howes. We can hardly go astray if we assume that before he
returned from Oxford to London the hand bell had been
procured, the bellman employed, the prayers and exhortation
approved by the bishop, and that thereafter whenever felons
in Newgate (across the street from the church) were to be
hanged next morning, the greatest bell of "Pulchers," as the
cockney called it, tolled at midnight, and the hand bell was
rung at the prison grate. This practice of tolling the great
bell continued until 1890. The use of the hand bell was discontinued much earlier, but the bell is preserved in a glass
case in the church.

William Shakespeare having returned in the autumn of
1605 to his lodging in Silver Street, within easy earshot of the
tower of St. Sepulchre, then for the first time heard this dread
midnight peal and shuddered, as would any sensitive man.
Thereafter a bell ringing in the night calls to his mind
Master Dow's "fatal bell-man" ringing his hand bell at the
grating of Newgate Prison to summon the poor condemned
wretch to heaven or to hell; and hence the great and vivid
imagery of these lines in *Macbeth*, written as this "stern'st
good-night" resounds in his ears.

I think Shakespeare began the composition of his play of
Macbeth at I, iii, 39, where Banquo asks three women standing by his pathway, "How far is it called to Forres?" * Others
have had the same impression; for Holinshed's wonder-
working tale thus began (p. 170):

Shortlie after happened a strange and uncouth wonder, which
afterward was the cause of much trouble in the realme of Scotland, as ye shall after heare. It fortuned as Makbeth and
Banquho journied towards Fores . . . there met them three
women. . . .

* This question is usually treated by actors as though addressed to
Macbeth, but the words "is it called" show that it was addressed to
persons thought to be inhabitants of the neighborhood. There were no
milestones on this heath.

What follows in the *Chronicle* is the material out of which the play is fabricated. Nothing before it is necessary to the story. The pictures of sorcery which now precede these lines in the play are not part of the story of Macbeth as found in Holinshed, and may best be thought of as a prelude written by Shakespeare as part of the final shaping up of his play; for he was most skilled in the art of quieting his audience before the main action begins, and these pictures are well calculated to accomplish this.

This prelude, when it came to be written, consisted at first of the twelve lines which constitute the first scene of the play, ending with the witches' words "Fair is foul and foul is fair." The dramatist then wrote the longer scene of sorcery which occupies I, iii, 1-37, and this required the interposition of a short scene to separate the two scenes of sorcery. But this interposed scene (the so-called "bleeding-sergeant" scene) was written last of all, and carries many indications of being a hastily written last-minute addition to the play. A later chapter (p. 332) is devoted to the examination of it.

The great drama of *Macbeth* really begins with the two captains journeying toward Forres and meeting the sisters, and the succeeding lines to the caldron scene flow on at high voltage. From the start Shakespeare took his obligation to write a play for his king very seriously. These scenes contain more tense action, powerful imagery, great poetry, and depth of character analysis than can be found in any other like amount of the Shakespearean canon. New depths and new meanings appear every time one reads them. In this sense they are quite unfathomable and unmatchable.* They

---

* Frederick J. Furnivall, a most excellent judge, has given his views upon this subject. He says (The Leopold Shakespeare, p. lxxviii):

My friend Mr. Peter Baynes holds that the analysis of Macbeth's ideas and motives is Shakespeare's greatest achievement. I think the third Act of *Othello* is that.

I agree with Mr. Furnivall that the third act of *Othello* is the most per-are written by a dramatist conscious of the plenitude of his powers and bound by no rule or precedent. Nothing can check the energy with which he creates as the action progresses. The extreme compression produces extreme resiliency. No other play of Shakespeare marches at so rapid a pace as *Macbeth*. It is not a play with plot and subplot as are so many of Shakespeare's, in which case presumably the main plot is set up first and the subplot later woven into it. This is what Shakespeare was doing at this time with his unfinished draft of *King Lear*. But *Macbeth* is different. It is made up of successive episodes closely concatenated but not interwoven.

This leads us to feel that this part of the drama was created *currente calamo*. The prophecy of the sisters, the planning and the execution of the murder of Duncan, the assassination of Banquo, the revelation of Macbeth's guilt, and on to the flight of Macduff and the visit of the frightened king to the witches were written while the fire burned—at white heat. The lines are at times not those of a dramatist but those of a rhapsodist, ignoring rules of meter or construction, if only the writer be delivered of the vivid picture already fully formed in the brain.*

---

fect and powerful dramatic act ever written. But I also agree with Mr. Baynes, and perhaps Mr. Furnivall would have agreed, that for continuous powerful dramatic expression nothing can equal the first three acts of *Macbeth*. Of course for varied and universal appeal *Hamlet* is greater, hence its greater popularity. In *Othello* the repulsive subject matter has lessened its popularity and *Macbeth's* position on the stage is handicapped because of the extreme difficulty of finding two actors who can competently assume the principal parts. An actor may make a great success of Hamlet and yet utterly fail in portrayal of the subtle impulses which govern Macbeth.

* I have been anticipated in this thought by that sound Shakespearean Gulian C. Verplanck. In his Introduction to this play he says: "Macbeth appears to me to have been completely meditated out before any part was written; so that it was presented to the poet's mind in all its parts as a single conception, and the actual composition then 'flew an eagle's flight, bold and forth on.' This is evidenced in the crowded rapidity of the action, and the hurried intensity of the varied passions,

Richard Grant White (*Works of Shakespeare*, X, p. 424) writes:

I . . . regard *Macbeth* as, for the most part a specimen of Shakespeare's unelaborated, if not unfinished, writing, in the maturity and highest vitality of his genius. It abounds in instances of extremest compression, and most daring ellipsis; while it exhibits in every Scene a union of supreme dramatic and poetic power, and in almost every line an imperially irresponsible control of language.

And elsewhere he writes that the play "was produced upon an emergency. It exhibits throughout the hasty execution of a grand and clearly-conceived design."

F. J. Furnivall in his Introduction to the Leopold Shakespeare (p. lxxviii) writes:

That the play was written in haste, the hurry of its action in its first acts, the want of finish in its first scenes, the difficulty of its expression, tend to prove. Most critics agree in this opinion.

An evidence of the high-speed production of this play is the frequency with which we find distasteful word repeti-

---

all bearing to one end." My only criticism of this language would be that the concept was not *meditated out,* it was *envisioned out.* Kittredge speaks of "the continuous burst of enthusiasm," in which this part of the drama of Macbeth was written (III, i, 3n.).

This play, more than any other of Shakespeare's plays, carries these marks of a birth fully grown as Minerva from Jove's brain. It is therefore strange that Dover Wilson should have mistaken the extreme compression of the play, which was a limitation which the dramatist placed upon himself, causing him to strike out words or to condense sentences as he was writing them, and should think that this evidences a condensation of a longer play written by himself some years previously, a theory which creates two new difficulties for every one it solves. When once it is found that I, ii, was hastily written after the play was otherwise finished, a great many of the difficulties about the play disappear. Mr. Wilson has been led in order to explain these to make what he calls "a very daring guess," that the play was originally written in longer form in the reign of Elizabeth and so played at that time *in Scotland,* but later shortened by the author for presentation in England in 1606. This is truly a bold and a dangerous conjecture which had best be avoided.

tion. Shakespeare usually took pains not to place a word in juxtaposition to itself or to one *idem sonans,* except where he was intentionally playing with the word. All writers are apt to violate this rule when they write too fast. Notice the following repetitions in *Macbeth:*

To beguile the *time* Look like the *time*   [I, v, 64–65].

<blockquote>
Well, I will thither.

Well, may you see things *well* done there   [II, iv, 36].
</blockquote>

Whom we to gain our *peace* have sent to *peace*   [III, ii, 20].

The tyrant has not batter'd at their *peace?*
No; they were well at *peace*   [IV, iii, 178–179].

Cleanse the *stuffed* bosom of this perillous *stuff*   [V, iii, 44].

We shall not *spend* a large *expense* of time   [V, viii, 60].

By the *grace* of *Grace* We will perform   [V, iii, 72].

Some of these may be intentional, but the others would not have occurred had not the play been written in haste. Textual editors have had no difficulty in suggesting changes which avoid this iteration. But Shakespeare did not stop to make these obvious changes. Nor was the delivery regular. The child was a footling, of which the vigor was evident before the features became clear. It could not await orderly development. Hence the frequency of the phenomenon of anticipation.* The audience must wait a little before the

---

* This sort of anticipation is a characteristic mark of the play of *Macbeth*. It is a product of the writer's excitement. It may be defined in the words of Lady Macbeth (I, v, 59) when she says, "I feel now the future in the instant." For example, the words "imperial theme" (I, iii, 129) require for their clarification the vision of the treble-sceptered king of IV, i, 121. I, iii, 139 is difficult to understand until we read what is stated in I, vii, 47 and 48. II, i, 7–9 is not explained until II, i, 20 has been read. When we are told (I, iii, 97) that a brave and experienced warrior is not afraid of the "images of death" which he makes, we feel the phrase to be a mere intrusion until we find that the same warrior later exhibits craven fear of the images of death created by his murders. And "nature's copy" of III, ii, 38 is a very empty phrase until we know

full meaning of the words becomes clear; for in the first three acts of the play there are many phrases and figures only explicable by what comes after. The poet's eye in fine frenzy rolling imputes to his audience either an imagination such as his own, which is able instantly to carry forward the scene, or a memory so strong that it can recall and interpret past words by what comes later. This creates an uncanny prescience which will be noted by rapidly but understandingly reading the lines from I, iii to IV, i, in which last-mentioned scene the true meaning of much that went before is made clear.

The rapid and inspired pace of the play slows down during Act IV. The necromantic scene proved a difficult one to write for it was to pass the scrutiny of a king who had written learnedly upon this technical science. Shakespeare had read the king's *Daemonologie,* no doubt soon after its reprinting in London in 1603, but it was only prudent for him to read it again, and to carefully con all that the king said about devils before showing his audience how witches can charm them and how they may deceive a conjurer seeking to learn the future from them. So the dramatist laid down his pen, and with it the mighty urge which brought forth the first three acts subsided, and the caldron scene was completed only after careful and perhaps even laborious study of a very recondite subject about which he had known very little. The scene is a very cunningly devised structure. A later chapter must be devoted to its analysis. The scene is also one of the two turning points in the character of Macbeth. The brave and noble Macbeth of the opening of the play who has a sensitive conscience and does not know fear yields to temptation and becomes a superstitious murderer who suffers torture of the mind, is shaken nightly with terrible dreams, and ever flees to the imaginary that he may not know himself. This continues until his visit to the witches "by the worst means to know the worst," at which point his con-

---

Macbeth's picture of the line of Stuart kings who favor their ancestor Banquo as told in IV, i, 112–121.

science is burnt out by the cautery and fear again disappears. He sleeps "in spite of thunder," but all control of his faculties has been lost; the body lives, but his soul is dead and "life's but a walking shadow." Thus has the dramatist exhibited in Macbeth first the "sound" conscience, next the "superstitious" conscience, and finally the "cauterized" conscience, according to the classification of the book which the king had written for the instruction of his son, of which more will be told in a later chapter. Evidently Macbeth suffering from this "leaprousie," as the king calls it, did not interest William Shakespeare as much as the superstitious Macbeth; nor does it so much interest the audience. Accordingly, in Act V we find this human interest transferred to the conscience-tortured Lady Macbeth.

There are short episodes in the earlier part of the play which may, and some which must, have been inserted by the dramatist after the fabrication of the main structure of the play, but before its completion. II, iv is a short scene which has the expository function of the chorus of the Greek play, telling what people outside Macbeth's castle are thinking about the strange goings on inside. It may have been written at any time. The drunken-porter episode contains one of these later additions. The same is true of the introductory pictures of witchery. The bleeding-sergeant scene was evidently written just before the first performance of the play, and V, ii, picturing the revolt of the thanes, also looks like a late insertion. Some of these are of high dramatic value, but they are not necessary to the development of the main theme.

Thus it would seem that when once the play was under way, Shakespeare kept straight on to the fourth act, maintaining the same grand initial key until Macduff fled to the English court, whereupon he stopped to take breath. This was in the first scene of the fourth act. As soon as the apparition utters the words "Beware Macduff," the audience knows how the play is to end. All of this was written, and most fittingly written, in London during the gloomy but exciting winter days which followed the discovery on November 5, 1605, of the Gunpowder Plot which was to have destroyed at a single blow the king and his royal family, the court and the Parliament.*

The great apotheosis scene near the end of IV, i, glorifying the line of the Scottish kings, marks the center of the drama, around which all else is grouped. While the Stuarts reigned it was full of meaning, and was chosen by Rowe for illustration in his edition. Let no intelligent auditor minimize it, even though today it has no popular appeal whatever, and is merely shuffled through on the stage. To know the play, one must have in mind the Stuarts as they were thought of in 1606, and not the disgraced dynasty of modern histories. In writing this scene the energy which the great picture of Macbeth's crimes had evoked seems to have exhausted itself. In consequence the completion of the play was not seriously undertaken until after it was known that King Christian was soon to visit his brother-in-law, and that a play suitable for performance before the *two kings* would be called for. This was in May, 1606.

In the earlier-written part of the play, the poetry is epic and wonderfully vivid. The force of the human imagination is a controlling theme; and of current events, the Gunpowder Plot and the equinoctial storms of the end of March, 1606, have produced quite visible and datable scars. Nerves are tense. The weather is foul or tempestuous. There is no sunshine.

We are conscious in the later parts of the play of a different atmosphere and different influences seem to be at work. The tempests are forgotten. Macbeth's hallucinations cease. He is by turns an automaton and a near maniac. The poetry

* From a number of other indications, which have been or will be mentioned, I think most of it was written during February and March 1605/6. At this date few or no performances were given at the Globe during Lent (Boswell's Malone, Vol. III, p. 65), so that the dramatist would probably have been free for a while after Feb. 19, 1605/6 to devote all his time to this task.

is no longer epic but elegiac. In consequence these later scenes of the play have a distinctly different flavor and a different tempo. Parts are written rather perfunctorily and others obviously hurriedly written. The scene of the murder of Lady Macduff, a disagreeable scene at best, was evidently written without fervor. Perhaps a scene showing an unsuccessful effort by Lady Macbeth to save her friend was to have preceded it and might have given it life. But the scene was never written. The scene in England lags even more painfully.*

In the drunken-porter scene the execution of Henry Garnet, the archequivocator, is pictured, but by sentences and phrases which bear marks of after insertion in an already written scene. They were probably written after the latter part of the play was taken in hand.

In the last two acts we distinctly trace the influence of the Profanity Statute, which went into effect May 27, 1606. Because in the fourth act the action flags, topical matter was introduced to hold the king's interest, including some use of the very latest news. In Scene ii of that act the sifting of the Jesuits in England by the Oath of Allegiance, which also went into effect May 27, 1606, is referred to.

Since a King of Denmark was to see the play, Siward, *the Dane,* was given a prominent and heroic part, and the Danes defeated by the Scots were politely converted into Norweyans. Later the uproar of July 31, 1606, as the royal procession passed through Cheapside, by which Concord's address was interrupted and Peace and Unity insulted in the presence of

---

* Barrett Wendell's impression of the third scene of the fourth act is interesting:

While taken straight from Holinshed it is so highly finished as to suggest either that it is the single remaining fragment of a more elaborate play than now remains, or else that it was either written in a momentary lapse of mood, or inserted later when the emotional impulse which pervades Macbeth had subsided.

The latter is the true explanation.

the two kings, was put into the play for condemnation. And King Christian's cannonade and his largess of 10,000 dollars were courteously acknowledged. These last two references to current events were worked into Act I, Scene ii, which was the very last portion of the play to be written, as a later chapter will show.

But these topical matters, of course, did not add to the dramatic interest of the play, which had by this time fallen far below the point which it had attained in the second and third acts. How the play was to end had been made clear in the first scene of the fourth act, and the play threatened to continue to its end without arousing any new interest or any tense feelings. At this point the dramatist rescued his great play from a weak ending by a feat of supreme genius. He interposed at the beginning of Act V the sleepwalking scene, and in but eighty-seven lines succeeded in again raising the tension of the drama to its highest pitch, for it is a scene that never fails to hold its audience bound motionless. It was a superlative achievement to put in one play two scenes showing the involuntary self-revelation of crime wrought by the conscience of the criminal, in Macbeth's case by his hallucinations and in his wife's case by her somnambulism. To differentiate them, Macbeth in the banquet scene speaks in ornate verse. Lady Macbeth in the sleepwalking scene speaks her mind in utter simplicity and in monosyllabic prose. Of the 170 words which she utters, all but twelve are of one syllable, and with the sibilant and dental consonants predominating. The great actress knows this and can utter them with startling effect. Shakespeare never did just this before nor again.

The sleepwalking scene tells us nothing of how, when, and why it was written. It is purely of the dramatist's own invention. Its author must be awarded the palm for having written the greatest short tragic scene ever produced. If King James had become sleepy toward the end of Act IV, he assuredly was wide awake as the last act opened, and gave his full attention to the boisterous battle scenes, the taking of the castle of Dunsinane, the downfall of Macbeth, and the proclamation of Malcolm as his successor.

Such lively scenes are the proper and expected place for the use of the heroic rimed terminal couplet, and it should surprise no one that the scenes of Act V contain an unusually large number of them, increasing the number of such couplets in the play to a high percentage. (See the table on p. 68 of D. L. Chambers's essay on *The Metre of Macbeth*.) I see no reason for suspecting, as some do, that Shakespeare was not the author of these rimed tags. They are effective and memorable on the stage. They are for the most part aphorisms of the Senecan variety such as one would expect to find in this Senecan play. People leave the theater repeating them; and *Macbeth* was written as a stage play and not merely for readers who may upon examination find some of these tags flat, for it is undoubtedly true that upon analysis some are feeble or repetitive. But the truth is that tags of this sort in an Elizabethan play are not really intended to advance the drama. They serve in many instances only to give the actor the bouncing exit and the *plaudite* which he craves and to notify the audience that the scene of the drama is about to change and that the next few lines must be attended to in order to find out where the new scene is laid. The modern reader, accustomed to a scenic stage, forgets this, but the theatergoer of Shakespeare's time knew it well.

Lines of this sort may have been put into the play at the request of the actor or of the stage director and may have been written by almost anyone, and we can never tell by whom. But if there is a reasonable possibility that Shakespeare wrote them, we should assign them to him rather than to "an inferior dramatist" or to anyone else. There are signs of hasty writing in the fifth act of this play, but I have found no lines in it that William Shakespeare may not have written, and therefore I put them all down as his until the contrary is proven. There is a discussion of this matter by E. K.

Chambers in Appendix G of his *Macbeth* in the Warwick Shakespeare, to which I refer anyone who may wish to pursue this matter further than is possible here.

The lines with which the play ends are inappropriate except as a concluding speech to the monarchs; for in *Macbeth,* as in the other great tragedies, the noble man who has fallen becomes at the end an object of pity and not of hatred. So Othello and Lear were treated. So does the audience feel toward the Macbeth of Act V, "tied to a stake" and fighting alone with harness on his back; and even more is his dead queen to be pitied. Therefore it is that the sensitive reader is jarred by Malcolm's reference in the last lines of the play to "this dead butcher and his fiend-like queen." But this phrase describes two regicides and was the last word concerning them as spoken by a king to two kings. Only for this reason is the line acceptable. "Coming from the speaker, 'this dead butcher' is quite proper. As Shakespeare's final designation of Macbeth, it will not do." * It is consequently omitted from all the modern stage versions of the play, for there are no kings now in the audience.

The late topical additions to the play mentioned on page 37 are very short. They might all have been written in an hour or so and tried out at the last rehearsal. They call for a date of performance a few days after August 1, 1606, and the showing must have taken place before August 10, when King Christian boarded his ship to go home. It thus becomes possible to fix the date of the first performance of *Macbeth* with satisfactory exactitude. In the year 1606 no performances were given at court by the King's Players after Shrovetide (February 19) until after the arrival of the King of Denmark, which was on July 17. During this visit the kings stayed mostly at Greenwich, but they visited Hampton Court on August 7 and only then. Three performances were given by the King's Players before the two kings, as evidenced by the following entry, which is found in the *Accounts of the*

---

* Sprague, *Shakespeare and the Audience,* p. 131.

Revels at Court as printed by the Old Shakespeare Society in 1842 at page xxxviii:

To John Hemynges one of his M^ts players upon Warrant dated 18th October 1606 * for three plays before his Matie and the kinge of Denmarke twoe of them at Grenewich and one at Hampton Courte

xxx [11]

Everything points to the performance at Hampton Court on August 7 as that of *Macbeth*. This is the only date late enough to allow time for the insertion of I, ii, 62 and IV, iii, 98–100. The Greenwich dates are too early unless, as is possible, the play was given there on August 8. But the accounts of the king's doings say that they rested that day after their journeys; therefore this date seems unlikely. Disregarding, then, this remote and unimportant uncertainty, August 7 at Hampton Court may be taken as the date and place of the first performance of *Macbeth*.

The play was then short but complete. Six years later forty-nine lines were added to it by someone who may conveniently be called Thomas Middleton, for it was likely he. This is explained on page 275. These lines should be stricken from our texts. No quarto edition of the play as acted during the dramatist's life has ever turned up. Our only text is that of the first folio, which was printed, seven years after Shakespeare's death, from a playhouse copy of the original manuscript in which, unfortunately, Middleton's lines had been interpolated. By removing these we get a fairly good text presenting no really serious difficulties, for which we may be thankful. It is practically as it came from the dramatist's pen, disclosing the author's constant effort to compress his thought so as to shorten the play, and even

---

* This is the date in the printed volume and in Peter Cunningham's transcript. In the original entry in the Rolls of Declared Accounts of the Audit Office in the Public Record Office, the date of the Warrant is 14 Oct., 1606.

disclosing some of the marginalia which were a by-product of this compression.

This is not the usual assessment of the folio text of *Macbeth*. Most editors have labeled it a faulty text and have struggled to better it, with the result that it has suffered much from unnecessary "emendation." To understand the play it is best to read it in the text of the first folio and give careful attention to the punctuation of the text, always being mindful of the fact that this text was written as an actor's text and not for readers of the play. If we do this, we will better catch its meaning. There will be found the usual number of compositor's errors and mislineations, which were the inevitable result of the printing process which produced the first folio, but for most of these the correction is obvious and unimportant. The really important and difficult thing is to get rid of the false emendations in our modern texts which distort the author's meaning.

This outline of how and when the play was written calls for proofs, and such evidences will occupy the balance of this book. They include examination of the external forces which influenced the construction of the play and the internal forces which molded its growth. Of the external forces one was the performance of Dr. Gwinn's *Tres Sibyllae*. The extent of this influence upon the play will be examined in a chapter entitled "The Imperial Theme." Another external force was a debate before the king while he was in Oxford on the question "Whether the Imagination Can Produce Real Effects." This is a persistent question in the play. To rightly understand the play one must know what the Elizabethans in general, and William Shakespeare in particular, were then thinking about the imagination. King James's thought as to the influence of the imagination is also of great interest and is necessarily involved. Fortunately, we have a good deal of information on these subjects, which will be set down at some length in chapters which follow.

The internal forces can only be known by peering into the laboratory of the dramatist's mind as he did his work. To do this it is important to know the tools which he had in his hands. Chief among these were two of the king's own books: the *Basilicon Doron* and the *Daemonologie,* in which are set forth the moral and philosophical standards which the dramatist built into his play; and next to these were Holinshed's *Chronicles* and some other historical sources which supplied him with the factual picture of eleventh century Scotland which is reproduced in the play. These were his most important working implements, and all must be considered.

The imagination plays so large a part in controlling and accounting for the actions of the characters of this play that it will be well to begin with an examination of the ideas of the Elizabethans, of King James and of William Shakespeare upon this subject, for it will not do to dispose of it by means of hasty generalizations such as are often to be found in discussions of this play.

THE EFFECTS OF IMAGINATION

For a word to designate the power of the mind to apprehend what is nonexistent, the Elizabethans often went to the Greek. They liked to call it *fantasy,* and its effect a *phantasma;* but still more often they used the equivalent Latin terms *imagination* and *image.* Many years before he wrote *Macbeth,* Shakespeare had opened his mind concerning this faculty in unforgettable lines (*Midsummer Night's Dream,* V, i, 1–22):

> *Hip.* 'Tis strange, my Theseus, that these lovers speak of.
> *The.* More strange than true: I never may believe
> These antique fables, nor these fairy toys.
> Lovers and madmen have such seething brains,
> Such shaping *fantasies,* that apprehend
> More than cool reason ever comprehends.
> The Lunatic, the lover and the poet
> Are of *imagination* all compact:
> One sees more devils than vast hell can hold,
> That is, the madman: the lover, all as frantic,
> Sees Helen's beauty in a brow of Egypt:
> The poet's eye, in a fine frenzy rolling,
> Doth glance from heaven to earth, from earth to heaven;
> And as *imagination* bodies forth
> The forms of things unknown, the poet's pen
> Turns them to shapes and gives to airy nothing
> A local habitation and a name.
> Such tricks hath strong *imagination,*
> That, if it would but apprehend some joy,
> It comprehends some bringer of that joy;
> Or in the night, imagining some fear,
> How easy is a bush supposed a bear!

Duke Theseus evidently considered devils to be the creatures of a diseased imagination; and he also knew well how easily

44

the poetical mind can give to "airy nothing a local habitation and a name." The world seems to have agreed that in these words of Theseus we truly hear the voice of William Shakespeare speaking through Theseus' mask.

As he advanced in maturity, the plays of Shakespeare increasingly magnify the subjectivity of supernatural effects and minimize their objectivity. In the early days of his dramatic career he was content to represent Joan of Arc as a traditional witch, with no questions raised or answered. Margery Jourdain seems to belong in the same category. But when he came to write the fairy tale of *Midsummer Night's Dream,* he put in the mouth of Theseus the lines just quoted in which the marvelous is rationalized—and dramatic propriety demands that the audience take Theseus as their mentor. Certain famous lines of Prospero in *The Tempest* (IV, i, 148–158) leave the audience in the same frame of mind. Even more obviously is it intended that those who see the *First Part of King Henry IV* acted shall side with Hotspur and not with Glendower in their discussion about the feats of the magician. The ghosts of the victims of Richard III and the ghost of Julius Caesar are dream ghosts. In the play of *Hamlet,* faced still more acutely with the problem of the nature of ghostly visitation, the ghost of Hamlet's father is shown in the early scenes playing a part (as the exigencies of the plot require) which compels an audience to think of it as a veritable objective reality—a character in the drama; and yet, as though to offset this, in the later closet scene there is a showing of the same ghost which anyone who will may take as a mere hallucination; and so it is with the ghost of Banquo in *Macbeth.* In *Cymbeline* the ghosts are stated by Posthumus, and also in the dramatist's stage direction, to be seen only in his sleep. Shakespeare's dramatic intent in this has been under critical examination for now a hundred years or more. Were his specters and spirits real or imaginary? There are persuasive arguments adducible both pro and con. These have been fairly set down by Professor

Elmer E. Stoll in the chapter on Ghosts in his *Shakespeare Studies.* But it may now be said, I think, that of late an increasing weight of mature critical opinion has judged that his art is intended to *invite,* but *not compel,* his audience to think of visions and ghosts as products of the excited imagination of the beholder. Only so can be explained the contradictions which the subject otherwise presents. It is not possible to think that Shakespeare was not aware of these. Reconciliation is found only in the assumption that he thus intentionally gave to the supernatural a dual aspect because he knew that most of his audience could not think of these things other than as realities, and yet he himself was sufficiently ahead of his time to carefully open a door for those who might think differently.

As we are now about to apply this generalization to the play of *Macbeth,* where it is most fully exemplified, this is the proper place to trace the books and other influences which seem to have had a part in leading Shakespeare to this position so much in advance of his time.

Three influences which greatly stimulated and affected his thinking on this subject are the Bible, Ovid, and Montaigne. These books brought him into full contact with Hebrew, Christian, pagan, and Renaissance thought concerning the supernatural and helped to produce the "myriad-minded Shakespeare" whose philosophy is a product of them all. Attempts to formulate either Shakespeare's philosophy or his religion have been and will remain futile; for his mind was in sympathy with contending philosophies and he did not try to define for us his reconciliation but made use of what he thought best in each one of them. This is to say that he was not a philosopher but only an unusually observant human being.

Both the biblical and the Ovidian pictures of witchcraft were familiar to William Shakespeare, and both have their reflections in his play of *Macbeth;* but before writing this play in which his thoughts about witches and other imaginary things were to find their most complete exposition, he had also read and thought about what Montaigne had to say on the subject. Montaigne's views were very different from those propounded in either the Bible or Ovid. King James, too, had been reading Montaigne in Florio's translation published in 1603; for his copy of this book, with what looks like the king's signature on the title page, is now in the Boston Public Library; while Shakespeare's copy, with his signature (now believed genuine) on the flyleaf, is in the Library of the British Museum.

In making his translation of Montaigne, Florio had been helped by his friends, Dr. Gwinn and Samuel Daniel, both of whom had been in Oxford during the king's visit when Shakespeare had his attention called to the story of Macbeth. John Florio, too, was an Oxonian and in 1604 had been appointed a groom of the king's privy chamber and so was almost certainly in Oxford at the same time. Therefore not only Shakespeare's own inclination but other influences seem to have conspired to lead him to Montaigne at this juncture.

Montaigne was the great introspectionist. He looked into his own mind and then into the minds of others, and having done this wrote down the result with more frankness and sincerity than other writers have been able to muster. His shrewd and pithy observations are scrappy in form, but the scrapbook which he thus produced and called *Essais* has since the date of its publication (1580) had a powerful influence on the world of thought. Shakespeare, it is clear, came into contact with these thoughts. He did not copy Montaigne's language, except once when he came to write *The Tempest*. Rather, these thoughts of the Frenchman were like seeds which found in the Englishman's mind congenial soil, so that they blossomed forth in this play of *Macbeth*, in which he shows the altogether dominant power over some persons of their imagination. This theme easily led him to show the responsibility of the imagination for the then almost universal belief in witches, for the same journey had first been made by Montaigne. Lecky considers Montaigne's *Essays* the chief influence which ultimately overcame the belief in witchcraft.

The minute introspection of Montaigne fitted very readily into this, the most Senecan of all of Shakespeare's plays.* English tragedy was still haunted by a Senecan style—five acts of sensational and bloody deeds done by men or women who have a way of reciting at length their thoughts about their crimes before they commit them. Recitals of this sort gave the dramatist the best possible opportunity of exhibiting the way the human imagination can do its strange work.

In the first book of *Les Essais de Montaigne* Shakespeare's eye had been attracted to Chapter XX, which begins thus:

DE LA FORCE DE L'IMAGINATION

Fortis imaginatio generat casum, disent les clercs.
Je suis de ceux qui sentent tres-grand effort de l'imagination.

---

* I recommend examination of what J. W. Cunliffe says on the Senecan influence in his book entitled *The Influence of Seneca on Elizabethan Tragedy,* one of the oldest and sanest attempts to trace this one of the forces which produced the Shakespearean tragedies. That the horror engendered in both Macbeth and his wife by the sight of their bloodstained hands is a reflection of the corresponding lines in Seneca's *Hercules Furens* I cannot doubt. Likewise is Seneca's "Curae leves loquuntur, ingentes stupent," back of Malcolm's lines in IV, iii, 254–256. J. A. Symonds, after pointing to this (*Shakspere's Predecessors,* p. 241), adds, "To neglect this instance of the Shakespearean alchemy, though unseasonable, was beyond my fortitude." Just so do I feel. Shakespeare had revolted against both Seneca's formalism and his fatalism, but his fondness for the Senecan ghost and the Senecan aphorism was never lost. And when Shakespeare's villains die they die in what T. S. Eliot aptly calls "the odour of Seneca." Macbeth in his death is no less evil a man than he was before, but the emphasis is now put upon his resolution and fortitude, so that the fickle audience may be coaxed to forget the evil and admire what is left. This is distinctly a Senecan art which Shakespeare inherited. Let me here point out that the fatalism of King Lear is that of an ancient pagan king and must not be imputed to the author of the play. F. R. Johnson's article on Shakespearean imagery and Senecan imitation published in the Adams Memorial Studies (p. 33) is the most recent study of this matter.

Chacun en est heurté, mais aucuns en sont renversez. Son impression me perse; & mon art est de luy eschapper, par faute de force à lui resister.

I have quoted this in the lively original, for Shakespeare probably knew the *Essais* before they were done into English. He seems to have pondered these words deeply. That the too great strength of the imagination may work the downfall of the man is the foundation upon which the play of *Macbeth* is built.* Montaigne says he could not resist it, but had learned to escape from it. Macbeth could neither resist nor escape and was overthrown by it.

After many examples of the working of the imagination, the same chapter proceeds (and I quote now from Florio's translation):

It is very likely that the principall credit of visions, of enchantments, and such extraordinary effects, proceedeth from the power of *imaginations*, working especially in the mindes of the vulgar sort, as the weakest and seeliest, whose conceit and beleefe is so seized upon, that they *imagine* to see what they see not.

In the play of *Macbeth,* more than in any other of his plays, Shakespeare has pictured people who "imagine to see what they see not." It is Macbeth, the Pictish poet, too full of black bile, who says, "Nothing is but what is not." He was of imagination all compact, and out of this abnormal imagination grew his fatal habit of trusting unreality instead of reality. Thus it is that *fortis imaginatio generat casum.*

This teaching of Montaigne, expressed with the freshness and exuberance of Renaissance thought, was itself no novelty.

* If, as I think likely, for he was musical, the boy Shakespeare while attending the Stratford School sang as a chorister at morning prayer in the church, he had often recited from the Fifth Psalm (Verse 11 in the Prayer Book version) these words: "Let them perish through their own imaginations." I owe this suggestion to my friend Dr. Frederick Fraley, a member of the Shakspere Society of Philadelphia.

The Greek philosophers had explored this field long before; and what is more important for our purpose, Shakespeare was familiar with what they had said, for when writing his Roman plays he had studied Plutarch's *Lives* in Sir Thomas North's translation and there had found these earlier philosophical discussions concerning the power of man's imagination. In the "Life of Marcus Brutus," which he used extensively in writing his play of *Julius Caesar,* he read of a conversation between Cassius the Epicurean and Brutus the Stoic on this subject which took place the night after Caesar's ghost appeared to the latter. Cassius is here reported to have said:

In our sect, Brutus, we have an opinion, that we do not always feel or see that which we suppose we do both see and feel: but that our senses being credulous, and therefore easily abused (when they are idle and unoccupied in their own objects), are induced to imagine they see and conjecture that which they in truth do not. For our mind is quick and cunning to work (without either cause or matter) anything in the imagination whatsoever. And therefore the imagination is resembled to clay, and the mind to the potter: who without any other cause than his fancy and pleasure, changeth it into what fashion and form he will. . . . But yet there is a further cause of this in you. For you being by nature given to melancholic discoursing, and of late continually occupied, your wits and senses having been over-laboured do easilier yield to such imaginations. For, to say that there are spirits or angels, and if there were, that they had the shape of men, or such voices, or any power at all to come unto us: it is a mockery.

Plutarch adds, "With these words Cassius did somewhat comfort and quiet Brutus."

We may rest assured that the dramatist was inclined to follow this portion of the Epicurean philosophy, for it so well accords with the views which he put into the mouth of Duke Theseus in *Midsummer Night's Dream* already quoted at the beginning of this chapter.

Another book well known to Shakespeare was Reginald Scot's *The Discovery of Witchcraft* (London, 1584). This was the first book in the English language to challenge the murderous belief in witchcraft. Scot boldly attacked with all his weapons of reasoning, irony, and ridicule this belief strongly rooted in popular opinion and upheld by both Church and state, disclosing the silliness and folly of the whole puerile system of demonology. The book is said to have been burned by the hangman * and, being ahead of its time, made little headway until in the seventeenth century, when it was several times reprinted and played its part in bringing about the repeal of the cruel witchcraft laws.

In Scot's *Discovery* (Bk. 15, Chapter XXXIX) is a chapter entitled a "Of visions, noises, apparitions and imagined sounds, and of other illusions, of wandering souls: with a confutation thereof." Here one may read how:

Many thorough melancholie do imagine, that they see or heare visions, spirits, ghosts, strange noises &c. . . . Many againe thorough fear proceeding from a cowardlie nature and complexion . . . are timerous and afraid of spirits and bugs &c.

In the play of *Macbeth* there is shown a melancholy man who imagines that he sees or hears the things enumerated by Scot and is by them made a coward and so destroyed.

Scot's book is often referred to as a source of the witch lore found in the play of *Macbeth*. I do not think it is. Shake-

---

* But certainly not by order of King James, as I hope all will agree after reading the chapters which are to follow concerning James's attitude toward witchcraft while he was King of England. It is true that many writers have charged James with this barbaric act without a particle of evidence to support the statement. The only basis for an assertion of the burning of this book is a statement in a German treatise published in 1659 that Scot's book was burned somewhere in England, without telling when, or where, or by whom. (See B. Nicholson's preface to his edition of Scot, pp. xxxvii to xxxix; and also the valuable bibliographical note prefixed to Montague Summers's edition of the work.) This myth is characteristic of the proneness of writers to thrown stones unfairly at James, concerning which more will be said later.

speare in writing this play wished to show a picture of the
witchcraft of Scotland. The English ideas about witches,
which he had known from his childhood, were too vulgar and
stupid. The continental ideas were too scientific for this
play. Scotland had produced a wilder and more imaginative
variety of witch, and to learn what such witches are like and
how they behave one must go to Scottish sources of information, the best known of which was the Scottish Kings'
Book on the subject. Therefore to that book he went and
reproduced in his Scotch play much that he found there.
But Reginald Scot's book has had an influence upon his play
in that it supplies the tempering thought of the power of
the human imagination as the only reasonable explanation
of such things. Those who would understand the fascination
which Scot's brave book had for William Shakespeare should
read Isaac Disraeli's praise of it in his essay entitled "The
Discovery of Witchcraft." He classes the book among those
which "mark an epoch in the history of the human mind."
And yet the book is almost forgotten, except by Shakespeareans, who have long known it to be one of the works which
had a notable influence upon the thought of the dramatist.
I am inclined to reckon Reginald Scot as the exciting influence which, supplementing and completing Montaigne's
formless exposition, instigated the dramatist to fully develop
Montaigne's thesis, "Fortis imaginatio generat casum," and
apply it to the delusions of witchcraft.*

* My admiration for this book induces me to quote a statement in the
article on Reginald Scot in the *Dictionary of National Biography* (XVII,
1002):

With remarkable boldness and an insight that was far in advance of his
age, he set himself to prove that the belief in witchcraft and magic was rejected alike by reason and religion, and that spiritualistic manifestations were
wilful impostures or illusions due to mental disturbance in the observers. He
wrote with the philanthropic aim of staying the cruel persecution which
habitually pursued poor, aged and simple persons who were popularly credited
with being witches.

Shakespeare had known from his boyhood the story of the Witch of Endor as told in I Samuel, 28. This was a stronghold of the demonologists. King James has gone into it at some length in his *Daemonologie* (pp. 2–5). But Scot had discussed it even more carefully (Bk. VII, Chaps. 8–14). The point at issue between Scot and the king was whether, as stated in the margin of the Geneva Bible and as James urged, it was the devil taking on the form of Samuel who was produced by the witch (for both agreed it could not really have been Samuel), or whether, as Scot argued, it was a trick practiced by a cozening old woman upon "the deceived mind and imagination" of a frightened king, "being now straught of mind, desparate, and a very foole." Shakespeare in the play of *Macbeth* pictures just such a distraught and frightened king seeking by the worst means to know the worst and learning that he is to lose his kingdom. Disraeli in his essay previously mentioned (*Amenities of Literature,* Vol. II) terms King Saul "the Israelitish Macbeth." It would be just as apt to call Macbeth the Scottish King Saul. The moody and murderous King Saul seeking out the witch who foretells his fall in the battle of Mount Gilboa is the prototype of the imaginative and murderous King Macbeth seeking the witches who foretell his fall in the battle of high Dunsinane, and King James will be sure to notice how exactly parallel are the two cases, for in his *Basilicon Doron* (p. 57) he had warned his son: "Consult therefore with no necromancier nor false prophet upon the success of your warres, remembering on King Saul's miserable end."

Finally, Shakespeare was in these days reading Harsnet's *Declaration of Egregious Popish Impostures,* published in 1603. More will later be said about this book, which furnished a good deal of the demoniac nomenclature used in *King Lear.* It contains a vivid picture of a man ruled by his imagination. Here Shakespeare had read (Chap. 21, pp. 131–132):

It is a question moved by Scaliger: Why men of a melancholick constitution be more subject to fears, fancies and imaginations of devils, and witches, than other tempers be? His answer is, *quia ab atra bile, atri & fuliginosi generantur spiritus, qui Cerebrum pingunt turbulentis phantasmatibus,* because from their black & sooty blood, gloomie fuliginous spirits do fume into their brain, which bring black, gloomy, and frightful images, representations, and similitudes in them.

Thus the books in Shakespeare's hands in 1605 abounded with suggestions that if he is to write a play based on the Macbeth legend as told by Holinshed, it would be most timely to endow this ambitious man with an abnormal imagination so strong as to lead him step by step through a career of crime to his downfall. Such a theme would be likely to appeal to thoughtful minds in England just at this time.

With this plan in mind and while turning over thoughts such as those of Montaigne and Scaliger and Reginald Scot upon this subject, Shakespeare heard about the debate at Oxford in the king's presence dealing with the same question. In these debates the king took great pleasure and an active part. The Venetian Ambassador Nicolo Molyno, in a dispatch dated September 14, 1605, writes:

I have just been to Oxford on his Majesty's invitation. . . . The King attended morning and afternoon at all the disputations which were held by each of the faculties, and not only did he take a share in the debate, but filled the role of "moderator," with such elegance and finish that he proved himself no mere superficial smatterer, but a profound student of these matters [*Calendar of State Papers—Venetian,* Vol. X, p. 270].

The Oxford debate which had most interest for Shakespeare occurred on August 29, 1605, as part of the Philosophy Act.* The question propounded was: "An imaginatio possit

* It is very unlikely that William Shakespeare, a noncollegian, was actually present at any of these Latin disputations in St. Mary's Church;

producere reales effectus." The following explanatory verses were read with the question:

> Qualia monstra parit, quot vis phantastica formas,
> Quam vaga fert Proteus, quam nova Nilus habet.
> Concipit Aethiopem dum foemina mente nigellum,
> Ventre simul foetum concipit alba nigrum.*

The first couplet is an enunciation of the subjective power of the imagination; the second, an unconvincing effort to show that it may have objective reality. The modern mind better understands the powerful influence of a vivid imagination, for hallucination is now a well recognized psychological phenomenon. Its effects are subjectively very real but have no objective reality.

The nature of the imagination and the reality of its results was no new subject for debate in England during the reigns of Elizabeth and James. The Reformation had put in question the old ideas as to ghosts or specters. To a Roman Catholic they were still veritable spirits of the departed returning to the earth from purgatory. But the Protestants, denying that there is any such place as purgatory, insisted that if a specter were a reality at all it was only a devil appearing as a dead body. Both Catholic and Protestant agreed that many ghosts or demons were purely imaginary. The specula-

---

but Wake expressly records that the two theses for the Philosophy Act were selected "jussu Regio." Being in Oxford, Shakespeare would learn this and would thus become conscious of the king's interest in the subject of the force of the imagination, and no doubt felt that he could tell him more about it than the disputants at Oxford.

* This may be literally translated:

> The force of the imagination brings forth such monsters and as many shapes
> As Proteus makes changes, or the Nile new things.
> When a white woman conceives in her mind a dusky Ethiopian,
> Straightway she conceives in her belly a black foetus.

The latter choice nosegay has been culled directly from Montaigne's essay on "The Force of the Imagination" (Liv. I, Chap. XX).

tions of the day therefore first tried to distinguish the real from the imaginary and then to settle whether the reality was ghost or demon. Shakespeare's play of *Hamlet* deals with the latter question, while *Macbeth* deals with the first.

Two books printed in London helped to stimulate interest in these controversies. The earlier of them was Lavater's *Of Ghosts and Spirits, etc.,* translated into English and so printed in London in 1572. Lavater was a learned Swiss Protestant believing in the spiritual world and in the reality of its wonders, and yet at the outset of his book he warns us that we must not be deceived by our imaginations:

And fyrste it can not be denyed, but that some menne whiche eyther by dispositions of nature, or for that they have susteyned greate miserie, are nowe become heavie and full of melancholie, imagine many tymes with them selves being alone, miraculous and straunge things. Sometimes they affirme in great soothe, that they verily heare and see this or that thing, whiche notwithstanding neyther they nor yet any other man dyd once see or heare. Which thing we sometimes see by experience to bee true in those men, whiche be troubled with greate headache or subject to other diseases of the body, or cannot take rest in the night or are distraughted of their wittes [p. 10].

It is highly probable that Shakespeare had read Lavater's book. Dover Wilson has shown how much its thought seems to have influenced the speculations found in *Hamlet*.

More recently interest in this subject had been revived by the publication in London in 1605 of an English translation of the Catholic answer to Lavater originally written in French in 1586 by Peter de Loier of Angiers.* This translation was dedicated to King James, and is entitled:

* His name is thus printed in the translation, and I follow it, although the common usage prints Pierre Le Loyer. His French work was in four books and under its French title was entered on the Stationers' Register Jan. 11, 1605. The English publisher only favored us with a translation of the first of the four books.

A
TREATISE
OF SPECTERS OR
straunge Sights, Visions and Ap-
paritions appearing sen-
sibly unto men.
Wherein is delivered, the Nature of
Spirites, Angels, and Divels: their
power and properties: as also of
Witches, Sorcerers, Enchanters
and such like.
With a Table of the Contents of the severall
Chapters annexed in the end of the Booke.
Newly done out of French into English.
AT LONDON
Printed by Val. S. for Mathew Lownes.
1605.

It seems likely that the belated publication by Z. Jones in
1605 of this translation was due to the great popularity in
England of the play of *Hamlet* during the years 1602 to 1605,
for the book deals largely with the nature of ghosts such as
that of Hamlet's father, as well as with such witches, sorcerers,
and enchanters as are shown in the play of *Macbeth*. At this
point we are chiefly concerned with what it tells about the
imagination.

De Loier begins his treatise with an effort to define specters,
"phantosmes," and visions. He explains that "some modern
physitians . . . do confound a specter and a phantosme together," but De Loier thus (p. 1) differentiates them:

A Specter or Apparition, is an Imagination of a substance without a Bodie, the which presenteth itself sensible unto men,
against the order and course of nature, and maketh them afraid.
. . . So that the severall and speciall kindes of the Imagination
are, the Specter or strange sight, the Phantosme, the vision & the
fantasie. . . . Suydas saith, That a Phantosme is an imagina-

tion of thinges which are not indeed, and doth proceede of the senses being corrupted: which Plutarch also doth seeme to confirme.

More specifically, they are thus to be distinguished:

The Specter hath a substance hidden and concealed, which seemeth to move the fantastique body, the which it hath taken. Moreover, the Phantosme (being as it is) a thing without life, hath not any will: whereas the Specter, if it will, doth appeare unto us: if it will not, it doth not appeare.

This seems to be an effort to define the distinction which we now make between the subjective effects of the imagination and the supposed or believed objective effects. The latter has no body but has "substance" and a will of its own; the former has neither substance nor will power.

There are statements in De Loier's book which seem to find their reflex in the play of *Macbeth*. We read in Chapter XI, page 112:

Now amongst the manifold numbers of those that have their consciences troubled, by reason of their wicked and lewd lives, and are perplexed and terrified with a million of feares; we may well account those tyrants, who by unlawfull and indirect meanes, have usurped a tyrannicall authoritie over their owne native countries, or in some strange estate, and have changed a good forme of common-wealth and government, into an unjust and tyrannicall power; putting to death thousands of persons, whom they suspected to bee men of noted vertue and honestie, and who might be able to resist their damnable attempts and usurpations. How often have we seene, that these men have bin troubled and tormented with most horrible phantosmes & imaginations, which do com into their heads both sleeping & waking: . . . How often have they supposed and imagined, that they have seene sundry visions and apparitions of those whom they have murthered, or of some others whome they have feared?

And on the next page we read that King Thierry, having slain Simmachus, saw "on an evening as he sat at supper . . . the face of Simmachus in a most horrible shape and fashion, with great mustachoes, knitting his browes, frowning with his eyes, biting his lippes for very anger, and looking awry upon him.''

This account of the "phantosmes and imaginations" which terrify the kingly murderer and tyrant, found in a book which was for sale on the book stalls of London in the year in which the play of Macbeth was about to take shape, has such close resemblances to what we find in the third act of the play that I cannot doubt that there is some connection.

In the Banquo tale of Hector Boece (and of those who had followed him, including Holinshed), Macbeth invites Banquo to a supper and causes him to be slain as he is returning home late at night. But it would seem that after reading Chapter XI of De Loier's book, the dramatist saw a great opportunity to better the tale of his predecessors. So the slaying of Banquo in the play occurs not as he is leaving but as he is coming to the supper, and his "phantosme" in horrible shape is soon afterward seen by Macbeth at the supper table; and it is this transformation which has given to Shakespeare's banquet scene its extraordinary dramatic power. Thus much does the world owe to "Z. Jones," who translated De Loier's *Treatise of Specters* into English, and so brought King Thierry's supper to the attention of William Shakespeare.

MACBETH'S IMAGINATION

In the play of *Macbeth* the dramatist has pictured the "vis phantastica," that is, the force of the imagination, more vividly than in any other play he, or perhaps anyone else, ever wrote. Dr. J. Q. Adams, in his discussion of *Macbeth*, puts it thus:

Indeed, his abnormal imagination almost completely dominates his mental processes. His thoughts take the form, not of ideas, but of vivid images. For instance, when the purpose to murder Duncan comes into his mind, it promptly shapes itself into a "horrid image." And this is characteristic of his mental activity throughout the play; everywhere we see his thoughts expressing themselves in images so vivid as scarcely to be distinguished from reality [ed. of *Macbeth*, p. 135].

And Dr. Kittredge writes that Macbeth has "an imagination of extraordinary power, which visualizes to the verge of delirium. Every idea that enters his mind takes instant visible shape. He *sees* what another would merely *think*" (ed. of *Macbeth*, p. xiv).

Macbeth's imagination is not only powerful; it is characterized by what has been happily called "the hallucination of self-credulity." The phrase is that of the elder Disraeli.* It is finely shown in Shakespeare's disclosure of the mind of Macbeth, who speaks of it as his "strange and self-abuse" (III, iv, 142). In modern parlance, "he fools himself by seeing things." Macbeth thinks about a certain thing. He may wish it true. He may fear it will be true. There follows quickly a state of rapture or ecstasy or hallucination which pictures the thing hoped or feared so vividly that he assumes

* The "Discovery of Witchcraft," in his *Amenities of Literature*.

it to be true, acts as though it were true, and is thus brought to ruin.

This elaborate development by Shakespeare of Macbeth's imagination becomes the more striking when we realize that Holinshed's Macbeth had no imagination at all. He was merely a brave warrior who became a cruel murderer.

This abnormal imagination has great dramatic significance, for the turning point of the plot of *Macbeth* is the exposure of the crime by the hallucination of the criminal. It has an even greater psychological interest, for it is the self-credulity of Macbeth's imagination led by his hopes which tempts him to violate his conscience; and the same powerful imagination led by his fears vastly increases the torments of his violated conscience. Furthermore, the succession of hallucinations created by this imagination is used by the dramatist to lead the king to a better understanding of the delusions of witch-craft, for King James was by now troubled about the relia-bility of the confessions of the witches whom fifteen years ago he had had tortured with the pilliwinks and burned. He had come to suspect that their stories might be the fictions of an unduly vivid imagination. Shakespeare thought so too, and used his royal play to show the king what extraordinary effects can result from the human imagination.

To do this he shows to us three old hags practicing sorcery and necromancy according to the beliefs of the Scottish people and professing to do strange things. But a running comment put in the mouths of those who see them constantly suggests that their awesome practices are due to hallucination of the beholder, very real subjectively, but objectively nonex-istent. When alone, they are only old women of flesh and blood professing sorcery as expounded by King James in his *Daemonologie;* but when Banquo or Macbeth sees them, the audience is kept aware that their doings and sayings are in-fluenced by the imagination of those who see them, suggesting at once to the "judicious" that witchcraft may be but a delusion.

Dr. Johnson failed to see this, and thought it necessary to apologize for the showing of sorcery in *Macbeth*. After describing "the doctrine of witchcraft at once established by law and by the fashion," he said:

Upon this general infatuation Shakespeare might be easily allowed to found a play, especially since he has followed with great exactness such histories as were then thought true; nor can it be doubted that the scenes of enchantment, however they may now be ridiculed, were both by himself and his audience thought awful and affecting [Johnson's Shakespeare, Vol. 6, p. 372].

This literalism is blind to the scope of Shakespeare's enduring art. At the other extreme is such a well phrased statement as the following taken from a short essay on *Macbeth* by William Preston Johnston:

The prophetic soul of Shakespeare accepted the popular beliefs as modes of expression, and employed them as symbols for the unseen forces of nature and spirit, in which dwell activities more potent than even superstition could conjure up. And it was through this high poetic and philosophic power, this eminent gift of imagination and understanding working together, that he produced the terrible and highly idealized conception of supernatural agency embodied in the Weird Sisters. These and Banquo's ghost, the apparitions, the omens, the air-drawn dagger, the mysterious voice, are but the signs and formulas through which he represents the problem of evil, with which Macbeth grapples, and which he solves to his own temporal and eternal ruin.*

Neither of these statements is satisfactory. The first is entirely characteristic of the unimaginative eighteenth century criticism which is now out of favor. The latter is a typical nineteenth century romantic generalization which does not take into account the minds of the audience who were to see the play in Shakespeare's day.

* New Orleans, 1887, pp. 15–16; reprinted in *The Prototype of Hamlet* (New York, 1890), pp. 54–55.

The twentieth century has found (as we must hope) the true via media. For an excellent statement of this position I quote the words of Allardyce Nicoll:

There are thus two distinct points of view from which we may regard the witches. We can see in them evil ministers tempting Macbeth to destruction, or we can look on them merely as embodiments of ambitious thoughts which had already moved Macbeth and his wife to murderous imaginings. The peculiar thing to note is that through Shakespeare's subtle and suggestive art we do not regard these two points of view as mutually antagonistic [*Studies in Shakespeare* (1928), p. 123].

So important is this that I subjoin in a footnote a few other statements to much the same effect, although in differing phraseology.*

The way in which the thaumaturgy of the dramatist works this wonder can be seen by the inquiring eye. There truly were on the heath three withered hags of whom Banquo inquired how far they were from Forres. But Macbeth, always prone to substitute the imaginary for the real, transmutes the mumblings of the third witch into greetings corresponding to the hopes which are in his own mind.

Banquo's reaction is different. He, too, is interested in the establishment of a "line of kings" in Scotland (the "imperial theme"), so as to end the lawless succession of fighting king-

---

* "Shakespeare meant the judicious to take the Ghost [of Banquo] for an hallucination, but knew that the bulk of the audience would take it for a reality." A. C. Bradley, *Shakespearean Tragedy* (1904), p. 493.

"The language and the imagery which he [Shakespeare] employed [in *Macbeth*] were such that each hearer could interpret according to his condition or temperament." Margaret Lucy, *Shakespeare and the Supernatural* (1904).

Shakespeare "distinctly leaves open the question whether these preternatural appearances [in *Macbeth*] are not in fact subjective visions." H. J. Bridges, *Our Fellow Shakespeare* (1916), p. 165.

"To his own generation one of the most amazing things about Shakespeare must have been his power to appeal to the 'generalty' and the 'judicious' at one and the same time." Dover Wilson, Introduction to the 1929 ed. of Lavater, p. xxvii.

lets who have ruled and ruined Scotland during the preceding
century.   Therefore he, too, welcomes words of the witches
which seem to promise this to his descendants; but his trouble
is that he is not at all sure that they really said it.   To his
honest mind they seem but "bubbles."   He asks them: "Are
ye fantastical [imaginary], or that indeed which outwardly
you show?"

And he asks Macbeth:

> Were such things here as we do speak about?
> Or have we eaten on the insane root
> That takes the reason prisoner?

This suggestion of the fantastical and imaginary character
of the words and doings of the witches runs through the play.
Not only does Banquo thus question the reality of the witches
but as Macbeth's imaginings take shape, his habit is to seek
confirmation from another.   When he sees the dagger in the
air, he debates with himself whether it really is there.   When
he sees Banquo's ghost, he debates its reality with his wife.
When he sees the procession of the kings, he asks Lennox
whether there was really anybody there.   The subtle suggestion of this will be lost on the crowd.   It still is.   To the
groundlings what the sisters do or say seems real.   To thoughtful men, including the king, the play presses home Banquo's
question, whether it is imaginary.   Thus the witchery of the
play has a different meaning to different people.

It is apt to be overlooked that this difference of opinion as
to the powers of the sisters is derived from the ancient sources.
Hector Boece writes (1575 ed., p. 249 v.):

Vana ea Maccabaeo Banquohonique visa. . . . Verum ex eventu
postea Parcas, aut nymphas aliquas fatidicas diabolico astu praedi-
tas fuisse interpretatum est vulgo.

Holinshed, freely translating this, states that the strange
words and doings of the three sisters were

reputed at the first but some vaine fantastical illusion by Macbeth and Banquo. . . . But afterward the common opinion was, that these women were either the weird sisters, that is (as ye would say) the goddesses of destinie; or else some nymphs or feiries, endued with knowledge of prophecie by their necromantical science, because everything came to pass as they had spoken. p. 171.

The sources thus specify three views: the sisters were (1) imaginary; or (2) the Fates or Norns; or (3) women practicing black art. Shakespeare projected question concerning this throughout his entire play with the result that discussion has continued to this day as to what the dramatist really wished his audience to think.

The first interpretation was the immediate reaction of Banquo and the ultimate acknowledgment of Macbeth, and they were the two who could best judge. It was, as I think, Shakespeare's view, and he hoped that it would be that of the king. The second interpretation has been much insisted upon by a few modern critics, but Dr. Bradley's refutation of it (*Shakespearean Tragedy*, p. 342) seems to me unanswerable.* The third is now, as then, the usual view and has always been the "common opinion," as no doubt Shakespeare expected it to be. Everyone is left free to decide whether the deeds of the witches are real or fantastical. For the dramatist did not know how far he might dare to lead his king. He had been told of the general trend of James's thoughts toward a rational position, but just where the king stood at the

---

* On April 20, 1611, that notorious scalawag Simon Forman saw *Macbeth* performed at the Globe Theater, and when he reached home he opened his Holinshed to help him to remember what he had seen, and wrote out a description of the play in which he called the sisters "3 women feiries or nimphes," thus evidencing his adhesion to the third hypothesis of Holinshed. One would not expect a professional magician to accept the Sisters' deeds as imaginary, but it is worth noting that he saw nothing on the stage to indicate that they were "goddesses of destiny."

moment he could not know; and so he left it for him to go as far as he pleased and no farther.

The temptation scene (I, iii, 116–142) is the full showing of how Macbeth's imagination operates. He clings to an evil thought while trying to shift responsibility for it. His hopes created the thought (I, iii, 118). He had already discussed it with his wife, and this had produced an image in his mind of King Duncan murdered that Macbeth may take his throne. The sight of the sisters brings this image again to mind and he yields to what he calls a "supernatural soliciting," although as he yields he knows it to be only a "horrible imagining," a *fantasy*, an unreal thing. His great fault is thus shown to be his habit of taking the unreal to be real, and allowing it to master him because it corresponds precisely with his wishes.* It is this reflexive element in the enticements of the witches which teaches the thoughtful auditor that their temptations are imaginary.

The important lines are:

> My thought, whose murder yet is but fantastical,
> Shakes so my single state of man that function
> Is smother'd in surmise, and nothing is
> But what is not.
>
> [I, iii, 138–142]

In these lines the dramatist took the first opportunity offered in his play to define with the accuracy of a psychologist the devious way in which the imagination of Macbeth does

---

* This correspondence may be traced throughout the play. Many thinkers have discovered this secret. Coleridge expressed it in his Bristol Lectures of 1813: "They [the witches] lead evil minds from evil to evil, and have the power of tempting those who have been the tempters of themselves."

The latest statement of it which I have seen is found in Prof. Morozov's lecture, delivered at the Shakespeare Conference in Moscow in April, 1942: "Macbeth killed Duncan not because they [the weird sisters] had come into his life; they came into his life because he wanted to kill Duncan." *Shakespeare Association Bulletin*, Vol. XVIII, p. 57.

its work. Unfortunately for the modern playgoer, the definition is expressed in words several of which are used in senses
now obsolete or unusual. It is therefore necessary in this
twentieth century to translate these lines into a more modern,
even though less vigorous, mode, thus:

The murder which is part of the design I have in mind,
though as yet existing only in my imagination, so shakes my
power to control myself, that action is overruled by imagination, and nothing exists for me but that which is not.*

Thus we are shown the workings of the mind of the worthy
Macbeth as he is transformed into the superstitious Macbeth,
a change which marks the first milestone of the play. He well
knows that he has put his actions under the control of his
imagination. He well knows that he ought not to do this.

Persons with this sort of imagination are at times beside
themselves. The mind leaves the body and watches it.
"Ecstasy," the Greeks called it. The Latins called it "rapture." Macbeth after first seeing the witches "seems rapt"
(I, iii, 57). The fit lasts for some time, until Banquo exclaims, "Look how our partner's rapt." Macbeth, too, knows
about these fits. He writes to his wife that he "stood rapt" at
the wonder of the witches. But this rapture is not involuntary. He can control the fit if he wants to do so. There is a
fine showing of this at the end of the murder scene. Macbeth has been racked by the sight of his bloody hands. To
escape his tormenting conscience, he at once flees from reality
to unreality. So is he rapt until his wife urges, "Be not lost
so poorly in your thoughts" (II, ii, 73). She knows that he
can control this matter. So does he. The next words, "To
know my deed?," in the folio text make a single line and, as
the Clarendon editors prefer (p. 109), should stand as Mac-

* This paraphrase uses definitions found in the *Oxford English Dictionary*. Reference is made to the following numbered definitions:
thought, 4d; fantastical, 1; single state of man (see footnote, p. 12);
function, 2; smothered, 3; surmise, 5.

beth's question. For if he obeys his wife, he will know his deed and from that he would escape. His next words, " 'Twere best not know myself," are his acknowledgment that he is deceiving himself. But the rapture ends, and as he comes to himself the pangs of remorse begin their torment and he wishes the loud knocking could wake Duncan. Again in the banquet scene we are shown the operation of one of Macbeth's fits, and both he and his wife describe the malady. He says, "I have a strange infirmity which is nothing to those that know me." She tells more. "My lord is often thus, and hath been from his youth. . . . The fit is momentary; upon a thought he will again be well." This process of hallucination and self-deception, begun in boyhood and developed until the mind has become diseased, is the process by which Macbeth's strong imagination brings about his downfall. "Fortis imaginatio generat casum."

The supreme exhibition of the power of Macbeth's imagination is the vision of the bloody dagger which the murderer sees as he goes to Duncan's chamber. The familiar lines (II, i, 33–49) are a debate, "an imaginatio possit producere reales effectus." The mind insists on the reality of that which the bodily sense asserts to be nonexistent. In the end the latter wins ("there's no such thing"), recognizing that the hallucination is due to Macbeth's wish, that is, "the bloody business." It is his responsibility. The handle is "toward his hand" for he wishes it so. It marshals him the way that he was going. The gouts of blood appear on the blade because he wishes them there. In III, iv, 62, Lady Macbeth says that her husband told her that this air-drawn dagger *led him to Duncan,* showing how well he knew that he had let his imagination thus tempt and control him in violation of his conscience.

The actor of this part must make the imaginary dagger so real that not only Macbeth but the audience see it. Burbage could do this. So could Garrick, Macready, Irving, and

Booth. For this reason the dagger is not shown to the audience, although some poor actors have called for it. I have seen it lying on a table and revealed by the spotlight. I have also seen it dangled in the air and turned to show the blood on it. Thus will the inferior actor crave help in depicting the imaginary, and thus will the stage strive to give it.

The bloody dagger is only *seen*, not *felt:* "Mine eyes are made the fools of the other senses or else worth all the rest." Other senses are soon brought in. Macbeth *hears* the voice crying, "Sleep no more." In the sleepwalking scene, Lady Macbeth (V, i, 56) *smells* the imagined blood spots on her hands; and Angus tells us (V, iii, 16) that Macbeth *feels* the clotted blood of his victims on his hands. Macbeth's "I have supp'd full with horrors" suggests the *taste* of blood. All of man's senses can thus deceive him.

In the banquet scene the ghost of Banquo is as purely imaginary as the bloody dagger, coming and going according to Macbeth's fitful hallucinations. By De Loier's test, it is a "phantosme" and not a "specter," for it "hath not any will of its own." Heretofore, image had followed the wish of Macbeth, but in this case it twice follows his feigned wish, expressed in a bravado which is really an expression of his fear. Again it occasions a debate as to its reality, this time with Lady Macbeth, terminating in the acknowledgment that it is an "unreal mockery."

We may accept as authoritative Dr. Schelling's estimate of this ghost as expressed in his *Elizabethan Drama* (Vol. I, p. 582):

Banquo appears among the guests unseen by them and purely as the subjective result of the concentration of Macbeth's mind on his murdered victim; and the apparition disappears as other figures replace the mental image, a phenomenon repeated in this case with cumulative effect most powerful.

There has been much critical pronouncement as to whether Banquo's ghost should appear physically. The stage direction calls for it, for Shakespeare wished to make sure that his audience should know how vividly and horridly Macbeth sees the gory locks. Yet many great actors have been able to attain the desired effect without it, and modernist sentiment generally extols its banishment. But the fact remains that whether or not this ghost should be shown on the stage is really dependent not upon critical literary judgments but upon the intelligence of the audience. My preference is for the manager who follows Shakespeare's stage direction. Playgoers of this age can be relied upon to know that Banquo's ghost, even though appearing visibly, is purely a creation of Macbeth's imagination. Furthermore, the stage direction at IV, i, 112, compels us to treat the procession of the kings as we do this ghost. If the latter is driven from the stage because imaginary, so too must be the kings, and this is most unfortunate. We do best when we follow the expressed judgment of William Shakespeare, dramatist, stage manager, and actor; for there is no good reason to think that anyone but he wrote the stage directions for the play of *Macbeth*.

Taking up next the necromantic scene, it appears that the oracles uttered by the apparitions are essentially subjective. Here it behooves us to advance carefully, for this proposition has been questioned by high authority.

The first apparition warns, "Beware Macduff," which, as Macbeth says, harps his fear. The second tells him, "Be bloody, bold and resolute." This was his own thought when he had recently called for a "bloody and invisible" hand to serve him in his crimes (III, ii, 48). The third says, "Be lion-mettled, proud, and take no care who chafes, who frets or where conspirers are." This, too, is the comfort he longs for. All of these oracles are "sweet bodements" to the frightened king, and spring from his own brain. But to the last two oracles are appended the familiar deceptive pronouncements concerning the man not born of woman and the coming of Birnam Wood, and these prophetical tags admittedly raise the difficulty which is discussed by Dr. A. C. Bradley in his *Shakespearean Tragedy* (p. 346). After expressing sympathy with the view that the play of *Macbeth* is psychological for those who will so take it, although for the groundlings it is "hard fact," he is led to a skeptical intermediate position in regard to the subjectivity of the apparitions, finding the theory which has been outlined "incomplete" and urging that although it applies to the prophecy of the crown and the warning to beware Macduff, yet the prophecies as to Birnam Wood and the man not born of woman "answer to nothing inward"; for which reason he considers that the theory breaks down at this point.

But this judgment needs to be tempered by noting that the two deceptive prophecies are not of Shakespeare's making, but are an essential part of the Macbeth story as known to King James and all the Scotchmen with him. It was necessary to retain them and weave them into the otherwise subjective prophecies which influence Macbeth's conduct; and the dramatist has done this with great skill, for they are only corollaries to words telling Macbeth just what he wants to be told. In this way this scene (otherwise wholly of his own invention) is caused to include the striking utterances which Holinshed records and to pave the way for the dramatic denouement of the play.

But the dramatist wished to make sure that his audience was not deceived by the visible showing of the apparitions and of the kings, and therefore for the third time he resorted to the device of an argument by Macbeth as to the reality of it all. In our current texts this argument is ruined by the unfortunate interpolation of seven lines with their stage directions put into the play later, probably by Thomas Middleton. What Shakespeare wrote (beginning at IV, i, 122) is the following:

> *Macb.* Horrible sight! Now, I see, 'tis true;
> For the blood-bolter'd Banquo smiles upon me,

And points at them for his. What? Is this so?
   First Witch. Ay, sir, all this is so. (*Witches vanish.*)
   Macb. Where are they? Gone. Let this pernicious hour
Stand aye accursed in the calendar!
Come in, without there! (*Enter Lennox.*)
   Len.   What's your grace's will?
   Macb. Saw you the weird sisters?
   Len.   No, my lord.
   Macb. Came they not by you?
   Len.   No, indeed, my lord.

These lines conclude the debate which began in the first act as to the reality of Macbeth's hallucinations; and they are proportionately important to an understanding of the whole play. No greater misfortune ever happened to a great play than when Thomas Middleton took *Macbeth* in hand and turned it into a spectacle with dancing witches, actually interposing a divertissement of this sort in the midst of Macbeth's argument. How this happened will later be examined in the chapter on the necromantic scene (p. 275).

Shakespeare's lines, when freed from the intrusion, tell us that Macbeth has seen his question concerning Banquo's issue answered as he did not wish it answered. But suddenly the "sight" fades, as is indicated in the text by the exclamation "What!" Being gone, the argument begins. Was the sight real or imaginary? The question "Is this so?" comes from a mind writhing in agony. The malign witch affirms it to be verity and immediately the witches, too, vanish. "Where are they? Gone?" Whereupon Lennox, who has come with the king to the door of the witches' house, is summoned and questioned. Did he see anything? Lennox twice affirms that he did not; whereupon with a groan, now knowing himself to be a slave to that which is not, Macbeth expresses the final judgment of the play:

> Infected be the air whereon they ride
> And damn'd all those that trust them.

Macbeth has been damned by his imagination for he will still trust them.

Thus has the Oxford question as to the reality of the effects of the imagination been woven into the texture of the play by showing Macbeth discussing in three different scenes the reality of what he imagines he has seen. The arguments constitute a progression showing how "fortis imaginatio generat casum," for the imagination creates fear, and each fear a greater one, according to the Senecan maxim, "Things bad begun make strong themselves by ill" (III, ii, 55).

The dramatist has been at pains to lead his audience to appreciate the power of the human imagination by carefully chosen gradations. Macbeth's imagination can shake him while yet only a murderous purpose. It can unnerve him by the vision of an unreal dagger. It can paralyze him with fear by the image of Banquo's gory corpse. It can deceive him by horrid apparitions. It can even picture to him that "horrible sight," the line of the future Scottish kings descended from Banquo. At what point in this progression are we to admit an objective reality? Here opinions have and will continue to differ. Every investigator may satisfy himself where the line is to be drawn, but he never has satisfied others. Shall we say they are all real? Or shall we assign all to the imagination? The dramatist strove to make the latter alternative easy for all to whom it is a welcome thought; but left all free to find a limit short of this if they please. The audience at the Globe Theater may take ghosts, devils, apparitions, and sights for verity, but some at Hampton Court and most modern playgoers will not.

When Gervinus says, "Shakespeare's spirit world signifies nothing but the visible embodiment of the images conjured up by a lively fancy," he is speaking to a modern audience in a modern world. The world of King James was very different, and no such convenient generalization is possible in reference to it. But one has only to look and see that Shakespeare wrote his plays with a view to their differing appeal to minds of differing calibers. This it is which has enabled these plays to endure the transformation of popular thought which has since taken place. Ben Jonson foresaw this when he said that his friend was "for all time."

But if King James is to see this play, the important question which at once arises is: What will be his attitude toward the witches, demons, specters, and sights with which the play is peopled? The answer is both interesting and unexpected; for strange as it may seem to those who have not looked into the matter, King James, too, was by this time skeptical concerning the witches of whom in his early years he had written so learnedly in his *Daemonologie*. So we may expect that Shakespeare, when writing a play for his king which exhibits the mighty power of the imagination, will venture to invite the king to take a more rational view concerning witches and necromancy by showing him what strange things the human imagination can do to us.

THE KING'S SKEPTICISM CONCERNING WITCHES

Had consideration been given to the changed view concerning demonology of King James when King of England, a different idea of the supernatural element in the play of *Macbeth* must have prevailed.   Editors and critics seem to vie with each other in asserting that King James of England was a confirmed believer in witchcraft, who had not only written a treatise on the subject, but who habitually persecuted witches, and whose influence caused Parliament to enact a statute designed to extirpate them even more effectively than the Statute of Elizabeth.*   Such mistaken pictures of the king are usually accompanied by derogatory adjectives; and are sure to be followed by the inference that the introduction of witchcraft into the play of *Macbeth* was intended to confirm the king's belief in sorcery.

The doughty reviewer William Gifford was the first to denounce the "audacious falsehoods" of these pictures.   His attack took the form of a long and acrid note appended to *The Witch of Edmonton* in his edition of the *Works of John Ford*.†   This vigorous pronouncement is as much needed

---

* This mistake is not confined to Shakespearean critics.   Even so learned and kindly a writer as Sir Walter Scott has been led, in his *Letters on Demonology and Witchcraft,* strongly to imply the king's responsibility for the English statute (1830 ed., p. 246).   And some of our great historians have likewise gone astray in their descriptions of James's attitude toward witchcraft.   Read, e.g., the eloquent passage in which the distinguished author George M. Trevelyan, in his *England Under the Stuarts* (p. 33), pictures King James as leader of this witch hunt, with William Shakespeare (Save the mark!) as pricker of the witch hounds.

† It is reprinted in Dyce's edition of the *Works of John Ford,* Vol. III, p. 273.   There is also a somewhat similar deliverance by the same pugnacious critic in his edition of the *Works of Ben Jonson,* appended

today as it was when written over a hundred years ago. It is still true that some who should know better "continue to run in the same vile line," for the habit of Shakespeareans to thus maltreat King James is deep rooted and hard to eradicate. To correct this line of thought the evidences must be carefully marshaled, for there is a weight of long-standing tradition and prejudice to be overcome. To do this will take some time and patience; but full examination of this matter is warranted, for a proper understanding of the play of *Macbeth* cannot be had without knowing what King James was doing to, or for, witches during the years from 1603 to 1606.

James VI, King of Scotland, did indeed, at the age of twenty-five, write a treatise on demonology in which he upholds the mysteries of sorcery and necromancy as verities, and this book has brought down upon him much denunciation. It was the quixotic effort of this young man to defend the cruel antiwitchcraft laws of Scotland and to exhibit his skill in the dialectic in which he was trained. But before he became King of England his views about witches had changed. He is not to be held responsible for the statute punishing witchcraft which was enacted by his English Parliament in the second year of his English reign; and all inferences which rest upon the idea that when King of England he had any genuine belief in witchcraft are erroneous. Since the appearance of Dr. Kittredge's examination of this subject * there is

---

as note 2 to the *Masque of Queens,* and to be found in Vol. VII, p. 128, of F. Cunningham's edition of Jonson (London, 1875).

    * "English Witchcraft and James I," by G. L. Kittredge, in *Studies in the History of Religions* (New York, Macmillan, 1912). Wallace Notestein's *History of Witchcraft in England from 1558 to 1781* (Washington, 1911) is full of information upon this subject but inconsistent in its conclusions concerning King James. Earlier in the book (but without adducing any evidence) he holds James responsible for the Statute of 1604 but later (p. 138) he finds him skeptical as to devils even before he came to England; and (p. 143) he records and accepts the evidence which shows that the king affirmed the workings of witches and devils to be but falsehoods and delusions.

no excuse for the further perpetuation of this falsehood. When King of England, James was skeptical of witches and was chiefly concerned in protecting those wrongfully accused of witchcraft and with the discovery of the frauds and delusions which account for the belief in witches. The present chapter will recount evidence, long known or accessible but neglected, which supports this proposition. The two following chapters will set forth newly developed evidence which enables us to know with particularity what were the king's ideas about witches from the year 1603, when he came to England, to the year 1606, when the play of *Macbeth* was written.

In his *Daemonologie, in forme of a dialogue,* the king supported the popular beliefs concerning evil spirits and their dealings with mankind, with, however, some significant additions and modifications of his own; and he urged severity in the execution of the laws for the suppression of witchcraft. Read beneath the surface, the book is a labored argument with himself to justify the laws of his kingdom.* If any one may be excused for such a performance, it is the young bridegroom whose bride had been delayed by storms and contrary winds as she sailed from Denmark to join her husband in Scotland; for a number of Scotch women had confessed in his presence that these delays were due to the fact that the devil had incited them to practice their diabolical arts of sorcery against this Lutheran princess. Their stories and their trials (which James attended) are recounted in a little tract published in London in 1591 and entitled *News from Scotland.* This nauseous Scotch morsel must be read and digested if

---

* In his Preface the young king states that his treatise is designed to show "both that such assaultes of Sathan are most certainly practized, & that the instruments thereof, merits most severely to be punished." His effort to sustain the first of these propositions by pure deduction is a failure; but granting its validity, the second proposition is convincingly sustained. When he became older he substituted induction for deduction with the result that he soon convinced himself that witchcraft was a delusion.

one would understand the king's vigorous even if short-lived support of the popular philosophy concerning witches. The *Daemonologie* was published in 1597. Very soon after this we find the king beginning to express skepticism about demons and witches. But this was really a reversion, or perhaps more properly a revulsion, for though the revelations of these witches caused him to yield to the popular view this proved but a temporary phase.* James was a learned, inquisitive, shrewd young man, essentially honest, and greatly interested in demonology. Having examined this subject in his book, he thereupon made it his practice to personally ex-

---

* Notestein states (*History of Witchcraft*, p. 138) that "there had always been a grain of skepticism in his make-up"; but this is an understatement. Dr. Henry More, the editor of Joseph Glanvil's *Sadducismus Triumphatus*, came into possession of, and reprinted, the latter's original papers concerning the trials of the Scottish witches in 1590 (1726 ed., pp. 396–400), and he records that prior to these trials the young king was inclinable to think witches "to be but a mere conceit."

The *Daemonologie* was written while the king was dominated by the events recited in the *News from Scotland*. It seems to have been first printed in Edinburgh in 1597, six years before he came to England. But it is possible that it was published at an even earlier date. Grässe in his *Bibliotheca Magica* (Leipzig, 1843), p. 55, quotes an edition of this book printed in Edinburgh in 1591. As this has never turned up, it is probably a mistake; and yet it would seem more likely that the *Daemonologie* was written at the time James was hearing the witches telling about their deviltry than that he wrote it some years later. The king's Preface to the Reader better fits the earlier date.

In 1603, while he was on his way to England to become king of that nation and before he reached London, the *Daemonologie* was reprinted by London booksellers along with some other books written by the king. Bishop Montagu again reprinted the book with the rest of the king's prose works in the year 1616, and a question has been raised as to why the king permitted this. But to have omitted it would have been a public confession of error, which James was never willing to make. The high-flown praise bestowed by the bishop on the king's other works contrasts strongly with his meager reference to this book in his Preface, his only remark about it being that it is "a rare piece for many precepts and experiments both in Divinity and Natural Philosophy." This cautious and cryptic sentence indicates that the king then looked upon his excursion into the realms of magic as merely an essay in experimental philosophy.

amine persons accused of witchcraft, and found that under
his cross-examination one after another broke down and revealed that their evil doings were due either to fraud or to a
diseased imagination. This caused him to warn his judges
not to allow the conviction of witches merely because of their
confessions. After this there followed a period of skepticism;
which ultimately led to his denial of the system of demonology concerning which in his youth he had written so con-
fidently.

The witchcraft law of the second year of James's English
reign corresponds with the end of the first of the above
periods. Having written down in his book that witches must
be severely punished, he allowed the statute so punishing
them to stand; but he determined to take care that none but
dangerous witches should suffer. Such cases proved hard to
find, and many convicted witches were pardoned by him.
Thus he reconciled his book, the statute, and his conscience
during the ensuing period of his increasing skepticism, and
it was during this skeptical period that the play of *Macbeth*
was written.

Even while writing his *Daemonologie* he was conscious of
an element of delusion in the operation of the witches' minds,
and on this account he rejected many of what he calls the
"innumerable absurdities" popularly attributed to them.
And the reason which he gives (Part II, Chap. III) for believing the marvels which he defends is: "lest that draw us to the
error that there is no witches"—truly a precarious foundation on which to build; but the laws of his kingdom founded
on the scriptural injunction, "Thou shalt not suffer a witch
to live," must be defended by him.

But the king's inquisitive mind could not rest here. Both
before and after he came to England he examined more and
more alleged witches and found more and more delusion;
thus the boundaries of legitimate demonology kept shrink-
ing. The belief in sorcery has always been dependent upon
a priori reasoning and has always yielded when subjected to

an examination of the facts. When James found by cross-examining alleged witches that their imaginations created real effects, which they indeed saw but which "were no ways so," the props which had sustained his theories concerning the devils' compacts with their victims began to crumble. Thereupon he instituted a brave and serious effort to discover what of truth and what of error was involved in the science of demonology. The personal examination of demoniacal possession became a habit with him. Dr. Godfrey Goodman in his *Court of King James I* (Vol. I, p. 3) tells that the king "was ever apt to search into secrets, to try conclusions, as I did know some who saw him run to see one in a fit whom they said was bewitched." We shall soon find how persistent he was in his examination of witches and how cleverly he often ferreted out the reasons for the bad reputation these poor creatures had among their neighbors. The inevitable result was that before long he found that his science was indefensible.

The first evidence of a modification of the king's views is found in the year 1597, the same year in which his *Daemonologie* appeared. Immediately following the extensive outburst of Scotch sorcery which in 1591 had endeavored to destroy the king and queen, the Scotch people found an over-abundance of witchcraft everywhere. For six years Scotland saw a contagious epidemic of witch-finding which resulted in the burning of several hundred poor half-crazed victims. So strong was the public pressure for the extermination of witches that the king had issued commissions for their trial to different tribunals, including the presbyteries of the Scottish Church. But the horror and violence of the result was such that in the year 1597 the king himself became alarmed about these executions and by a single executive act revoked all of the special commissions for the trial of witchcraft then in force.*

---

* *Privy Council Register 5*, pp. 409–410; Spottiswoode (4th ed., pp. 449–450).
The fullest account of this occurrence will be found in an article

After this, King James took up the task of personally examining witches, and this soon became a habit with him. A letter written by him to one of his judges is printed on page 124 of Volume II of Halliwell's *Letters of the Kings of England*. It lacks the year date but seems to belong to the Scotch period. It reads as follows:

March 5th.

Trusty and well-beloved, we greet you well: and whereas ye remember how that in late time we discovered and put to flight one of those counterfeits, the like whereof ye now advertise us, by this bearer we send unto you instructions suited for such an occasion, willing you leave nothing untried to discover the imposture, trying by any deceits ye can devise to expose the cheat, as I am sure no mortal yet living could last for so long a time with a small cup of charnigo; and whereas ye advertise us that she has been straitly guarded when as she lay so in a trance, I desire ye to see that those persons who do that office may be chosen from out of your own retinue, and by no means trust any who may be a leaguer or assister with her of her own sending; for we let you to wit that miracles like those of which you give us notice should be by all ways and diligently tested, according to what Agrippa says, "Many there are now-a-days who sanctify and believe miracles, when it is past the power of man to test them, who would not have believed them had they lived in the time in which they are alleged to have occurred, and the more especially if they knew the people who had a hand in the manufacture of them." It therefore becomes us to lose no opportunity of seeking after the real truth of pretended wonders, that if true we may bless the Creator who hath shown such marvels to men, and if false we may punish the impudent inventors of them.

James R.

When he wrote this it seems that he had found at least one counterfeit witch. He soon found more, as we learn from another letter of the king which is printed on page 102 of the

---

entitled "Witchcraft in Scotland," by F. Legge, published in October, 1891, in the *Scottish Review*, Vol. XVIII, p. 264.

same book. It was written in 1603 to Prince Henry in Scotland. After giving advice on other subjects, he says:

I am also glad of the discovery of your little counterfeit wench. I pray God ye may be my heir in such discoveries. Ye have oft heard me say that most miracles now a days prove but illusions, and ye may see by this how wary judges should be in trusting accusations without an exact trial, and likewise how easily people are induced to trust to wonders. Let her be kept fast till my coming; and thus God bless you, my son,

Your loving father,
JAMES R.

Again in the same book, Volume II, page 124n., Halliwell states that he took the following account from a manuscript history of Wiltshire, by John Aubrey:

In the reign of King James I., one Mrs. Katherine Waldron (a gentlewoman of good family) waited on Sir Francis Seymor's lady of Marlborough. She pretended to be bewitched by a certain woman . . . and pretended strange things, &c. . . . She had acquired such a strange habit, that she would endure exquisite torments, as to have pins thrust into her flesh, nay, under her nails. These tricks of hers were about the time when King James wrote his Daemonologie. His majesty being in these parts, went to see her in one of her fits; she lay on a bed, and the king saw her endure the torments aforesaid. The room, as it is easily to be believed, was full of company. His majesty gave a sudden pluck to her coats, and tossed them over her head, which surprise (it seems she had some innate modesty in her), not imagining of such a thing, made her immediately start, and detected the cheat.

His Majesty was in Wiltshire a large part of September and October, 1603. This was the year the *Daemonologie* was published in England, and this was probably when this incident occurred.

Contemporary evidence of James's later views on witchcraft is given us by Francis Osborne, a now forgotten acrimonious essayist who had every opportunity of knowing the truth.   In 1659, the year in which he died, Osborne published *A Miscellany of Sundry Essayes, etc.*   In his preface to this volume Osborne gives us to understand that these essays were written before he was twenty.   This puts them in the first half of James's English reign.   Osborne was then Master of Horse for William Herbert, Earl of Pembroke, who was high in the king's favor and much in his company.   It was the king's habit after he dined to sit long chatting with his inti-mates while his tongue was loosed with wine, and often his pithy talk filtered through to his entourage.

In the first essay of this *Miscellany* (pp. 3-5), after inveigh-ing against those who discourage "prosecution after Knowl-edge by branding Reason with an Imputation of Atheism: and Hanging what they understand not, under the Notion of Witchcraft," he tells of King James's views upon atheism and witchcraft:

It was the Custom of King James, (and no question, of no small Improvement to his Understanding) to Discourse during Meals, with the Chaplain that said Grace, (or Other Divines) Concern-ing some point of Controversie in Philosophy.   And falling one Day upon Atheism, He did by undenyable Arguments maintain, No Man could be found so Irrational, as to deny a First Cause: (which could be no other then that Power we call God.)   And Therefore, no such thing in Nature, as an Atheist.

What his Judgement was of Witchcraft, you may, in part, find by His Treatise on that Subject, and Charge he gave the Judges, to be Circumspect in Condemning those, Committed by Ignorant Justices, for Diabolical Compacts.   Nor had he Concluded his Advice in a Narrower Circle, (as I have heard) Then the Denyal of any such operations, but out of Reason of State: and to gratifie the Church, which hath in no Age, thought fit to explode out of the Common-peoples minds, An Apprehension of Witchcraft. The greatest Miracles, now extant, making their Apparitions, in the Dark Corners of this clouded Imagination.*

* One of the collections of the pithy sayings of James (*Flores Regii, or Proverbs and Aphorisms, Divine and Moral, as they were at several*

Osborne in the same essay tells about a demented boy named Smythe who accused three silly women of witchcraft before Sir Humphry Winch, which account concludes thus:

The King being gratified by nothing more, then an Opportunity to shew his Dexterity in Discovering an Imposture, (at which, I must confess Him, The Promptest Man Living) upon his Arrival convented The Boy. Where, before Him, (possibly daunted at his Presence, or Terrified by his Words) he began to faulter, so as The King discover'd a Fallacy.*

With Osborne's information agrees the more weighty and more clearly expressed statement of Thomas Fuller in his *Church-History*. In detail these accounts are wholly different, but the conclusion is the same. Fuller's great work, long in preparation, was published in 1655. In Book X, page 74, after an account of the "extatical phrensies" of a number of sham demoniacs, we read:

K. James remembring what Solomon saith, It is the honour of a King to search out a matter, was no lesse dexterous than desirous to make discovery of these Deceits. Various were His Waies in detecting them, awing some into confession with His presence, perswading others by promise of pardon and fair usage

---

times upon sundry Occasions spoken by his most excellent Majesty James of famous memory King of Great Britain. Collected by J. L. S. London 1627) includes this sentence: "20 The Devil always avoids the mean, and waits upon extremities; so hath he sought to devide the world betwixt Atheism and Superstition." This might well have been culled from the same postprandial discourse which gave rise to Osborne's report of his sayings upon these two subjects. Another of the king's sayings reported by J. L. S. (who has never been identified) runs thus: "188 False miracles and lying news are the food of superstition, which by credulity deludes ignorant people." This was the trend of James's thought throughout his life in England.

*In his later days Osborne was of the Parliamentary party and violently opposed to King James. When he says anything good about the king, we have the more reason to believe it to be true. His style is quite outrageous and confused, and this caused him to be maligned by Dr. Johnson (as we may read in Boswell's *Life*), but he is really a very observant and entertaining writer.

. . . The frequency of such forged Possessions wrought such an alteration upon the judgment of King JAMES, that he receding from what he had written in his *Demonologie* grew first dissident of, and then flatly to deny the workings of Witches and Devils, as but Falsehoods and Delusions.

This is an unqualified statement by a divine who had lived during the days of King James, had every opportunity of knowing the truth, and whom Coleridge called the most sensible and least prejudiced great man of his age. Its measured terms should be accepted at their face value.

Next comes a piece of evidence which is very persuasive because derived from a detractor of King James and because it is unstudied and incidental rather than argumentative. A certain Michael Sparke, who had for a time had some connection with James's household accounts and who knew things about him that others did not know, wrote a vituperative attack upon him entitled *History of the First 14 years of King James I.* This he first published in 1651, when because of the Commonwealth James could be freely maligned. The book contains curious and valuable information about the Essex divorce and the Overbury murder. When it was reprinted in 1692, it carried a new address To the Reader in which (p. A4) is to be found the following:

It may be said [of James] he divided his time between his Standish, his Bottle, and his Hunting; the last had his fair weather, the two former his more dull and cloudy; so that no wonder if his Writings are so variable; and after he had pleaded for Witchcraft, and the Pope's being Antichrist; Somerset affair, and the Spanish Match cured him of both.*

This statement, in which we gather truth from the words of an enemy, is repeated by James Wellwood, a much more temperate writer, in his account of the times of King James which is found in his *Memoirs* published in 1700 (p. 36).

---

* This address bears marks of having been written much earlier, but the Restoration prevented its publication until after the Revolution.

Finally, the Devonshire nonconformist William Harris, a bitter detractor of the Stuarts, in his *Life of James I* (London, 1753, p. 42) closes his account of the king's *Daemonologie* with this endorsement of Fuller's statement:

I have said above, that I supposed James did believe the doctrine of witches. But, in justice to his character, I must here add, that after his being in England, having met with a number of forgeries and cheats, they wrought such an alteration upon his judgment, that at first he grew dissident of, and then flatly denied the workings of witches and devils.

While many of the so-called "sorcerers" and demonized persons examined by the king turned out to be pure frauds, others were found to be the victims of a diseased imagination. Lies and imposture are usual concomitants of hysteria; hence fraud and delusion are often jointly responsible for the tricks of those thought to be demonized. These workings of the morbid mind were also taken in hand by the king. In Arthur Wilson's *History of Great Britain* (London, 1653, p. 111), the author, after giving a lengthy account of the frauds of William Perry, the bewitched boy of Bilson, adds:

The King took delight by the *line* of his *Reason* to sound the depths of such *brutish Impostors,* and he discovered many. . . . Some others, both men and women, inspired with such *enthusiasmes,* and *frantique fancies,* he reduced to their right *senses,* applying his *Remedies* suitable to the *Distemper,* wherein he made himself often very merry.

In truth James was a good detective in his own way, and somewhat of a psychiatrist. He boasted of his skill in such matters. His effort was not to punish these poor deluded wretches, for he enjoyed trying to restore them to sanity, and in this he was sometimes successful, as we shall see. His progress in the study of demonism was a gradual one. When he came to England he was skeptical of most witches (so he wrote to his son); but he still believed there might be some. Soon after he became skeptical of all witches. Later he denied that there were any witches.

It has been questioned by some whether James, although skeptical, ever wholly lost his belief in sorcery. The only evidence which I have seen which might support such question is the following statement by William Sanderson, who was an adherent of the House of Stuart, maintaining at all points the rectitude of the motives of both James and Charles. Evelyn in his *Diary* (1857 ed., Vol. II, p. 107) tells us that Sanderson was "the author of two large but mean histories." The first of these is his history of the reign of James which was printed in 1656, the year after Thomas Fuller's statement, already quoted, had been printed in his *Church-History*. In obvious criticism of what Fuller says, Sanderson writes (p. 215):

I know, how it hath been of late urged, that King James was not of the same mind alwaies; and very tender of his Judges proceedings, ignorantly condemning some innocent Melancholly simple old women; whose miserable poverties, made them weary of life, and easily to confess themselves guilty, of they knew not what, though in sad condition, otherwise; liable to Satans suggestions and deceipt.

And so busied himself with curious perspicuity, into tryal examination and discovery of sundry counterfeits, pretenders to be possessed by evill spirits. But yet, to my knowledg, he was ever constant to his former opinion, of witches and witchcraft, in particulars I can evidence.

As he mentions no such particulars, his evidence bears little weight. Sanderson was himself a firm believer in witchcraft and hoped that James was too, for to disbelieve in witches was to be a Sadducee and therefore little better than an atheist, and against such a charge he wished to defend the king, who is held up as in all respects a virtuous man and a model king. And it is also true that King James never publicly repudiated the views expressed in his *Daemonologie*. His kingly courage failed him at this point, and he was thus sometimes placed in an inconsistent position; as, for example, in 1613 during the infamous divorce proceedings between the Earl and Countess of Essex. The king's efforts to further this divorce led him to argue before the commission upon grounds which some have thought to imply that he still believed there are some witches. Such inconsistencies made possible Sanderson's statement which has been quoted. But the weight of the evidence compels us to follow Thomas Fuller rather than William Sanderson.

However interesting may be this question of the king's ultimate denial of all witchcraft, it is not involved in the examination of the play of *Macbeth,* for when that was written he had only reached the stage of serious skepticism whenever a case of witchcraft was brought to his attention. To this attitude the play has been attuned.

In all discussions of this subject one should have in mind some clear idea of the causes and nature of the outbreaks of witch mania which were so prevalent in Europe during the sixteenth and seventeenth centuries.

What went under the name of witchcraft was a web of fraud, folk-medicine, fairy tale, hysteria, and hypnotic suggestion, including physical and physiological phenomena still unclassified [Andrew Lang's *History of Scotland,* Vol. II, p. 432].

The disease was highly contagious. Seeing the delusions of witches and hearing exaggerated accounts of them produced and multiplied similar delusions in the victims. In these phenomena James became so interested that he soon found the views expressed in his *Daemonologie* quite untenable and was honest enough to change his mind, even if not honest enough publicly to confess his error.

Those who would pursue this matter further should read Hutchinson's *Historical Essay Concerning Witchcraft* (1718 ed., pp. 178–180), where will be found some account of the progress of the king's enlightenment. Hutchinson's general conclusion is "that King James himself came off very much from these notions in his elder years." More modern and more full discussions will be found in Gifford's note already referred to, and in the works mentioned in the note (on page 76 near the beginning of this chapter). Especially must Kittredge's essay be examined. For many unwise, unjust, and wrong deeds King James has a heavy reckoning to meet, but defending sorcery when King of England is not among them. Of this charge he must be acquitted, and instead he must receive the commendation which Robert Southey in his *Book of the Church* (Vol. II, p. 339) accords to him:

He [James] had written a treatise upon demonology; and yet in consequence of what he afterwards observed, and the discovery of many impostures which were detected by his sagacity, he was perhaps the first person who shook off the superstitious belief of witchcraft, and openly proclaimed its falsehood.

James was not the first to do this, as we shall soon see; nor did he ever publicly proclaim his change of view, but he was far ahead of his time in his dealings with this subject and for this open-mindedness he is entitled to due credit.

JAMES AND THE WITCHES OF 1603

Having found the trend of the mind of King James on the subject of witchcraft, it remains to determine what progress he had made in his journey from superstition to reason when Shakespeare wrote his play of *Macbeth* in 1606. This field has not yet been investigated. Much evidence is available. To set it forth adequately will occupy this and the next chapter of this book.

First we should know the attitude toward demonology of his English advisers. These men had helped him to gain his English throne, and were of his council, so that he was much influenced by them.

Witchcraft had a strong hold upon most Englishmen during the reigns of Elizabeth and James; but Reginald Scot's book had not been written in vain, and there were in those days some highly intelligent opponents of the popular view among the better intellects, especially among the higher clergy, even though most of them thought it best to hold their peace.

When James came to England early in 1603, he chose as his mentor in state affairs the diligent, shrewd, inscrutable Robert Cecil, who had guided the affairs of the kingdom during the last years of Elizabeth. Ennobling him as Earl of Salisbury, he gave into his hands much of the guidance of the state; and because he was a small but very useful man, he called him his "little beagle." Cecil was in sympathy with the medical and philosophic views of an eminent physician of London, Dr. Edward Jorden, who was an outspoken opponent of the whole system of witchcraft and whose acquaintance we are soon to make.

Second to Cecil in the council of James was Henry Howard,

Earl of Northampton, a learned and able but sinuous and unscrupulous man, who along with Cecil had taken part in the secret correspondence which arranged the terms on which James upon the queen's death was to take possession of the English throne. As a result Northampton had a strong hold on King James and in turn was used by James for the management of many affairs calling for indirect rather than straightforward dealings. Northampton's family were Roman Catholics, but he seems to have been a skeptic on the subject of demonology. In 1583 he had published a treatise entitled:

A Defensative against the Poyson of supposed Prophecies. Not hitherto confuted by the Pen of any man, which being grounded, either upon the warrant and Authority of Old painted Books, Expositions of Dreames, Oracles, Revelations, Invocations of damned Spirits, Judicials of Astrology, or any other kind of pretended knowledge whatsoever, De futuris contingentibus; have been causes of great disorder in the Common-wealth, especially among the simple and unlearned people.

This work is wordy, discursive, very erudite, but without arriving at any clear conclusions. James once said that Northampton's letters were "Asiatic and endless," a phrase which well applies to the earl's book. It leaves the impression (which the subsequent career of the earl confirms) that, although interlarded with pious phrases, the author had no principles and very little belief in anything.

This man was James's evil genius who led him into the gross missteps of the latter part of his reign. But the king was in his power and had made his nephew, Thomas Howard, Earl of Suffolk and Lord Chamberlain; so that when Salisbury, Northampton, and Suffolk urged any course upon the king he generally took it. These three men were supporting the Bishop of London in his efforts to suppress exorcists, and I think that their influence was thrown in the scale to induce the king to change his views as to devils.

To help him in ecclesiastical affairs, James chose Richard Bancroft, Bishop of London, whom he made Archbishop of Canterbury upon the death of Archbishop Whitgift. Referring to this succession, Arthur Wilson in his *History of Great Britain* (p. 8), after stating that Whitgift died on February 29, 1603/4, writes that he left "a Name like a Sweet perfume behind him. And Bancroft, a sturdy peece, succeeded him, but not with the same spirit; for what Whitgift strove to do by Sweetness and Gentleness, Bancroft did persevere in with Rigor and Severity." In the Martin Marprelate controversy, Dr. Bancroft had stirred up a swarm of writers to defend the cause of the prelates. In the Darrel controversy of the last years of Elizabeth, he performed a similar function, urging his pamphleteers to adopt a smart, vituperative style in imitation of the Martinists. Bishop Bancroft is credited with being the author of a famous paragraph attacking the popular belief in witches (often quoted and often misquoted) found in Harsnet's *Declaration of Egregious Popish Impostures,* which is recited at length later in this chapter (see page 99). His chaplain and secretary Dr. Samuel Harsnet wrote most of the work just referred to, but it was generally held that parts were written by the bishop himself (Darrel's *A Detection of that Sinful, etc.,* pp. 7, 8). Part of the paragraph to be quoted later is attributed by John Swan to Dr. Harsnet, but Lewes Hewes attributes it to the bishop and so does Andrew Lang in quoting it in 1902 in his *History of Scotland* (Vol. II, p. 431). That the whole pamphlet accurately reflects the bishop's views can hardly be doubted. It shows how far the leading prelate of the Church of England was prepared to go in his effort to overthrow the popular views as to demonology, and to this position the already skeptical mind of King James found it not hard to adjust itself.

But for the king, the book he had written was an obstacle. A king must not admit mistakes. James must still be able to say that somewhere in Scotland there might perhaps be *some*

witches such as he had written about, even though all whom
he had examined had turned out to be either frauds or
demented.   As far as the people and the courts were concerned, there was no special need at this time for the King
of England to try to check their eagerness to suppress the bad
deeds of malicious or murderous witches.   There was no particular excitement about the subject.   The execution of a few
evil-minded scolding hags was quite in accord with the other
cruel laws of England as to felony, which annually relieved
the kingdom of the burden of a number of useless and usually
harmful subjects.

James's plan, therefore, was not to attack the laws, but to
caution his judges to be careful about allowing convictions
of witches, and to temper the execution of their sentences by
pardoning them whenever he believed them to be demented
or the victims of an excited popular sentiment.   But he
would not interfere in cases where the alleged witchcraft had
resulted in death.   This plan might take a good deal of his
own time; but it would prevent cruelty and would save his
face.   He carried it out; and as a result less than forty executions for witchcraft are known to have occurred in England
during James's reign of twenty-two years (Kittredge, p. 65;
Notestein, pp. 105, 114), and in most of these cases the alleged
witchcraft had resulted in the death of a victim, probably
by poison.

While in this frame of mind, the king was confronted,
when his first Parliament came to Westminster, with an
urgent popular call for amendment of the Elizabethan statute
against witches.   Kittredge has shown at great length the special influences which led to the passage of the new law and
has exonerated James from any part in it.   In fact, no one
has ever shown that he had any such part.   His alleged par-
ticipation is an unfounded traditional assumption.   The
statute was somewhat harsher than that of Elizabeth, but the
most that its passage indicates is that the king in 1604 was
not courageous enough to oppose his Parliament, which

thought that witches must be severely dealt with, and that to do so would please their king.

As the best evidence of James's plan of pardoning convicted witches, unless he believed them to be murderers, we must know what judicial proceedings were had under either the old or the new statute between April, 1603, when King James arrived, and the summer of 1606, when *Macbeth* was finished and performed; for over these proceedings the king kept a watchful eye. When he reached England, there were two women in jail who had been convicted under the statute of Elizabeth and sentenced for the crime of witchcraft.

Elizabeth Jackson was held in Newgate under sentence by Chief Justice Anderson for alleged bewitching of Mary Glover. The king had her released. There will be occasion a little later to examine this case more at length.

Mary Pannel was under like sentence in Yorkshire. It is an obscure case, mentioned only in Mayhall's *Annals of Yorkshire* (London, 1878). She was executed for a "killing" committed in 1593.

Christian, wife of Thomas Weech of the County of Norfolk, was convicted of witchcraft in the year 1604 (Kittredge, p. 47). She received a pardon from the king on April 16, 1604. Let it be noted that she was again convicted as a witch in 1610 and again pardoned by the king.

There is no record during the period under examination of any other conviction for witchcraft under either the old or the new statute. There were accusations and examinations before ecclesiastical authorities or magistrates but no other judicial trials or executions.*

---

* I have omitted reference to the case of Joan Harrison, for it may be apocryphal. If real, it was a lurid murder case. All we know of it is to be learned from the pamphlet entitled, *The most cruel and bloody murder committed by an Innkeepers Wife called Annis Dell and her son George Dell four years since . . . with the several Witchcrafts and most demnable practices of Johane Harrison and her daughter upon several persons men and women at Royston, who were all executed at*

On January 26, 1605, James Montagu, the king's chaplain, writing to Robert Cecil, states that as yet there had been no judicial interpretation of the statute of James.

The fact is therefore established that during his first years in England James was not on a witch hunt, as his detractors would have us think; but on the contrary, if his judges allowed witches to be convicted, he pardoned them unless he thought them murderers.

There was one aspect of demonology about which James, arriving in England, found the public mind much excited. This was the matter of demoniacal possession, and the doings of some who professed extraordinary powers of expelling by their exorcisms the evil spirits inhabiting demoniacs. James had discussed this in his *Daemonologie* (p. 70), putting the question: "Whereby shal these possessed folks be discerned fra them that ar trubled with a natural Phrensie or Manie?" As we shall find, during his first years in England he spent much time trying to find the answer.

The Bishop of London, with Dr. Harsnet to assist him, had for some six years been fighting the battle against these fraudulent exorcists and sham demoniacs. The public excitement grew out of the apparent success as an exorcist of the puritan preacher John Darrel. Full details as to Darrel may be found in Hutchinson's *Essay Concerning Witchcraft* (1718 ed., pp. 193–209), or in Notestein's *Witchcraft in England* (pp. 75–87). For present purposes it is sufficient to state that in 1597 a boy named William Sommers professed to be bewitched and inhabited by a devil. Darrel was able by his proceedings, which included prayer and fasting by the whole community, to drive the demon out; but after a short time the boy was "repossessed" and the exorcism had to be repeated. This continuous performance greatly excited the

Hartford the 4th of August last past 1606 (London, 1606) (*Short-Title Catalogue,* 6553).

clergy and the good people of Nottingham. Darrel was examined by the Archbishop of York, before whom Sommers
confessed his dissimulation and acted over all his tricks; but
he later retracted this confession and reasserted the reality of
his possession. Over a dozen books issued from the press ad-
vocating opposing views about the Darrel case, with the result
that the Privy Council summoned him before a high commission which included Archbishop Whitgift and Dr. Bancroft, then Bishop of London. This commission examined
Darrel at Lambeth on May 26, 1599, and made a report condemning both Sommers and Darrel as fraudulent impostors.
The latter was degraded from the ministry, and both suffered imprisonment. Throughout this controversy the
pamphleteers on behalf of the Church were John Deacon,
John Walker, and Dr. Harsnet. The treatises of the two
former are very lengthy, and their dreary wastes of scholastic
argument cannot be followed by the modern mind. But
Dr. Harsnet's pamphlets are very readable, and some reference must here be made to them.

In 1599 Harsnet printed *A Discovery of the Fraudulent
Practises of John Darrel* as his contribution to the effort of
the Church to refute the claims of this puritan exorcist.
Shortly afterward there came into the hands of Dr. Bancroft
the lengthy examinations and confessions of some women
from whom many devils were said to have been driven out by
the exorcisms of certain Jesuits. The confessions showed the
whole performance to be a piece of miserable trickery, and
Bishop Bancroft prepared to take advantage of this disclosure.
He therefore wrote or caused to be written *A Declaration of
Egregious Popish Impostures* and had it published anony-
mously in 1603 by order of the Privy Council. It was reissued
in 1604 and 1605. Its greatest vogue was just after the Gunpowder Plot in 1605. Its influence upon both King James
and William Shakespeare is of significance. The latter read
this book as well as Harsnet's earlier book. The attack upon

the puritans in the *Discovery* colored the picture of Malvolio as "a kind of puritan," as was first pointed out by Joseph Hunter in his *New Illustrations* (Vol. I, pp. 380–390). The attack upon the Jesuits in the *Declaration* printed in 1603 is well known as the source of the demonology of Edgar in *King Lear.**

But even after these vigorous attacks upon both puritan and papist exorcists by the authorities of the English Church, a belief in the rightfulness of exorcism by "prayer and fasting" continued among many of the clergy. Darrel notwithstanding his condemnation maintained a large and vociferous following (see the *Dictionary of National Biography* under "John Darrel"). To meet this emergency the bishops determined to put a stop to all exorcism. A new canon was adopted forbidding any minister without license "to attempt upon any pretense whatever, either of possession or obsession, by fasting and prayer to cast out any devil or devils under pain of imputation of Imposture or Cousenage and Deposition from the Ministry." * By this canon the Church of England took its present position, from which it has never deviated, alongside the Calvinistic and Reformed churches (but in opposition to the Lutheran and Roman Catholic churches) against exorcism. This canon (LXXII) immediately appeared in the revised edition of the *Constitutions and Canons* printed in 1604.

---

* That Edgar's feigned demonism is a timely satirical picture of this variety of fraud and derived from Bishop Bancroft's book was first pointed out by Theobald in a long note (29) to *King Lear* in his edition of 1733. Dr. Furness in his New Variorum quoted part of this note and pointed out additional topical details. A fuller analysis of Shakespeare's use of the book may be found in Anders's *Shakespeare's Books*, pp. 109–112. Modern editors, although explaining that Shakespeare took the names of his devils from this book, are apt to ignore the fact that not merely Edgar's devils but the entire showing of his feigned possession is derived from what was disclosed in the examinations of six confessed fraudulent accomplices of the Jesuit exorcisors as printed in an appendix to the book, a matter of intense interest to

Dr. Harsnet was one of a growing body of thinkers in England who saw where the trend of affairs was leading them. The Church would not as yet officially deny that there were evil spirits who at times entered into compacts with men and women, but they denied that these witches could cast devils into men and women and they ridiculed the pretenses of the clergy who asserted they could cast them out. Whatever phenomena of this sort had existed during biblical times had ceased, and in modern times both the exorcised and the exorcists were in collusion and carried on their practices for the sake of gain or notoriety. This was the official ecclesiastical position.

As James approached his English capital, he found another controversy similar to the Darrel case raging over the doings of Mary Glover of London, from whom a devil had recently been expelled by the exorcism of a number of puritan ministers. Soon we find him enlisted on the side of the Bishop of London in his opposition to exorcism, for this accorded with his own developing skepticism on the subject of demons. But his ratiocinating mind saw the weakness of the Church's halfway position. Demoniacs always accused witches of having bedeviled them. If, in fact, the former had no devils, perhaps the latter had no devils. Both Osborne's account and Fuller's account of the king's change of view recite the putting down of sham demoniacs as the step which led him to discredit all witches. The Bishop of London, too, saw that the Church's position was vulnerable, and in his eagerness to suppress exorcism he found it necessary to attack all witchcraft and demonism. The result was that the belief in witchcraft is denounced in the *Declaration of Egregious Popish Impostures* and in no uncertain terms. Let no one

---

people in the days of the Gunpowder Plot, when their fury raged against the Jesuits.

* Only one Episcopal license under this canon was ever issued. (See Dedication of Hutchinson's *Essay Concerning Witchcraft*.)

say that when James came to England everyone believed in witches. It is not possible to quote all of Chapter 21, entitled, "Of the strange formes, shapes, and apparitions of the devills." But after a recitation of the origins of sorcery, the argument proceeds (pp. 136–137):

Out of these is shaped us the true *Idea* of a Witch, an olde weather-beaten Croane, having her chinne, & her knees meeting for age, walking like a bow leaning on a shaft, hollow eyed, untoothed, furrowed on her face, having her lips trembling with the palsie, going mumbling in the streetes, one that hath forgotte her *pater noster,* and hath yet a shrewd tongue in her head, to call a drab, a drab. If shee have learned of an olde wife in a chimnies end: *Pax, max, fax,* for a spel: or can say Sir *John of Grantams* curse, for the Millers Eeles, that were stolne: *All you that have stolne the Millers Eeles,* Laudate dominum de cælis: *And all they that have consented thereto,* benedicamus domino: Why then ho, beware, looke about you my neighbours; if any of you have a sheepe sicke of the giddies, or an hogge of the mumps, or an horse of the staggers, or a knavish boy of the schoole, or an idle girle of the wheele, or a young drab of the sullens, and hath not fat enough for her porredge, nor her father, and mother, butter enough for their bread; and she have a little helpe of the *Mother, Epilepsie,* or *Cramp,* to teach her role her eyes, wrie her mouth, gnash her teeth, startle with her body, hold her armes and hands stiffe, make anticke faces, girne, mow, and mop like an Ape, tumble like a Hedgehogge, and can mutter out two or three words of gibridg, as *obus, bobus:* and then withall old mother *Nobs* hath called her by chaunce, idle young huswife, or bid the devil scratch her, then no doubt but mother *Nobs* is the Witch: the young girle is Owle-blasted, and possessed: and it goes hard, but ye shal have some idle, adle, giddie, lymphaticall, illuminate dotrel, who being out of credite, learning, sobriety, honesty, and wit, wil take this holy advantage, to raise the ruines of his desperate decayed name, and for his better glory wil be-pray the jugling drab, and cast out *Mopp* the devil.

They that have their braines baited, and their fancies distempered with the imaginations, and apprehensions of Witches, Conjurers, and Fayries, and all that Lymphatical *Chimera:* I finde to be marshalled in one of these five rankes, children, fooles, women, cowards, sick, or blacke, melancholicke, discomposed wits. . . . *Horace* the Heathen spied long agoe, that a Witch, a Wizard, and a Conjurer were but bul-beggers to scare fooles: . . .

And *Geoffry Chaucer*, who had his two eyes, wit, and learning in his head, spying that all these brainlesse imaginations, of witchings, possessings, house-hanting, and the rest, were the forgeries, cosenages, Impostures, and legerdemaine of craftie priests, and leacherous Friers . . .

It would seem that Dr. Harsnet had been reading Scot's *Discovery of Witchcraft* and particularly Chapter 12 of Book 4, where Scot quotes Chaucer's attack upon the popular beliefs found near the beginning of his "Wife of Bath's Tale." Furthermore, the reference to "a little helpe of the Mother" indicates knowledge of the medical views of Dr. Jorden, which will be told about a few pages later. At all events the witty diatribe just quoted was printed and promulgated under the aegis of the Bishop of London just as James approached London after his journey from Scotland, and we are told by John Swan that the book was at once put in the king's hands. Furthermore, John Swan immediately wrote and printed a reply which he addressed to and sent directly to the king, so that James found the issue sharply drawn as he approached London.

Three questions were involved:

Are there really witches acting in collusion with devils?

Are there really people inhabited by devils?

Can exorcists cast out these devils?

These questions were intensely interesting to him as a past expert in the science of demonology, and we shall now see how much time he spent in the next few years in trying to settle them experimentally.

A digression is here made which may interest those who enjoy searching out the tricklets which ultimately become the mighty streams affecting the destiny of our race. In the library of the Episcopal Palace at Lambeth there still rests a little volume which was the property of Richard Bancroft when Archbishop of Canterbury. It is beautifully bound, with his initials in gold on the covers, and it contains five tracts:

The Apprehension and Confession of three notorious Witches arraigned and by Justice condemned in the County of Essex the 5 day of July last past [London, 1589].

News from Scotland, Declaring the Damnable life and death of Doctor Fian, a notable Sorcerer, who was burned at Edenbrough in January last [London, 1591].

A most wicked Work of a Wretched Witch (the like whereof none can record these many years in England) wrought on the person of one Richard Burt, servant to Maister Edling . . . by G. B. Maister of Artes [London, 1593].

The most Wonderfull and true Storie of a certaine Witch named Alse Gooderidge of Stapenhill who was arraigned and convicted at Darbie at the Assizes there. As also a true report of the strange Torments of Thomas Darling, a boy of thirteen years of age, that was possessed by the Devil, with his horrible Fittes and terrible apparitions by him uttered at Burton upon Trent, in the Countie of Stafford and of his marvellous deliverance [London, 1597].

A true Narration of the strange and grevous vexation by the Devil of seven persons in Lancashire [London, 1600].

The first four of these are the tracts used by Dr. Harsnet in writing his *Discovery of the Fraudulent Practises of John Darrel*. Judge their contents from their titles. Although all were written by profound believers in witchcraft, it would be hard to find five accounts of sorcery in which the real nature of the delusion is more horribly and evidently revealed.

Both Dr. Bancroft and Dr. Harsnet were men of vigorous reasoning powers. I think that both determined that witchcraft was a senseless and wicked delusion, which they must try to check; for they did try very hard to do so. But it took

over a hundred years to alter the deeply rooted superstitions
of the nation. It called for courageous attacks by many brave
crusaders for truth, and it was not until 1736 that the English
statute punishing witchcraft was stricken from the books.
Since then the infamous thing has never dared to rear its head
among English-speaking peoples. The writers in England
to whom special praise must be awarded for this riddance are:
Reginald Scot, whose *Discovery of Witchcraft* was printed
in 1584 and reprinted in 1651; Samuel Harsnet, whose tracts
above referred to were printed in 1599 and 1603; Edward
Jorden, whose *Brief Discourse, etc.* was printed in 1603; Sir
Robert Filmore, whose *Advertisement to the jurymen of
England* was published in 1653; John Wagstaffe, whose *Question of Witchcraft Debated* was published in 1669; John
Webster, whose *Displaying of Supposed Witchcraft* was pub-
lished in 1677; Francis Hutchinson, whose *Essay Concerning
Witchcraft* was published in 1718. And Lecky is surely right
in awarding a place in the crusade to Montaigne, so that John
Florio's English translation of his work (1603) should also be
included.

Third in order in the above list is the name of Dr. Edward
Jorden. When James came to London, Dr. Jorden was practicing medicine in that city. The doctor's special interest was
in hysteria, or "the mother," as it was vulgarly called. He
had just published a treatise on this subject entitled:

A brief discourse of a disease called the Suffocation of the
Mother, written upon occasion which hath beene of late taken
thereby, to suspect possessions of an evil spirit, or some such like
supernaturall power. Wherein is declared that divers strange
actions and passions of the body of man, which in the common
opinion, are imputed to the devill, have their true naturall causes,
and do accompanie this Disease.
By Edward Jorden, Doctor in Physicke. London, Printed by
John Windet, dwelling at the Signe of the Crosse Keyes at
Powles Wharf. 1603.

Dr. Jorden was far ahead of his time. "He had the singular boldness and enlightenment to maintain that cases of so-called demoniacal possession were really due to fits of the mother or, in modern language, hysteria" (*D.N.B.*, Vol. X, p. 1089). Particularly note his phrase *"natural causes"* as responsible for diverse strange human actions. It constantly reappears in the discussions of the next two or three years. Dr. Jorden uses the word in contradistinction to the *supernatural causes* which the demonologists believed to be responsible for these actions (*O.E.D.* 3b).

There are two lives of Dr. Jorden written by Dr. Thomas Guidott.* From these we learn that Dr. Jorden took his degree of Doctor of Physick at Padua, and then "returned home, practiced at London, became an eminently solid and rational philosopher and physician and one of that famous and learned society, The Kings College of Physicians in London." We also learn that Dr. Jorden had *"a good share in the affection of King James,"* who "committed the queen to his care when she used to bathe." He removed to Bath and there treated not merely the queen but the Earl of Salisbury in his decline.

How Dr. Jorden's novel point of view influenced the king's thought on witchcraft must now be looked into, and this will require investigation of the facts as to the alleged bedevilment of Mary Glover.

Mary Glover was the fourteen-year-old daughter of Timothy Glover, a merchant in Thames Street, and granddaughter of Robert Glover, one of the Marian martyrs of whom we read in Foxe's book. She was troubled with violent fits which she said were cast upon her by the witchcraft of

---

* One of these lives is prefixed to Dr. Jorden's work entitled *Discourse of Natural Baths and Mineral Waters* as edited by Dr. Guidott and printed in London in 1669. The other was published in London in 1677 in *The Lives and Character of the Physicians of Bathe.* Having succeeded to Dr. Jorden's practice, Dr. Guidott had ample information on which to base his biographies.

Elizabeth Jackson, an old charwoman who was accordingly
arraigned as a witch, tried, and convicted by a jury in the year
1602 before Chief Justice Anderson and committed to Newgate. But the Bishop of London intervened. He and his
secretary, Samuel Harsnet, asserted that Mary Glover, like
the boy Sommers, was a fraud and "did but counterfeit,"
and that Elizabeth Jackson was wrongfully convicted. The
Chief Justice at the bishop's request ordered that Mary
should be produced before Sir John Croke, the Recorder of
London, to be by him examined to see if she was truly a
fraud. The proceedings which ensued are told us by Lewes
Hewes, a Welsh puritan clergyman later active in the affairs
of the Island of Bermuda. Hewes had been present during
the examination before the recorder and was sure that the
maid did not counterfeit.*

The recorder's proceedings are of much interest. He
caused Mother Jackson, disguised as a slatternly market
woman, to be brought into Mary's presence (p. 12):

As soone as she was come into the Chamber, the Maide suddenly
fell downe backwards on the floore, with her eyes pluckt into
her, her tongue pluckt into her throat, her mouth drawn up to
her eare, her bodie stiffe and sencelesse, her lipps being shut
close, a plaine and audible loud voice came out of her nostrels
saying, *hang her, hang her.*

Mary was then barbarously tested with a lighted candle and
with "a long pinne" and found insensible to all pain. Other
tests which were applied convinced the recorder that there
was no fraud (p. 13):

---

* This occupies pages 12–15 of the tract entitled *Certain Grievances,
or The Errors of the Service-Booke,* by Lewes Hewes, printed in London in 1641. In the Bermuda records he is variously named Lewis
Hughes, Hugh's, Hues, Hewes, Heughes, or more frequently Mr. Lewis.
(See *Memorials of the Bermudas* [London 1877], Vol. I, p. 685.) In
John Swan's pamphlet he is always "Mr. Lewis." This must be borne
in mind by anyone trying to piece together the various accounts about
Mary Glover. His Welsh name was Lewis ap Hugh, so that either
designation was correct.

Whereupon the Recorder looking upon the Witch said, Lord have mercy on thee woman, and sent her to *Newgate;* then as soone as she was gone, the voice that came out of the maids nostrells ceased, and the maide came to her selfe, and went home with her mother.

But Mary Glover's fits kept on recurring every second day, even though Mother Jackson was in jail. The recorder, hearing of this, blamed the puritan ministers for not exorcising the devil out of Mary. Accordingly, on December 14, 1602, but with great secrecy lest the Bishop of London should deprive them of their livings, six "godly ministers," along with eighteen other persons, including Mary Glover's parents, met at Mistress Ratcliff's in Shoreditch and spent the entire day from 8:00 A.M. to 7:00 P.M. in a ceremony of exorcism. Lewes Hewes was one of these ministers and also John Swan, a divinity student, who has left us a secretly printed and very detailed account of the extraordinary doings of that day in a seventy-one-page pamphlet (entitled *A True and Brief Report, of Mary Glovers Vexation . . . by John Swan . . . Imprinted 1603*) of which the copy in the British Museum seems to be unique.

A modern psychiatrist will find this account of intense interest; and all biblical students who desire a better understanding of the Gospel accounts of people possessed with evil spirits should ponder the deeds and sayings of Mary Glover. Nothing could have been better calculated than these proceedings to cause poor Mary to believe that she was possessed by a devil, and she responded most completely to the suggestion and did all the things that one so possessed ought to do, not omitting a prayer for the woman who had bewitched her. Truly she did not counterfeit. It was a typical case of hypnotic suggestion. Accordingly, when the ministers reached the end of the exorcism the devil was cast out and she became normal.

Lewes Hewes goes on to relate that the day after this he went to Sir John Croke and told him what had occurred and was advised to make immediately a full statement to Bishop Bancroft. He says:

I did so, but could have no audience, and for my paines I was called Rascall and varlot, and sent to the Gatehouse, where hee kept mee foure moneths, and did set forth a booke wherein he called me and the rest of the Ministers, that did joyne with me in that holy action, Devill finders, Devill puffers, and Devill prayers, and such as could tare a devill in a lane, as soone as an hare in *Waltham Forrest*. All the rest, being men and women of good esteeme and credit, he called, a rout, rable, and swarme of giddy, idle, lunatick, illuminate, holy spectators, of both sexes, and specially a sisternitie of nimps, mops, and idle holy women, that did grace the devill with their idle holy presence [p. 15].

This when noised abroad occasioned much ado. The puritans asked for a public debate on the subject, which was held at Cambridge. The question first proposed for discussion was, "Nulla est his diebus possessio ac dispossessio demoniorum"; but the university authorities insisted that the field of debate be limited by inserting the word "ordinaria" before "possessio" (Swan, p. 58). The curious reader should consider the implications of this. The affirmative is free to assert that there may yet be some witches with their demons somewhere even though all tests give negative results, thus paralleling the well known but highly unsatisfactory remark of Joseph Addison: "I believe in general that there is and has been such a thing as witchcraft; but at the same time can give no credit to any particular instance of it."

By this time Mary Glover's case had resulted in a serious conflict of authority between the Chief Justice of the Court of Common Pleas and the Bishop of London which could only be resolved by the royal authority. Immediately a pamphlet war broke out even more violent than that produced by the Darrel case. Harsnet wrote for the Church; Hewes, Bradwell, and Swan for the puritans; while Dr.

Jorden propounded his rationalizing position which it was hoped might reconcile all differences.

The conflict reached its climax during the last weeks of the life of the queen. She was obviously dying and the royal authority was in the hands of her principal secretary, Robert Cecil. I have no doubt that it was he who, when the bishop's pamphlet was about to be published by order of the council, saw to it that Dr. Jorden's quiet but accurate reasoning about the effects of hysteria in cases of this sort should be published at the same time, for, statesman as he was, he hoped to end this conflict by propounding this *tertium quid*. So it came about that while King James was journeying to London for his coronation and at about the time that he was writing to his son about the discovery of counterfeit wenches, he learned of the imprisonment of Elizabeth Jackson in Newgate for witchcraft by reason of Mary Glover's testimony, and that the eminent Dr. Jorden had examined Mary Glover and had pronounced her a victim of the "mother," while the Bishop of London gave it out that she was a fraud. The question raised was of great interest to him. On his way south he stopped from May 3 to May 7, 1603, at Theobalds, the home of Robert Cecil, and there, if not previously, we may be assured that Dr. Jorden's book, just off the press, was put into his hands. On July 22, 1603, the king spent the entire day with Dr. Bancroft at his Episcopal palace at Fulham. No doubt the bishop and Dr. Harsnet discussed with him the latter's book and repeated their contention that Mary was a fraud. Soon after this the king received John Swan's little book assuring him that Mary was truly possessed by a devil which the ministers had expelled. Swan's prefatory address to the king pertinently asks him:

Who can be a fitter judge in such a cause than a Prince, whose book (of the like case) proclaymes his knowledg, and whose Princlye disposition and resolution, is to find out and maintayne, all truth? . . . They have not forborne to offer that immodest book [by one S. H., a chaplain to the Bishop of London] to your Majesties owne hands, notwithstanding the same (in the 21st cap p. 137, lin. 8) giveth a most dishonorable counterbuffe to your Highnes Treatise, which handleth that argument.

His special accusation against S. H. is that "in his said last book he broacheth a concept as if there were no witches at all, yea it seemeth by his so dallying with Modu his Devil that he is of mind there is no Devil at all." He further tells the king that those who opposed the puritan proceedings were stirred (meaning by the bishop) to this

vehement and eager opposition, in this and such other cases: whereby they have even shaken the land. Yet, (as I heare) they have as it were, now given over their first charge of this Mary Glover touching any counterfeiting: and now they maintain (and that specially by the means of a physician) that her affliction proceeded only from a naturall cause; who also hath written and published to that effect.

Thus we know that both Dr. Harsnet's and Dr. Jorden's books were printed and in the king's hands before Swan printed his little book and sent it to the king. The imprints of all three are dated 1603.*

* The bibliography of the three works just referred to is interesting and confirms statements made in the text.

Dr. Jorden's book was the first of them entered on the Stationers' Register. The full title of his book has already been quoted on page 102. From the first lines of this title we may know that the book was written after Dr. Jorden had given his opinion upon the case of Mary Glover. His preface is dated March 2, 1602/3. The Register entry reads as follows:

14° Martii (1602/3)
Master Windett / Entred for his Copie vnder thandes
of the Lord Bishop of LONDON
and the wardens a booke of *the*
Suffocacon of the mother . . . vjd /

Windet was an old established and reputable London printer who in the year 1603 was appointed printer to the City of London. In the ordinary course of business he would have gotten this small book out

Thus were the issues drawn. Was Mary Glover possessed, or was she a fraud, or was she insane? If she was possessed, Elizabeth Jackson alone should be punished. If she was a fraud, both she and Elizabeth Jackson should be punished.

---

promptly, so that we may assume that the book was on sale some time in April. The book was allowed by the Lord Bishop of London personally. He was not usually present in person. This informed the bishop that people would soon be told that Mary Glover did not counterfeit but was only a victim of hysteria. This was not the bishop's view of the case, and he wished that his book about counterfeit demoniacs be read before judgment was passed on Dr. Jorden's theory. So only two days later we find the following entry:

> 16o martij (1602/3)
> master Robertes   Entred for his Copie vnder thandes
> of the wardens / A booke called
> *A Declaracon of egregious popishe*
> *ympostures &c* / . . . . vjd

The full title of the bishop's book is as follows:

A Declaration of egregious Popish Impostures, to with-draw the harts of her Maiesties Subjects from their allegeance, and from the truth of Christian Religion professed in England, vnder the pretence of casting out deuils. Practised by Edmvnds, Alias Weston a Iesuit, and diuers Romish Priests his wicked associates. Where-vnto are annexed the Copies of the Confessions, and Examinations of the parties themselues, which were pretended to be possessed, and dispossessed, taken vpon oath before her Maiesties Commissioners, for causes Ecclesiasticall.
At London Printed by Iames Roberts, dwelling in Barbican. 1603.

The main part of the bishop's book has no reference to the case of Mary Glover. It is only a clever attack upon certain Jesuits; but on p. 166 there is a paragraph which I quote:

And if they want devils in Italy, to exorcise, and aske Oracles of: let them come but over into London in England: and wee have ready for them, *Darrells wife, Moores Minion, Sharpe, Skelton, Evans, Swan, & Lewis;* the devil-finders, and devil-puffers, or devil-prayers: and they shal start them a devil in a lane, as soone as an Hare in *Waltham* forrest, that shall nick it with aunswers, as dead as *Westons,* and *Dibdales* devils did. And wee shal as easily finde them a route, rable, and swarme of giddy, adle, lunaticke, illuminate holy spectators of both sexes, but especially a Sisternity of mimpes, mops, and idle holy women, that shal grace *Modu* the devil, with their idle holy presence, and be as ready to cry out, at the mowing of an apish wench, and the lowing, or bellowing of a brainlesse empty fellow: *O the glory of God: O the power of prayer:* as the Romish guls did troupe about *Sara, Fid,* and *Anne Smith,* and cry out at the conjuration of the Exorcist: *O the Catholique fayth! O the power of the fayth Catholique. Haec tempora, hi*

If she was insane, nobody should be punished. The result will show the king's mind, which is what we want to learn. It was a novelty to have a king who would interest himself in such questions, but so it was. The printed briefs supporting

mores. These are the times, wherein we are sicke, and mad of *Robin good fellow,* and the devil, to walke againe amongst us: and (I feare) the latter times, wherein lying signes, faigned wonders, cogged miracles, the companions of Antichrist, shall prevaile with the children of pride, giddines, and misbeleefe.

The last four exorcists named are four of the six puritan ministers who were present on Dec. 16, 1602, at the exorcism of Mary Glover, some of whom were sent by the bishop to the gatehouse. I very much suspect that this paragraph was hastily inserted in the bishop's book after he found that Dr. Jorden's book was to be printed, so that the public might know that his attacks upon counterfeiting demoniacs applied to Mary Glover as well as to the other confessed frauds named in the book. Roberts was a well known London printer accustomed to getting books out in a hurry. He had long been the printer of the playbills for the Globe Theater. We have a right to assume that this book, too, appeared about April, 1603. It was reissued in 1604 and again in 1605 by the same bookseller.

John Swan's book was written later than either of the other two, for they were entered on the Register before the queen died, whereas Swan's book refers to the king as the reigning sovereign, and in his Preface he makes specific reference to the fact of the publication of both of the other books. The Preface also refers to the prevalence of the plague, but in such a way as to leave the impression that it was in its earlier stages. I should assign its publication to midsummer, 1603. The full title reads as follows:

A True and Briefe Report, of Mary Glovers Vexation, and of her deliverance by the meanes of fastinge and prayer. Performed by those whose names are sett downe, in the next page. By John Swan, student in Divinitie. Psal.34.6 *This poore man cried, and the Lord hearde him, and saved him out of all his troubles.*
Imprinted: 1603.

It was never entered on the Stationers' Register nor does the name of any printer or bookseller appear in the imprint. It is a very small quarto (6 + 71 pages with 7 pages of verse added) no doubt secretly printed and cautiously circulated. Its author, John Swan, signs his name as "student of Divinitie." He was therefore not an ordained clergyman with a living of which the bishop might deprive him, and this is probably why he was chosen to be responsible for the book rather than any of the other clergy who took part in the exorcism of Mary Glover.

each of these three theses were before him, and he had time to read them and reach his conclusions, as he spent the autumn of 1603 in places near London, fearing to enter the city because of the plague. The result was that Elizabeth Jackson was released from Newgate and from her sentence. Nothing was ever done to Mary Glover.* Thus we see that the king followed neither the teachings of the book he had written nor the position of the Church of which he had recently become the head, but adopted the independent views of a rationalizing philosopher with whom he had now come into contact and who said that "the cause was natural." James was really beginning to see the light.

This account of Mary Glover has been extended to greater

* Those who wish to examine the case of Mary Glover in greater detail should read not only the books of John Swan and Lewes Hewes to which reference has been made, but another account of the same case written in 1603 by Stephen Bradwell, a member of the College of Physicians, entitled:

Marie Glover's late woefull case . . . upon occasion of Doctor Jorden's discourse of the Mother, wherein he covertly taxeth, first the Phisitiones which judged her sicknes a vexation of Sathan and consequently the sentence of Lawe and proceeding aginst the Witche, who was discovered to be a meanes thereof, with a defence of the truth against D. J. his scandalous Impugnations.

This treatise never appeared in print, but the MS remains in the British Museum as Sloane MS 831. It gives very detailed accounts of Mary Glover's symptoms and presents a ponderous medical argument in opposition to Dr. Jorden's diagnosis of the case. Some further information about the case may be gathered from *Certain Grievances, etc.*, by Lewes Hewes (London, 1641, pp. 12–14). Two previous books by the same author and with very similar titles but dated 1640 contain no account of Mary Glover. For later references to this case see: *Satan's Invisible World Discovered*, by George Sinclair (Edinburgh, 1685; reprinted 1871); *Kingdom of Darkness, or the History of Daemons, Spectres, Witches, etc.*, by Richard Burton (London, 1694; 4th ed., London 1728); *Essay Concerning Witchcraft*, by Hutchinson (London, 1718) in which, on p. 37, is the entry, "Mother Jackson condemned in London 1642." He was led by Burton to thus mistake the date. Notestein's *History of Witchcraft in England* has short references to the case (pp. 138, 355, 395), and Kittredge in his *English Witchcraft and James I* refers briefly to the case on p. 29. Both of the latter works have gone astray as to the facts of the case.

length than had been anticipated; but the story has never been told before. The incident is practically unknown to historians and yet it is not without interest and is of some importance, for it throws light on the mind and character of King James and discloses the beginning of influences which much affected him in the later years of his reign.

JAMES AND THE WITCHES OF 1605

During the year 1604 there seem to have been no notable cases of demoniacal possession or of witchcraft for the king to look into. James was extremely busy this year. His first Parliament met and showed him that his rights as King of England were not as divinely derived as he had thought. He summoned the Hampton Court conference, where he treated the puritan ministers very roughly. He also had to entertain the Spanish embassy which came to make the peace.

But the next year his interest in demonology was re-awakened by things which will now be set forth. The king, as everyone knows, was inordinately fond of hunting, spending much of his time in the saddle as an escape from affairs of state. Not so well known is it that he spent much time during these trips interviewing witches.

Early in January, 1604/5, the king hurried away with his boyhood friend, Jocky O'Sclaittis, or more respectfully, the Earl of Mar, and his older friend Edward Somerset, Earl of Worcester, to his favorite hunting ground at Royston in Hertfordshire, about fifty miles north of London. Concerning this trip Chamberlain wrote to Winwood on January 26, 1604/5 (*Memorials,* Vol. II, p. 46):

The King went to *Roiston* two Days after Twelfth-tide, where and thereabout he hath continued ever since, and finds such Felicity in that Hunting Life that he hath written to the Councill, that it is the only Means to maintain his Health, which being the Health and Welfare of us all, *he desires them to take the Charge and Burden of affairs and foresee that he be not* interrupted nor troubled by too much Busyness. . . . You have heard of the putting off of the Parliament until October. . . . Tho' he [the king] seek to be very private and retired where he is, yet he is much importuned . . . with foolish Prophecies of Danger to ensue, and great Speech we hear of a strange Apparition lately at *Berwick* of two Armies that fought a long time with Horse, Foot and Ordinance.

This hunting trip occupied full ten weeks, with the exception of two weeks in February during which the king returned to London. The often quoted letter of Sir John Harington to his cousin Sir Amyas Pawlett, dated "Jan. 1604," describes Sir John's reception by the king on some day during this trip. It is sometimes cited as though it evidenced the seriousness of the king's belief in witchcraft. The pertinent sentences are these:

His Majestie did much presse for my opinion touchinge the power of Satane in matter of witchcraft; and askede me with much gravity,—"If I did trulie understande why the devil did worke more with anciente women than others?" I did not refraine from a scurvey jeste, . . . He . . . saide he had soughte out of certaine bookes a sure waie to attaine knowledge of future chances [*Nugae Antiquae,* Vol. I, p. 368].

To me this language appears to require quite the opposite construction. It does indeed show that the king's mind was at this time running on the subject of witchcraft and prophecy, and we shall soon see why it was; but his reference to "anciente women" as troubled by the devil sounds like a question asked with the merry gravity of a skeptic.

The king's idea of hunting was a little different from that of other people. On January 26, 1604/5, the Earl of Mar wrote to Cecil:

We are here continually busied either at hunting or examining of witches, and although I like the first better than the last, yet I must confess both uncertain sports [*Calendar of MSS at Hatfield House,* Part XVII, p. 37].

And a few days later the king wrote to his "little beagle" that he was "ever kept busy with hunting of witches, prophets, puritans, dead cats, and hares" [*ibid.,* p. 121].

Information as to the witches, prophets, and puritans which the king was hunting is contained in the letters sent by the king's intimates to Robert Cecil at this time.* These are for the most part familiar letters and consequently more informative as to the king's state of mind than official correspondence. The king devoted an astonishingly large amount of his time during this trip to these matters of purely psychological interest. Both sorcery and conjuration (matters particularly interesting to the king) were involved in the utterances of the prophets and the witches. The names of the principal prophets were Morton and Butler, the former a harmless deluded puritan minister, and the latter a disreputable quack doctor. The alleged witches were named Frances and Beatrice. These witches had for some time exhibited strange and violent symptoms which they and others attributed to the conjurations, some said, of the poor crackbrained Morton, or, others said, of Butler. Both of the latter were reputed to be prophets foretelling some great national disaster, and the witches were the disseminators of these prophecies. All thus involved had first been sent to certain neighboring magistrates for examination. When the king reached Royston, reports of the magistrates about the matter were put in his hands and he ordered all of the parties to be brought before him, spending much of his time during the last two weeks of January personally examining them. He soon found that Morton was wrongly accused and ordered him to be released. Butler turned out to be an old offender who had been punished for conjuration during the days of Elizabeth. The king brought him to confess that he had been "meddling in witchcraft and sorcery" but "what he confessed one day he denied the next." James took him with him to Whitehall when he returned there on February 4, for

* Cal. of MSS at Hatfield House, Part XVII, pp. 19, 22, 31, 33, 36, 37, 65, 121, 222, 223; Cal. of State Papers—Domestic, 1603–1610, p. 218; Letter, Coke to Cecil, Jan. 29, 1605, British Museum Additional MSS 6171, p. 403.

on that day Rowland Whyte writes from Whitehall to the Earl of Shrewsbury: "Here are also foolish wizards, that deny this day what the other day they confessed, and speak they know not what" (Lodge's *Illustrations,* 1836 ed., Vol. III, p. 123). This is the last we hear of Butler. But the king's chief interest was in the witches, for they exhibited symptoms similar to those of Mary Glover. James's secretaries were hoping and expecting that the witches would be immediately turned over to magistrates and held for trial by the courts under the new witchcraft statute. But James thought other-wise. He sent Frances and Beatrice to Cambridge University with instructions to the vice-chancellor that they be examined by the learned doctors there. These were the men who two years before had taken part in the public debate on the sub-ject of bedevilment. They were now to report to the king their diagnosis of these two witches, who must have been dif-ficult cases, for they were being kept at the university in charge of "four keepers." When James returned to Royston he received their report, and on February 23 the king's secre-tary writes to Richard Bancroft, now Archbishop of Canter-bury:

The physicians of Cambridge have certified his Majesty that the disease of the maidens is natural, and they are much amended. I wish they were rid of them for their charge grows great [Part XVII, p. 65, *Hatfield House MSS*].

Evidently the physicians agreed with Dr. Jorden that hysteria was responsible for their symptoms. On the same day Dr. Cowell, the vice-chancellor of the University of Cambridge, writes to Cecil:

Since his Majesty's coming to Royston last, I sent thither a bill of those charges, which the University has been at for these two visited maidens, sent unto us by his commandment, since their coming to Cambridge. I received direction from the Dean of the Chapel [the king's secretary] that the king had appointed the money to be paid out of the privy purse [*ibid.*].

But the king was not prepared to let the two maids go home so soon, and they were kept under observation at Cambridge for three months longer. There is a warrant under the privy seal dated May 22, 1605, authorizing the following payment:

> For the charges of two maids suspected to be bewitched and kept by our commandment at Cambridge for their trial,* such sums of money as from the Earl of Salisbury, our Principal Secretary, Chancellor of that University, you shall be required so as the same exceed not the sum of £100 [*ibid.* p. 222].

Accompanying this warrant is a bill itemizing the charges:

> March 25 to May 14—diet, lodging, firing, candle, washing, etc., for the two maids Frances and Beatrix together with those for their four keepers, and for their apothecary's bill—£39 – 15 s. – 4 d.
>
> [Signed] Jo. COWELL, *Vice-Chancellor*

> The maids charges from May 14 until the end of 20 days after for so much time as your Lordship alloweth them to prepare themselves for their dismission [*ibid.,* pp. 222–223].

And again, in another handwriting: "Besides their Majesty's reward to the physicians—£20" (*ibid.* p. 223).

Previous investigators have slighted James's interest in this case. Kittredge has a few lines (p. 56) about it suggesting that James intrusted the investigation of it to someone else. Notestein tells a little more (p. 139) but mistakenly says that James "turned the whole thing over to the courts," which is just what he did not do. To neither of these historians were the *Hatfield MSS* available. Had they been, both would have seen how much of the king's own time and money was spent in his effort to find the real cause of the affliction of the maids, and that again the opinions of Dr. Jorden as expressed in his book prevailed.

During the month of April, 1605, the king's psychological curiosity took another turn. He heard of Richard Haydock

---

* "Trial" here means medical testing, not judicial.

of Oxford (see *D.N.B.*), "the sleeping preacher" who could preach wonderful sermons, but only at night and when sound asleep in bed. The king had him brought to Whitehall (Packer to Winwood, London, April 6, 1605, *Memorials,* p. 56), sat up all night in order to hear his midnight sermon, and soon discovered his practice to be fraudulent, but after his public confession the king relented and forgave him and offered him preferment in the Church.*

We now pass on to October, 1605, when at the end of the month Sir Roger Wilbraham entered in his journal:

The king's majestie, sithence his happie comyng, by his owne skill hath discovered 2 notorious impostures: one of a phisicion that made latyne & lerned sermons in the slepe: which he did by secret premeditacion: thother of a woman pretended to be bewitched, that cast up at her mouth pynnes, & pynnes were taken by divers in her fitts out of her breast [*Journal of Sir Roger Wilbraham, Camden Miscellany,* Vol. X, London, 1902].

The sleeping sermonizer was, of course, Richard Haydock.

The other and more notorious case is that of the woman who had pins in her.† Her name was Ann Gunter. She

* There is an interesting statement of the king's analysis of this case in the Earl of Worcester's letter to Cecil dated "April 29, 1605 at 11 at night" (Lodge's *Illustrations,* 1838 ed., Vol. III, pp. 154–155). There is a longer account of Haydock's confession and pardon by the king in Lascelles's letter to the Earl of Shrewsbury dated April 30, 1605 (*id.,* pp. 157–160).

† In this connection note what Dr. Kittredge says (p. 56) concerning the importance of the symptom of vomiting pins in the diagnosis of demoniacs. But the popular belief went far beyond this. It asserted that the most effective test of bedevilment was that no amount of pin-pricking pained the victim. One of the books produced by the Darrel controversy was the *Summary Answer, etc.* of John Deacon and John Walker (London, 1601). On p. 34 the following occurs in the course of a dialogue between Physiologus, who represents the medical point of view, and Exorcistes, who is John Darrel:

Physiologus. Give me leave (M. Orthodoxus) to argue this point. Come on *Exorcistes,* rehearse some few of the *straungest* of those your supposed *actions* or *passions:* which so highly surmounted the whole *faculitie, skill* and *power* of *nature.*   (continued on next page)

lived at Windsor and was a young woman of some respectability, but evidently slightly deranged. She was subject to strange delusions, had attacks of hysteria, announced that she was possessed by a devil, and at the instigation of her father carried out tricks of her own. It was therefore a case of combined delusion and trickery. The history of her case has come down to us only in disconnected scraps which have not, I believe, before been pieced together. The picture of this philosophic king spending his time studying the psychology of hysteria is something of a novelty and will be here set out from the records.

Fuller's *Church-History* contains this reference to her: "Anne Gunter a Maid of Windsor, gave it out she was possessed of a devil, & was transported with strange Extaticall Phrensies" (Bk. X, p. 73).

In October, 1605, Walter Yonge, J.P. and M.P., wrote in his diary:

This year there was a gentlewoman and near kinswoman to Doctor Holland's wife, Rector of Exon College in Oxford, strangely

---

Exorcistes. With verie good will. First therefore, the *youngman* (having pinnes thrust verie deepe into his *legges,* and other *parts* of his *bodie*) he was without *sense* or feeling thereof: a thing utterlie impossible to *nature.*

Physiologus. Hee himselfe hath eftsoones *deposed,* and confessed since then, that he hath *felt* the *pinnes,* and plucked them forth: although (for the present) he whollie dissembled the *paine,* as if he had been altogether in a *sensles* condition. Howbeit, because in this, and those other his *deposed reports* which directly doe *crosse* your idle conceit, you usuallie give him the *lie:* let us therefore, the more stricktly examine this your *sensles opinion,* concerning his supposed *sensles condition.*

This is followed by two pages of ponderous discussion as to the sensations produced by the pricking of pins, which let him who can endure it read in the original.

So firmly had this belief taken hold of people that sham demoniacs sprang up everywhere, for mock hysteria is very contagious. A common form of vagabondism in England at this time was the "Abraham man." Such stuck pins into their arms, and, pretending that they were senseless to any pain from it, asserted that they were demonized and terrified the country people. Dekker's *Bellman of London* (1608) describes the beggar who swore he had been in Bedlam and had pins stuck in his flesh.

possessed and bewitched, so that in her fits she cast out of her nose and mouth pins in great abundance, and did divers other things very strange to be reported [*Diary of Walter Yonge, Esq.* (London, Camden Society)].

Dr. Thomas Holland was Regius Professor of Divinity at Oxford and a very learned man. He had taken active part in the debates in the Divinity Act before King James at Oxford at the end of August, 1605.

We find that King James, immediately upon leaving Oxford, interested himself in the case of Ann Gunter. He suspected her bewitchment to be due either to hysteria or to fraud, and chose as his experts to diagnose the case Dr. Jorden and Dr. Harsnet, one of whom believed that demoniacal possession is the result of hysteria, and the other that it is the result of fraud. His choices show that the king was seeking enlightened opinion totally at variance with the pronouncements embodied in his own book on demonology.

The first expert to whom he sent Ann Gunter was Dr. Jorden. Dr. Guidott gives the following account of the resulting diagnosis:

Whilst he practised in London there was one Anne Gunter troubled with such strange and unusual symptomes, that she was generally thought and reported by all that saw her to be bewitch'd. King James hearing of it, sent for her to London, and pretending great pitty to her, told her, he would take care for her relief, in which thing he employed Dr. Jorden, who, upon examination, reported to the king, that he thought it was a cheat; and tincturing all she took with harmless things, made her believe that she had taken physick, by the use of which, she said, she had found great benefit. The doctor acquainting his majesty that he had given her nothing of a medicinal nature, but only what did so appear to the maid, and also, that though when he repeated the Lord's Prayer, and Creed in English, she was much out of order, yet at the rehearsal of the same in Latin she was not concern'd, the king was confirmed in what he had suspected before, and the doctor had suggested. Whereupon the king dealing very plainly with her, and commanding her to discover the truth unto him, the maid, though at first very unwilling to disclose the juggle, yet, upon the king's importunity and promise to her of making up what damage should accrue from the discovery, confessed all, and his majesty received from her own mouth this account: That sometime before, there happened a difference between a female neighbour of her father's and himself, and having in his own apprehension no better way to be avenged of her then this, impiously caused his daughter, on the receiving of the sacrament, to engage to imitate one bewitched and ascribe it to that woman, which she did, and acted this part in so exact and wonderfull a manner, that she deceived all the country where she lived, who thought it to be a truth. After which confession she was very quiet, and the king giving her a portion, she was afterwards married, being, by this subtle artifice, perfectly cured of her mimical witchery [Preface by Thomas Guidott to Jorden's *Discourse of Natural Baths,* 3rd ed., London, 1669].

Concerning the king's interviews with the woman we have more full information, and it comes from the king himself. His first interview was in London in September, 1605, when he sent her to Dr. Jorden.   After this he had her brought before him at Finchingbrook where he was hunting and had an interview with her on October 9, 1605.   The next day he saw her again and the case was solved.   There was no devil, but some hysteria, some delusion, and much fraud.   After her confession the king at once sat down and wrote this letter to his "little beagle":

For your better satisfaction touching Ann Gunter we let you wit that whereas not long ago she was a creature in outward show most weak and impotent, yet she did yesterday in our view dance with that . . . dexterity of body that we, marvelling thereat to see the great change, spent some time this day in the examination of her concerning the same.   And we find by her confession that she finds herself perfectly cured from her former weakness by a potion given her by a physician, and a tablet hanged about her neck; that she was never possessed with any devil nor bewitched;

that the practice of the pins grew at the first from a pin that she put in her mouth, affirmed by her father to be cast therein by the devil, and afterwards that and some other such pin-pranks which she used together with the swelling of her belly, occasioned by the disease called the mother, whereunto she was oftentimes vehemently afflicted, she did of long time daily use and practice make show to be matters of truth to the beholders thereof; and lastly that she hath been very far in love with one Appleby, servant to the Lord of Canterbury, and is still, hath sought his love long most importunately and immodestly (in manner unfit to be written) and now she doth most humbly and earnestly crave our furtherance that she may marry him; and this last is confessed also by himself. Whereof ye shall hear more by the next messenger; in the meantime we have sent you this letter enclosed for the better satisfaction of my Lords and yourself [*Hatfield House MSS*, Part XVII, p. 450].

The "potion given her by a physician" was, of course, Dr. Jorden's "harmless" physic. It confirmed the diagnosis. Note that the tone of the letter indicates that it was written to one who would be pleased with the finding that no devil was concerned. But the king wished his diagnosis confirmed by Dr. Harsnet, who had recently become rector of Shenfield in Essex. He therefore directed Dr. Richard Neile (who was chaplain to the Earl of Salisbury) to take Ann Gunter to Shenfield for further examination. This examination occurred later in the same month. On October 30 the king, who had been hunting at Royston, went to Ware, not far from Shenfield, and directed the earl to require Ann Gunter and the experts to come to Ware for still another consultation. Cecil did this, and a letter written that day by Dr. Richard Neile to the earl tells what happened:

Your letters signifying his Majesty's pleasure for Ann Gunter's attending him this night at Ware came to Mr. Harsnet's hands about one o'clock this Wednesday; at what time we were in the midst of our examinations and no way fit for his Majesty. Besides we had there neither coach nor any other provision fit for her conveying thither.

I have therefore sent my man to Ware with letters that his Majesty may be the better satisfied for her not coming, desiring him to let her attend him at Whitehall or some other convenient place hereafter. Whatsoever she has formerly confessed voluntarily, she has now confessed upon her oath. I sent your letters enclosed, that his Majesty may see there was no slackness in you to fulfil his pleasure herein. My fellow-chaplain commends himself very kindly to you. Shenfield, Wednesday, Oct. 30, *hora 2da pomeridiana,* 1605 [*Hatfield House MSS,* Part XVII, p. 471].

At this point the preoccupation of James and of Cecil in the delusions of Ann Gunter was suddenly interrupted for a time. While the king was at Royston, Lord Monteagle had received on October 26, 1605, the cryptic letter which led to the discovery of the Gunpowder Plot. He was at Ware on the night of Wednesday, October 30, on his way back to Whitehall and reached his palace on October 31. On November 1 Salisbury showed the king the letter and the tracing of the plot began. The powder beneath Parliament House was found on Monday, November 4.

But Dr. Neile and Dr. Harsnet had been directed by the king to complete their examination of Ann Gunter and to report their findings to him. They took her to London as foreshadowed in the above-quoted letter to Cecil; and no punishment was ever inflicted upon her. We may therefore assume that when the report was duly received it confirmed Dr. Jorden's diagnosis. The woman's restoration to some measure of health and decency seems to be established by Dr. Guidott's statement that the king gave her a portion so that she might marry. But in the course of her examinations she had revealed the fact that her father had committed an offence which required correction even though neither the witchcraft statute nor the common law provided any adequate remedy. In order to vent a grudge, he had induced his daughter to make a false accusation of witchcraft against a female neighbor. Such a despicable proceeding (all too common in the days of witchcraft) could not be punished in the law courts but only in the king's Court of Star Chamber, which had special jurisdiction of this sort of slander cases, and accordingly such proceedings were under consideration. And there is one more letter which tells about this. Unfortunately, the letter has no date except the endorsement "1606." When it was written, Ann Gunter's examination by the doctors must still have been under way and deemed of such weighty importance as to be ground for excusing Dr. Harsnet, who had just been appointed vice-chancellor of the University of Cambridge, from going to that city for induction into his new office. And the statements which had been made by Ann Gunter were being laid before King's Council and the clerks of the Star Chamber, but with what ultimate result seems not to be recorded. The letter is holographic from Dr. Richard Neile to Robert Cecil, Earl of Salisbury, and reads as follows:

I am bold to move you to sign this letter enclosed to the University, touching Mr. Harsnett, who is by the University chosen Vice-Chancellor for the year to come. If he should now go down to Cambridge to be admitted he would greatly hinder the prosecuting of Anne Gunter's business, in which we cannot have either his Majesty's learned counsel or any of the Clerks of the Star Chamber, to do anything longer than myself or Mr. Harsnett do ourselves attend them. The admitting of the Vice-Chancellor in this sort by proxy is a thing ordinary [*Hatfield House MSS*, Part XVIII, p. 423].

Hawarde's reports of cases determined in the Court of Star Chamber during this period reveal the trial of no such case. All we know of the outcome is that James had kindliness enough to help poor Ann Gunter. We must not fail to recognize what was involved in the king's sending Ann to Dr. Harsnet, the man who had so recently affirmed in print that those who believe in witches are either children, fools, women, cowards, or of discomposed wits. Clearly the king was sympathetic with the most enlightened opinion upon this subject in England and was making a sincere effort to discover the truth.

The accounts of this affair contained in the foregoing documents are supplemented by an interesting account of it written by a certain Robert Johnston. Johnston (see D.N.B.) was a Scot of Edinburgh, one year younger than James. He was a Burgess of that city, but came to London with his king in 1603, received favors from him and greatly admired him. He wrote a Latin history of his own times, in the form of a chronicle (apparently compiled from contemporary notes) covering the period from 1572 to 1628. This was not printed in his lifetime and first appeared in Amsterdam entitled *Historia Rerum Britannicarum—Auctore Roberto Johnstono Scoto-Britanno. Amstelaedami, Sumptibus Johannis Ravesteynii*, MDCLV.

Under the year heading of 1605, immediately following an account of the king's visit to Oxford, he proceeds (p. 401) to tell of Ann Gunter's performances and of this the following is a literal translation:

Whil'st the King was staying at Oxford a young girl about eighteen years of age excited the wonder of the people of Britain on account of her strange cleverness in deception, which imposed upon the astonished multitude. Whereupon James was seized with the desire of seeing one so celebrated in popular report. Therefore she was at once brought to the King. To the great wonder of the bystanders she lacked all sense of pain when she was stuck with pins. The strangeness of this created great astonishment. Not only was this wonderful in the eyes of those who were present, but she also cast out of her mouth and throat needles and pins in an extraordinary fashion. The King wondering whence she vomited forth so many pins so suddenly, plied her with repeated questioning but she remained firm; asserting that this happened to her by a miracle and that the sense of feeling taken away from her for the time being would soon return to her by divine providence. The King being skillful in untangling deceptions and considering the thing incredible, ordered physicians to determine whether this occurred by some natural cause

or by human fraud. By recommendation of the theologians and
the entreaty of the physicians, who differed widely concerning
this novel and unusual thing, he committed the young girl and
the investigation of the matter to the archbishop of Canterbury,
in the hope of detecting the fraud. The archbishop, when he
accomplished nothing by threats, warning and promises, called
in the services of Samuel Harsnet, his chaplain, whom he honored
above others. Led by a hint from the archbishop he induced a
very proper youth in the retinue of the archbishop to entice the
girl into love; who discovering the secret and promising marriage
easily procured her favor. Thereafter he gradually neglected her
on the pretext of her magical vanities, and the infamy of witchcraft, widespread through all Britain. But she (as is characteristic of womankind) inclined to lust, revealed all her tricks,
committing fame and safety to the mastery of the youth. Thus
was fraud laid bare and detected by the lack of self-control in a
woman. In the end the glory of detecting the fraud was awarded
the King, and ridicule for their vanity was awarded to its actors.

There are slight discrepancies between Johnston's account
and that previously given but these are readily reconciled.
James evidently first heard of Ann Gunter when he was in
Oxford and first sent her to Dr. Jorden, but the important
steps towards uncovering her frauds seem to have been made
by Archbishop Bancroft and his chaplain. Their very ques-
tionable method of tripping her had met with success before
the king had his interviews with her which are described in
his letters of September and October 1605. The dower which
the king offered Ann to enable her to marry Appleby looks
like an effort on the king's part to make some small repara-
tion for the shabby treatment that both had received from his
clergy. Of course, the king, notwithstanding this, claimed
and received all the credit for the discoveries which were
made and was by the voice of the populace praised as the
sagacious detective who had ferreted out the mystery.

Here ends our information about the clinical aspects of
this case; but its extraneous results are more far-reaching.
The royal interest made it a *cause célèbre*. That King James,

instead of persecuting witches, was trying to find the nature
of the strange malady which underlies such delusions, and to
restore the deluded victims to health and normal life—this
was indeed a novel development in which people became
greatly interested. So it is that we find an immediate reaction to it upon the stage—"the abstract and brief chronicles
of the time."

During the last months of 1605, three notable stage plays
were in the making, and this excursion of an inquisitive king
into the realm of psychiatry has left its mark upon all three.

Ben Jonson is about to write *Volpone,* which was first
performed the following March (*Modern Language Notes,*
Vol. XX, pp. 164–165). To compliment the king on his successful solution of Ann Gunter's case, he brings into the play
a fraudulent demoniac named Voltore, whose trick it is to
vomit pins in his pretended spasms but who is successfully
unmasked and punished.

Shakespeare is writing *King Lear,* in which Edgar plays the
sham demoniac thrusting pins into his bare arm and pretending to be infested with devils. To learn the tricks of this
kind of fraud, he is reading Harsnet's book. He is also reading Dr. Jorden's book, in which (Cap. 2) we too may read:
"This disease is called by diverse names . . . Passio Hys-
terica. . . . In English the Mother, or the Suffocation of the
Mother, because most commonly it takes them with choaking
in the throat." So in *Lear* (II, iv, 56) he writes:

> O! how this mother swells up toward my heart
> Hysterica passio! down.

Shakespeare is also about to write *Macbeth,* in which,
while depicting just such sorcery as the king has described in
his *Daemonologie,* he persistently surrounds it with questioning of its reality; and so powerfully paints the extraordinary
effects of the human imagination as to show this philosophic
king that the same hysterical imagination which was responsible for Ann Gunter's foolish pranks can account for the

phenomena of witchcraft. He even coins a phrase to designate the pseudohysterics of women like Ann Gunter, calling it *"modern ecstasy"* (IV, iii, 170). This is found in Ross's speech where he contrasts the terrible sorrows of Scotland under the tyranny of Macbeth with all lesser sorrows, so that the latter in comparison seem but a "modern ecstasy."

Editorial exposition of the phrase "modern ecstasy" began with Warburton, who said: "that is no more regarded than the contorsions that Fanatics throw themselves into. The author was thinking of those of his own times." This was sound. But a few years later Dr. Johnson led us all into a blind alley, for after quoting Warburton, he added: "I believe 'modern' is only foolish or trifling." There is no doubt that during Shakespeare's lifetime, and for a short time afterward, the word "modern" did sometimes carry this implication; that is, it meant *modern and therefore trifling or commonplace,* and Shakespeare so uses it, but not always (for example, *All's Well,* V, iii, 216). Following Dr. Johnson's lead, we find editors offering the following paraphrases for modern ecstasy:

an ordinary fit of sorrow	Capell
an ordinary excitation	Staunton
a slight nervousness	R. G. White
a common malady	Mull
a trivial excitement	Manly
a commonplace delirium	Liddell
an everyday ordinary or commonplace emotion	Cuningham
common fits of madness	Parrott
cheap passion	J. Q. Adams
slight mental disturbance	G. B. Harrison
an ordinary, commonplace fit of excitement	Kittredge

This list is doleful reading. Each editor feels the weakness of his predecessors' versions but fails to better them; for they all involve an unwarranted dilution of the word "ecstasy." The Clarendon editors, seeing this, explained: "The emphasis must be on 'modern,' as 'ecstasy' is not antithetical to 'violent' or 'sorrow'." But no emphasis on "modern" can justify an equating of ecstasy with mere excitement. Dr. Johnson's lead must therefore be abandoned, or rather pushed to a more legitimate conclusion. At the time *Macbeth* was being written, the people of England had been much aroused by this epidemic of sham demoniacs which broke out consequent upon the notoriety of the Darrel case. Their doings were customarily referred to as "ecstatical frenzies," and were believed to be mere fraudulent trickery for the sake of gain. Therefore when Shakespeare in his play spoke of "a modern ecstasy," the phrase carried with it the implication, not of a commonplace, but of a fraudulent or sham trance or fit of hysteria.

It was the accepted doctrine of the Anglican Church that miracles such as had characterized the early Christian Church had ceased and that the later miraculous doings proclaimed by the Roman Church were fraudulent. That exorcism had been successfully practiced in the early Church was not to be denied. But the gift, like others, had ceased, and modern exorcism and modern ecstasy were merely deceptive practices such as the king had detected in the case of Ann Gunter. He better than others would understand the antithesis between "modern ecstasy" and "violent sorrow."

In thus using their plays to show to the king their sympathy with his efforts to uncover the delusions and deceits of the demonized, the players did not incur any royal disapprobation; for Ben Jonson repeated and emphasized this sort of satire in his later play, *The Devil Is an Ass,* given by the King's Players at the Blackfriars in 1616. That this play is utterly contemptuous in its attitude toward witchcraft and demonology has long been noted. (See Kittredge's essay published in *Modern Philology,* Vol. IX, p. 193.) The play was intended (as had been the plays of 1606) to compliment the king on his sagacity in detecting sham demoniacs, and to satirize his judges for their childish credulity in witchcraft cases.

Putting these indications together, we have persuasive evidence that William Shakespeare knew that the debate at Oxford as to the reality of the effects of the imagination had made its impression upon the mind of this learned and inquisitive king and that James's examination of Ann Gunter had strengthened the impression; that the play of *Macbeth* was intended to take advantage of the opening thus afforded; and that the insistence which we find in the play that the human mind may be convinced of the existence of nonexistent things was intended to be William Shakespeare's contribution to the argument.

The excuse for this long account of these psychiatric explorations of King James must be that they have never before been examined, and that it is only by realizing what was being done and talked about concerning witches and devils in the year 1606 that one can form any adequate idea of the atmosphere into which the play of *Macbeth* was born.

THE KINGLY GIFT

A play for a king should accord with the thoughts of the king; and because England's new king had written books this could more easily be accomplished. In the spring of 1603, as James was slowly journeying from Edinburgh to be crowned at Westminster, several of his earlier works were reprinted in London in large editions. Two of these, the *Basilicon Doron* (Kingly Gift) and the *Daemonologie,* have much influenced the play of *Macbeth.* The effect of the latter is seen only in certain parts of the play, but the influence of the *Basilicon Doron,* which he wrote for the instruction of his eldest son in good morals and kingcraft, permeates the entire play. The outraged and avenging conscience which Shakespeare has painted at full length in this play was sure to hold the interest of the king, for in his book the king had made a serious effort to look into this subject and to tell his son about it. A king's heavier responsibility to his conscience, because not subject to other control, is the foundation on which the king's book is built.

It is only a little book. It was highly approved in England. In some other places it was anathema. On December 24, 1605, the Venetian ambassador in Rome wrote to the Doge of Venice:

The inquisitor of Venice has sent to the Congregation of the Index the King of England's book containing instructions to his son. As it expresses many impious and detestable sentiments, entirely opposed to our fundamental dogmas, consultation was held as to what ought to be done. Some opined that one of the Cardinals should be deputed to refute it, but seeing that this would add to the importance of the work, and would stimulate many heretics to a rejoinder, it has been resolved to put it on the Index [*Calendar of State Papers—Venetian*].

But all Englishmen who could do so bought the book and read it during the early days of King James's rule over them, for they wished to know more about their new sovereign, and the book is most readable.* As the king approached London in May, 1603, an address on behalf of the sheriffs of London and Middlesex told him that they were assured of their hopes by "some bookes now fresh in every man's hands" which set forth "those excellent wholesome rules your Majesty will never transgresse, having bound your Princely Sonne by such heavy penalties to observe them after you" (Nichols's *Progresses of James,* Vol. I. p. 132*).

William Shakespeare had evidently read the *Kingly Gift* carefully, and consequently its standards and instructions reappear in the play which he wrote for his king two years later. The lofty ethical tone which pervades the book finds its complete exemplification in the play of *Macbeth* as in no other play which Shakespeare wrote.

There is no reasonable doubt of the sincerity with which the young king had written this book. He assured his readers in his prefatory address that his book "must be taken of all men for the true image of my very mind," and the candid reader feels this to be true. We must deplore the fact that James's later character failed to exemplify the good principles which he had laid down for his son. The luxurious life of an English sovereign proved a fatal seduction to this well educated young Scot, and his high ideals gave way to the temptations of ease and flattery. But this was not yet apparent in 1606, and so Shakespeare took the king at his word and put into the play the moral standards which he read in his book.

* In the early days of the reign of King James a gentleman's library was deemed incomplete if it did not contain: the Bible, Hooker's *Ecclesiastical Polity,* Plutarch's *Lives,* Camden's *Britannia,* Holinshed's *Chronicles,* Tully's *Offices,* James I's *Basilicon Doron,* Sidney's *Arcadia* (see Trevelyan's *England Under the Stuarts,* p. 55). We may assume that William Shakespeare had some acquaintance with all of them. The influence of all except Hooker may be distinctly traced in his works.

The first part of the book concerns a king's duty toward
God. A good king is "conserved by conscience" (p. 6). Of
this James gives a crisp and somewhat original account:

And as for conscience, which I called the conserver of Religion, it is nothing else, but the light of knowledge that God hath
planted in man, which ever watching over all his actions, as it
beareth him a joyfull testimonie when he does right, so choppeth
it him with a feeling that hee hath done wrong, whenever he
committeth any sinne. And surely, although this conscience bee
a great torture to the wicked, yet is it as great a comfort to the
godlie, if wee will consider it rightly. For have we not a great
advantage, that have within ourselves while wee live heere, a
count booke and inventarie of al the crimes that wee shall be
accused of, either at the houre of our death, or at the great day
of judgement; which when wee please (yea though wee forget)
will chop, and remember us to look upon it; that while we have
leasure and are here, wee may remember to amend [p. 14].

A man whose heart knocks at his ribs * (I, iii, 136) when
he entertains the thought of murder would remind James of
the chopping (that is, "knocking," O.E.D., v¹, 12) conscience he had written about (p. 15). That this conscience
urges a man to look upon the "count book and inventarie"
of his crimes is a characteristic turn given to his thought by
the king; and we find this same turn in the play, as the criminal, rejecting the urgings of his conscience, expresses his fear
of looking upon the evidence of his crimes. When Macbeth
determines (I, iv, 52) to commit his first crime, he says: "yet
let that be, Which the eye fears, when it is done, to see."

* Why do I yield to that suggestion
Whose horrid image doth unfix my hair
And make my seated heart knock at my ribs
Against the use of nature? [I, iii, 134–137]

Liddell has a good analysis of these lines. "Suggestion" connotes
temptation. "Seated" means fixed in its seat. "Against the use of nature" means contrary to Macbeth's customary disposition. Although
Macbeth had a very steady heart, yet this temptation unseated it so that
it knocked against his ribs.

And when he has committed the crime, he says: "Look on 't again I dare not." In his last hour the count book of his crimes against the Macduff family whom he has slaughtered causes him to tell Macduff that his "soul is too much *charged* with blood of thine already" (V, viii, 5).

The author of the *Basilicon Doron* would assuredly be interested in the showing of a good king who has been "clear in his great office," who has borne his faculties so meek that his "joys are plenteous," and who retires at night in "measureless content"; as compared with a bad king whose people curse him, whose mind is "filled with scorpions," and who at night "lies in restless ecstasy."

All these thoughts expressed in the play must have had special appeal to the king. With Furnivall we must call *Macbeth* "the play of conscience" (Introduction to the Leopold Shakespeare, p. lxxvii).

Having described the conscience in the words which have been quoted, the king thus further admonishes his son:

Above all then, my Sonne, labour to keepe sound this conscience, which many prattle of, but over few feele: especiallie be carefull to keepe it free from two diseases, wherewith it useth oft to be infested; to wit, Leaprosie, and Superstition: the former is the mother of Atheisme, the other of Heresies. By a leaprouse conscience, I meane a cauterized conscience, as Paul calleth it, being become senselesse of sinne.

The dramatist in his play, after picturing the sound conscience of Macbeth prior to the commission of his first great crime, proceeds to show Macbeth suffering first from the disease which King James calls "superstition" and later from the disease which he calls "leaprosie." Tracing the symptoms of these two diseases which successively afflict Macbeth's conscience is a help in understanding the play. The sound conscience of "worthy" Captain Macbeth appears in I, ii, and is minutely described by his wife in I, v, 17–26. But when Macbeth hears the prophecies of the witches, he falls at once under the thrall of "superstition," which James calls the mother of heresies, instancing two varieties: that grounded upon the arrogant vanities of the Church's authority, and that of those who are ruled by the "ignorant fantasie" of "your own conceites and dreamed revelations" (p. 19). The dramatist, choosing the latter, shows Macbeth supporting his conceits by wordy arguments. He begins by asserting that the "supernatural soliciting" cannot be ill because of its promise of success, and continues in a succession of high-sounding, sophisticated, self-deceptive phrases (I, iv, 48–53; I, vii, 1–10; II, ii, 73; III, i, 71; III, ii, 55; III, iv, 135–140). This disease of superstition afflicts Macbeth throughout Acts II and III; but ends when, convinced that "blood will have blood," he hurries to the witches, "by the worst means to know the worst." Here he contracts the disease of "leaprosie" (or "cauterized conscience") which is "the mother of atheisme." James told his son ever to eschew "wilfully and wittingly to contrarie your conscience" (p. 16). The "fiend of Scotland" does just that. "For mine own good all causes shall give way" (III, iv, 135); and throughout the last two acts of the play a wicked Macbeth willfully cauterizes his conscience. Sophistry is done with. Instead, "be it thought and done" (IV, i, 145–154). This "leaprosie" is a mortal disease. He has lived long enough. Life is but "a tale told by an idiot."

This systematic development of Macbeth's conscience according to the philosophy of the king's book will be more fully examined in a later chapter which points out how the dramatist transformed the Macbeth of Holinshed's *Chronicles* into the Macbeth of the play, with a conscience illustrating the three phases of which the king had told his son.

The second part of the king's book concerns "a king's duty in his office." Four pages (24–27) are devoted to "the true difference between a lawful, good king and an usurping tyrant." He thus defines this difference:

A good King thinking his highest honor to consist in the due discharge of his calling, . . . and as their natural father and kindly maister thinketh his greatest contentment standeth in their prosperity, and his greatest suretie in having their hearts . . . where by the contrarie an usurping Tyrant thinking his greatest honour and felicitie to consist in attaining *per fas, vel nefas,* to his ambitious pretenses, . . . building his suretie upon his peoples miserie. . . . [Some good kings] may bee cut off by the treason of some unnaturall subjects, yet liveth their fame after them; and some notable plague faileth never to over-take the committers in this life, besides their infamie to all posterities hereafter. Where by the contrarie, a Tyrannes miserable and infamous life, armeth in end his owne subjects to become his burreaux [that is, *bourreaux:* hangmen].

This passage was of great notoriety when the book was printed, and for long afterward it was the subject of much favorable comment. Shakespeare determined to use his play to illustrate this difference as thus defined by his king, and he accordingly shows us in his royal play a good and kindly king cut off by the treason of an unnatural subject who becomes "an usurping tyrant," lives a "miserable and infamous life," building his surety upon his people's misery, until he is slain by his own subjects.

The dramatist has thus been supplied with his theme. His forthcoming play will exhibit the downfall of the noble as instanced in a man who murdered his king but was thereafter tormented and hunted down to his death by an avenging conscience. In this part of the book (pp. 84–100) is also found a reasoned catalogue of the princely virtues with an execration of a king's vices very like what is said about these things in the play (IV, iii, 91–100).

Supplementing the ethical teachings of the first two books of the *Basilicon Doron* is a third book telling his young son

how a king should behave "in indifferent things." These
rules of propriety were read by the dramatist and in writing
the play of *Macbeth* he showed the minds of three successive
kings of Scotland—Duncan, Macbeth, and Malcolm. All of
Duncan's speeches, and Malcolm's speech after he became
king, are good samples of James's teaching in Book III, p. 115,
on the subject of a king's proper language. These two kings
fill all of King James's requirements as to what a king should
be and do, but the other shows the bad result of the failure
to fill these requirements.

Another influence of the *Basilicon Doron* must not be
overlooked. It is very generally recognized that some parts
of *Macbeth* are written with a disregard of grammatical structure and metrical regularity, unusual even among Shakespeare's late plays. Haste may, and I think must, in part
account for this. But it is still easier to understand if we
assume, as we have a right to do, that William Shakespeare
knew his play was to be judged according to the standards
written down by King James in his book for the instruction
of his son. The king had written poetry as well as prose and
had explained "the Reulis and Cautelis to be observit";
nevertheless, in his book he told his son (p. 119):

And if ye write in verse, remember that it is not the principal
part of a poëme to rime right, and flow well with many pretie
words: but the chiefe commendation of a poëme is that when the
verse shall be shaken sundrie in prose, it shall be found so rich
in quick inventions and poëticke flowers, and in faire and pertinent comparisons; as it shall retain the lustre of a poëme, although in prose.

Shake the irregular verse of *Macbeth* down into prose and
it will at once appear that it is above all else rich in quick inventions and poetic flowers, and that it abounds in fullest
measure with "pertinent comparisons." Miss Caroline F. E.
Spurgeon, after spending ten years in the classification of
Shakespeare's Imagery, writes (p. 324):

The imagery in *Macbeth* appears to me to be more rich and varied, more highly imaginative, more unapproachable by any other writer, than that of any other single play. . . .

The ideas in the imagery are in themselves more imaginative, more subtle and complex than in other plays.

The dramatist needed not to watch so carefully his metrical step in writing this play because of his fulfillment of the more important test laid down by his king.

Earlier influence of the *Basilicon Doron* may, I think, be traced in another play. As he read the book, Shakespeare's eye had lit upon this advice of his father to Prince Henry:

And in case it please God to provide you to all these three king-domes, make your eldest sonne *Isaac,* leaving him all your king-domes; and provide the rest with private possessions. Otherwaies by dividing your kingdomes, ye shall leave the seede of division & discorde among your posteritie: as befell to this Ile, by the division & assignment thereof, to the three sonnes of *Brutus, Locrine, Albanact,* and *Camber* [p. 83].

An anonymous play of *Locrine,* printed ten years pre-viously, had shown the division of the kingdom amongst the three sons of Brutus to be unsatisfactory material for a play; but Shakespeare also knew the story to be found in his Holins-hed of the similar division of his kingdom into three parts by King Lear. This story had been used some years earlier, by an unknown dramatist who called his play the *History of King Leir and his Three Daughters.* It had lately been re-vived and was printed early in 1605 (Stationers' Register, May 8, 1605). This revival may have made it clear to Wil-liam Shakespeare that the king's advice could be well illus-trated by Lear's case. Therefore we may suspect that Shake-speare's play of *King Lear* was projected and perhaps begun before he went to Oxford in the summer of 1605, and would have been finished next after *Othello,* if certain things which

occurred in Oxford had not changed the plan.   For the writing by Shakespeare of the *True Chronicle Historie of the life
and death of King Lear and his three Daughters* proved to
be a laborious task occupying many months and subject to
interruptions.   It seemingly did not reach the stage until,
as is stated on the title page of the first (Pide Bull) quarto,
"it was played before the Kings Maiestie at Whitehall upon
S. Stephans night in Christmas Hollidayes by his Maiesties
feruants playing usually at the Gloabe on the Bancke-side."
The date of performance thus recorded is December 26, 1606.

This information leads to the conclusion that *Lear*, which
like Macbeth carries marks of the powder plot and of the
March hurricane, was written at the same time as *Macbeth*,
but not finished and performed until more than four months
after *Macbeth* had been given before the king.*

Two criticisms of the book are inserted here in the hope
that I may thereby induce others to read the king's book.

* There are many evidences of the contemporaneous writing of
Lear and *Macbeth*.   *Macbeth* I, iii, 6 borrows from *King Lear* III, iv,
127.   *Macbeth* IV, i, 59, uses words taken from *King Lear* III, ii, 8.
The simile in *Lear* (III, vii, 54) by which Gloucester likens himself to
a bear tied to a stake and baited is used again with verbal repetition
by Macbeth (V, vii, 1).   Cordelia's answer in I, i, 98 ff., indicates that
Shakespeare had been reading the story attributed to both King Ina
and King Lear as told in Camden's *Remaines* (pp. 182–183), which was
published early in 1605 (S.R. Nov. 10, 1604).   As this book will later
be referred to more than once, it is here noted that on p. 8 of its
section headed "Poems" there occurs the name "William Shakespeare"
among the names of the "pregnant wits of these our times, whom succeeding ages may justly admire."   When a man learns that he has been
thus eulogized in print, he is apt to get the book and read it at once.
Gloucester's speech, I, ii, 98 ff., refers to the double eclipse of Oct.,
1605; and from this Aldis Wright concludes that it is highly probable
that Shakespeare began to write *King Lear* toward the end of the year
1605.   We may be sure that such a massive play occupied many months
in the writing.   Although it is not capable of proof, my own belief
is that the main structure of the play of Lear was commenced in the
first half of the year 1605, but that the subplot which has been woven
into it did not take shape until after the disclosure of the powder
treason near the end of that year.

The Bishop of Winton in his preface to the 1616 edition of the king's works called it:

A book so singularly penned that a pomegranate is not so full of kernels as that is of excellent counsels.

Sir Walter Scott (*Somers Tracts,* Vol. III, p. 260) said:

It is composed in his Majesty's very best manner, exhibiting that extraordinary mixture of learning and pedantry, sense and folly, reason and prejudice, vanity and prudence which most deservedly procured James the character of the wisest fool in Christendom.

This latter judgment has been influenced by a fondness for antithesis. There is certainly pedantry in some of the king's books, but I do not find it in this one, nor do I think it should be accused of folly. That there is much prejudice and some vanity I will at once agree. This gives it its intense interest, for it is a human document written by a man in whom was a singular intermixture of that which was good with that which was not good. Such mixtures fascinated William Shakespeare; so before writing his play he studied and absorbed the thought of the book, with the result that a careful reader of the play is conscious of the influence of two minds.

"Macbeth" is an instance of a piece written for a reason external to and independent of the promptings of his own breast [Dr. Richard Garnett in Forshaw's *At Shakespeare's Shrine,* p. 6].
    The play gives a plainer indication than any other of Shakespeare's works of the dramatist's desire to conciliate the Scottish King's idiosyncrasies [Sir Sidney Lee's *Life of Shakespeare* (1929), p. 394].

The philosophy of the play is in truth a fusion of the thoughts of two minds. But there was here no contradiction. The ethics of King James, although Shakespeare may not have cared for his precise and theological form of expression, were the ethics of the people of England, and those of the dramatist, and were readily molded to fit the latter's pattern for his high tragedies.

Shakespeare could the more easily thus build his play upon King James's morals because his art was not much influenced by the great Greek tragedies, of which he had read only the Latin imitations by Seneca, with whose Roman stoicism he was not in sympathy. Had it been otherwise, we might have seen his heroic noble characters overthrown by an unreasoning fate, a theme which, though exciting our pity, does not better our lives. The Shakespearean dramatic pattern consistently differs from the Greek in that it emphasizes man's responsibility for the bad habit which, by suffering one faculty to dominate the others, overthrows man's self-control.

And consequent upon this, a Shakespearean tragedy compels us to feel how unjust is the "general censure" which forgets all the original noble substance and refuses forgiveness because of the particular fatal fault. Shakespeare never did this. Pity and forgiveness combine to produce the chord with which all of his great tragedies end when properly acted.

The king's book will be better appreciated by those who know about its writing and original reception. To William Shakespeare it meant much more than it can to the modern reader. Very dead now, it was a very live book when the play was written. So extensive is the influence of the thought of this book upon the play of *Macbeth,* and so little recognition has been given to it, that there seems justification for adding a short bibliographical account of this forgotten book for those who may wish to know more about it. Those not interested in bibliography should pass on directly to the next chapter.

The original MS of the *Basilicon Doron* in James's own hand is preserved in the British Museum. The book was not written for publication but for the private instruction of his young son and heir, then but six years old. James had seven copies of the work, and no more, privately printed by Robert Waldegrave, his printer in Edinburgh. One of these he gave to his son, one he kept for himself, and the other five he distributed among trusty friends under instructions to replace the prince's copy should it be lost. Of these seven copies at least three seem to have survived, one of which is in the British Museum. The volume is a finely printed quarto in large italic type and with the following title page:

ΒΑΣΙΛΙΚΟΝ ΔΩΡΟΝ.
Devided/into three/Bookes,
Edinburgh
Printed by Ro-
bert Walde-grave Prin-
ter to the Kings
Majestie. 1599.

That the King of Scotland had written this book soon became known; and as he was likely soon to be King of England, the English people were curious to read it and by 1602 manuscript copies were being freely circulated in both countries.* This curiosity, James says, "hath inforced the un-timous divulgating of this book," by which he means that he had it again printed by Robert Waldegrave in Edinburgh—this time for general circulation. Our first knowledge of his intention to do this is derived from a letter from Chamberlain to Carleton dated London, October 18, 1602, which informs us that King James of Scotland "is printing a little work with a Greek name, a last will of remembrance to his son; and because it has gone abroad subject to many constructions, and much depraved by many copies, he will now set it out under his own hand." So it was that very shortly before

---

* Information as to how transcriptions of the *Basilicon Doron* came into circulation is to be found on p. 223 of William Sanderson's *History of the Reigns of Mary and James* (London, 1656). See also Spottiswood's *Church History* (4th ed., London, 1677), p. 457.

Queen Elizabeth died the work appeared with the following title page:

BAΣIAIKON ΔΩPON
or
HIS MAIESTIES IN-
STRVCTIONS TO HIS
DEAREST SONNE,
HENRY THE
PRINCE.
(Royal Arms of Scotland)
EDINBVRGH
Printed by Robert Walde-grave
Printer to the Kings Majestie.
M. D. C. III.

Immediately after the queen died, and while James was preparing for his journey to Westminster to be crowned King of England, he wrote a letter to his son Henry from which the following is quoted:

I send you herewith my booke latelie prentid; studdie and profite in it as ye wolde deserve my blessing; and as thaire can na thing happen unto you quhairof ye will not finde the generall grounde thairin, if not the verrie particulaire pointe touched, sa mon ye levell everie mannis opinions or advyces unto you as ye finde thaime agree or discorde with the reulis thair sett down, allowing and following thair advyces that agrees with the same, mistrusting and frowning upon thaime that advyses you to the contraire [Ellis's *Letters*, Series I, Vol. 3, pp. 78–79].

But this book was not merely a reprint, for the text was carefully revised by the king. The original had been written in Scottish dialect and spelling. This was modified to make the book more readable by Englishmen, although the work thereby lost something of its rich Doric tang; and furthermore there was added a prefatory address To the Reader in which James with great adroitness defines his views on certain matters of interest to the English people. In it he inserted the following laudatory reference to Queen Elizabeth which fell gratefully upon English ears:

there is a lawfull Queene there presently raigning, who hath so long with so great wifedome & fælicity gouerned her kingdoms, as (I must in true sinceritie confesse) the like hath not bene read nor heard of, either in our time, or since the dayes of the Romane Emperour Angustus; it could no wayes become me, farre inferiour to her in knowledge and experience, to be a busiebody in other Princes maters. . . .

Obviously this was written before he learned by the word of Sir Robert Carey on the evening of Saturday, March 26, that the queen had died early in the morning of March 24.*

James felt that dissemination of this book in England with this new preface would make his reception as king more agreeable to the English people. To this end copies were sent to the English Council, who proceeded to have it quickly printed in England and widely disseminated. A printer and bookseller named John Norton held the office of "printer in Greek, Latin, and Hebrew to the Queen." Perhaps because the book bore a Greek title the Council entrusted the publishing to Norton, but to cheapen the book they limited the price at which he might sell it. To expedite its publication the printing was carried on in several different printing establishments simultaneously. The queen died on March 24. The copy for this book was entered on the Stationers' Register on March 26, and on March 30 John Manningham

---

* Of the copies of this book which the printer sent to the King, one was beautifully bound in ornamented vellum and bears on the middle of the front cover this impression:

A[nna]   R[egina]
(Thistle)
I[acobus]   R[ex]

This copy is now in the Library of Harvard University. The stamp seems to indicate that the copy was received before the king had heard of the death of Queen Elizabeth and also probably indicates that the king had turned it over to his queen.

wrote in his diary: "The King's booke Basicon Doron came forth with an epistle to the reader apologeticell."

All this shows with what haste the book was put forth.

The first London printings dated 1603 were for "John Norton, according to the copie printed at Edinburgh." Some of these were printed by Felix Kyngston and some by Shakespeare's friend Richard Field. Such was the demand for copies that a stationer named Edward White had another edition printed by E. Alde in contravention of Norton's entry. For this he was on April 13, 1603, fined by the Stationers' Company. This action was appealed by Alde to the Court of Star Chamber, which affirmed the proceedings. Notwithstanding all this, Alde and Edward White printed a "Second Impression," for which they were further punished. Alde made his final submission to his company on June 6, 1603.

The hasty dissemination of this book had a double purpose. The king wanted his book printed officially and not from incorrect manuscript copies; and both he and his council wished to use the work as propaganda to make easier his peaceful entrance into his English kingdom.

Public interest in the book was intense. Everybody wanted to read it, for it showed what sort of a man was the new king. The work was most timely. Spottiswood in his *Church History,* 4th ed. [London, 1655], p. 457) says that it raised in all men's hearts an admiration of King James's piety and wisdom, adding, "Certain it is that all the Discourses that came forth at that time for maintaining his right to the Crown of England, prevailed nothing so much as did this treatise." Spottiswood made the journey from Edinburgh to London along with his king, and therefore his estimate carries weight. Francis Bacon wrote of the book that "it filled the whole realm with a good perfume." On May 18, 1603, in the Court of Star Chamber, Robert Cecil called the book "the mirror of virtue" (Baildon's ed. of Hawarde's *Cases in the Star Chamber,* p. 163).

Thy Kingly gift, if thou dost keepe,
How happie are thy English sheepe.

is a sentiment addressed to the new king by the University of Cambridge in "Sorrowes Joy" (Cambridge, 1603; see Nichols's *Progresses of James,* Vol. I, p. 13). And Camden writes, "Incredible it is how many hearts and affections he won unto him by his correcting of it" (*id.* Vol. I, p. 148).

The work as printed in London must have had a very large circulation, for copies are still easily obtainable. A Cambridge puritan, William Willymat, at once versified the book in both Latin and English. This was printed as *A Prince's Looking Glass* in Cambridge in 1603. It was also turned into Latin quatrains by Henry Peacham, who sent his MS to the prince. The nature and reasons for the interest thus evidenced are recounted in the reports of the Venetian ambassador to his Doge and Senate as printed in the *Calendar of State Papers—Venetian* (1603–1607, pp. 10, 65, etc.). The king and his council evidently did all they could to further the circulation of his book. From 1603 to 1605 it was distinctly "The book of the day."

But the interest was not confined to English readers. The book was immediately translated into several other languages and so published at various places of which a list may serve to show how widespread an interest the book evoked.

Latin translations were published in:

> London, 1604
> Hanau, 1604 (twice) and 1607
> Frankfort-on-the-Oder, 1679 and 1682.

French translations were published in:

> Paris, 1603, 1604 (twice), 1616, 1617, and 1646
> Poitiers, 1603
> Rouen, 1603, 1604 (three times)
> Lyons, 1603
> Hanau, 1604.

German translations were published in:

> Hamburg, 1604
> Spires, 1604.

Dutch translations were published in:

> Amsterdam, 1603 (twice).

Welsh translations were published in:

> London, 1604
> Cardiff, 1931.

Swedish translation was published in:

> Stockholm, 1606.*

In the year 1616 the *Basilicon Doron* was printed along with the other prose works of the king in the large folio volume edited by the Bishop of Winchester. In his preface to this work the bishop reminds his readers of the "applause" with which the *Basilicon Doron* was greeted when it was published. "How did it inflame men's minds to a love and admiration of his Majestie beyond measure; inasmuch that coming out just at the time his Majestie came in, it made the hearts of all his people as one man, as much to honor him for Religion and Learning, as to obey him for Title and Authority." This entire volume was translated into Latin, and thus printed in London in 1619 and reprinted in Frankfort-on-the-Main in 1689. But as the king grew older and lost favor with his people, so did his book. Nevertheless, twice during the seventeenth century the work again took on political significance.

As the conflict between King Charles and his Parliament was approaching its climax, there appeared a bitter little

---

* This list of the translations of the *Basilicon Doron* is for the most part taken from the list given by Dr. James Craigie in his article in *The Library*, Fifth Series, Vol. III, No. 1, June, 1948, pp. 22–32. For his kind permission to use this material, as well as other helpful information on the subject of the *Basilicon Doron*, I am much indebted to Dr. Craigie.

tract entitled *A Puritane set forth in his Lively Colours: or K. James his discription of a Puritan. London, Printed for N. B. 1642.* This is a collection of distorted excerpts from the *Basilicon Doron* in which King James had expressed his distaste for the puritans. In the same year was printed a more considerable quarto pamphlet, *The Dutie of a King in his Royal Office—written by the High and Mightie Prince, James King of Great Brittain,—London, Printed for I. B.—1642.* I am unable to comprehend what purpose was achieved by this mongrel tract. The first three pages are a verbatim re-print of that part of James's speech to his Parliament on March 21, 1609, which is the high-water mark of his assertion of the divine right of kings, where he says, "by God himself they are called Gods"; but immediately following this, without the slightest indication of any change of source or date, and with some petty garbling and patching made necessary to conceal the joint between the two parts, follows the entire second book of the *Basilicon Doron*. The combination seems devised to give publicity and emphasis to the king's definition of the difference between "a lawful good King and an usurping tyrant," and to make sure that the reader will not know that he is reading a hodgepodge.

Forty years later political interest in the *Basilicon Doron* flared up again as a result of the violent controversies between Whig and Tory which marked the last years of King Charles II. Some of the book was reprinted in 1681 in a little pamphlet entitled *Vox Regis: or the Difference betwixt a King Ruling by Law and a Tyrant by his own Will.—London, Printed &c 1681.* (See *Harleian Miscellany,* Vol. 1, p. 13.) These pages again print the king's distinction between "good Kings" and "usurping tyrants," which evidently was of perennial interest.* Much more discussion of the same subject, with further quotation, is found in *A just Vindication of the Honour of King James, London, Printed for*

---

* See Epigram 399 in Sir John Harington's *Letters and Epigrams,* ed. McClure (Philadelphia, 1930).

R. Oswell, 1683. In the meantime King Charles II, to coun-
teract this piecemeal and garbled use of his grandfather's
book, ordered the publication of a complete but cheap reprint of the entire *Basilicon Doron,* which appeared with a
London imprint dated 1682.

But as the Stuart dynasty came to its end, interest in the
book fell off and it seems to have been well nigh forgotten
for some two hundred years. Of late, however, an antiquar-
ian and linguistic interest has occasioned four new editions.
In 1887 fifty copies of a sumptuous reprint of the original
Edinburgh edition of 1599 were printed by Wertheimer for
the Roxburghe Club. There is a cheap reprint in Professor
Henry Morley's Universal Library, Volume 63. In 1918 an
edition of the *Political Works of James I,* including the
Basilicon Doron, was published at Cambridge, Massachusetts,
under the editorial direction of Charles H. McIlwain. And
finally, as a crowning tribute to the lasting interest in this
neglected book, there has appeared under the aegis of the
Scottish Text Society a most useful and interesting edition in
which the text of the king's MS, that of the first Edinburgh
edition, and that of the second and final edition are printed
alongside each other on the page so that the reader may note
the progressive changes in the thought of the young king as
he evolved this book. This edition is edited by Dr. James
Craigie and bears the Blackwood imprint.

Lack of knowledge of this book by the present generation
is unfortunate. One who is indoctrinated with James' antithetical teachings about "lawful good kings" and "usurping
tyrants," can better appreciate the sharp contrast which the
play creates between Duncan and Macbeth. To read the
book will not prove laborious and will only take an hour or
so. The reader will find a continuing interest as he follows
the workings of a very curious mind acutely discussing in
strong northern dialect ethical problems, many of which find
expression in the play.

THE DRAMATIS PERSONAE

The list of the characters appearing in the play of *Macbeth* is of particular interest. It is at once evident that the dramatist expected his play to be given before an audience acquainted with the *History of Scotland* as written by Hector Boece and on which Holinshed's *Chronicle* is based. In his other plays based on Holinshed, Shakespeare added or omitted characters as he saw fit, but in this play he used only the names which occur in the *Chronicle,* adding no new ones. Several persons unknown to Holinshed appear as speaking characters in the play, but they are left unnamed. In making this statement, the Middletonian scene, in which Hecate appears, is ignored, for Shakespeare did not write it. (p. 275.)

The dramatist seems to have planned a play in which the characters, grouped in families, are Macbeth and his wife, Duncan and his sons, Banquo and his son, Macduff with his wife and child, and the three witches, who seem to be sisters as well as members of the same coven. Later old Siward and his son were added. These are the principal characters of the drama and they are all designated in the play as they are in the source.*

Five of these characters were deemed to be ancestors of King James; namely, Duncan, Malcolm, Banquo, Fleance, and old Siward. The dramatist was careful to keep these progenitors of his king free from anything which might seem unworthy of the royal family. The play attributes no untoward act or word to any one of them.

---

* Except for changes in the spelling of the names. For example, for Makbeth or Mackbeth he substituted Macbeth

    for Cawder   "   "   Cawdor
    for Banquho   "   "   Banquoh or Banquo
    for Donald Bane "   "   Donalbain

If anyone can find usage earlier than this play of the spelling "Donalbain," he may find a clue to one of Shakespeare's unrecognized sources.

THE HONOURABLE PREDECESSOURS OF KING JAMES

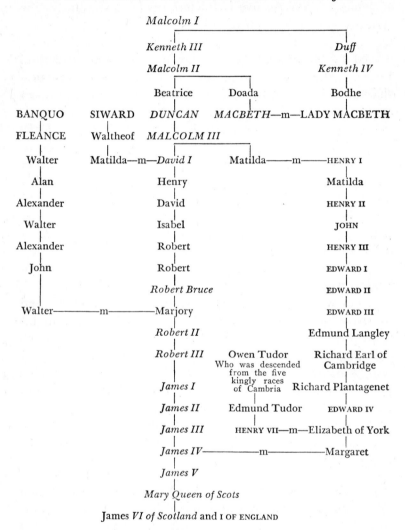

Names printed in CAPITALS are those of characters in the play. Names in *italic* were kings of Scotland. Names in SMALL CAPITALS were kings of England.

The genealogical table here given shows the royal descent of James from these five characters traced according to the genealogy current when the play was written. The Banquo line is set down as it is recorded by Hector Boece (and repeated by Holinshed). The same line is given by Bishop Leslie. The line of kings is as given in the genealogical chart of "The Race of the Kings of Scotland" found in Skene's *Scots Acts* (ed. of 1597). In 1722 Richard Hay, the Scottish antiquary, published *An Essay on the Origin of the Royal Family of the Stewarts* in which he assailed the historicity of Banquo and Fleance, asserting that "there never were any such two persons in the world." * This view has prevailed notwithstanding the attempt of J. K. Hewison (*Bute in the Olden Time,* Edinburgh, 1895) to reinstate the Banquo pedigree. But to interpret the play of *Macbeth* we need not know the modern view of history. In fact we should forget it. We are concerned only with the history of Scotland as it was accepted by King James and his age.

James was a genealogist. Only one who keeps in mind the passionate interest which this learned king had in his royal ancestry (from which he deduced his alleged divine right) can understand certain parts of the play. In his *Kingly Gift* he assured his son Henry, "Yee are come of as honourable predecessours as anie prince living" (p. 33). He gave full credence to the tables which carried his royal line back to King Fergus, who was said to have flourished over three hundred years B.C., and of this ancient lineage he boasted to his English Parliament.

Curiously enough, not only King James but King Christian IV of Denmark, who was also to see the play, was descended from King Duncan and King Malcolm. Whether Christian knew this before he saw the play is to be doubted, but James must have known it. In the year 1585, when James was at-

* See also Andrew Stuart's *Genealogical History of the Stewarts* (London, 1798), p. 2.

taining the age of twenty, his council urged him to marry; and several choices were before him, one of which was that he should marry a princess of the Danish royal family. At first he thought rather meanly of that family; but Sir James Melvil (*Memoirs*, 3rd ed., p. 329) told him it was "an old and royal stock," and this caused him to change his mind. After satisfying himself of the honorable descent of the Danish king from nearly all the royal houses of Europe, he sent an embassage to Copenhagen to discuss the matter. It was found that the elder princess was forespoken, but that the younger and more attractive sister, Princess Anna, was subject to negotiation. Her beautiful miniature was brought to James, and after examining this and also her genealogy he was convinced that Anna would be a suitable consort, and thereupon the marriage was arranged and shortly took place.*

* Because the English king was a student of genealogy, English and Welsh genealogists produced for him many tabular genealogies and family trees showing his royal descents. In 1604 a Welshman named George Owen Harry sent him a book with many plates of his genealogies; and in 1608 Morgan Colman sent him a very large and truly magnificent family tree. A print of this, cut up into ten sheets, is to be found in the British Museum, no other copy being known. I suspect that this Colman tree was never finished, for one corner is incomplete. But it gives very fully the royal descents of Queen Anna, and therefore of King Christian. Colman traces King Christian's descent from King Duncan through the houses of Plantagenet and Brunswick. The Plantagenet descent has already been traced to King Henry II of England in the table already given and need not be repeated. Henry II had a daughter, Maud Plantagenet, who married Henry the Lion, of Saxony; and their son, William I of Saxony, was the father of Otho the Little, Lord of Luneborg, from whom the descent of the line of the Dukes of Brunswick runs in regular succession as follows:

Albert the Great
Albert the Fat
Magnus the Holy
Magnus with the Chain
Henry
William the Victorious
William the Younger
Henry the Elder
Catherine
Dorothy, who married Christian III of Denmark who was the father of Frederick II, the father of Christian IV.

In addition to these principal characters Shakespeare needed a number of subordinate ones to fill his stage and maintain the dialogue. These he named Lennox, Ross, Angus, Menteith, Caithness, and Seyton. The way in which these six names came to be chosen is informative.

Holinshed states in his *Chronicle* that, after the death of Macbeth, Malcolm made a number of his thanes to be earls, then a new title in Scotland. Eight such newly created earls are listed by him: Fife, Menteth, Atholl, Levenox, Morey, Cathnes, Rosse, and Angus. The first of these, Macduff, Thane of Fife, had been assigned a principal part in the play. For the minor characters seven names remained. Of these he used five, but did not use either Atholl or Morey, although more names were needed, for in III, vi, "another Lord" enters and speaks twenty-two lines of verse, but is given no name.* Why did the dramatist strike Atholl and Morey from Holinshed's list? The answer is not difficult. History tells that Duncan was the head of the house of Atholl, that is, he was in Shakespeare's language Thane of Atholl; therefore he could not bring another Thane of Atholl into the play. Likewise, Macbeth was Mormaer, or Thane of Morey, so that this title could not be used for another thane. Buchanan knew this, for in his *History of Scotland* he records that the three women saluted Macbeth as "Thane of Morey"; and it was this learned George Buchanan who first taught James as a little boy his history of Scotland. How, then, did William Shakespeare learn enough about the early history of Scotland to avoid falling into Holinshed's error concerning the thanes of Atholl and Morey? †

* This so troubled Dr. Johnson that he assigns the lines to Angus. Dyce prefers to assign them to Ross. But the reason for this shortage of names is sufficiently clear; all of Holinshed's names of the nobility which were available to him had been exhausted.

† Information about the lines of Morey and Atholl in Macbeth's time may be found in E. W. Robertson's *Scotland Under her Early Kings*, Vol. 1, Chaps. V and VI. Or see Andrew Lang's *History of Scotland*, Vol. 1, p. 53; or a pamphlet entitled *Mac Beth*, written by the Hon. R. Erskine of Marr, which was published at Inverness in 1930.

Two answers are possible. He might have learned it from Buchanan's history, with which he certainly had some acquaintance; but this seems unlikely because of the meagerness of what Buchanan says on the subject. Or—and this is more likely—he may have sought the aid of some well informed Scot to keep him from falling into errors about the history of Scotland. Further evidence of such assistance will appear later. Had the dramatist been writing this play (as he did the others founded on Holinshed) for the audience of the Globe Theater, no such caution would have been necessary. No one there knew or cared who really were the Scottish thanes in the days of Edward the Confessor, nor does the modern audience know or care. But the king was a very learned man, well versed in the history of Scotland, so that it was important in writing this play to be seen by the king to be careful about matters of this sort as to which he would otherwise have paid little or no attention.

Of the five thanes remaining on his list, Levenox, or Lennox, bore the name most grateful to King James; for his paternal grandfather, Matthew Stewart, had been Earl of Lennox; and now his cousin and trusted friend, Ludowic Stuart, was Duke of Lennox, Great Chamberlain, and High Admiral of Scotland. It was therefore peculiarly fitting for the play to show a thane of Lennox standing by good King Duncan and his sons as chief adviser and Chamberlain. Angus, too, who accompanies Lennox, usually as *persona muta,* would remind James that through his father he was heir to the house of Angus, for Darnley's mother, Margaret Douglas, was the daughter of the Earl of Angus. Ross is used chiefly as the *nuntius* of the play. "Haste looks through his eyes," and he is apt to speak in excited hyperbole. The other two thanes, Menteith and Caithness, have little to say and are lacking in characterization.

When Macbeth was deserted by his thanes, someone was needed to carry on the dialogue. In Holinshed there is a list of gentlemen of Scotland who received their family surname at the hands of Malcolm.   The fourth of these is Seiton. This name was in peculiar favor with King James.   Alexander Seton, Lord Fyvie, an honorable and learned councilor of the king, had held many state offices in Scotland, and from 1597 to 1604 was the personal guardian of Prince Charles. He had recently been in England as one of the commissioners for the union of the two kingdoms, and for this valuable service James on March 6, 1606, created him Earl of Dunfermline.   So Shakespeare, writing the fifth act of his play, chose "Seyton" as the name of the guardian of the queen in her disability, the one trusty shieldbearer who remained faithful to his king when all the thanes had fled and even the doctor had said, "were I from Dunsinane away and clear, Profit again should hardly draw me here."

In this royal play to be performed before the King of Denmark, it was very fitting to show "the war-like Siward" helping Malcolm to regain his kingdom; for Siward was a Dane, usually referred to in history as "the great Dane, Siward the Strong" (Freeman's *Norman Conquest*, 3rd ed., Vol. I, pp. 526, 791; Vol. II, pp. 50, 370).   He was the son of Beorn, the son of Ulf, the son of Spratling, the son of a polar bear, a pedigree of great celebrity in Danish annals and no doubt well known to King Christian.   Shakespeare followed authentic history in making him a supporter both of the English king, Edward the Confessor, and of Malcolm Canmore, the heir to the Scottish throne.

The play shows a studied effort to extol this Danish ancestor of the king.   He is pictured as the ideal old soldier: "Good Siward, an older and a better soldier none That Christendom gives out" (IV, iii, 191).   He first appears with Malcolm's army in V, vi, where his bearing is that of an experienced warrior heartening his troops.   In this scene he is Malcolm's "worthy uncle" and is given command of the "first battle" (that is, the vanguard of the army).   Having taken Macbeth's castle, he courteously delivers it to Malcolm as its rightful master. When he learns of his son's death, he asks:

> Had he his hurts before?
> *Ross.* Ay, on the front.
> *Siward.* Why then, God's soldier be he!
> Had I as many sons as I have hairs,
> I would not wish them to a fairer death.

Thus has Shakespeare painted this grand old warrior-earl for us with peculiar care so as to make him worthy to be the ancestor of kings.*

Donalbain, the second son of King Duncan, has a very minor part in the play, and is but a foil to his brother Malcolm. Immediately after the murder of their father, the brothers separate themselves and their *fortunes* (II, iii, 145), a fact of no small significance to King James and a Scottish audience. The history of Scotland tells the story of how the

* Although he is now forgotten by all but students of history, people in the days of Shakespeare knew about "Siward, the powerful earl of Northumbria, a giant in stature, whose vigor of mind was equal to his bodily strength" (Henry of Huntingdon's *Chronicle,* Bk. VI, 1052). In Worsaae's *Danes and Norwegians in England* (p. 143), he is called "the celebrated Danish jarl Siward, surnamed Digre [strong], who in the year 1040 became jarl in Northumberland." His question about his son's death was a common anecdote. Shakespeare may have read it in Holinshed's *Chronicles of England,* as most commentators explain, or he may have taken it from Camden's *Remaines,* published the year before *Macbeth* was written. Camden thus records it on page 188:

Sywarde the martiall Earle of *Northumberland,* feeling in his sickness that he drew towards his end, arose out of his bed and put on his Armour, saying, *That it became not a valiant man to die lying, like a beast:* and so he gave up the Ghost standing: As valiantly both spoken and performed, as it was by Vespasian.

When the said *Siward* understood that his sonne whom he had sent in service against the Scottishmen, was slaine, he demaunded whether his wound were in fore part or hinder part of his body, when it was answered in the fore part, he replied: *I am right glad, neither wish any other death to me or mine.* (Hen. Huntingdon.)

The lines which Shakespeare has assigned to Siward (V, viii, 52–53) as to a warrior's death gain point if we have in mind the two incidents recounted by Camden.

wild Celtic tribes of the north were gradually transformed into a people speaking an English language and following many English modes. King James, seeking to unify his kingdoms, was interested in every past step of this process. Historians point to the reign of Malcolm as one during which the Anglicizing process made much progress; but after Malcolm's death his brother Donalbain became King of Scotland and his reign marked a reaction against the civilizing influences of the "English epicures." As Holinshed tells this, upon the accession of Donald Bane,

manie of the poeple abhorring the riotous maners and superfluous gormandizing brought in among them by the Englishmen, were willing enough to receive this Donald for their King, trusting (bicause he had been brought up in the Iles with the old customes and maners of their ancient nation, without taste of the English likerous delicats) they would by his severe order in government recover againe the former temperance of their old progenitors [*History of Scotland*, p. 180].

Consciousness of this antithesis is to be sensed several times in the play (I, ii, 12; II, iii, 143–147; III, iv, 75–80; V, ii, 7–8; V, iii, 8). This explains why, as the revolting Scottish thanes march to join the English, we must hear Caithness ask whether Donalbain is coming with his brother Malcolm, and hear Lennox assure him that Donalbain is not with the English forces. This talk has no dramatic value. Its purpose seems to be to remind the audience of the differing attitudes of the two brothers toward the English. Malcolm is to be admired because he is helping to unite the two kingdoms; while Donalbain is to be discredited as an opponent of this unifying process. A modern audience fails to appreciate this, but the point was of moment to the Scots in the original audience.

"Three Witches," according to the direction, occupy the stage as the play opens. It is important to know what sort of creatures these are, for on no question in the play have more contradictory opinions been expressed. Are they Fates? Are they Norns? Are they sibyls? Are they witches?

In our current texts they are six times designated "The Weïrd Sisters," but this is not so in the original text. In the first folio, and therefore presumably in Shakespeare's MS, the terms used are:

Weyward sisters, I, iii, 31; I, v, 8; II, i, 20; and

Weyard sisters, III, i, 2; III, iv, 133; IV, i, 136.

These readings were continued by Rowe and Pope, but in 1733 Theobald, to the serious and lasting injury of the play, changed "weyward" to "weïrd" and in support of the change subjoined a seemingly learned but really quite misleading note. A just protest against this alteration of a good meaningful reading was registered by Hunter (*New Illustrations*, Vol. II, p. 162); and there are still better reasons why we should retain the folio text.

The word "weyward" (the Elizabethan spelling of the modern "wayward") means, as Theobald explains, *perverse, froward, moody, obstinate, intractable*—fit adjectives to describe the Witches of Forres. Such bad women glory in such epithets. It cannot be a copyist's or printer's error, for it is repeated six times; and still more clearly because Shakespeare's verse requires a dissyllabic word, which "weyward" is; while "weird" is always monosyllabic. Recognizing this difficulty, Theobald was compelled to impose a clumsy and unwarranted diaeresis upon the word.

Theobald justified his change of "weyward" to "weïrd" by reference to the passage in Holinshed which tells that some thought that the women who met Macbeth and Banquo were "the weird sisters, that is, as ye would say, the Goddesses of Destiny." From this expression he drew the inference that Shakespeare must have written in his play "weird sisters." This reasoning ignores the fact that Shakespeare habitually changes or adapts Holinshed's words as he sees fit. It would have been perfectly normal for him to change Holinshed's "weird" to "weyward" as a more fit description of the witches he wished to show in his play, and this I believe is just what he did. Dr. Gwinn in his verses, influenced by the picture he found in his 1577 edition of Holinshed, had converted the weird sisters of Holinshed into sibyls. Shakespeare wished his malicious midnight hags to be Scotch witches and considered "weyward" (suggested by, but quite different from, "weird") a suitable adjective to describe them. We should allow him to have his way.

He has shown in the play veritable Scotch witches motivated by devilish malignity, bound by contract each to her own familiar devil, tempting but not controlling Macbeth. This was a notable and far-reaching gain to his drama, which we must not lose because some modern scholars, conscious of the connection of "werd" or "weird" with "fate" (a connection which probably never entered Shakespeare's head), desire to find a fatalistic philosophy in the play which Shakespeare nowhere put there. The issuance twenty years ago of Volume X of the *O.E.D.* (see p. 273a, Weird a) should have caused Theobald's emendation to be reexamined. I add this to previous protests by Joseph Hunter (Vol. II, p. 162) and M. H. Liddell (p. 17) which have gone unheeded. A Shakespearean tradition, hallowed by age, is as hard to change as the law of the Medes and Persians.

Sweno takes part in the battle with which the play opens (I, ii, 61). Holinshed calls him King of Norway and brother of Canute the Great and puts him at the head of an invading army of *Danes* who defeated Macbeth and Banquo but were later tricked to their destruction so that few escaped. In contrast to this, Shakespeare puts Sweno at the head of an invading band of *Norwegians* whom Macbeth defeats with attendant circumstances taken from another account in Holinshed of the defeat of another invading fleet of *Danes*. Shakespeare calls them "the stout Norweyan ranks" and "those of Norway," although Holinshed knows of no such invasion and speaks only of *Danes*. The reason for this substitution of *Norwegians* for *Danes* is that the play was to be shown before a King of Denmark as well as before a King of Scotland. To depict before these two kings the ignominious defeat of Danes by Scots would have been impolite and most unseemly.

This change deserves further examination in order to see how it was brought about. More of Holinshed must be read than is usually to be found in our critical editions of the play, or even in Boswell-Stone's useful edition of *Shakspere's Holinshed;* and one must know the circumstances under which the second scene of the first act of this play was written. This is to be examined in a later chapter, "The Bleeding-Sergeant Scene," to which further examination of the part played by Sweno and his Danes transformed into Norwegians will be deferred.

THE IMPERIAL THEME

To Macbeth and Banquo approaching Forres the witches make four pronouncements: (1) Macbeth is Thane of Glamis; (2) he is Thane of Cawdor; (3) he is to be king; and (4) Banquo is to "get kings," which Macbeth interprets (III, i, 60) as being "father to a line of kings." Macbeth, having been promised the first three, has set his heart also upon being father to a line of kings. He calls the last two his "black and deep desires" (I, iv, 51); and more fully defines the last when, having attained the first three, he bitterly laments the prophecy that no son of his is to succeed him and calls upon fate to champion him against Banquo that he may attain the fourth (III, i, 60–72).

It was immediately after the first two had come true that he disclosed the full extent of his ambition as he mused:

> Two truths are told
> As happy prologues to the swelling act
> Of the imperial theme.* [I, iii, 127]

Thus we see that already in his mind the witches' words have taken shape as a dramatic crescendo: Glamis, Cawdor, king, empire. The first two are but prologues finding a place in Act I of the play. Act II depicts Macbeth attaining kingship. In Act III Macbeth sees Banquo as "father to a line of kings," and in Act IV the kings of this line bear treble scepters and stretch to the crack of doom, betokening a truly imperial dynasty, which should be his, not Banquo's. This "imperial theme" is a very insistent motif of the play. It is what Scotland in Macbeth's time had not known but sorely

---

* The "swelling act" of the imperial theme should be contrasted with the "lingering act" which feeds contention (*Henry IV, Part 2*, I, i, 156).

needed, and was to attain when, at the end of the play, Malcolm succeeds Macbeth, thus founding the dynasty of which when the play was written King James held the scepter. The audience who were to see the play had an inherited predilection in favor of the stable government of a state by a strong monarch the legitimacy of whose dynastic rule could not be questioned, and the author shared this with his time. To him and to his audience the phrase "imperial theme" was a more real and definable thing than is the diluted and modernized imperialism of the twentieth century. To our present-day ears the phrase is vague. But as we see this play our ears should be tuned to the sixteenth and not to the twentieth century usage.

The phrase "imperial theme" did not come into the play from Holinshed, who gives the prophecy to Banquo in these words: "Of thee those shall be borne which shall governe the Scotish Kingdome by long order of continuall descent." But Dr. Gwinn, writing his *Tres Sibyllae* in Latin, tells that the sisters foretold to Banquo, "*Imperium sine fine* tuae, rex inclyte, stirpis," that is, "An *endless empire*, O renowned King, to thy descendants." This became in Shakespeare's hands "the imperial theme."

It is necessary to realize in what grandiose terms Dr. Gwinn had described this *imperium* in his verses recited before King James at Oxford on August 27, 1605. As these verses are unfamiliar, a translation of the first twenty lines of Gwinn's Latin text follows:

1.   There is a story, O renowned King, that once in the olden time the fateful sisters foretold to thy descendants an endless empire [*imperium sine fine*]. Famed Lochabria acknowledged Banquo as its Thane; not for thee O Banquo, but for thine immortal descendants [*nepotibus immortalibus*] did these sooth-saying women predict immortal sceptres [*sceptra immortalia*] as thou didst withdraw from the court to the country for rest. We three sisters in like manner foretell the same fates for thee and thine, whilst along with thy family

thou dost return from the country to the city, and we salute thee:

Hail thou who rulest Scotland.

2. Hail thou who rulest England.

3. Hail thou who rulest Ireland.

1. Hail thou to whom France gives titles whilst the others give lands.

2. Hail thou whom Britain, now united though formerly divided, cherishes.

3. Hail thou supreme British, Irish, Gallic Monarch.

1. Hail Anna, parent and sister and wife and daughter of Kings.

2. Hail Henry, heir apparent, handsome prince.

3. Hail Charles, Duke, and beautiful Polish princeling, hail.

1. Nor set we bounds nor times to these prophecies; save that the world is the limit of thy dominion and the stars of thy Fame. Bring back great Canute with his fourfold kingdom; Greater than thy ancestors, O thou who hast been crowned with a diadem to be rivalled only by thy descendants.

This is the imperial theme in its full glory. Shakespeare did not stoop to such flattery as this, but the theme rang in his ears as he wrote his play, and he did take care to picture to the king the *endless* line of his descendants (IV, i, 117) and the *imperial* expansion of his dominions (IV, i, 121); both thoughts being supplied by Dr. Gwinn and not by Holinshed.*

To appreciate the art with which the dramatist gave this

---

* Evidence that Shakespeare was familiar with Dr. Gwinn's verses is quite convincing. Not only does the "imperial theme" spring from this source. The crown passing to descendants as described in the verses is to be contrasted with Macbeth's chagrin that he wears a "fruitless crown"; and the "immortal sceptres" of the verses are similarly to be contrasted with Macbeth's "barren sceptre" (III, i, 60–61). Canute's "fourfold kingdom" of the verses called forth the "treble sceptres," and Britain "now united though formerly divided" produced the "two-fold balls" of IV, i, 121. The "immortal descendants" which Gwinn awards to Banquo recur in the play as a line of kings which "stretch out to the crack of doom"; and James "crowned with a diadem" is reflected in the play as the nobility of Scotland see Malcolm "compassed" with his "Kingdom's pearl."

imperial theme appropriate place in his play, there must be kept in mind (*a*) what had happened in Scotland during the reigns which preceded those of Duncan and Macbeth, for this makes clear what the phrase meant as spoken by Macbeth; and (*b*) what had happened since, for this makes clear what the dramatist meant the phrase to mean for his king. Both happenings must be pictured, not in the terms of modern histories, but solely in terms of the knowledge of the Elizabethans, including King James, and more particularly of William Shakespeare.

a) The dramatist had read (and with care, for he made much use of them) the pages of Holinshed's *Description of Scotland* which tell of the reigns of King Duffe and of his successors Kings Culene, Kenneth, Constantine, Gryme, and Malcolm II. The last of these was the grandfather of both Duncan and Macbeth. These pages tell a sorry and a bloody story. There was nothing like "empire" in Scotland. Kingship was not hereditary. There was no "line of kings"; but there were several families descended from Kenneth MacAlpine, from whom kings were *elected* in a system of alternating succession. Sometimes a king proclaimed his son Prince of Cumberland, in hopes of thus securing his succession; but the chieftains at once appealed to the "custom and ancient order used by their elders" which required them to choose as king that member of the MacAlpine family whom they deemed most able to maintain his rule. It resulted that a king usually seized power by the slaughter of his predecessor or rival and held it only so long as he was able to hold it with his sword. Of the ten successive kings of Scotland who preceded Macbeth, all had been slain. This had brought ruin and misery to the people of Scotland, for while the chieftains were fighting among themselves the Danes took occasion to invade and harry the land.

Andrew Lang gives a succinct account of the evil state of Scotland under these descendants of Kenneth MacAlpine. It leads him to conclude that "there is no worse form of political rule than that of elective monarchies" (*History of Scotland,* Vol. I, pp. 41, 42). He thus sums up his account: "A dynasty, founded in Pictland by a Scot [Kenneth MacAlpine], and rent asunder by the jealousies necessarily aroused by the curious system of succession, consolidated Scotland; only to hand it over to a dynasty half English in blood and wholly Anglo-Norman in creed, language, sentiment, and education." This latter dynasty, founded upon Macbeth's death by Malcolm Canmore (the Malcolm of the play) and his wife Margaret the English princess, was the first true dynastic succession Scotland had known. The line of their descendants, coalescing with the line from Banquo, has endured as an imperial succession to this day.

Imperium was the term then in use to designate this desired dynastic succession initiated by Malcolm Canmore. To know this we have but to notice the words used by Hector Boece, who tells that it was Malcolm's great-great-grandfather Kenneth III who first made an attempt to abrogate the older law of electoral succession in Scotland and to establish such new laws as would bring about the hereditary descent of the crown. He then proclaimed his son Malcolm II Prince of Cumberland. But upon Kenneth's death the electors ignored his laws and insisted upon the old law, and ahead of Malcolm thrust in Kings Constantine and Grime, who ruled for twelve years; but when Gryme was slaughtered Malcolm II was at last chosen king. Thereupon this Malcolm II at Scone, in the presence of the Scottish chieftains, refused to receive the crown unless they would swear to confirm his father's laws of hereditary descent. This they did and Boece thus relates it.

Quo conveniente Scotica nobilitate, Malcolmus *nomen insigniaque imperii* negavit se prius recepturum quam legum creandi regis a patre Kennetho latum denuo cuncti firmarent.

Bellenden translates this:

Malcolme declarit that he wald nocht ressaif the *diademe im-periall*, quhill the lawis maid afoir be his fader Kenneth war approbaitt [*The Chronicles of Scotland, Compiled by Hector Boece, Translated into Scots by John Bellenden,* Scottish Text Society, 1938, Vol. II, p. 127].

But notwithstanding the acceptance by the chieftains of Kenneth's laws, a precarious situation arose when Malcolm II died, for he left no male issue, but two daughters. A choice had then to be made between Duncan, the son of one of these daughters, and Macbeth, the son of the other. And when the play of *Macbeth* opens, this choice has been made in favor of Duncan, who has proved to be but a feeble king. He has been compelled to rely upon his cousin Macbeth to quell the late serious disorders, and before doing this Macbeth has spoken "much against the King's softness, and overmuch slackness in punishing offenders" (Holinshed, *Chronicles,* 1587, *Description of Scotland,* p. 169a).

All this was well known to the dramatist and to his Scottish audience; and the above-quoted language used by both Boece and Bellenden shows that the idea of an "imperial diadem" was connected by Scots of the sixteenth century with the more stable hereditary dynasty which both Kenneth III and Malcolm II had unsuccessfully tried to found, but which Malcolm Canmore * ultimately succeeded in establishing and

* Malcolm Canmore was crowned King of Scotland at Scone on April 25, 1057. The Holy Roman Empire, and the feudal system of government with which it was associated, had then long exerted what was in the main a stabilizing effect upon the peoples of Europe. This system, along with a feudal nobility, came to England with William the Conqueror only nine years later. But many years before this the terms *imperator* and *imperium* had been in use to designate a desired supreme hereditary monarchy as contrasted with the disordered rules of Angles, Saxons, and Danes in England and of Celts in Scotland. See E. A. Freeman, *History of the Norman Conquest of England* (1877, Vol. I, pp. 145–147, 548–565, and William Stubbs, *Constitutional History of England* (4th ed., 1883), Vol. I, p. 195.

It is sometimes said that Malcolm Canmore (1058–1093) first brought feudal institutions to Scotland. He did pave the way. But the feudal system did not really find lodgment in Scotland until the reign of

which culminated in the long line of the Stuart kings. Dr. Gwinn evidently knew this when he designated this line an "imperium"; and this designation was thus perpetuated in the play of *Macbeth,* for the talk of the three witches near the beginning of the play about kingship and the getting of kings opened up the whole question of this dangerous state of affairs, the need for a well defined rule of succession and a stable government, and the corresponding ambitions of both Macbeth and Banquo. Bellenden's "diadem imperial" it is that Macbeth longs for more than for the kingly crown of the Celtic kings of Scotland. His soliloquy about "the swelling act of the *imperial* theme" was the natural expression of his desire to be father to this coming line of kings rather than to see Banquo thus favored.

b) But the dramatist had more than this in mind. He was writing a play to be exhibited to Duncan's descendant in the eighteenth generation, and in like degree a descendant of Banquo, and the words *"imperial theme"* were to take on a still more pregnant meaning. It is not only an imperial dynasty that is pictured, but a dynasty which to its great advantage had since the days of Robert Bruce produced a line of nine Stuart kings who had taken the throne of Scotland by direct *lineal succession.* This may conveniently be thought of as the *Stuart theme.*

When Hector Boece in 1526 wrote his *History of Scotland,* James V was king and the scepter had passed in the Stuart line directly from father to son by seven consecutive descents. To emphasize this notable fact, Boece invented a mythical ancestor of the Stuarts whom he named Banquo and a

---

Malcolm's son David I (1124–1153). But Shakespeare has claimed the dramatist's privilege of advancing the date. Several expressions in the text of the play witness this; and on the stage it is played in a feudal setting and in feudal costumes. So romantic a drama is better framed if the castles of Inverness (where Duncan is murdered) and of Forres (where the banquet takes place) and of Dunsinane are huge feudal structures.

prophecy promising to Banquo's issue kingship *"longa nepo-tum serie."* By the time Holinshed wrote, there had been eight such direct descents; and when Shakespeare wrote his play there had been nine, with a Prince of Wales living who if he were to attain the throne would be the tenth. For length of *lineal,* that is, unbroken direct descent from father to son, royal genealogy cannot match the Stuart line. The longest lineal descent which has occurred in the English royal family is that of five Plantagenets, from King John to King Edward III. Holinshed, with this phenomenon in mind, thus speaks of the Stuart line:

I shall in few words rehearse the originall *line* of those kings, which have descended from the foresaid Banquho, that they which have injoyed the kingdome by *so long continuance of descent, from one to another, and that even* unto these our daies, may be knowen from whence they had their first beginning [*ibid.,* 172b].

Lord Chancellor Ellesmere, in rendering his judgment in June, 1608, in the great case of the Post-nati, thus expressed it:

The King our Soveraigne is lawfully and *lineally* descended of the first great Monarchs & Kings of both the Kingdomes; and that by *so long a continued line of lawfull discent, as therein he exceedeth all the Kings that the World now knoweth* [1609, p. 59].

King James was fully conscious of the glory conferred upon him by reason of this *lineal* and long-continued succession of the Stuart kings from which he sprang. In his *Basilicon Doron* he told his eldest son: "Enjoy . . . this whole isle according to God's right and your *lineal descent.*" In his *True Law of Free Monarchies* (1603) he speaks of the happy continuance in Christian commonwealths of the "lineal succession of Crowns." In his speech to his first Parliament he thanked them for "receiving of me in this Seat, which God by my Birthright and *lineal descent* had in the fulness of time provided for me." And on March 21, 1607, speaking to his third Parliament, he said, "I desire a perfect Union of Laws

and Persons, and such a naturalizing as may make one body
of both Kingdoms under me your King that I and my posterity (if it so please God) may rule over you *to the world's
end.*" In the same speech he advocated "those laws, whereby
confusion is avoided, and their King's descent maintained,
and the heritage of the succession of the Monarchy which
hath been a kingdom to which *I am in descent three hundred
years before Christ,*" a boast obviously founded on the traditional line of the Scottish kings from Fergus I (330 B.C.) in
which Duncan stands as the eighty-fourth king.*

But it is not alone King James who is to be pleased by the
promise of this line of kings. The English people, who in
past years had gloried in the virginity of their queen, experienced upon her death distressing anxieties concerning the
succession due to the failure of the issue of King Henry VIII.
This produced a revulsion, and as soon as James was firmly
set on his throne they began to extol a propagating king each
one of whose ancestors had been capable of producing a royal

---

* Some of the pedigrees of which James was so proud may be found
in George Owen Harry, *The Genealogy of the High and Mighty
Monarch James, etc.,* 1604. It twice traces the line from Banquo.

Boece, who first mentioned Banquo, Thane of Lochaber, tells nothing of his paternity, but later writers provided Banquo with a royal
ancestry. He was said to be the son of Kenneth, the son of Ferquhard,
the son of Murdoc, the son of Doir, the son of Ethus, the son of Kenneth MacAlpine (called Kenneth the Great), King of Scotland from 839
to 860 and the sixty-ninth king in the famous line from Fergus I. Thus
was this mythical line rendered even more desirable for King James
and the people of Scotland; for it gave to the House of Stuart an
unbroken line of male succession from the ancient line of Scottish
kings, whereas the line through Robert Bruce involved several descents
by female lines. All of this adds pertinency to what was written by
Sir George Mackenzie in 1686 in his Epistle Dedicatory to King
James II of England which is found in his work on *The Antiquity of
the Royal Line of Scotland.* After speaking (p. A2) of "that right of
precedency, which is due to your Royal Race, as the most Ancient
Monarchy which we know," he told King James that those who deny
the authenticity of the royal line "destroy one of the great Foundations, whereby your Majesty's Grandfather (James I of England), your
Father, and your Last Parliament have further engaged and encour-
aged the Loyalty of this your Ancient Kingdom."

son and heir for so many successive generations.   There are
dangers to a monarchic state when the crown must pass to a
collateral of the last sovereign, as recent experience had
proven.*   It is much safer to have a direct lineal succession.
Early in 1606 Parliament passed an act granting James three
subsidies in which the following is recorded:

We cannot but with unspeakable joy of heart consider of that
blessing, which having respect to later times in this state, is rare
and unwonted, which is the blessed fruit and Royal Issue of
singular towardness and comfort, which God hath given your
Majesty, with great hope of many the like; these being indeed as
arrows in the hand of the Mighty, able to dant your Enemies, and
to assure your loving subjects, and to safeguard your Royal person, and to shield and protect each other, and to be a pledge to
us and our posterity, of future and perdurable felicity.

This idea of a line of kings taking the throne in *direct
lineal* succession seems not to have influenced Dr. Gwinn's
verses, nor was it apparently in Shakespeare's mind when he
wrote the first act of his play, for the prophecy to Banquo
there pronounced only foretells that he will "get kings" or
that his "children shall be kings."   But before he came to the
third act of the play, a new source of imagery and language
concerning the Banquo line came into the dramatist's hands
and seized upon his mind, and is thereafter used by him to
foreshadow the Stuart direct line of kings as known to King
James and to history.

The story of the prophecy to Banquo, invented by and
told by Boece in Latin in 1527, had been translated into other
languages, but it had never been independently retold by any
historian until John Leslie, Bishop of Ross, an ardent Roman
Catholic and loyal supporter of Mary Stuart as Queen of
Scots, published in 1578 in Rome, where he was then living
in exile, his *De Origine, Moribus, et Rebus Gestis Scotorum.*

* Thomas Wilson in his *State of England* A.D. *1600* (*Camden Miscellany,* Vol. XVI, pp. 2–5) names the twelve collaterals of the queen each
one of whom claimed the right of succession.

This history contains a lively recasting and compression of the story of Banquo in new terms, accompanied by a very striking cut showing the Banquo line in the form of a family tree. The dramatist saw this book and from it seems to have derived both the language and imagery which he uses to picture the glories of the Stuart line in the third and fourth acts of his play. Some of Leslie's language will be quoted, for the book is difficult of access and seemingly unknown to Shakespeareans.

Leslie had given an account in his book of the reigns of Duncan and Macbeth without mentioning the prophecy of the sisters; but later when he comes to the reign of King Robert II (1371–1390) he stops to tell about the prophecy to Banquo; for at this point the descendants of Banquo merge with the Bruces, who descend from Duncan, because of the marriage of Walter Stewart with Marjory, daughter of Robert Bruce, whose son (Robert II) was the first of the descendants of Banquo to be crowned King of Scotland.

Leslie here relates:

Verum cum post mortuum Davidem maribus & Bruseorum familia desideratis, matrimonii certa lege, juris sanctione recta, & ordinum justa assensione Stuartis regni nostri gubernacula tradita fuerint, & ab his ad hoc usque tempus feliciter administrata; locus hic videtur omnino postulare, ut Stuartorum originem altius repetitam tam breviter pertexam, quo manifeste liqueat omnibus, quam justa serie Reges nostri ex Regibus parentibus continenter fuerint nexi, & quanta gloria vel rei militaris in bellis, vel consilii in pace, Stuartorum familia apud nos semper floruerit [p. 257].

This may be translated:

But since after David's death, the males and family of the Bruces having failed, the government of our kingdom by the established law of matrimony, the proper sanction of law, and with the full assent of all ranks has been passed down to the Stuarts and to this present day happily carried on by them; this place seems to require that I briefly review the previously traced origin of the Stuarts in order that it may become perfectly clear to all in how *direct a line our kings have been bound together in unbroken succession from their parent kings,* and with what great glory both in military affairs in war, and in council in peace, the family of the Stuarts has ever flourished among us.

This is the Stuart theme in its full glory.

Thus it came about that what began in Act I of the play as the *"imperial theme"* as glorified by Dr. Gwinn became transformed or merged throughout Acts III and IV of the play into the *Stuart theme* as glorified by Bishop Leslie.

Following this quotation, Leslie tells that a certain thane of Lochaber called Banquo was a man of great name in his day and then proceeds to show how it was that his issue (*soboles*) came to royal dignity. He says that Macbeth had learned from the prophecy of certain devils disguised as women (*"ex vaticinio quarundum mulierum, seu potius Daemonorum, qui mulierum personas ementiti"*) that his own issue failing, there would spring from the blood of this Banquo those who would reign in a *long line* (*"qui longa serie regnarent"*). Consequently, by his machinations certain assassins were induced to attack Banquo and Fleance. Banquo was killed, but Fleance escaped. Then follows the tale about Fleance and the daughter of the Welsh king, and how from their union the Stuart line originated. This is traced (pp. 258–259) to Walter Stewart, who married Marjory Bruce. This account of the issue of Banquo is too long to be quoted; but one who reads it will better appreciate the soliloquy (III, i, 49–57) which the dramatist puts in the mouth of Macbeth in which he expresses both his praise of, and also his fear of, the royalty of nature, which is deeply rooted in Banquo and is personified as his Genius, for this is transmissible to his issue. Following this, Leslie explains:

A Bruseis ad Stuartos, qui ex Bruseorum sanguine juste profluxerant, regni nostri successio devoluta est. Hujus cognominis justi haeredes nostram Scotiam ad hanc usque; aetatem ita temperaurunt, ut nex Reip. nostrae ullis Regibus florentior, nec ulli

Reges nostra Rep. feliciores fuerint. Quorum singulorum vitas suo quasque ordine postea fuse persequemur; & nomina (ut Regum ex Regibus series perpetuo filo contexta manifestius liqueat) huic tabulae in arboris forman descriptae, quae Genealogiam familiae Stuartorum ab ejus prima origine continet, subjecimus [p. 259].

That is to say:

From the Bruces to the Stuarts who truly flow from the blood of the Bruces, the succession of our Kingdom has devolved. The true heirs of this name have so ruled our Scotland even to this day that neither has it ever been more prosperous under any other of the Kings of our state nor have any of these kings been more happy. Hereupon we will fully set forth the lives of these Kings each in its own order, and (in order that *the line of Kings from Kings united by a perpetual thread* may appear more clearly) we annex their names to this properly arranged table in the form of a tree, which discloses the Genealogy of the family of the Stuarts from its first origin.

At this point is inserted in Leslie's book the interesting cut of the Banquo tree here reproduced.*   This cut was done in

* The bibliography of Leslie's history has not yet been adequately set down. The original work, published in Rome in 1578, was a book of (40) + 588 + (32) pages in quaternions entitled:

> De Origine Moribus, et Rebus Gestis
> Scotorum Libri Decem. . . . . Authore Ioanne
> Leslæo, Scoto, Episcopo Rossensi
> (Printer's device, Peter & Paul)
> Romae, In Aedibus populi Romani. MDLXXVIII.

The terminal colophon is similarly dated.

Of this book Father Dalrymple made in 1596 a MS translation into the Scottish vernacular which was printed for the first time by the Scottish Text Society in two volumes in 1884–1895.

The original Latin book was reprinted in 1675 (Bohn's Lowndes says "printed in Holland"). It is a nonpaginal reprint on a smaller page and not so well printed. It usually bears on its title page the following imprint.

> Romae, in Aedibus Populi Romani M.D. LXXVIII
> Nunc denuo recus. Anno Domini M.D. CLXXV

(continued on next page)

LESLIE'S CUT OF THE BANQUO TREE

Rome in 1587 while Mary Stuart was still living a prisoner
in England. John Leslie and the Romans held that Mary's
abdication was obtained by duress and was a nullity. She
was still Queen of Scots, and her son, although he had been
crowned King of Scotland when a year old, was still only
"Scotorum Princeps." Leslie therefore asserted in the title
of the cut that the family of the Stuarts "Scotiae sceptrum
Octo posteriorum regum recta serie et successione obtinet."
To the Englishman this was not true. There were in 1578
nine Stuart kings in the direct line, not eight.

The poet's eye, struck by this pictorial showing of the
Stuart line, allowed it to create the imagery used by him in
Acts III and IV.

Banquo (III, i, 5) rephrases the prophecy concerning his
children as he sees himself "the *root* and father of many
kings." Macbeth's fears stick deep (are deeply rooted) in
Banquo (III, i, 49) because he is to be "father to a *line of
kings*" ("*series perpetuo filo contexta*"). The tree of Banquo
in the cut bears not only leaves and flowers, but globular
fruit, eight of which united in a direct line are crowned; and
Macbeth sees that he has murdered Banquo only to make

But some copies bear the following imprint.

> Romae, in Aedibus Populi Romani, M.D. LXXVIII
> Londini, excusum pro Roberto Boulter,
> ad insigne Capitis Turcae, ex adversum
> Mercatorio Regali, in vico vulgo Cornhill
> dicto. MDCLXXVII

For the reprint all of the cuts in the original book were copied, but in
smaller size, with less skillful engraving, and with correction of some
errors and a few minor changes.

The cut of the Banquo tree in the original book is of distinctly finer
work than in the reprint. So far as I can ascertain, Shakespearean
scholars have had no knowledge of this cut. A copy of the smaller cut
in the reprinted book is in the Bodleian Library (Sutherland 211) and
was reproduced in *Shakespeare's England* (1916), Vol. II, p. 536. It has
been extracted from the reprinted book and could not have been seen
by Shakespeare. What he did see and use was the original cut in the
book printed in Rome in 1578, and here given.

these *"seeds"* of Banquo kings.* Macbeth's thwarted ambition imagines the serpentine trunk of the tree as drawn in the cut to be a "snake" he cannot kill (III, ii, 13), or a "serpent" (III, iv, 29). The picture of this trunk showing *"quam justa serie Reges nostri ex Regibus parentibus continenter fuerint nexi"* is seen as "that great bond" which keeps Macbeth pale and which he wishes "torn to pieces" (III, ii, 49). And finally, in the fourth act it is a show of eight (not nine) kings, for the title of the cut speaks of a series *"octo posteriorum regum."*

But the dramatist wished to develop the Stuart theme in other ways in addition to those suggested by Bishop Leslie, and proceeded to do so. He so staged the procession of the kings that it would show son continually succeeding father, and transmitting both Banquo's "royalty of nature" and the color of his hair in apparently endless succession. This family likeness is "nature's copy" † which Lady Macbeth hopes

---

* Shakespeare wrote "seeds" (III, i, 70), but following Pope nearly all editions mistakenly change the expressive plural, as found in the folios, to "seed." H. Elwin, *Shakespeare Restored* (1853), p. v, retains the plural, explaining that "by multiplying the ordinary plurality of the term *seed* it is rendered emphatically significant of far-extended descents." With the Leslie cut before him, Shakespeare quite naturally pluralized the word, and our texts should read *"seeds."*

The whole great soliloquy, III, i, 48–72, takes on consistency and new significance if we realize that Macbeth does not fear the man Banquo. Why should he? Banquo is not to be a king (I, iii, 67). What he fears is Banquo's "royalty of nature," or his "being" (= nature, O.E.D. 3); for this will be transmitted to his seeds," i.e., the succession of valorous and wise kings rooted in Banquo and pictured in the cut as seeds which are crowned. Against this, fate must champion him. This idea of Banquo as a natural organism consisting of root, trunk, and seeds continues in Macbeth's mind. He asks the murderer, "Are you so gospelled to pray for this good man *and for his issue?*" He says of Fleance after his escape, "The worm that's fled hath *nature* that in time will venom breed."

† "Nature's copy" is the copy which nature makes in causing the son to look like the father. Some have found in this phrase a reference to copyhold tenure. This is, I think, misleading (see P. S. Clarkson and C. T. Warren, "Copyhold Tenure and *Macbeth*," *Modern Language*

is "not eterne." This is why Macbeth viewing the "show of eight kings" is startled as he notes that the first is "too like the spirit of Banquo." The second with "haire" like the first. The third like the former, until he exclaims, "What will the *line stretch out to the crack of doom?*" It is a *direct lineal* unbroken succession of kings to the world's end. And it is an imperial dynasty, the future rulers of which are to carry "double balls and treble scepters." When Malcolm is proclaimed king, he is seen as compassed by his "Kingdom's pearl," an uncompleted simile which needs to be filled out. Malcolm is about to take his place as ruler of what these ancient Scottish chiefs looked upon as the coming feudal empire of Scotland, of which all the thanes were to be feudatories. They are about to be proclaimed earls, a feudal title hitherto unknown in Scotland. The head of such an empire is crowned by an imperial diadem, which differs from the golden fillet of a kingly crown in that it is studded with pearls representing the dependent fiefs. Accordingly, when Macduff calls upon the rest of the thanes to hail Malcolm as their king (V, viii, 54–59), he appropriately likens them to the "Kingdom's pearl," that is, the pearls of the imperial diadem which is to compass Malcolm's head. This is the suggestion of the Clarendon editors which is repeated by Dr. Furness at the close of his list of previous less satisfactory ones. It accords with Bellenden's reference to the "diademe imperiall" of Scotland; and this designation of the crown of the Stuarts was continued by King James VI after he became King of England. Four days after the death of Queen Elizabeth, he wrote a greeting to the Lord Mayor of London in which he speaks of that city as "the Chamber of our Imperial Crowne" (Nichols's *Progresses of James I,* p. 41). James could not

---

Notes, Vol. lv (1940), pp. 483–493). What Shakespeare really thought about "nature's copy" is more fully developed in *Winter's Tale* (II, iii, 95–107). Lady Macbeth hopes that the lineal descent from Banquo (in which each son will favor his father), will not last forever.

fail, therefore, to know what the dramatist meant by the words "the imperial theme."

The feudal terms used by Shakespeare in thus exhibiting the devolution of imperial sovereignty upon Malcolm Canmore and from him descending to his present sovereign are in full accord with the earlier act of his father King Duncan (I, iv, 35, printed with the capitalization of the folio):

> Sonnes, Kinsmen, Thanes,
> And you whose places are the nearest, know,
> We will establish our Estate upon
> Our eldest, Malcolme, whom we name hereafter,
> The Prince of Cumberland: which Honour must
> Not unaccompanied invest him onely,
> But signes of Nobleness, like Starres, shall shine
> On all deservers.

These words concern not merely Malcolm's succession to his father's throne. They are the decree by which Duncan puts into effect the law which his grandfather had exacted from his thanes abolishing the older law of tanistry, which placed brothers or cousins on the throne before sons. Duncan was thus creating in Scotland a hereditary monarchy; and as part of this enactment he converts his kinsmen and chieftains into a feudal nobility to whom he promises grants which will enable them to sustain this relation to their overlord. It was grateful to James and his nobility to hear the words by which their long-lived Scottish dynasty was established.

This brings us to the difficult task of painting the picture of the show of the eight Stuart kings as staged by the King's Company. In part the difficulty arises from the contradiction between the stage direction of the folio and the text, for the former puts Banquo last with a glass in his hand, while the text puts the glass in the hand of the eighth king. Editors always amend the stage direction, but in varying ways. It should, I think, read: "A show of Banquo and eight kings, the last with a glass in his hand," for line 112 is more intelligible if Banquo's spirit enters first and stands near the first king.* The other difficult question is: Who is the eighth king bearing the glass? The *History of Scotland,* like the Leslie chart, names eight, and only eight, sovereigns of the Stuart line reigning between Banquo and James, and the last of these was Mary Queen of Scots. Because they are collectively called "kings," most editors refuse to allow Queen Mary a place in the procession. I think it likely that this delicate matter was intentionally left vague, and I suggest that following the seven kings, all well known to the Scots in the audience, there came a muffled figure peering down into a large glass and therefore unrecognizable. But as James hears the words:

> And yet the eighth appears who bears a glass
> Which shows me many more. And some I see
> That two-fold balls and treble sceptres carry,

he will inevitably see in this figure his own mother triumphing in her issue over the barren queen who signed the death warrant.

The ball surmounted by the cross (later called the orb) is that part of the regalia which symbolizes kingship by divine right; whilst the scepter betokens actual kingly power. King James thought he was appointed by the "divine predestinate will" to unite all Britain, formerly divided into England and Scotland. The ball is therefore "two-fold." But he carries a "treble sceptre," corresponding to the first three salutations of the sibyls in Dr. Gwinn's verses, as King of Scotland, England, and Ireland. Lord Chancellor Ellesmere in delivering his judgment two years later in the case of the Post-nati (p. 64)

---

* T. M. Parrott suggests to me that the dramatist originally wrote, "A show of eight kings, the last with a glass in his hand," but subsequently wrote "Banquo" in the margin, intending it to be inserted before "eight kings," but the compositor put it after. That Banquo enters first and stands pointing as the procession passes is clearly shown in the plate for this play found in Rowe's edition of 1709. This has high authority as a true showing of the usage of the Restoration stage.

accurately defined the king's sovereignty thus: "King *James* hath now the Kingdomes of *England, Scotland* and *Ireland,* and the Isles of *Gernsey* and *Jersey* by discent; all these be his Dominions, and under his subjection and obedience."

The fourth salutation of the sibyls explains why he carries no scepter for France. The channel islands did not constitute a kingdom.

But most important of all is it that the procession of the kings should be given with historical accuracy and with proper dignity; for it should be a true apotheosis scene. It is usually shabbily staged as a tiresome and meaningless tableau.

King James having been shown his royal line, it was timely to ennoble the strain. When Malcolm accuses himself of foul crimes, Macduff tells him that he "does blaspheme his breed. Thy royal father was a most sainted king: the queen that bare thee, oftener upon her knees than on her feet, died every day she lived." This praise of King Duncan and his wife, the father and mother of Malcolm, who is the Malcolm Canmore of history from whom the Stuarts are descended, is introduced *ex industria.* There is no warrant in the *Chronicles* for the assertion that Duncan "was a most sainted king"; and still less for the praise of Duncan's wife. Finding nothing at all recorded in Holinshed concerning Duncan's wife, Shakespeare read on a few pages and found that Duncan's son Malcolm subsequently married Margaret (sister to Edgar Aetheling), "a woman of great zeal unto the religion of the time . . . (otherwise called for her holiness of life Saint Margaret)." So he transferred the recorded virtues of St. Margaret to her mother-in-law, and thus increased the attractiveness of his picture of the ancestry from which King James sprang.

Modern criticism of this play, while recognizing that praise for the Stuart line is a note several times heard in it, does not seem able to hear the full chord which the dramatist has struck in his effort to remind his king of the glories of the

Stuart dynasty. Or if heard, it is as a discord. The history
of the play shows why this is so. Before King James died, his
initial popularity had turned to contempt, and the play of
Macbeth had been laid aside. Davenant's spectacular perver-
sion of the play was the form in which it appeared on the
Restoration stage, and this omits reference to the "imperial
theme," nor does it mention the "two-fold balls and treble
sceptres." This version held the stage until Garrick revived
Shakespeare's play in the middle of the eighteenth century at
a time when the Stuarts were classed as public enemies because of the Jacobite rising which terminated at Culloden.
Garrick and his successors were able to hold their audiences
by relying upon the dramatic power of the play, and preferred, in deference to public sentiment, to slur over all that
glorified the Stuarts. Neither Garrick's version nor Kemble's
contains the line as to the balls and scepters. This habit of
mind has unconsciously permeated later criticism and interpretation of the play, and exists today. It remains for our
generation to put the play back into harmony with the
thought of the king which obtained in the year 1606.

We cannot reverse the verdict of history; but it may help us
to a more sympathetic attitude toward the dramatist's glorification of his king if we recall that while the play of *Macbeth*
was being written, the scholars of the kingdom were engaged in the production of the King James version of the
Holy Scriptures. Their prefatory address to the king begins
thus:

Great and manifold were the blessings, most dread Sovereign,
which Almighty God, the Father of all mercies, bestowed upon
us the people of England when first he sent Your Majesty's Royal
Person to rule and reign over us. For whereas it was the expectation of many, who wished not well unto our Sion, that
upon the setting of that bright Occidental Star Queen Elizabeth
of most happy memory, some thick and palpable clouds of darkness would so have overshadowed this Land, that men should
have been in doubt which way they were to walk; and that it

should hardly be known, who was to direct the unsettled State; the appearance of Your Majesty, as of the Sun in his strength, instantly dispelled these supposed and surmised mists, and gave unto all that were well affected exceeding cause of comfort; especially when we beheld the Government established in Your Highness, and Your hopeful Seed, by an undoubted Title, and this also accompanied with peace and tranquillity at home and abroad.

We should grant to the dramatist the same right to honor his king that we grant to the translators. And all who see the play of *Macbeth* should bear in mind that King George VI is directly descended from King James I in the eleventh degree. The question, "Will the line stretch out to the crack of doom?" is no less interesting and important today than when Macbeth first asked it.

HOLINSHED'S CHRONICLES AS A SOURCE
OF THE PLAY

Volume I of Holinshed's *Chronicles* (edition of 1587) contains 464 double-column pages prefaced by this special title page:

THE DESCRIPTION OF SCOTLAND,
Written at the first by Hector Boetius in Latine,
and afterward translated into the Scotish Speech
by John Bellenden Archdeacon of Murrey, and now
finallie into English by R. H.

Here Shakespeare learned that the prophecy to Banquo, which Dr. Gwinn had told about, was accompanied by a contrasted prophecy to another thane named Macbeth who was thereby incited to murder the mild King Duncan in order to gain his crown. This Macbeth story disclosed subject matter fit for a great drama; a noble man possessed of bravery, vigor, and ambition, who yielding to the deceptive prophecy of three sisters was led to murder his king and seize the throne; after which he became a murderous tyrant who was ultimately slain by his own subjects by whom the rightful king was restored to his kingdom. The Tudor ideal of an ordered kingdom had a strong hold on the people of Elizabethan England and on William Shakespeare. This attracted him to the showing exemplified in the Macbeth story of the difference between good kings and usurping tyrants.* It was

---

* This subject has been developed by E. M. W. Tilyard in his *Shakespeare's History Plays*. Shakespeare's respect for hereditary monarchy is expressed in this play in such phrases as "due of birth" (III, vi, 25); "truest issue of thy throne" (IV, iii, 106); but they may be due to King James's own insistence upon the divine right of inherited kingship, and the "imperial theme" of the play.

therefore apparent that the progress of the "vicious mole" which worked the corruption and downfall of Macbeth might be so pictured by the dramatist as to contrast a good king, such as Duncan, with a usurping tyrant, such as Macbeth became, as King James had contrasted them on pages 24 to 26 of the book which he had written for his son's instruction. This Macbeth might also be shown to experience the tortures of the accusing conscience of a murderer by transferring to him the torments suffered by King Kenneth after he had poisoned his nephew, as pictured a few pages earlier in the same volume of Holinshed. Thereby Macbeth's career would disclose to us a noble man who became a murderous usurper and was overthrown by his avenging conscience.

Holinshed's story of Macbeth told how a good King of England helped an exiled King of Scotland to regain his kingdom. With a little embellishment it could be used to show the wickedness of regicide and its terrible punishment in terms matching King James's denunciation of its infamy. It could be made to trace King James's descent from Banquo. James was a diligent student of his genealogy. It could include pictures of sorcery and necromancy. James had written a book about demonology. It could show the English and Scotch as friends. James's passion was to unify his kingdoms. It could be molded to exhibit the traitorous murder of a King of Scotland by a subject in whose castle he was a guest. Just such a danger had King James narrowly escaped in 1600 when the Earl of Gowrie tried to kill him while guest at Gowrie House in Perth. But to do this the Macbeth story must take upon it certain details, also related by Holinshed, of the treacherous assassination of an earlier King Duffe by Donwald the captain of his castle.

As Shakespeare studied in his Holinshed the history of the reigns of King Duffe, King Kenneth, King Duncan, and King Macbeth, he made choice of what he would use, what he would reject, and what he would change. The changes which he made are sometimes only to make the story of the play more dramatic, but sometimes they are made so as to show the workings of the minds of the characters whereby the human interest of the play is increased. Such changes let us into the secret of the working of the dramatist's mind. They are evident and purposeful. Some of these will now be examined to find why the dramatist made them. The first to be noted are those which created Shakespeare's Macbeths, for in the play there are not one but three Macbeths.

a) According to Holinshed, Macbeth before his great crime was a valiant gentleman but had shown himself "somewhat cruel of nature." The dramatist changed this to make more worthy the Macbeth with whom the drama opens. Instead of being cruel he is "full of the milk of human kindness," wishes to obey his conscience, and fears to violate it. He is conscious of judgment both here and in the life to come: he dares do all that may become a man but no more. Such is the sound Macbeth.

But when the play opens, a sore temptation has come to him. He was an ambitious man and had some claim to the throne. Unable to control his rebellious subjects, Duncan had sent for him and asked his help. He told the king that he would go in person against the rebels and put them down (I, iii, 91). When commissioned to do this, his pride was aroused, and he broke to his wife the thought that since Duncan did not know how to rule he should be done away with (I, vii, 48). She welcomed this thought; but he put it aside because it involved a "murder" (I, iii, 139) and therefore deep damnation (I, vii, 20). The second scene of the play shows how he vanquished the rebels, and the rest of the first act shows how it transpired that in but two days' time the temptation mastered him.

Some modern criticism refuses to agree that such a man could be guilty of so great a crime. It therefore minimizes or sets aside the original soundness of this Scottish thane whom Shakespeare has substituted for Holinshed's naturally cruel Macbeth. Thus is the play belittled, and bloody melodrama substituted for this most magnificent idealistic and romantic drama which shows how easy it is for a good man to fall under the sudden impact of a great temptation.

b) According to Holinshed, after Duncan's murder "the prick of conscience caused [Macbeth] ever to fear lest he should be served of the same cup as he had ministered to his predecessor." Out of this grew Shakespeare's analyzed picture of the second Macbeth, who has violated his conscience and become a murderer. Macbeth before his crime has no fear of "strange images of death" (I, iii, 97), but after it dares not look upon the images of his victims. Before the murder he wished to attain his ambitious ends without doing wrong —"holily" is the word his wife uses; but yielding to a "supernatural soliciting" he committed his monstrous crime. Not five minutes after the murder he wishes the knocking at the gate could "wake Duncan." The pricks of conscience become the stings of scorpions. He can never cleanse the hand that did the bloody deed. Remorse creates the fear which leads to his next great crime.

To learn more of the torments of a violated conscience, Shakespeare read about the remorse of King Kenneth after he had poisoned his nephew, as recorded both in Holinshed's *Chronicle* and in Buchanan's *History of Scotland*. Holinshed says: "It chanced that a voice was heard [by Kenneth] as he was in bed. . . . The King with this voice being stricken into great dred and terror, passed the night without any sleep coming in his eyes." Shakespeare seized upon this picture. The voice which Macbeth heard on the murder night dooms him to "sleep no more." Thereafter his "rugged looks" proclaim that he is shaken nightly with terrible dreams (III, ii, 18). He envies Duncan his sound sleep of death. When his wife says: "You lack the season of all natures, sleep," he eagerly agrees, "Come, we'll to sleep" (III, iv, 141); and emboldened by the assurance of the apparition, hopes to "sleep in spite of thunder" (IV, i, 86). So has Kenneth's loss of sleep been multiplied by the dramatist to exhibit the punishment by insomnia of the superstitious, conscience-smitten murderer Macbeth.

It is quite possible that Shakespeare's choice of insomnia as the punishment for Macbeth's great crime was due to his knowledge that King James himself suffered from sleeplessness. Sir Theodore Mayerne, the king's physician, amongst memoranda concerning the king has recorded: "Male naturaliter dormit, et inquiete: saepissime expergiscitur noctu, vocatque cubicularios, neque nisi legente Anagnoste obrepit somnus ut plurimum" (MS Sloane B. M. 1679); that is, he slept ill, waked often in the night, and called his chamberlains, nor could sleep be again induced unless some one read to him.*

c) At the end of Scene iv of Act III are found the terrible words by which Macbeth makes final choice of evil as his good. After this the drama shows us the third Macbeth, who has cauterized his conscience. Holinshed tells only that "after the contrived slaughter of Banquo . . . Macbeth began to make those away by one surmised cavillation or other whom he thought most able to work him any displeasure." But in Shakespeare's play the Macbeth of the last two acts does not stop to cavil. All excuse is thrown aside. That his conscience had formerly troubled him was due to his inexperience. It must be quieted by "hard use" (III, iv, 142–144). "Things bad begun make strong themselves with ill" (III, ii, 55). Crime is to be practiced without being scanned, because although the young criminal may fear punishment, the hardened murderer will outgrow this weakness. After this Macbeth hears only "curses not loud but deep." He has "supp'd full with horrors" and has "lived long enough."

King James in his book (p. 16) calls this "a deliberate

* Ellis's *Letters,* Series II, Vol. III, p. 199.

resolution to breake the bridle of conscience" and he solemnly
charges his son to eschew ever "wilfully and wittingly to contrarie your conscience," thus enforcing it.

And if yee followe the contrarie course, I take the great God to
record, that this booke shall one day be a witnesse betwixt me
and you; and shall procure to bee ratified in heaven, the curse
that in that case here I give unto you. For I protest before that
great God, I had rather not bee a Father, and childlesse, then be
a Father of wicked children [End of the Epistle].

The variations from Holinshed's picture thus made by the
dramatist produced the contrasts between the originally
sound conscience of Macbeth and his "superstitious" conscience after he committed his first great crime, and later with
his "cauterized conscience become senseless of sin" which
marked the end of his wicked career. King James was particularly interested in the analysis of the conscience, and had
described at some length these very steps (*Basilicon Doron*,
p. 15) which mark the degeneration of this originally valiant,
red-faced, yellow-haired Pict with the big blue eyes which
were constantly seeing things which fascinated, tormented,
and misled him.

How the play expresses this strongly marked character development needs some words of explanation. A dramatist
has an advantage over a storyteller in that character can better
be shown by actors' dialogue than by historical narration.
But better still, Shakespeare could use the actor's face to reveal character. In no play of Shakespeare's is such opportunity given a good actor to use his facial muscles as is given
one who can sufficiently contrast the face of the worthy Captain Macbeth with that of the conscience-tortured King
Macbeth, and later with that of the conscience-hardened
tyrant of Dunsinane. These changes cannot be fully con-
veyed to the audience by the text of the drama; but Shakespeare could and did tell Burbage how to do it, for we find
that the text of the play again and again reminds the actor

of Macbeth what his face must show, and Lady Macbeth keeps telling her husband that his thoughts are revealed by his face.*   This face revelation it is, and not merely the dramatic story of Macbeth, which grips the discerning audience.   John W. Hales stated this long ago (*Transactions of the New Shakspere Society*, 1874, p. 509):

There is no play more complete in its physiological development than is *Macbeth*.   All competent critics concur in this.   There is scarcely perhaps elsewhere in literature a decay of soul represented with such completeness.   The biography is absolute.

d) Nothing in Holinshed indicates that Macbeth's imagination is an active one, but Shakespeare paints this man as a poet, a seer of sights, and a dreamer.   His fell of hair rises at the dismal sound of a night shriek; and this hypersensitive imagination frequently produces the phenomenon of hallucination, † a word which is thus defined in Shakespearean terms in the *Century Dictionary.*

In *pathol.* and *psychol.*, the apparent perception of some external thing to which no real object corresponds.   The mistaking of a bush for a bear in the dark is not hallucination, but only illusion; but the hearing of a voice when no sensible acoustic vibrations strike the ear is a very common hallucination.   Hallucination may be of sight only, or of hearing only, or of both together. It may be consistent with perfect sanity and the absence of any

---

* In the following lines the text of the play seems designed to inform the actor of Macbeth what his countenance should express: I, iii, 51, 57, 142; I, iv, 51; I, v, 63–67, 72; II, ii, 72; III, ii, 9, 27, 34, 54; III, iv, 21, 67, 116; V, iii, 3.

† The word "hallucination" did not come into use until shortly after the time of William Shakespeare.   Instead, the word "sight" was in use with much the same meaning; indeed, one of the earliest uses of "sight" is to designate a thing seen with the eye which is considered strange or found to be nonexistent.

King James called such things "sichts," and William Shakespeare in the play of *Macbeth* so uses the word "sight" to designate both the ghost of Banquo and the procession of the kings (III, iv, 114 and 116; IV, i, 122 and 155).   We retain this meaning in the phrase "second sight."

false belief, and may even become an object of observation and study to the person affected.

Shakespeare's Macbeth has both the power and the habit of substituting image for reality, and in II, i, 33 he practices observation and study of his own hallucination. Images and sounds which originate in Macbeth's own mind and which are subject to his control lead him, because he chooses not to control them, to the precipice from which he falls. Thus has the dramatist shown in this play the power of a strong imagination, and the danger of the delusions it can create.

But did any earlier Macbeth story suggest this? Boece and Holinshed did not. But in Wyntoun's *Chronicle,* written about 1420, it is recorded (infra p. 208) that "Macbeth aye in fantown frettis had gret fay," that is, had great faith in his phantom imaginings. "Frettis," "freets," or "freits" is the Scottish name for the superstitions to which common people give credence.* One is strongly tempted to regard this as the germ from which grew the imaginative and superstitious Macbeth of Shakespeare's play; although it is not easy to see how the dramatist came in contact with this old *Chronicle* which had not been printed. It might have been by way of some well read Scot who told him about it.

e) According to Holinshed, Macbeth's wife (and the same is true of Donwald's wife who helped to murder King Duffe) is only an ambitious, evil woman. In place of these revolting

---

* King James uses this word in his *Basilicon Doron* at p. 109, where he says:

Take no heede to any of your dreams; for all Prophecies, visions, and prophetick dreames are accomplished and ceased in Christ. And therefore take no heede to freets either in dreames or any other things: for that errour proceedeth of ignorance.

I am told that the word "freits," although nearly obsolete even in Scotland, is still used by older people in some places. If the word were well understood in these days, it would be proper to say that the play of *Macbeth* is the showing of a man who gave too great heed to freits.

females Shakespeare has pictured that wonderful creature, the Lady Macbeth of his play. After the murder of Duncan she disappears from Holinshed's pages. Purely a Shakespearean creation is the wicked lady who fell into collapse when she heard that her husband had killed not only the king but two more innocent victims; who soon found "nought's had, all's spent"; whose hand was ever after bloody and hell murky; and who in the end took her life. Her conscience is in contrast to that of her husband. He can sear his conscience. She can not. When he tells her that he will wade deeper in blood, she would turn back. This rift with her husband it is which breaks her spirit.

In at least one other respect she discloses characteristics in which James was particularly interested, for she is a somnambulist who sees things in her sleep which do not exist. King James in his *Daemonologie* says (p. 74) that the devil illudes "the senses of sundry simple creatures, in making them beleeve that they saw and hearde such thinges as were nothing so indeed"—a clear enough description of hallucination. The king next asks, "may not the devil object to their fantasie *their senses being dulled and, as it were, in a sleep, . .* whatsoever such like wherewith he pleaseth to delude them?" This is a good description of what happened to Lady Macbeth.

f) Holinshed at the end of his history of Macbeth's reign observes that his downfall was caused "by illusion of the devil." This opened the door to what is perhaps the most magnificent theme a dramatist can set before himself. Shakespeare, taking this hint, also attributes Macbeth's temptation and fall to the devil (I, iii, 107; III, i, 69; V, v, 43; and V, viii, 14), thus raising the question, as old as the human race, of the origin of evil. Was Macbeth's fall caused solely by the devil or was it his own free choice? The dramatist made no effort to avoid this hard question, for he knew the king's answer. Near the beginning of the *Daemonologie* (p. 4) the king had written that God will permit the devil to deceive "only such, as first wilfully deceives themselves, by running unto him, whome God then suffers to fall in their owne snares, and justlie permittes them to be illuded with great efficacy of deceit, because they would not beleeve the trueth (as *Paul* sayth)." This was good Calvinism based on St. Paul's exposition in II Thessalonians, 2 : 9–12, and James was a Calvinist. These verses were often quoted by those who argued about the deeds of the devil (see, for example, Gifford's *Dialogue Concerning Witches,* pp. B4r and K1v). Some have even thought the play of *Macbeth* to be a discourse on this passage of Scripture (see Professor Henry Morley's *English Writers,* XI, p. 39, and E. I. Fripp's *Shakespeare,* p. 647). I think it more likely that Shakespeare took his theology on this subject from King James, and molded his play of *Macbeth* so as to cause it to exemplify the royal reasoning.

Shakespeare (as Marlowe before him and Goethe afterward) shows us a man tempted by the devil and making very starkly his choice of evil as his good at the price of his soul. Early in the play (I, iii, 130–142) Macbeth discusses with himself the question whether the "supernatural soliciting" is good or evil. The lines are a signal to the audience to follow the tergiversations of his mind as he pronounces it evil, and yet proceeds to make one bad choice after another, until at III, iv, 135–140, the final choice is reached. He has committed two foul murders. He is deep in blood, and now the world knows it. His wife hopes he will wade no more, but instead he determines to run to the devil, and announces that he will visit the weird sisters at once in order that he may know "by the worst means the worst." For his own good all causes must give way. Evil is to be his good. He has made his compact with the devil and given his "eternal jewel to the common enemy of man" (III, i, 68). His conjuration (IV, i, 52–60) requires the devil to do his part of the compact even though by its terms Macbeth accepts destruction, which he likens to a shipwreck. And when the devil has done his part, and Macbeth is to die, his invocation, "Blow wind, Come wrack," invites the very penalty recited in his conjuration; for as James expressed it in his *Daemonologie,* the devil contracts with his victims "that he may have the better commodity thereafter, to deceive them in the end with a trick once for all; I mean the everlasting perdition of their soul and body." The play is built in accord with the king's philosophy. This accord will be further developed in later chapters of this book.

g) In Holinshed the supernatural element is multifarious. Three women "resembling creatures of elder world" hail Macbeth and Banquo with prophetic greetings. "Certain Wizzards" warn against Macduff; and "a certain witch" pronounces the delusive prophecies. Shakespeare, the dramatist, reduces these to a single trio of witches pictured strictly in accordance with the ideas of Scotch (not English) sorcery. Scotch witches are bad women who have attendant devils who teach them evil practices, including the art of destroying kings by deceptive prophetical phrases, as for instance in the case of King Natholocus and the witch of Colmekill (Holinshed's *Description of Scotland,* p. 69a).

The effort of some scholars to liken the witches of the play to the Parcae of the Latins or to the Norns of Scandinavian mythology is without foundation in the play. Other critics, influenced by their own imaginings, speak of Shakespeare's bearded hags as "august" or "awe-inspiring." The shipmaster's fat wife knew better when she cried out to one of the sisters "Aroint thee witch" (I, iii, 6). The play depicts three Scotch witches of the Jacobean variety and nothing else. Visibly they are old and withered hags. They have some knowledge of the future and they are capable of invisible flight in the air, but this is solely because of the knowledge and powers of the little devils who are their masters and who in every witch scene stand by them, teaching them evil deeds or transporting them through the air.

Artists and critics have allowed their imagination to erect a demonic philosophy about these hags for which there is no justification in the text of the play. They have thus been led into all manner of extravagances. It is well to read in Curry's *Shakespeare's Philosophical Patterns* his second chapter on the "Demonic Metaphysics of Macbeth" and note his citations (p. 56) which show what distant flights our imaginative faculties may make when stimulated by such metaphysical philosophy. The variance between the different flights proves their subjectivity. The play of *Macbeth* affords a fertile field for such speculation. Shakespeare could easily have put such ideas into his play, and no doubt was tempted to do so, for Holinshed's text encourages it. But the king would not have liked to see Scotch witches thus dignified and he did not do so. We should respect this restraint, and accept the play as it was written. For in the play, as in the king's demonology, the witches are only ugly old women who have no supernatural powers. Only the visible devils have any such powers, and to these such critics are apt to shut their eyes. The stage is partly responsible for this, for the devils are usually invisible and inarticulate.

The sisters of destiny, which some imagine they see in the play, could have controlled Macbeth's fate. Witches can only tempt him to ruin. A fate-driven Macbeth would not have appealed to the author of the *Basilicon Doron,* and would never have carried this play to its supreme position among the dramas of the world. It is the picture of Macbeth tempted by lying witches to blood guilt in violation of his conscience that has secured this world audience. To dramatize this picture Shakespeare substituted the phrase "weyward sisters," in place of the conventional "weird sisters" as the proper designation of his coven or sisterhood (see p. 159) and put a veritable little devil alongside each witch to instigate them to their evil deeds. This bold step Shakespeare took, relying upon the king's book for justification. "Weird sisters" have no devils to help them. Nor do Fates nor

Norns nor sibyls.   To visibly incorporate the king's philosophy in the play, he shows the witches of Forres in Scotland as hags accompanied by visible devils who instruct them how to cause the murders by which Macbeth is brought to ruin.

A serious attempt to trace the process by which Holinshed's weird sisters were thus changed to witches was made by T. A. Spalding in his *Elizabethan Demonology,* published in 1880, (pp. 86–124).   Had Spalding's reasoning been noted by later editors and critics, they would have been saved from some of their mistaken ideas concerning the "weird sisters."   This subject will be more fully examined in chapters of this book which follow.

h) In Holinshed's account, Macbeth, near the end of his reign, built Dunsinane for his protection, and among the thanes summoned to help build this strong castle was "Macduffe, thane of Fife," a man whom he had not previously mentioned.   Because he refused to come, Macbeth threatened to "ride him with a snaffle," whereupon he fled to England and promoted the revolt which put Malcolm on the throne. In contrast with this, in the first act of the play Macduff is found among the court of King Duncan and he is given no small part to enact before his flight to England.   Why did the dramatist thus enlarge Macduff's role?

King James was an extreme proponent of the divine right of kings.   He strongly condemned the justification of tyrannicide put forth by George Buchanan in his *De Jure Regni.* Regicide was in James's opinion always wrong, and in his treatise *The True Law of Free Monarchies* he asserts that subjects may never rebel against a bad king "in respect they had once received and acknowledged him for their king." In the *Basilicon Doron,* after stating that a tyrant's infamous life may incite his subjects to revolt, James adds, "although that rebellion be ever unlawful on their part" (p. 26).   There is no exception to the divinity that doth hedge a king.   He must never be slain by his people, "how wicked soever he be." For many years this was a hotly debated issue, until it culminated in the execution of James's son by his subjects.

But in the play Shakespeare is writing, the audience must see a tyrannical King of Scotland killed by the Scotsman Macduff, and King James as well as the audience must justify the deed. Therefore Macduff must be kept free from the charge of regicide or from violation of his allegiance in his killing of Macbeth. This explains the part assigned to Macduff in the first three acts of the play. He is the first to discover the murder of Duncan. With instant vigor he denounces the "sacrilegious murder" of the king, "the Lord's annointed temple." These are right Jacobean phrases. He suspects Macbeth and refuses to go to Scone to swear allegiance to, or attend the coronation of, the man whom he believes to be only "an untitled tyrant." Any titles he might thus gain would not sit so easily upon him as the old robes with which he was invested by King Duncan (II, iv, 35–38). He will not make "friends of foes." Instead he retires to his own domain of Fife, never goes to Macbeth's court (III, iv, 128–130), and when summoned to do so replies with an absolute, "Sir, not I"; and immediately flees the country (III, vi, 40).

Thus has the dramatist been at pains to free Macduff from any tie of allegiance to Macbeth, and so from the crimes of rebellion and regicide which King James so hated. No one in the audience questions the justice of his challenge of Macbeth. They may condemn, as did James, the overthrow of Nebuchadnezzar and of Nero, but they will not condemn this tyrant's just punishment by Macduff.

i) In Holinshed the rebellion in Lochquhaber which Macbeth and Banquo put down was headed by *Makdowald*, "one of great estimation among them," to whom had come from out the Western Isles many people, and from Ireland "no small number of Kerns and Gallowglasses."

James in his book had told his son that the people of the
Western Isles were "allutterlie barbares," and directed him
(p. 36) to "followe foorth the course that I have intended . . .
rooting out, or transporting the barbarous & stubborne sort,
and planting civility in their roomes," and was just now busy
about this. At the time the play was written, a certain Angus
Macdonald possessed as chieftain the southern section of these
isles, including Islay, where he and his rebellious islesmen
were giving trouble to the king. In 1605 the government was
making special efforts to suppress Macdonald and restore
order in these islands, some account of which affairs may be
read in Hume Brown's *History of Scotland* (Vol. II, pp. 255–
256). Shakespeare accordingly changed the *Makdowald* of
Holinshed to "the merciless *Macdonwald*," and attributed
the "skipping Kerns" not to Ireland but to the Western Isles
(I, ii, 12–13). Macbeth, quelling a rebellion of islanders led
by Macdonwald, thus suggested the success of James's own
efforts to restore order to his Western Isles.

j) In Holinshed, Duncan is a lenient, ineffective man totally lacking in kingly vigor. As Duncan was the ancestor of
both King James and King Christian, this was changed. In
the play he is shown as a gracious and kindly king exercising
his office with modesty but with vigor and with no qualities
subject to criticism in a king, in fact the most ideal king that
Shakespeare has drawn. He is too old (V, i, 45) to fight personally in battle but nowise lacking in courage or firmness.
Of late a succession of critics have failed to see this and have
charged him with cowardice because taking no part in the
battle with which the play opens. This is a misconception
of Duncan, and at variance with Shakespeare's intention.
There was a royal palace at Forres upon the "battlements" of
which the rebel's head was set up (I, ii, 23). The two fights
of the day are not far from these battlements, and the old
king might have remained safely in his stronghold. Instead
he with his two young sons and his chamberlain, Lennox,

have gone forth from their castle so as to be near the engagement and direct the fight, the elder son taking an active part and narrowly escaping capture by the rebels. No reflection upon Duncan's bravery is indicated and none should be permitted. Thus the drama gains. It is the slaughter of a friendly king which makes Macbeth's crime so hateful. A good king is thus contrasted with a usurping tyrant as James has contrasted them in his book; and the two kings at Hampton Court see what an attractive king their royal ancestor was.

k) In Holinshed, Banquo is actively concerned in Macbeth's conspiracy to murder Duncan. In the play the king's ancestor must be kept clear of crime, and therefore Shakespeare omits anything which would implicate him in Macbeth's crime. From this we may know that those critics who are suspicious of Banquo's integrity are mistaken. Macbeth knew Banquo intimately, and lines 50 to 54 of III, i, are his estimate of Banquo's character. No other estimate now made is likely to be as good. We shall go far astray if we follow those knowing moderns who nurse suspicions of Banquo by reason of a misunderstanding of his soliloquy at the beginning of Act III. Rightly interpreted, this is the dramatist's showing of Banquo subject to the same temptation which overthrew Macbeth, but without yielding to it. At the end of line 10 Banquo repels the evil suggestion of the preceding lines, and a really good actor giving these lines has the opportunity by the play of his face muscles to exhibit the struggle and the victory as the tempted and troubled face relaxes and with a joyous smile exhibits a face of integrity firmly checking the tempter with the words "no more." The drama thus gains force as the whole responsibility for the murder is put upon Macbeth and his wife; and Banquo's resistance is contrasted with Macbeth's yielding to the identical temptation.

l) In Boece the sisters preface their three salutations with "Salve," which Bellenden translates "Hail." Holinshed changed the first and third, *but not the second,* salutation to "All hail." Shakespeare noticed this oversight and changed the Cawdor salutation also to "All hail" and repeated this in Macbeth's letter:

Whiles I stood wrapped in the wonder of it, came Missives from the King, who *all hailed* me "Thane of Cawdor"; by which Title before, these weyward Sisters saluted me.

In Shakespeare's mind the salutation "All hail" was associated with treachery as a result of the gospel account of the Judas-kiss.

Third Part of King Henry VI, V, vii, 33
To say the truth, so Judas kiss'd his Master, and cried "all hail," when as he meant "all harm."

Love's Labour's Lost, V, ii, 399
  King. All hail, sweet madam, and fair time of day!
  Prin. "Fair" in "all hail" is foul, as I conceive.

King Richard II, IV, i, 167
      Yet I well remember
  The favours of these men: were they not mine?
  Did they not some time cry, "all hail" to me?
  So Judas did to Christ.

The witches' three "All hails" carry on this thought and stamp the three sisters as foul and treacherous. Holinshed says that after Macbeth's victory over Sweno the Scots thanked God "that had sent them so fair a day over their enemy." But in the play Macbeth calls it "so fair and foul a day," the "foul" looking forward to the treacherous "All hails" of the witches which follow a moment later, and looking back to the "Fair is foul; and foul is fair" of the witches in the prelude.

m) Holinshed described four portents associated with the murder of King Duffe seventy years earlier. Three of these Shakespeare transferred to the murder of King Duncan; namely, the cannibal horses, the hawking owl, and the dark day. The dramatist read in Holinshed that after Duffe's murder, "Horses in Louthian, being of singular beautie and swiftness, did eate their own flesh, and would in no wise taste anie other meate." Thereupon he wrote in his play:

> *Ross.* And Duncan's horses—a thing most strange and
>   certain—
> Beauteous and swift, the minions of their race,
> Turn'd wild in nature, broke their stalls, flung out
> Contending 'gainst obedience, as they would make
> War with mankind.
>   *Old Man.* 'Tis said they eat each other.
>   *Ross.* They did so, to the amazement of mine eyes,
> That look'd upon 't.   [II, iv, 14-20]

This was a striking transformation and betterment. He improved Holinshed's portents (1) by assigning the horses to Duncan, thus dramatizing the event; and by converting the strange behavior of the horses into a protest against the inhumanity of man, anticipatory of Swift's Kingdom of the Houyhnhnms; (2) by transforming the hawking owl into an image of the witches' malign power as is pointed out on p. 268 of this book; and (3) by confining to the murder day the darkness which the *Chronicle* ruinously diluted by protracting it for six months. Thus out of commonplace suggestions of another mind was created precisely the atmosphere needed for this play.

Here pardon this investigator a personal reference by way of parenthesis. As a very small boy he was powerfully moved by the frontispiece to the play of *Macbeth* found in Charles Knight's Pictorial edition. This fine woodcut shows the air of Scotland full of portents. Clouds obscure the sun; an owl

pursues a falcon; and wild horses snorting and biting each
other rush forth from all control whilst Ross and the Old
Man occupy the foreground.   This picture built up around
this play such an atmosphere of fear and wonder as to cause
this boy over seventy years ago to read it with creeps and
duckskin; and this atmosphere has never passed away, no
matter how many times he may since have read the play or
seen it on the stage.   This tribute to the power of the first
twenty lines of II, iv, is overdue and is gladly rendered.   The
Greek dramatists accomplished the same end by holding a
chorus in readiness throughout the play to tell the audience
what might be thought of it.   These twenty lines of Shakespeare's play accomplished the same end more vigorously
and more shortly.

No one can compare the origins of the Macbeth story with
their development by the dramatist without coming to realize
that the mind of William Shakespeare was subject to a
notable idiosyncrasy.   His creative mind could have created
the characters and events of his plays solely from his own
imagination, but it was his inveterate habit to seek for suggestions from other minds on which to build.   So highly developed was this trait that at every point it is well to look
for, and if possible find, the external suggestion which started
the building process.   Many such are indicated in this book.
There will always be those who ask why William Shakespeare
should have gone so constantly to other minds to get suggestions, and who feel that we should rather assume that he
wrote his plays without seeking outside help.   Let such ask
themselves why he made use of King Duffe's portents, which
occurred years before Macbeth murdered Duncan, when he
could more easily have himself invented others.   I believe
the answer to be that he found a pleasurable exhilaration in
choosing a source and adapting it to his purposes *with betterment;* so much so that this happy faculty became habitual

with him and he instinctively sought opportunity to exercise it. It is our privilege to trace these origins and use them as guides to interpret his drama.

Of the changes made by the dramatist as he used the Holinshed story, the most important are those concerning the personalities of Macbeth and of his wife. These changes created the characters which have held the world's attention ever since. They mark Shakespeare's reaction against Senecan fatalism. Shakespeare had read some of the *Ten Tragedies,* probably in Latin while he was at school and no doubt later in Newton's English translation. They revealed to him Roman stoicism, with which he had also met as it is reproduced by Marlowe and Kyd; but any attraction this had for him waned as he advanced in maturity, and in writing *Macbeth* he repudiated it entirely. Seneca's *Hercules Furens* nearly approaches the theme of *Macbeth.* Liddell in his Introduction has traced its influence. Some of the Senecan aphorisms found in *Macbeth* are reflections of similar aphorisms in this Latin play.* In his earlier career as a dramatist, Shakespeare often made use of Seneca's rhetorical tricks, but as his art matured he shook off these formalisms. He likewise revolted from Seneca's fatalism, and this revolt created the immeasurable difference between Macbeth yielding to a supernatural soliciting which makes him mad and Hercules driven by the gods into madness. Thus can we measure the distinction between the Roman thought and the Elizabethan. Hercules is abused by the gods and for this is to be pitied. Macbeth suffers from a strange and self-abuse. His choice between evil and good is his own responsibility, all supernatural influences to the contrary notwithstanding. It is the difference between black and white. This insistence upon Macbeth's freedom of choice, so

* Dover Wilson in note 1 on p. xliii of his Introduction to this play satisfactorily sums up the evidence of the indebtedness of the play to Seneca's *Hercules Furens.*

heavily emphasized in this play, is the more impressive when we consider that in *King Lear,* which was written at about the same time, we find not a little fatalistic philosophy. But *Lear* is a pagan play whose characters swear by the pagan gods and act on pagan principles.

SHAKESPEARE'S KNOWLEDGE
OF SCOTTISH HISTORY

Shakespeare, writing for the stage, built his play upon the picturesque fables concerning Macbeth which for the most part originated in the fertile brain of Hector Boece and thence found their way into Holinshed's *Chronicle*. But it must not be supposed that his information concerning Macbeth, King of Scotland, was thus limited. The coming in 1603 of King James VI of Scotland to his English kingdom had compelled the Englishmen to give attention to the history of the northern kingdom. Furthermore, the dramatist knew that the Scottish people relied upon a more recent *History of Scotland* written by George Buchanan, the learned humanist who had been King James's tutor and who had taught him in his youth the Macbeth-Banquo story. Prudence dictated that the play for his king should not show ignorance of the history in which the king was schooled.

It is generally held, and is no doubt true, that Shakespeare had no personal access to the various versions of the Macbeth story which antedate Holinshed (1577). But of later histories it should surprise no one that we have already found (p. 172) that he was acquainted with this story as told in John Leslie's *De Origine, Moribus, et Rebus Gestis Scotorum* (1578), and that we are about to find evidence that he had read what Buchanan tells of Macbeth in his *Rerum Scoticarum Historia* (1582). We are on safe, although neglected ground, in attributing to him knowledge of these two historians of his own day. Nor are we at liberty entirely to ignore the older sources, for they were known to Buchanan and to Leslie and to Dr. Gwinn, as well as to many Scots in London with whom he may have conversed, and thus they

seem in some indirect fashion to have influenced the story
told in the play.

This chapter will consider what historical material in addition to Holinshed was in the hands of the dramatist as he
wrote his play; and also whether his materials were by him
treated as fact or fiction. We must allow him more liberty
in the use of fictions than when dealing with what he deemed
to be facts.

No nation possessed so strange a written and accepted history as did Scotland in the time of King James. The Scots of
that age prided themselves upon a line of kings said to be
descended from King Fergus who nearly two thousand years
previously had taken possession of Scotland as an almost un-
inhabited territory, whereby he owned the whole country as
king by first entry, and exercised absolute sovereignty there-
over. This ownership and succession had been passed down
from king to king in unbroken succession. Numbers were
assigned to each of these kings. Fergus was number 1 and
King James was number 108. No other country possessed
such a kingly line. The power and authority of a King of
Scotland was not limited as it might be in countries where
kings obtained their title from other sources or in other
ways and often subject to some understanding with their
peoples. King James possessed unfettered authority by
divine right.

On May 18, 1603, in the Court of Star Chamber, Lord
Coke announced that "the kinge's ma^tie, in his lawfull, juste
& *lineall* title to the Crowne of Englaunde, comes not by
succession onelye, or by election, but from God onelye, (so
that there is no *interregnum,* as the ignoraunte dothe suppose, untill the ceremonie of coronation), by reason of his
lineall discente" (ed. Baildon, *Les Reportes del Cases,* p. 163).

Again on February 13, 1604/5, in the same court, the Lord
Chancellor stated: "The kinge's Matie, as it were inheritable
& descended from god, hathe absolutelye monarchicall power
annexed inseparablye to his Crowne and diademe, not by

Common lawe nor statute lawe, but more auncyente than eyther of them" (*id.*, p. 188).

William Shakespeare was fully conscious that his play for the king must harmonize with this thought, and his reading of Scottish history was under this influence. To understand the dramatist's use of the then accepted history of Scotland, we must rigorously exclude from our minds this history as it has been laboriously reconstructed during recent years by modern historians using modern methods. Modern history denies the sacrosanct claim that the Scottish royal line was derived by continual succession from Fergus I, who ruled 330 years B.C., after whom the King Duncan of the play was counted the eighty-fourth king in unbroken descent. It tells us that the Scots entered Scotland a thousand years later than Fergus. It gives an entirely different account of King Macbeth. But in this play for his king the traditional line and history of the Scottish kings must be accepted. King James was the "truest issue" (IV, iii, 106) of the throne, and in his *True Law of Free Monarchies* based his claim to an unfettered monarchical authority upon this descent.

A résumé of the historians who had portrayed the history of this line of kings will reveal something of the origin of the mythical history which is embodied in the play.

The earliest Scottish chronicles are little more than lists of the regnal years of kings. All one can read about Macbeth in the contemporary *Historia Britonum* is, "Macbethad mac Fin mic Laig XVI annis regnavit"; but by these and other similar documents we are well assured that there was in fact a King of the Scots named Duncan who reigned from A.D. 1034 to 1040, in which latter year he was slain and succeeded by Macbeth, who ruled in Scotland for about sixteen years until he, too, was slain in battle and succeeded by Duncan's son Malcolm Canmore, who thereupon became the founder of the dynasty which still reigns in Scotland and England.

This mere framework of known historic fact tempted the industrious chroniclers of later centuries to make their works more readable by filling the factual gaps with picturesque but traditional or imaginary stories detailing what they thought might have happened during Macbeth's reign; and it is this fictitious history, built into the framework of fact, which we see on the stage when the play of *Macbeth* is performed. But it must always be kept in mind that in the days of King James these stories were received as sober history.

Four active brains had thus worked in succession upon the romance which has developed into the play which William Shakespeare wrote. These four were John of Fordun, Andrew of Wyntoun, Hector Boece, and George Buchanan; and as we enjoy reading the greatest of all tragic dramas we should give credit to each of these for his contribution.

The first to attempt to write a detailed history of the reign of King Macbeth is *"Venerabilis vir dominus Johannes Fordun, presbyter."* He died in 1385, having written a *Latin Chronicle of the Scottish Nation* which has survived. The following is a condensation of his account:

Duncan, a good and kindly king, was privily wounded unto death by Machabeus, son of Finele, and being carried to Elgin, died there. This Machabeus, hedged round with bands of the disaffected, seized the kingly dignity in A.D. 1040 and reigned seventeen years, maintaining his power by cruelty and tyranny. During this time Malcolm, the eldest son of Duncan, was protected by Edward the Confessor at his court. Some of the chiefs of the Scottish kingdom for a long time planned to recall Malcolm and raise him to the throne. The chief of these was a distinguished, noble, and trusty man named Macduff, Thane of Fife. His loyalty being suspected by the king, he fled to England, and with great difficulty persuaded Malcolm to attempt to gain the Scottish throne. With the aid of Siward, Earl of Northumberland, they entered Scotland. Many of the apparent friends of Machabeus took the part of Malcolm. Accordingly, Machabeus made his way to the north of Scotland. Malcolm, following at a quick pace, a battle took place between them on December 5,

1056, at Lunfanan, in which Machabeus was slain, all of his followers having forsaken him and fled.

This is prosy enough, but it is notable for introducing us to the trusty Macduff, Thane of Fife, whom we would otherwise never have known. His enmity to Macbeth, his flight to England, the confiscation of his domain and castle, and finally his conversations with Malcolm at the court of Edward the Confessor are described at great length by Fordun and reappear in the fourth act of the play of *Macbeth*, for Hector Boece took this part of the story from Fordun, Bellenden took it from Boece, and Holinshed took it from Bellenden.

Andrew of Wyntoun, the prior of St. Serf's Inch in Loch Leven, wrote his *Orygynale Cronykil of Scotland* in versified northern English not many years later *(ca.* 1420). He seems to have written without knowledge of Fordun's *Chronicle*. He relates strange tales about Macbeth but always with a cautious skepticism. "Thre werd systrys" pronounce prophecies to Macbeth but this occurs "in hys dremying." It is "the fantasy thus of hys dreme" that moves him to the murder of Duncan. After "Sward, Lord of Northwmbyrland," had come into Scotland with Malcolm to help him gain his rightful heritage, they stopped at Brynnane. The account then proceeds:

> Syne thay herd, that Makbeth aye
> In fantown Fretis had gret Fay,
> And trowth had in swylk Fantasy
> Be that he trowyd stedfastly
> Nevyre dyscumfyt for to be,
> Qwhill wyth hys Eyne he suld se
> The Wode browcht of Brynnane
> To the hill of Dwnsynane.*

These lines are to be noted by anyone tracing the growth of the Macbeth legend to its full proportions in the Shakespearean play. Here begins the picture of the superimagina-

* *The Orygynale Cronykil of Scotland* (London, 1795), p. 238.

tive Macbeth seen more distinctly in Shakespeare's play; and of the weird sisters who were the predecessors of Shakespeare's witches; and of the sayings concerning Birnam Wood and the man not born of woman and of the "gret Hows of Ware apon the hycht of Dunsynane." That William Shakespeare had not read either the *Chronicle* of Fordun or that of Wyntoun may, I think, be taken for granted, for when the play was written these chronicles existed only in manuscripts preserved in places not easy of access. But that in some way he had heard of Wyntoun's saying that Macbeth had great faith in phantom "fretis" is quite likely, for this is the Macbeth whom Shakespeare depicts.*

John Major, the learned schoolman, published his *Historia Majoris Britanniae* in Paris in 1521. It includes an account of Macbeth based on Fordun, but this is short, compendious, unromantic, and of little interest to the reader of the play of *Macbeth*.

Hector Boece wrote his *Scotorum Historia* in Latin and published it in Paris in 1527. The greater part of the story

---

* It may be of interest to trace the origin of Shakespeare's strange name Sinel, Thane of Glamis (I, iii, 71). The name of Macbeth's father was Findlaech, Mormaer of Moray. In the *Annals of Tighernac* (A.D. 1088) we read of Macbethadh Mic Findlaich. In the *Duan Albanach* it is Macbeathadh son of Fionnlaoch. In the *Chronicle of the Scots* (1165) we find Macheth Filius Findleg. In the continuation of the *Chronicle of the Picts and Scots* which is dated 1251 it is written Macbeth mac Finlen, but in a later continuation written 1280 we read, "Macbeth mac *Sinley* reigned 16 years and was kiled by Malcolm." A copyist had mistaken *f* for *s*; and thereafter we find both initial letters. Both Fordun and Wyntoun retain the initial *F*. On the other hand, Boece gives us "Maccabaeus filius Synele," from which comes John Bellenden's "the thayn of Glammys, namytt Synell, on quhom wes gottin ane wailyeand [valiant] man namit Makbeth": and hence Holinshed's Macbeth son of Sinell, and Shakespeare's "Sinel." Had Shakespeare read Fordun or Wyntoun, he would likely have corrected the mistake of Boece.

It is a curious coincidence that in like manner someone wrote "Soris" (I, iii, 39) for "Fores" (so in Holinshed), a mistake which passed into the first folio of Shakespeare and perpetuated itself until Pope corrected it.

of Macbeth as unfolded in the play finds its original in this book. The tale there told is most readable. Imitating Livy, the author gives life to his narrative by putting speeches in the mouths of his characters which reveal the personality of the speaker; and whenever recorded facts are lacking, he invents them that there may be no vacuum. His book has been attacked by later historians, and properly so, on the ground that he believed too many miracles and invented "too many lies"; * but perhaps for this very reason it had instant and widespread popularity, and for a hundred years and more it was the accepted history of Scotland; so much so that for a Scot to question it was not far removed from treason.† It glorified the antiquity of the line of the Scottish kings and therefore was in great favor with King James. When the play was written, Boece's fictitious story was at the height of its popularity.

Banquo and Fleance and the prophecy of the line of kings were among the inventions of Boece. So too Lady Macbeth taunting her husband for cowardice when he hesitated to murder his king; and the tyrant Macbeth maintaining spies in the houses of his rebellious subjects.

It is not impossible, but unlikely, that Shakespeare possessed a copy of Boece's book, for all of its subject matter was available to him, in English rather than in Latin, by reason of his possession of a copy of Volume II of the *Chronicles* of Raphael Holinshed, which volume includes an English

---

* Leland's epigram must be recalled:

> Hectoris historici tot quot mendacia scripsit
> Si Vis ut numerem, lector amice, tibi,
> Me jubeas etiam fluctus numerare marinos
> Et liquidi stellas connumerare poli.

† Sir George Mackenzie, King's Advocate, declared in 1685 that if any in Scotland attempted to refute in print the antiquity of the line of Scottish monarchs reaching back to Fergus I, it would be his duty to prosecute the offender.

translation of what Boece told about this period of Scottish history.

The way in which the Latin work of Boece was transmuted into the English of Holinshed is of more than ordinary interest. Immediately after it appeared, King James V of Scotland requested a certain John Bellenden to translate it into the Scots vernacular.* This translation was completed in 1531. It is not likely that Shakespeare ever saw Bellenden's work. This was his loss, for Bellenden's style is crisp and racy and suggestive. Instead he was limited to a competent, if less lively, translation of Bellenden's Scotch into English made by William Harrison. This came about as follows:

Raphael Holinshed's *Chronicles* were compiled according to the then usual method of amassing together whatever previous writers had told. When it came to Scotland, previous English writers had told very little, therefore Holinshed determined to incorporate all that was to be found in Boece on the subject, and to this end requested his friend William Harrison to translate Hector Boece's work into English. Harrison in his dedication tells us:

> I have chosen rather, onlie with the losse of three or foure daies to translate *Hector* out of the Scotish (a toong verie like unto ours) than with more expense of time to devise a new, or

* There is also a *Metrical Chronicle of Scotland* written in 1535 by a certain William Stewart, likewise based on Boece but not printed until 1858 (Rolls Series). Of this particular work we have no knowledge of the existence in Shakespeare's time of more than a single manuscript, so that it seems most unlikely that he ever saw it. (See *Athenaeum* for July 25, 1896.) I can believe that William Shakespeare may have had access to most printed books that were pertinent to his purposes, but I cannot picture him examining old manuscripts.
Since writing the above, I find that Dover Wilson thinks that Shakespeare may have used this *Chronicle* (*Macbeth*, Introduction, pp. xvii–xviii, [Cambridge, 1947]). But of the five parallels to Shakespearean passages which he adduces, I find that the first and fourth are more closely paralleled by Bellenden's book, which was in print. The second and third are not at all close parallels. And the fifth is more closely paralleled by Dr. Gwinn's verses.

follow the Latin copie, which is far more large and copious. How excellentlie if you consider the art, *Boetius* hath penned it, and the rest of his historie in Latine, the skilfull are not ignorant: but how profitablie and compendiouslie *John Bellenden* archdeacon of Murrey his interpretor hath turned him from the Latine into the Scotish toong, there are verie few Englishmen that know, because we want the books.

I have referred to the book which is the chief source for Shakespeare's play of *Macbeth* as "Holinshed," and this usage will be continued notwithstanding the fact that it is now clear that the dramatist owed his Scottish information rather to William Harrison than to Raphael Holinshed.

Thus far only Scottish historians who wrote before Holinshed have been mentioned. We now come to Scottish histories of later date. These were all in print, and I think Shakespeare took some pains to consult them.

John Leslie, Bishop of Ross and Queen Mary's active advocate, published in Rome in 1578 his history of Scotland in ten books, *De Origine, Moribus, et Rebus Gestis Scotorum.* He used the prior histories of both Major and Boece, explaining that the former is *"vera sed non satis ornata,"* and the latter *"ornata sed non satis pressa oratione."* The book is noteworthy for the genealogical tables with which it is illustrated. Among them is the family tree of the Stuarts, showing their descent from Banquo, which has been reproduced at p. 174 of this volume. I have no doubt that Shakespeare studied this tree of Banquo with care, and read in the text of Leslie's book the description of the lineal descent of the Stuart kings and also the author's diagnosis as to the real nature of the weird sisters.

Last of all we come to George Buchanan, the Scottish historian who was held by some to have written the history of Scotland "better than Livius did that of Rome." His work (*Rerum Scoticarum Historia*) was written in fluent Latin and was first printed in Edinburgh in 1582. He made free use of all the preceding material and did not wholly ignore their fictions.   He described the salutations of the three women to Macbeth, but it was in a dream.   It was merely bruited abroad by evildoers that Banquo's issue should some day reign.   The "flytting wode" was no more than a march of triumphant soldiers with green sprays in their caps, the rest of the legendary material of Boece being thrown aside with the satirical remark: "Multa hic fabulose quidam nostrorum affingunt; sed quia theatris, aut milesiis fabulis sunt aptiora, quam historiae ea omitto" (74 v.).

Because of his own and his king's skepticism concerning the professed powers of witches, Shakespeare, while adopting Holinshed's fanciful and magical story as the basis of his play, took pains to endow Macbeth with such a vivid imagination that the king and others might, if they chose, attribute the supernatural elements of the story to Macbeth's hallucinations.   That the play is capable of this dual construction— magical for the commonalty, and psychological for the judicious—has long been observed; but it has not been sufficiently emphasized that this double appeal finds its origin in the historical method of George Buchanan, who after excluding the supernatural from his Macbeth history, adds that strange stories were in existence about this history which in his judgment were only *fit for the stage*.   Shakespeare, agreeing with this thought, founded his play on these strange stories but did not ask his audience to accept them as verity.

It is here proper to show by examples how the dramatist made use of Buchanan's *Rerum Scoticarum Historia*.

1. According to Holinshed, Macbeth before entering upon his career of crime was "a valiant gentleman and one that if he had not been somewhat cruel by nature might have been thought most worthy the government of a realm."

Buchanan awards him higher praise and nobler qualities: "Erat enim Macbethus acri ingenio, animo prorsus excelso, et magnarum rerum cupido: cui si moderatio accessisset quamvis magno imperio dignus erat" (For Macbeth had keen intelligence, was absolutely high minded and desirous of great things; had moderation been given to him he would have been worthy to exercise power howsoever great) (Ed. of 1582, p. 72 v.).

Holinshed makes no reference to this keenness, magnanimity, or ambition; but in I, v, 19–22, of Shakespeare's play, Macbeth is described by his wife in words paraphrasing Buchanan:

> Thou wouldst be great;
> Art not without ambition, but without
> The illness should attend it: what thou wouldst highly,
> That wouldst thou holily.

And the lack of moderation mentioned by Buchanan is the fault on which Shakespeare has seized to show how Macbeth was ruined by his violent imaginative impulses which led him on to the "valiant fury" of V, ii, 14.

2. Buchanan, the humanist and philosopher, was interested in depicting the workings of Macbeth's mind, concerning which not much is suggested by Holinshed. Buchanan describes the psychological effect of Macbeth's struggle first with temptation and then with remorse. Three women saluted him as king in his dream, whereupon we are told: "Hoc somnio animus cupiditate & spe aeger, vehementer in citatus, omnes regnum adipiscendi vias secum volvebat" (By this dream his mind, sick with desire and hope, was so profoundly stirred that he kept turning over with himself all the ways for obtaining the kingdom) (p. 73 r.).

In the play (I, iii, 127–142) we are shown this mind of Macbeth sick with desire and hope as it is plagued with horrible imaginings.

After he has killed the king we are told by Buchanan: "Regiae (ut credibile est) caedis stimulis animum elatum in praeceps impellentibus, imperium, perfidia partum, in cru-

delissimam tyrannidem vertit" (The stings of the king's murder drove his overwrought mind to a precipice, as he turned
his rule gained by perfidy into a cruel tyranny) (p. 73 v.).   In
V, ii, 13–25, the thanes give a like picture of the effect which
Macbeth's remorse has had upon his overwrought mind.
Thus from Buchanan came suggestions about Macbeth's sick
and overwrought mind out of which have grown the horrible
imaginings and pestered senses of the Shakespearean Macbeth.

3. In Holinshed, Macbeth did not plan to obtain the kingdom until after he had met the weird sisters, but in Buchanan
before he met them Macbethus *"regni spem occultam in
animo alebat"* (that is, cherished in his mind a hidden hope
of being king) (p. 73 r.).   The sisters only confirmed a previous
determination; and so in Shakespeare's *Macbeth* we find Lady
Macbeth referring to Macbeth's earlier formed murderous
plan (I, vii, 48).*

Observe Buchanan's emphasis on the fact that Macbeth hid
his hopes.   It was *spes occulta*.   This is magnificently rendered in Macbeth I, iv, 50–54:

> Stars, hide your fires;
> Let not light see my black and deep desires:
> The eye wink at the hand; yet let that be,
> Which the eye fears, when it is done, to see.

4. Dr. Furness in his New Variorum (p. 383), followed by
Boswell-Stone in his *Shakspere's Holinshed,* noticed that
for the picture of Macbeth's remorse following his crime the

---

* Those who would place the responsibility for Macbeth's crimes on
the Fates fritter away Lady Macbeth's clear declaration (ll. 48–54).
They would have us believe that the first breaking of the enterprise
to his wife by Macbeth was immediately after I, v.   But assuredly with
King Duncan approaching the castle, and the "night's great business"
left in charge of his wife, it could not be said that neither time nor
place were propitious.   No.   The dramatist was at great pains to leave
us in no doubt on this subject.

dramatist was indebted to the account of the remorse of Macbeth's great-grandfather King Kenneth after he had poisoned his nephew. Concerning this, Holinshed tells that Kenneth feared lest his wicked practice should come to light, "for so commeth it to pass that such as are pricked in conscience for any secret offense committed have ever an unquiet mind. But (as the fame goeth) it chanced that a voice was heard as he was in bed in the night time to take his rest." This voice said that he should be punished, and the account proceeds: "the king with this voice being stricken into great dread and terror passed that night without any sleep coming in his eyes."

It was Liddell in his Introduction to his edition of *Macbeth* (p. xxv) who first pointed out that Buchanan's much more detailed portrait of the torture of Kenneth is seen in the Macbeth of Acts II and III of Shakespeare's play. Liddell has gone fully into this and has developed the parallels clause by clause, so that this procedure need not be here repeated. Not merely Kenneth's sleepless night as described by Holinshed, but Buchanan's picture of a Kenneth foully troubled day and night by an accusing voice heard by his diseased mind has been reproduced by the dramatist. Buchanan says:

Tamen animus, conscientia sceleris inquietus, nullum solidum & sincerum ei gaudium esse permittebat, sed intercursantibus per otium cogitationibus sceleris foedissimi interdiu vexabatur; & per somnum observantia visa horroris plena quietem interpellabant. Tandem sive vere, quod quidam tradunt, vox coelo edita est, sive turbatus animus eam sibi ipse speciem finxerat [p. 68 r.].

Literally translated, this may be read:

Nevertheless his mind, disturbed by consciousness of his crime, permitted him to have no solid and real joy, but all day long, during his leisure, was foully troubled by the in-rushing thoughts of his crime; and during his sleep fantasies full of horror seen by him forbade him any rest. At length a voice was either truly, as some say, given forth from heaven, or his diseased mind itself deceived him with such a thing.

Compare this with the great remorse scene of Macbeth (III, ii). Macbeth has "filed" his mind by the murder of Duncan and "on the torture of the mind" lies "in restless ecstasy." Lady Macbeth says that they "dwell in doubtful joy." Macbeth makes companions of "sorriest fancies," has "put rancours in the vessel of his peace," "eats his meal in fear," while his mind is "full of scorpions." He "sleeps in the affliction of terrible dreams that shake him nightly."

5. In Holinshed, Lady Macbeth's part is thus told: "Specially his wife lay sore upon him to attempt the thing, as she that was very ambitious, burning in unquenchable desire to bear the name of queen."

Buchanan puts it thus: "Animus etiam per se ferox prope quotidianis convitiis uxoris (quae omnium consiliorum ei erat conscia) stimulabatur." (His [Macbeth's] mind, bold enough of itself, was spurred on by the almost daily taunts of his wife, who shared all of his plans) (p. 73 r.).

This latter is the Lady whom Shakespeare has drawn, as William Guthrie, was the first to point out, in his *Remarks on English Tragedy,* page 20. She is not herself ambitious. We hear nothing of her desire to be queen. But we find her sharing all her husband's plans and reproaching him bitterly when he hesitates to carry them out. Her first soliloquy (I, v, 16–26) is but her repetition of the arguments which she had been continually pouring into his ears. What Buchanan calls *"quotidiana convitia"* she calls the valor of her tongue. I, viii, 35–60, is a sample of the sort of tongue-lashing of which she was capable.*

---

* Porter and Clarke cite a description of her tauntings as written out by Bellenden (but not in Holinshed), and conclude, I think too hastily, that Shakespeare used Bellenden at this point (*Shakespeare Studies,* "Macbeth," pp. 49–50). The passage in Bellenden represents Lady Macbeth as desirous of being a queen, calling her husband a feeble coward "nocht desirus of honouris" and contrasting his lack of manhood and courage with what others had dared. Shakespeare does indeed show her calling her husband a coward, but in other respects the

6. In Holinshed the only reasons assigned for Macbeth's assassination of Banquo are these:

the prick of conscience caused him ever to fear lest he should be served with the same cup as he had ministered to his predecessor. The words also of the three weird sisters would not out of his mind, which as they promised him the kingdom, so likewise did they promise it at the same time unto the posterity of Banquo. He willed therefore the same Banquo and his son named Fleance to come to a supper.

Shakespeare felt the inadequacy of this explanation of the motive for the crime and was at pains to show further justification in Macbeth's mind for the second murder. He found it in Buchanan, who wrote:

Igitur veritus ne homo potens, & industrius, & Regio jam sanguine imbutus exemplum ab ipso propositum imitaretur, eam cum filio ad coenam familiariter vocatur curat redeuntem per insidias interimendum.

This may be translated:

Whereupon [Macbeth] fearing lest [Banquo, who was] a powerful man and a very resourceful one and with royal blood in his veins, might imitate the example set by himself, he in a friendly way invited him and his son to supper, and procured his assassination as he came.

In Shakespeare's play this becomes:

> Our fears in Banquo
> Stick deep; and in his royalty of nature
> Reigns that which would be feared: 'tis much he dares
> And to that dauntless temper of his mind

Shakespearean development contradicts Bellenden. According to Shakespeare, Macbeth does greatly desire the crown but is restrained by his scruples. His lack of daring is contrasted, not with what others had dared, but with his previous readiness. I think, therefore, that the Shakespearean passages are more likely a development of Buchanan's *"quotidiana convitia"* than of Bellenden's "Artation."

He hath a wisdom that doth guide his valour
To act in safety. There is none but he
Whose being I do fear.

[III, i, 49–54]

Furthermore, notice Buchanan's use of "familiariter" in connection with Macbeth's invitation. How much would be
lost from Shakespeare's *Macbeth* if he had not taken this hint
from Buchanan and cast Macbeth's murderous invitation in
the familiar and therefore doubly treacherous tone so wonderfully expressed in III, i, 15–40?

The proper generalization is that upon the picturesque
background of imaginary facts supplied by Holinshed, Shakespeare imposed ideas suggested by Buchanan; but they are
ideas relating to the workings of the minds of the characters
rather than to their acts. Reasons and motives were shrewdly
analyzed by the philosopher Buchanan, and his analyses were
well considered by the dramatist Shakespeare.

William Guthrie, in his *Remarks on English Tragedy*
(1757), first observed this, insisting that Shakespeare took his
portrait of Lady Macbeth from Buchanan, pointing particularly to the latter's account of Lady Macbeth which has just
been quoted (p. 217). Richard Farmer *(Essay on the Learning of Shakespeare,* 2nd ed. 1867, p. 54) refers to this as repeated by someone (whom I have not been able to identify)
in these words: "whose [Buchanan's] spirit, as well as words,
is translated into the play: and it had signified nothing to
have pored only on *Holinshed* for *Facts*." Dr. Farmer tried
to refute this, for he denied Shakespeare's Latinity. But the
Scotsman Guthrie better caught the flavor of Buchanan and
better sensed the play of *Macbeth* than did the indolent but
much loved Master of Emmanuel College who insisted that
Shakespeare's knowledge of Latin began and ended with *hic,
haec, hoc*. Mrs. Stopes, another native of Scotland, has
pointed out Shakespeare's debt to Buchanan *(Shakespeare's
Industry,* p. 94). Liddell also has noticed it.

One other source which seems to have had some part in forming the picture of Macbeth found in the play is here to be mentioned. It is one which apparently has not heretofore been noticed as having influenced the play.

At the time Shakespeare wrote his play there was current among the people of Scotland an official epitome or "Table" of the reigns of the kings of Scotland which had been prepared, under the direction of King James, by Sir John Skene, Clerk of Register. It was published, together with his digest of the laws of Scotland, in Edinburgh in 1597. The book was commonly called *Skene's Scots Acts,* and the Privy Council required a copy of the book to be purchased by all subjects of sufficient "substance and habilitie" (*D.N.B.* XVIII, 337). The table is to be found near the end of the book and is entitled: "A Table of all the Kinges of Scotland, Declaring quhat zeir of the warld and of Christ they began to reigne, how lang they reigned, and quhat qualities they were of." In this table we read:

LXXXIIII, *Duncane* 1, *Beatrix, Malcolme* the Second his daughters Sonne, began to reigne in the zeire of the warld 5004. In the zeare of Christ 1034, a gud and a modest Prince. He was slaine by *Macbeth* traiterouslie, in the sext zeire of his reigne.

LXXXV *Mackbeth, Dovada Malcolme* the second his daughters Son, began to reigne in the zeir of the warld, 5010. In the Zeir of Christ. 1040. In the beginning of his reigne he behaved himselfe as a gud and just Prince, bot thereafter he degenerated into a cruell tyrant. He was slayne by his Successour *Malcolme* 3. in battle, in the 17 zeir of his reign.

This table was many times reprinted during the following century, and was not only received as a convenient summary of the history of the Scottish kingly line, but as the official endorsement of the historicity of the descent from Fergus, for King James had directed that along with the laws of the kingdom, there should be printed "ane Chronology of the Kings of this realm, our maist Noble progenitors."

Stripping these sentences of their chronology and genealogy, the residue concerning the two kings is "quhat qualities they were of." *Duncan, a good and a modest prince, was traitorously slain by Macbeth, a good and just prince, who thereafter degenerated into a cruel tyrant.* This is what Shakespeare has shown in his play. Three notable qualities are designated by Skene.

a) Duncan is "a gud and a modest Prince." This gives him a better character than did Holinshed, who takes note of his "softnes and overmuch slackness in punishing offenders." Buchanan, too, speaks of Duncan's *"lenitas quam illi ignaviam interpretabantur."* So too Leslie. But Skene's language fits the Duncan of the play. I, vi, 10–14, are difficult lines unless read as the dramatist's effort to exhibit the modesty of Duncan.* In the play Duncan shows no slackness in punishing offenders (I, ii, 63–64). He is "Clear in his great office" (I, vii, 18).

b) Macbeth slays Duncan "traiterouslie." According to Holinshed, Macbeth slew Duncan in a fight and in assertion of his claim to the throne.

c) Most significant is Skene's statement that Macbeth "degenerates." Holinshed's *Chronicle* creates no such impression upon the reader. It says that the good deeds of the beginning of Macbeth's reign were a "counterfeit zeal of equity shewed by him partly against his natural inclination." But Skene says he was good and just at the outset, and so Shakespeare has drawn him.

---

* These lines have been paraphrased many times, with more or less success, which must be the excuse for another effort. The modest Duncan dislikes the pomp and ceremony of a royal visit. The visit is therefore a "trouble" to both the host and the royal guest. But it is also the means by which both show their love. Therefore the king thanks his host for his trouble, because showing love, and so teaches his host to thank the king for his trouble for the same reason.

Shakespeare has chosen another very subtle method of causing these lines to disclose Duncan's modesty. Seven times in five lines the king speaks in the first person. Six of these employ the royal plural of ceremony, but once the king allows himself to slip into the more familiar first person singular. The ceremonious plural is his trouble. He really prefers the more affectionate singular.

While *Macbeth* was being written, Sir John Skene was in England as a member of the commission for the union of the kingdoms. His "Table" was easily procurable and constituted the official catalogue of the Kings of Scotland. It was obviously desirable that any play for King James which depicted any of his royal progenitors should attribute to them the "qualities" which are given to them in the table, and this is what Shakespeare has done.

The following diagram indicates the relation of Shakespeare's play to these sources:

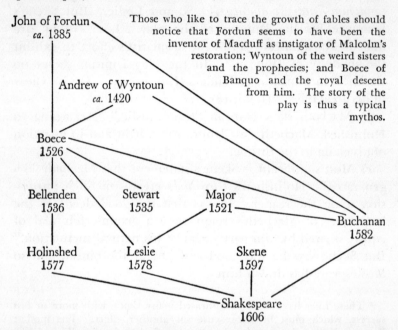

John of Fordun
ca. 1385

Those who like to trace the growth of fables should notice that Fordun seems to have been the inventor of Macduff as instigator of Malcolm's restoration; Wyntoun of the weird sisters and the prophecies; and Boece of Banquo and the royal descent from him. The story of the play is thus a typical mythos.

Andrew of Wyntoun
ca. 1420

Boece
1526

Bellenden
1536

Stewart
1535

Major
1521

Buchanan
1582

Holinshed
1577

Leslie
1578

Skene
1597

Shakespeare
1606

The diagram cannot indicate the differing ways in which Shakespeare used these sources. He wrote *Macbeth* with his Holinshed open before him, appropriating both the thought and the language whenever he wanted to do so. He probably used neither Bellenden nor Boece; nor had he seen either Fordun or Wyntoun, although some information about the latter's poem may have reached him. He had read what Buchanan tells of Macbeth and also Skene's table, and these gave him suggestions as to characterization. Bishop Leslie's book suggested the picture of the Stuart line found in Acts III and IV of the play. These were the stimuli which he used, but he used them freely, always remolding and bettering them.

To these sources of information must be added Dr. Gwinn's playlet glorifying the Banquo legend. Of course, Shakespeare may have seen the performance of *Tres Sibyllae* at Oxford, or he may have obtained one of the copies of Gwinn's verses which were hung upon the walls of St. John's; but I think it more likely that he had come in contact with the author either in Oxford or in London and thus obtained from him not only the verses but some knowledge of where to go for further information about Macbeth and Banquo than is to be found in Holinshed's *Chronicles*.

When William Shakespeare had secured his information about Scottish history, to what conclusion did he come as to the verity of the Macbeth story?

We are here dealing with inferences which cannot be verified; but it is admissible to state the conclusion to which the present excursion into this debatable land leads one. Shakespeare, endowed with a skeptical and very far-seeing mind, suspected that the tale of Boece was, as Buchanan had termed it, a Milesian fable; but he knew that to the king and the Scots surrounding him it was undeniable truth. Therefore, the play treats the tale as verity, while yet dealing with it as freely as though it were, as it is, but a gorgeous romance. This was his warrant for surrounding Macbeth with incidents which Boece recounted concerning Kings of Scotland who had lived nearly a hundred years earlier, and for attributing St. Margaret's piety to her mother-in-law; for as every reader of the play knows, he has shortened Macbeth's reign from sixteen years to only three or four months, and has put into these months some things which happened years earlier or years later, not to mention his transformation of Danes into Norwegians, of which more hereafter.

The author has succeeded in giving to his Scottish play a truly Scottish atmosphere. This has sometimes been attributed to a hypothetical trip of Shakespeare to Scotland. This is an unnecessary assumption, for his knowledge of Scotland is in most instances sufficiently explained by the careful study which he evidently gave to his Scottish sources.

There are other instances where it may best be attributed to help from a native of Scotland. For example, according to Holinshed and Buchanan old Siward is Duncan's father-in-law and Malcolm's grandfather; but Shakespeare designates him as Duncan's brother-in-law and Malcolm's uncle (V, ii, 2 and V, vi, 2). This is now supported by authority, for Malcolm's mother was in fact a sister of Siward.*

Again, historians know that Lady Macbeth had by a previous husband a son named Lulach (called Fatuus or the Simpleton) who lived for a short time after Macbeth was dead. Fordun refers to him as Macbeth's cousin Lulath surnamed the simple; Holinshed calls him "one Lugtake, surnamed the foole, being either the sonne, or (as some write) the cousin of the late mentioned Macbeth"; while Leslie and Buchanan more shortly call him Luthlac the son of Macbeth. But Shakespeare had evidently found out that he was really the son of Lady Macbeth by Gilcomgain her first husband; for in the play, although Macbeth is childless, Lady Macbeth speaks of her child (I, vii, 54).

Also, he had heard that Sir Alexander Seton of Touch had long ago been appointed "hereditary armour-bearer and squire of the body" to the king (*A History of the Family of Seton* by George Seton [Edinburgh, 1893], Vol. I, p. 337). Consequently, in the play Seton is Macbeth's armor-bearer (V, iii, 33, 48 and 58).

Another notable proof of the possession by the dramatist of unusual information concerning the affairs of Scotland in the ancient time is afforded by his rejection of the thanes of Atholl and Morey from his character-list, for reasons which have been previously stated on page 154.

As to the source of this information, consider the follow-

* William F. Skene, Historical Introduction to *Fordun's Chronicle* (Edinburgh, 1872), p. xxxv; John Hill Burton, *History of Scotland* (Edinburgh, 1897), Vol. 1, p. 346; G. R. French, *Shakespeareana Genealogica* (London, 1869), p. 285.

ing: Lawrence Fletcher (an old Scottish name) had traveled in Scotland along with a company of English comedians as early as 1595, at which time he was a favorite of King James. In the records of 1601 he is one of the "Kingis servandis," and is called "Comediane to his Majestie." *   He seems to have come to England in 1603 with King James, for when the King's Company was created in May of that year, his name was put in the Letters Patent ahead of the names of the members of the Lord Chamberlain's Company.   He was with the King's Company in 1604, and as a Groom of the Chamber had his grant of scarlet cloth.   When Augustine Phillips, a member of the King's Company, made his will on May 4, 1605, he gave legacies both to his "fellow" William Shakespeare and to his "fellow" Lawrence Fletcher.   Apparently Fletcher acted rarely in England, if at all, for his name does not appear in the list given in the first folio of the "principall actors" appearing in the plays of Shakespeare. This was probably due to some illness or disability, for he lived on in London in Maid Lane very near the Globe Theater until 1608, when he died.   If he could not act in the play of *Macbeth*, at least he could have given the dramatist much information about Scottish scenery, Scottish manners, and Scottish history, and I should like to think that Fletcher did this in an effort to repay his king for his advancement.

* Tytler, *History of Scotland* (1845 ed.), Vol. VII, pp. 386–387; Dibdin, *Annals of the Edinburgh Stage*, pp. 21 ff.; Chambers, *Elizabethan Stage*, Vol. II, pp. 266–270; Murray, *English Dramatic Companies*, Vol. II, p. 195.

THE GUNPOWDER TREASON

On November 5, 1605, everything in London stood still. The Gunpowder Plot was suddenly unmasked and a pall of horror and terror thrown over all. This astounding piece of atrocity had been in part hatched in Warwickshire. Shakespeare's close proximity to the matter was first pointed out by J. W. Hales in an article entitled "Stratford on Avon in 1605." * Trevelyan spoke of it in his *England Under the Stuarts* (p. 95). Leslie Hotson has gone still more fully into it in his recent book entitled *I, William Shakespeare*. Clopton House, which was a rendezvous of the plotters, was near Shakespeare's land, and he had known several of these men since childhood. Those who would get a detailed picture of the plot, the conspirators, and the relation in which they stood to William Shakespeare should read Chapter VIII of Dr. Hotson's book.

It was a foul, bloody, treacherous conspiracy, bold in design and extensive in its ramifications. At the time it was believed to be of still greater extent than it was in reality. The popular feeling may be judged from Sir Edward Philips's arraignment of the traitors at their trial on January 27, 1606. He called it treason "of such horror and monstrous nature, that before now the tongue of man never delivered, the ear of man never heard, the heart of man never conceited, nor the malice of hellish or earthly devil ever practiced." Anthony Nixon, writing of current events as late as May, 1606, calls his book *The Black Year*.

All things considered, it seems likely that William Shakespeare was either in Stratford or in Oxford when the news of the powder plot reached his ears, and that part at least of

* Originally published in *Fraser's Magazine* (April, 1878) and since reprinted in his *Notes and Essays* (1884), p. 25.

his company was on tour, for he no longer journeyed with them but contented himself with being on hand during the London season. The prevalence of plague had postponed the opening of this until December 15. But it cannot have been long after he heard the news of the plot that he found himself in London examining his Holinshed to learn more about the subject of his forthcoming royal play, and found the story of Macbeth especially suitable and timely because it could show the treacherous assassination of a king and the fit punishment of the assassin. It is no mere coincidence that as the play of *Macbeth* opens we hear the words "foul is fair," see a "bleeding sergeant," and listen to the summary condemnation of a traitor; nor that bloodshed and foulest treachery stain all its pages. Everyone will judge for himself how far this response to the thoughts of the times was the conscious act of the dramatist and how far it was a reflex; but there it is. It means that Shakespeare, like any other human being, was sensitive to, and affected by, the nerve-racking events which were going on around him, and that his mood showed itself in his work.

A medal was struck to glorify the sagacity of the king in detecting the plot.* It shows a serpent lurking among flowers, with the inscription "DETECTUS QUI LATUIT S.C." The same simile was in Shakespeare's mind as he caused Lady Macbeth to tell her husband to "look like the innocent flower, but be the serpent under it" (I, v, 66).

The plot was a deed of darkness in fact as well as in the language of the time. The plotters worked at night to dig their tunnel, got into a vault under the Parliament House, and there hid their powder barrels. There Guy Fawkes was found lurking at night with a dark lantern in his hand and a slow match in his pocket. That evil is associated with darkness is a very old thought, but it became the universal

* A reproduction of this medal is to be found in Henderson's *James I and VI* (Goupil, 1904), p. 211; and also in Hawkins and Frank's *Medallic Illustrations*.

thought of England in the winter of 1605–1606, and this has strongly affected the play of *Macbeth*. Miss Spurgeon in her book *Shakespeare's Imagery* (p. 329), has shown how constantly there recurs in it the symbolism that darkness stands for evil. I will not repeat her analysis of this, but here insist that the abundance of this imagery in the play is a product of the events of the days when it was being written. With Dowden we must agree that its dramatic effect may be summed up in the words,

> Good things of day begin to droop and drowse
> Whiles night's black agents to their preys do rouse.
> [III, ii, 52–53]

Another idea which the popular mind associated with the powder plot was that of universal destruction. The question everywhere under discussion was: How far would the effects of the explosion have reached? Would it have destroyed only Westminster, or would all of London have been laid waste? * The king undertook to answer these questions when he addressed his Parliament only four days after the plot was discovered. He first spoke about what had occurred during Noah's Flood, and what would happen at the last judgment, and then went on to explain that the conspirators had planned

not only for the destruction of my Person, nor of my Wife and Posteritie onely, but of the whole Body of the State in generall; wherein should neither have beene spared, or distinction made of yong nor of olde, of great nor of small, of man nor of woman: The whole Nobilitie, the whole Reverend Clergie, Bishops and most part of the good Preachers, the most part of the Knights and Gentrie; yea and if that any in this Societie were favorers of their Profession, they should all have gone one way: The whole Judges of the land, with the most of the Lawyers and the whole Clerkes.

* See Osborn's *Memoirs on the Raigne of King James* (London, 1658), p. 33.

Following this, he affirmed that "thefe wretches thought to haue blowen vp in a manner the whole world of this Island" (*His Majesties Speach* 1605, B2v and C3v).

Reflecting this attitude of mind, in the play Macbeth would "let the frame of things disjoint, both the worlds suffer" (III, ii, 16); and when overtaken by his fate wishes "the estate o' the world were now undone" (V, v, 50). This language now seems highly extravagant. But in the winter of 1605–1606 such phrases were in people's mouths and in the play only served to put Macbeth in the class with the powder plotters.

The failure of the plotters to kill the king has led Shakespeare unconsciously to cause Macduff when he sees his murdered king to say, "Confusion *now* hath made his Masterpeece" (II, iii, 69).

When Macbeth wishes (I, vii, 4),

> that but this blow *
> Might be the be-all and the end-all here,

and when Lennox speaks (II, iii, 63, 64),

> "Of dire combustion and confused events
> New hatch'd to the woeful time,"

we hear the phrases in the mouth of an Englishman of the year 1605 rather than of a Scot in the year 1040. The same is true of several lines in *King Lear*. Both plays owe something of their gloomy grandeur to the murky air of London during the months when all the talk every day was of the details of the plot, the search for, and the death or capture of the conspirators, and the successive revelations at their trials of the deviltry which underlay this attempt to simultaneously blow to pieces the king, the royal family, and the

---

* The word "blow" was commonly used as a name for the plot, for the letter to Lord Monteagle (which disclosed the plot) had stated that "they shall receyve a terrible blowe this parleament." See *His Majesties Speach* (1605), pp. K2v, L2r, and elsewhere.

Parliament; followed by the conviction of the plotters on January 27, 1606, and their execution on January 30 and 31. The trial of Father Garnet for failing to reveal his knowledge of the plot took place on March 28 following. His execution occurred on May 3, 1606. During this interval of six months the greater part of the play of *Macbeth* was planned and written.

To know what the people of London in general, and William Shakespeare in particular, thought about the plot, the "King's Book" should be read. This is the highly colored official account of the treason. It was printed at the end of November, 1605, and circulated early in December. Prior to this date William Shakespeare can have heard only the irresponsible rumors and hearsay reports which were flying around. This book told enough about the plot to set the pattern of his thoughts. The title page of this little quarto reads:

His Majesties Speach in This last Session of Parliament . . . Together with a discourse of the maner of the discovery of this late intended Treason . . . Imprinted at London by Robert Barker, Printer to the Kings most Excellent Majestie. Anno 1605.

As the dramatist read of these stirring events in this book, images and phrases formed themselves in his mind and sank into his brain. A few weeks later, as his drama was being evolved, these images and phrases were drawn upon and may sometimes be recognized. We are here dealing with imponderables, and therefore analysis is futile, but an example may help. The fleeing powder conspirators were surrounded by the sheriff's posse at Holbeach in Staffordshire. Some were killed, and some were taken alive and sent up to London. The *King's Book* (M2), explained that people wished to see them "as the rarest sort of monsters; fools to laugh at them; women and children to wonder, all the common people to gaze—" In the play, when Macduff has brought Macbeth to bay, he uses the same language as he taunts him (V, viii, 23–26):

Then yield thee coward
And live to be the show and gaze o' the time:
We'll have thee, as our rarer monsters are,
Painted upon a pole.

Although the plot had failed, people had been so terrified
by it that it was several months before their nerves became
steady again and during this interval they suffered much from
nervous apprehension.   The result was a singular occurrence
in London on March 22, 1606.   A baseless and senseless
rumor suddenly spread over the city that another attack had
been made upon king and Parliament, and a state of utter
terror resulted from nothing at all.   Arthur Wilson said of it:

A rumour was spread (by what strange means unknown) that the
King was stabbed . . . with a poysoned knife: The *Court* at
Whitehall, the *Parliament* and *City* took the *Alarum,* mustering
up their Old Fears, every man standing at *gaze* as if some new
Prodigie had seized them; such a Terrour had this late *monstrous*
intended *mischief* imprinted in the *spirits* of the People, that
they took Fire from every little Train of *Rumour,* and were
ready to grapple with their own *Destruction* before it came [*History of Great Britain,* p. 32].

To appreciate properly the extraordinary panic which
seized upon London that day, one should read the accounts
which have come down, many of which are to be found in
Nichols's *Progresses of James,* Volume II, pages 38–43.   Not
many days after this, Shakespeare's pen wrote:

Cruel are the times, . . . when we hold rumour
From what we fear, yet know not what we fear.
[IV, ii, 18]

A mass of diffuse annotation has striven to explain these
obscure lines.   A better way to know what Shakespeare
meant is to read the pages in Nichols which tell about this
panic.   The people of London had laid hold of a rumor
created by their fears without knowing of what they were

afraid. So had Lady Macduff. We need not suppose that Shakespeare was intentionally calling the recent panic to the attention of his audience. He was merely using phrases which had been in his and everyone else's mouth only a short time before.

This reflection in the play of the events of the powder plot helps in the dating of parts of the play. It is a fairly reliable inference that Act I, Scene iv, was not written until after the execution of Sir Everard Digby on January 30, 1605/6; and it is even more clear that the porter scene was not finished until after the execution of Henry Garnet on May 3, 1606.

To follow the first inference calls for examination of what the play tells of the Thane of Cawdor. Holinshed had told that "the Thane of Cawdor, being condemned at Forres of treason against the king committed, his lands, livings and offices were given of the king's liberality to Macbeth," and nothing more. Shakespeare wished so to enlarge and apply the picture of this traitor as to evoke from Duncan when he heard of Cawdor's execution the aphorism, "there is no art to find the mind's construction in the face," * uttered just as Macbeth enters and is effusively thanked by the victim he is

---

* A key thought of the play. Cf. I, v, 65; I, vii, 82; II, iii, 123, 146; III, ii, 27, 34; III, iv, 139. Geffrey Whitney's *Choice of Emblemes* was a common table book. On p. 100 is an emblem headed "Frontis nulla fides," under which two lines read:

> But man is made, of such a seemelie shape,
> That frende, or foe, is not discern'd by face.

Shakespeare had often seen this book. The powder plot may have brought the idea back to him. If, as is probable, he had read Juvenal when he was a schoolboy, he may have remembered "Frontis nulla fides" (*Satires* II. i. 8); but Whitney seems more likely as the immediate source, for "Friend or foe" is what neither Cawdor's nor Macbeth's face reveals. See Baldwin's disquisition in his *William Shakspere's Small Latine and Lesse Greeke*, Vol. 1, pp. 650–651, and compare this with what he says on p. 589 of the same volume.

about to murder. It was his habit thus to prepare for his ironies with both subtlety and care; and while he might have painted this picture wholly from his imagination, this time he chose, as great artists sometimes do, to make use of a contemporary model, in the person of Sir Everard Digby, one of the powder-plot traitors.

George Steevens, and others following him, have seen that the account of Cawdor's execution (I, iv, 1–11) looks like a piece of portrait painting. He thought it a picture of the execution of the Earl of Essex. But that had occurred five years previously. A more likely original of this portrait is to be found in the year 1606 rather than in the year 1601.

Most of the powder plotters were desperate fanatics maddened by the exactions which the law of England was inflicting upon them as Roman Catholics. Catesby, Percy, the Wrights, the Winters, and Guy Fawkes all belonged to this class. Francis Tresham and Ambrose Rokewood were in a different class but had never come into personal relations with the king they planned to kill.

Sir Everard Digby was of an old family long seated in the County of Rutland. He was young, had married a beautiful and very wealthy wife, had two little children, and everything man could desire. He was of large stature, great physical strength, fond of outdoor sports, an expert horseman, and yet of a serious nature and marked by a particularly *fine face*. In early youth he had come under the guidance of the Jesuit father John Gerard and had become a zealous Roman Catholic. The anti-Catholic laws had not borne hardly upon him in his midland shire, but he was deeply affronted by what he deemed the injustice done to many of his coreligionists.

In the spring of 1603, when making his way from Edinburgh to London, King James stopped at Belvoir Castle, and there Everard Digby, a most attractive young man of twenty-one years, was presented to him and received knighthood, for the king thought that he could make use of this goodly gentleman with the head of Apollo. He liked to surround himself with such men, and counted on his support.

Sir Everard had nothing to do with the origination of the plot. It was well advanced when he was told about it. He had nothing to do with the digging of the tunnel or the placing of the powder beneath the Parliament House, but he did take the sacrament and oath of the conspirators, and he had agreed to help them seize the Princess Elizabeth and make her a puppet queen over a new parliament which would reestablish the Catholic religion. He sent the conspirators large sums of money and ammunition and many horses, and when the plot was discovered he joined them in their flight to the Welsh border but was apprehended and taken to the Tower of London.

It was a surprise to the king to find his handsome young friend thus involved in this conspiracy against his life, and there was general comment as to this treason committed by a man who had everything to lose and nothing to gain by it. Digby confessed his guilt, received the death sentence, and on Thursday, January 30, 1606, with three others, was dragged on a hurdle to the scaffold in Paul's churchyard and there hung, drawn, and quartered. It is not at all unlikely that William Shakespeare witnessed this execution so near to his lodging place.

Most of the traitors were defiant or sullen at their trials and executions; but Sir Everard Digby was thoroughly penitent and made a moving speech. Howes (Stow's *Chronicle*, 1615 ed., p. 881) gives this account of his execution:

Sir Everard Digby protested from the bottom of his heart, he asked forgiveness of God, the king, the Queen, the Prince, and all the parliament, and if that, hee had knowne it first to have been so foul a treason he would not have concealed it to have gained a world; requiring the people to witnes he died penitent and sorrowfull for this vile Treason, and confident to be saved in the merits of his sweete saviour Jesus, &c. He praied kneeling about half a quarter of an howre, often bowing his head to the ground.

Shakespeare has thus reproduced this picture:

When Sweno invaded Scotland, Cawdor was "a prosperous gentleman" and one on whom the king "built an absolute trust." He turned out to be "a most disloyal traitor." "Whether he was combined" with the invaders,

> or did line the rebel
> With hidden help and vantage, or that with both
> He labour'd in his country's wreck,
>
> [I, iii, 111–116]

was not known. When his treason was disclosed the king announced:

> No more that thane of Cawdor shall deceive
> Our bosom interest: go pronounce his present death.
>
> [I, ii, 63–65]

Those who saw him die thus reported of his execution:

> . . . very frankly he confess'd his treasons,
> implored your highness' pardon and set forth
> A deep repentance: nothing in his life
> Became him like the leaving it; he died
> As one that had been studied in his death
> To throw away the dearest thing he owed,
> As 'twere a careless trifle.
>
> [I, iv, 5–11]

Whereupon Duncan says, "There is no art to find the mind's construction in the face." And a little later (I, vii, 82) Macbeth: "False face must hide what the false heart doth know." And then (II, iii, 119) Malcolm:

> To show an unfelt sorrow is an office
> Which the false man does easy.

And again (III, ii, 33) Macbeth:

> We must . . . make our faces visards to our hearts,
> Disguising what they are.

Plainly the dramatist was in this play trying to drive home this thought. If we keep the picture of Sir Everard's face and the memory of his deeds in mind, all these lines gain in meaning. If this inference is well founded, the first act of *Macbeth* was not begun until the early days of February, 1605/6. Several other circumstances to be mentioned later corroborate this.

To cheer himself and his court during this gloomy winter, the king imposed upon his company of players more work than ever. On March 24, 1606, a warrant was issued for £100 in payment for ten performances which had been given at court by the King's Company during the holidays. To relieve the surrounding gloom, the Lord Chamberlain probably arranged that these should be comedies. We do not know their names. Some have conjectured that *Macbeth* might have been one of these plays, but this cannot be, for the equivocator knocking for admission at Hell Gate calls for a date after the trial on March 28, 1606, of the arch-equivocator, Father Henry Garnet, or, more likely still, after his execution on May 3 following. No proper understanding of the influence of this trial and execution upon the play can be had until we know the history and meaning of the word "equivocation" at the time the play was written, for the word occurs six times in the play (II, iii, 10–13, 36–40, and again at V, v, 43). The following chapter will endeavor to trace the shift in the meaning of this word which was at this time under way, and the part that it played in the trial of, and at the execution of, Father Garnet.

GARNET'S DOCTRINE OF EQUIVOCATION

The word "equivocation" came into Middle English from the Latin and was used until near the end of the reign of Elizabeth with no sinister implications whatsoever. A word may have several meanings, and to distinguish these meanings, or to play with them (as in punning), is equivocation. The Hamlet of the old northern legends was a punster. So was William Shakespeare. Nothing more is involved in the first use made of the word by Shakespeare, which is in the play of *Hamlet* when the gravedigger puns with Hamlet until he says, "I fear equivocation will undo us."

But not long before *Macbeth* was written, Englishmen began to hear about quite a different thing called by the same name. It was a highly technical Jesuitical doctrine, invented in Italy and France, and thence in process of transplantation into England. It justified speaking untruthfully by the use of words with equivocal meanings accompanied with mental reservations; but this sort of deception might be practiced only in accordance with a set of contorted moral principles justifying such means because of the end to be attained. One may "equivocate," but it must be "for God's sake." *

During the latter years of the reign of Elizabeth, the Jesuits, though excluded by law, made a systematic effort to enter England by infiltration. They brought with them this doctrine of equivocation to help them evade interrogation by magistrates on matters which they deemed outside the magistrates' proper province. It was also a convenient way to help English Catholics to conceal the whereabouts of their

* In Harsnet's *Declaration of Egregious Popish Impostures,* published in 1603, on p. 165 we read, "May the Jesuits *in ordine ad deum* cog, lye, aequivocate, etc.? Oh, they may do what they list *in ordine ad deum.*"

Jesuit visitors. But this "damnable doctrine" gained no currency in Elizabethan England and its meaning was not understood. It had consequently found no place in English printed books. Notwithstanding some discussion about equivocation which occurred at the trials of seminary priests during the latter years of the reign of Elizabeth, the word (in this sense) did not find its way into print in England prior to 1600. The *O.E.D.* names Sir Edwin Sandys's *Europae Speculum*, a work written in Paris in 1599, as its first occurrence. Even as late as January 27, 1605/6, at the trial of the gunpowder plotters the Earl of Northampton in his speech charged one of the defendants with shifts "of lately devised equivocation" (*True and Perfect Relation, etc.,* M r.).*

But after the trial of the powder plotters the people of England knew not only the facts of the plot but had for the first time learned a good deal about the Jesuits' doctrine of equivocation.

Soon after the discovery of the plot, Francis Tresham, one of the conspirators, died in prison. Among his belongings was a manuscript bearing the following enlightening title:

A treatise of Equivocation, wherein is largely discussed the question whether a Catholic or any other person before a Magistrate being demanded upon his oath whether a Priest were in such a place, may (notwithstanding his perfect knowledge to the contrary) without Perjury and securely in conscience answer, No: with this secret meaning reserved in his mind, That he was not there so that any man is bound to detect it.

Detect here means to "divulge or reveal" (*O.E.D.* 2b). So

---

* Life of Robert Southwell in *D.N.B.; Salisbury Papers,* Vol. X, p. 213; Harrison's *Last Elizabethan Journal,* p. 111 and pp. 217–219; Parson's *Brief Apology* (1602); *Shakespeare and His Legal Problems,* by G. W. Keeton, p. 184.

The derivative noun "equivocator" and the verb "equivocate" are entered in the *O.E.D.* as first appearing in literary English in Sandys's *Europae Speculum,* written in Paris in 1599 and printed in England in 1605. (Note that in one place the *O.E.D. misprints* the date as 1590. It should read 1599 as in the second place.)

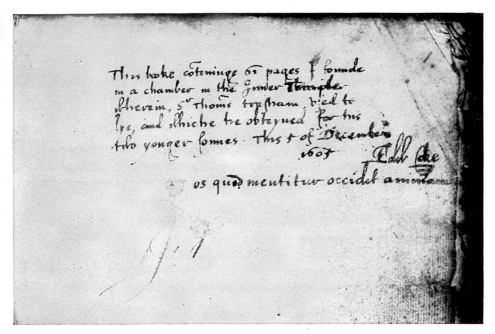

LORD COKE'S ENDORSEMENT
ON THE FIRST FLY LEAF OF MS
CONTAINING A TREATISE OF EQUIVOCATION

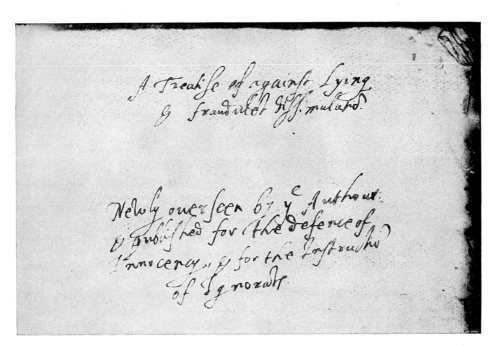

GARNET'S SUGGESTION
FOR A NEW TITLE WRITTEN ON THE
SECOND FLY LEAF OF MS

A TREATISE OF EQUIVOCATION

~~wherein is largely discussed the question wher~~

Whether a Catholicke or any other person before
a Magistrate beyng demaunded vppon his
oath whether a Preiste were in such a
place, maysnotwithstanding his perfect know
ledge to the contrary) wthout Periury
and securely in conscience answere, No
wth this secreat meaning reserued
in his mynde. That he was not
there so that any man is

~~newly aunswered by the author~~ bounde to detect it.

Although Mr Southwell hym selfe (with a
most fitte allegation of the examples of o Sauiour
and of the case of her Ma owne royall person,
(beyng not permitted to say, in that behalfe so much as
he coulde and was desyrous) did yet sufficiently
ynff to syleuce those wth speake against hym; yet
becaufe I perceaue this kynd of doctrine seemeth
straunge bothe to Hereticks and also to diuers Catholicks
I haue thought it necessary to difcuffe it more greatly.
Wherin for that I am principally to deale wth Hereticks
my purpose is not to trouble them much, wth the testimony of Schoolemen and Canonists (except in place
where we may, geue more light vnto the matter wthout
vrging theire authorityes at all) but our proofes shall all

startling is this title that it is here reproduced together with inscriptions on the two preceding leaves. On one of these Sir Edward Coke has written an account of where he found the book, and on the other Father Garnet has written a substitute harmless title after he had first tried his hand at tinkering with the original. The finding of this tract and its production at Garnet's trial had important consequences. Parliament was in session and was framing the Oath of Allegiance which is quoted on page 354. The affiant must swear that he speaks "without any equivocation or mental evasion or secret reservation whatsoever," a phrase devised to meet the special exigency which this doctrine of equivocation had created. As a result of this precedent, many statutory oaths both in England and in America conclude with the phrase "without equivocation or mental reservation," and some of these oaths are still in use today.

This manuscript played a considerable part in the trial of Father Henry Garnet, Superior of the Order of Jesus for England, for treason, for Garnet defended the doctrine of equivocation set forth in it. That for this reason his testimony could not be believed was the unanswerable argument of Lord Salisbury.

Many historians have endeavored to ascertain the actual facts involved in this famous trial. We are not so much concerned with this as we are to know what William Shakespeare, the king, and his court believed to be the facts, and what they thought of this new doctrine of "equivocation."

As to what James and his court thought, we may judge from a letter written early in April, 1606, by the Venetian ambassador to the Doge. After telling that the king was present incognito at the trial "of the Jesuit Provincial of England," he proceeds:

The interrogation [of Garnet] did not afford that satisfaction which Catholics expected, nay he has scandalized the very heretics, and greatly disgusted his Majesty. For beside being on his own confession—not wrung from him by torture, as he affirms, but compelled by irrefutable evidence—cognisant of the plot, he further endeavoured to excuse his previous perjury, in affirming that he was ignorant of it, by a disquisition on *Equivocation,* maintaining a certain doctrine which has shocked the ministers and especially the King who is particularly versed in such matters, and has caused a great outcry against the Roman religion [*Calendar of State Papers—Venetian,* Vol. X, p. 500].

This was written by a Venetian, and yet we find that to him "equivocation" was still vaguely but "a certain doctrine," which the king better understood than others, and the king was shocked by it.

We must next inquire how, when, and what William Shakespeare learned concerning Henry Garnet's doctrine of equivocation.

Garnet's trial was a highly political affair. The government wished to excite public opinion against the Catholics in general, and particularly against the Jesuits, and so strengthen James's hold upon the throne. To accomplish this, as soon as the trial was over, Salisbury caused an account of it to be printed.* Copies of this official but highly in-

---

* The original title page for this book reads:

A True and Perfect Relation of the proceedings at the several Arraignments of the Late Most Barbarous Traitors [ornament].
Imprinted At London by Robert Barker, Printer to the Kings most Excellent Maiestie. Anno 1606

On the reverse appear the royal arms, indicating the king's authorization. The book was in fact written by Robert Cecil and Francis Bacon but read over and edited by King James. After the trial of Garnet, publication was delayed to await the writing by the Earl of Northampton of a long speech, occupying some 250 pages. But before this speech was set up in type, Garnet's execution had occurred on May 3, 1606. Accordingly, six printed pages telling of the execution were hastily added and the work immediately issued with, however, the now entirely inadequate original title page. We may safely assign this first issue to a date early in the month of May, 1606. Copies of this issue are rare. Soon another and more accurate title page was substituted reading:

A True and Perfect Relation of the Whole proceedings against the late most barbarous Traitors, Garnet a Jesuite, and his Confederats; Contayning

flammatory pamphlet were circulated throughout England during May, 1606. It contains Coke's arraignment of Garnet at his trial, of which this sample will suffice:

He [Garnet] hath many gifts and endowments of nature, by Art learned, a good Linguist, and by profession a *Jesuite*, and a Superior, as in deed hee is Superior to all his predecessors in devilish Treason, a Doctor of *Jesuites*, that is, a Doctor five *Dd.* as Dissimulation, Deposing of Princes, Disposing of Kingdomes, Daunting and deterring of subjects, and Destruction. Their Dissimulation appeareth out of their doctrine of Equivocation. Concerning which it was thought fitte to touch something of that which was more copiously delivered in the former Arraignment, in respect of the presence of *Garnet* there, who was the superiour of the Jesuits in England, concerning the treatise of Equivocation seene and allowed by *Garnet,* and by *Blackwell* the Arch priest, wherein under the pretext of the lawfulnesse of a mixt proposition to expresse one part of a mans mind, and retaine another, people are indeed taught not onely simple lying, but fearefull and damnable blasphemie. And whereas the Jesuites aske why wee convict and condemne them not for heresie; it is for that they will equivocate, and so cannot that way be tryed or judged according to their words [pp. T1, T2].

Accordingly, when Garnet rose to reply, his first words were:

1. Concerning Aequivocation, whereunto he answered, that their Church condemned all lying, but especially if it be in cause of Religion & faith, that being the most pernicious lye of all others, and by S. Augustine condemned in the Priscillianists: Nay, to lye in any cause is held a sinne, and evill, Howsoever of 8.

---

sundry Speeches delivered by the Lords Commissioners at their Arraignments, for the better satisfaction of those that were hearers, as occasion was offered; The Earle of Northamptons Speech having bene enlarged upon those grounds which are set downe. And lastly all that passed at Garnets Execution [ornament]. Imprinted at London by Robert Barker, Printer to the Kings most Excellent Maiestie. 1606.

Examination of numerous copies shows that this last title page was issued in at least three variant printings, suggesting a large circulation. For continental readers the work was translated into Latin by George Camden and thus circulated in 1607.

degrees which S. Augustine maketh, the lowest indeed is to lye for to procure the good of some without hurting of any: So then our Aequivocation is not to maintaine lying, but to defend the use of certaine Propositions.* For a man may bee asked of one, who hath no Authoritie to interrogate, or examined concerning something which belongeth not to his cognisance who asketh, As what a man thinketh, &c. So then no man may Aequivocate, when he ought to tell the trueth, *Otherwise he may* [V4r.].

In answer to this the Attorney General said:

For Equivocation, it is true indeed that they doe outwardly to the world condemne lying and perjury, because the contrary were too palpable, and would make them odious to all men: But it is open and broade lying and forswearing, not secret and close lying and perjury, or swearing a falshoode which is most abomina-ble, and without defence or example. And if they allow it not generally in others, yet at least in themselves, their confederates and associates in treasonable practises, they will both warrant and defend it, especially when it may serve their turne for such purposes and endes as they looke after.

Thus, and much more, was the distinction between lying and equivocation discussed during this famous trial.

The jury retired and in less than fifteen minutes returned with a verdict of Guilty.

All this occurred on March 28, 1606; but extra leaves bound in the pamphlet tell that Garnet's execution took place on May 3 upon a scaffold at the west end of St. Paul's

---

* To understand what Garnet means, we must turn back to Coke's arraignment of the traitors. Speaking of the treatise of equivocation which Coke said Garnet had "seen and allowed," he went on:

Now in this Booke there is *Propositio mentalis, verbalis, scripta,* and *mixta,* distinguishing of a mentall, a verball, a written, and a mixt proposi-tion, a very labyrinth to leade men into error and falshood. For example, to giue you a little taste of this Art of cousning.

A man is asked upon Oath this question, Did you see such a one to day? he may by this doctrine answere: No, though hee did see him, *viz.* reseruing this secret meaning, not with purpose to tell my Lord Chiefe Justice. Or, I see him not *visione beatifica,* or, not in Venice, &c [p. Iv.].

church. As Garnet mounted the ladder, the Recorder of London, whom the king had sent to represent him at the execution, urged him *not to equivocate* with his last breath. Garnet said, "It is no time now to equivocate: How it was lawfull, and when, he had showed his mind elsewhere. But, saith he, I do not now equivocate, and more than I have confessed I do not know." Immediately he "was turned off, and hung till he was dead" (p. FFF³).

That William Shakespeare read this little book eagerly about the middle of May, 1606, is not to be doubted, for all London did so. From it he learned all he needed to know about the new meaning of the word "equivocation."

When this pamphlet came to Shakespeare's hands, he had written the greater part of his play of *Macbeth*. Conscious that the scene of the murder of Duncan might create a nervous tension so keen as to endanger the dramatic effect for which he sought, he had determined to interpose a low comedy scene to give a short relief, but this was a bold and a difficult thing to do. If this high tragedy is to be thus interrupted, a mood of the bitterest possible irony must be evoked. Shakespeare worked it out in this way.* Macbeth's castle of Inverness has by the murder just committed become very Hell, and the drunken porter stumbling to the gate is indeed the devil-porter of hell-gate. What can this porter talk about with sufficient satisfaction to the king and his courtiers to justify their listening at this critical moment to his drunken mumblings? The dramatist had pictured an engrossing farmer and a thieving tailor applying for admission to hell; one in the name of Beelzebub and the other in "th' other devils name"—apparently so far only two of them. But when he heard and read of Garnet's execution, he saw an opportunity to insert more apt material. He thought of Garnet

---

* This is one of the few occasions where a Shakespearean judgment of Samuel Taylor Coleridge has been completely reversed by the court of public opinion. De Quincey first led the attack. Then came Hales, followed by a chorus of approval of his view (*Transactions of the New Shakspere Society*, 1874, p. 498).

the equivocator hanging from the gibbet and going straight to hell. So the tailor was given third place and these words inserted:

Faith, here's an equivocator, that could swear in both the scales against either scale; who committed treason enough for God's sake, yet could not equivocate to heaven: O, come in, equivocator, Knock, knock, knock! Who's there?

This language most certainly refers to Henry Garnet, arraigned, tried, convicted, and executed for *treason* "for God's sake," notwithstanding his effort to escape the consequences of this treason by means of *equivocation*. The Jesuit poet Robert Southwell had been convicted ten years before under the Statute of 27 Elizabeth, by the terms of which every Jesuit found in England was guilty of treason. He had admitted at his trial that he was a Jesuit, but had pleaded that he was "not guilty of any treason," and had argued with great force the injustice of a law which made his mere presence in England treason, without proof of any treasonable act. Very different from this was the case of this equivocator who asks the porter of hell-gate to admit him. He has committed "treason enough," for Garnet had admitted his knowledge before the fact of the existence of the powder plot, only defending because this knowledge had reached him through the confessional.

The scene was, and is still, a dramatic triumph. Even to an audience with no knowledge of Garnet or of his doctrine of equivocation, and therefore no idea of what the porter is talking about, it is effective. But to King James and his court, to whom the implications of these words were instant and clear, it must have been electrifying.

But the dramatist could not thus shortly drop this pregnant subject, and so further matter suggested by Garnet's distinction between equivocation and lying was inserted between lines 25 and 45. The dialogue discusses the effects of drink. The porter says that "much drink may be said to be an *equivocator* with lechery." Read what follows with Garnet's arguments in mind and the unsavory similes become full of meaning. They are a burlesque upon the examples of equivocation which had been recited by Attorney General Coke in the course of his arraignment. At the end: "It *equivocates* him in a sleep, and giving him the *lie,* leaves him." Thus the drunken porter with a poor pun disposes of Garnet's argument that *equivocation* differs from *lying*. The scene soon changes, but the words "equivocate," "lie," "equivocate," "lie," continue to ring in the dramatist's ears, and as he returns to the part of the play he was writing, he causes Macbeth to say:

> I pull in resolution and begin
> To doubt th' *equivocation* of the fiend
> That *lies* like truth.

> [V, v, 43]

Some words about the engrosser and the thieving tailor are in order.

An engrosser is one who buys corn when it is cheap with intent to sell it in time of drought at an exorbitant price. During the reign of Elizabeth there had been constant efforts to prevent this cornering of foodstuffs, and these continued into the reign of James. Stringent orders against engrossing were promulgated by James's Privy Council on June 1, 1608. Malone tells that corn was plentiful in London and very cheap in the year 1606, so that the suicidal farmer, long on corn, may have been much in evidence during that year. But others look for a more pertinent incident to account for Shakespeare's picture:

Knock, knock, knock. Who's there i' the name of Beelzebub? Here's a farmer that hanged himself on the expectation of plenty: come in time; have napkins enow about you; here you'll sweat for't.

Such incident is supplied by referring the lines to Sordido in Ben Jonson's *Every Man Out of His Humour.* He is a miserly old farmer who has engrossed much corn, and who spends his time examining his almanac in hopes of bad weather.* He is "one that never pray'd but for a leane dearth, and ever wept in a fat harvest." Entering with a halter round his neck in Act III, Scene ii, he exclaims:

Now, now, when the sunne shines and the ayre thus cleere. Soule if this hold, wee shall shortly have an excellent crop of corne spring out of the high waies: . . . Go to, Ile prevent the sight of it, come as quickly as it can, I wil prevent the sight of it. I have this remedie heaven.

He clambers up and suspends the halter to a tree, ties the noose around his neck, and after some further chatter, we read: "I have hid it [my gold] as deepe as hell from the sight of heaven and to it I goe now *(falls off)*."

Here is a farmer who hanged himself in the expectation of plenty, preparing to go immediately to hell. King James liked Jonson's play. It made sport of the use of tobacco. It was owned by the King's Company, who gave it before the king at Whitehall on January 8, 1605. It may have been played again during King Christian's visit. If we can picture these two plays in juxtaposition, everything becomes clear. If the kings liked to see the earthly fate of the engrosser, they would also be interested in his fate in the next world. Joseph Hall had written in 1597 (*Satires,* Bk. IV, Sat. 6):

Each muckworm will be rich with lawless gain
Altho he smother up mowes of seven years grain
And hang'd himself when corn grows cheap again.

Perhaps Ben Jonson copied Hall, and Shakespeare copied Ben Jonson as I have surmised, or it may be that the jibe was at the time a commonplace due to the constant efforts the ministry was then making to suppress engrossing.

* Halliwell-Phillipps finds Shakespeare thinking of Sordido's almanac in *Antony and Cleopatra,* I, ii, 155.

The tailor is brought in to make place for the pun about cooking his goose. Again Malone has shown the special appositeness just at this time of the English tailor who steals out of a French hose. The same Anthony Nixon who published our earliest account of King James's visit to Oxford also published in the year 1606 (S. R., May 9, 1606) a little pamphlet called *The Blacke Yeare: Seria Jocis,* in which he says:

Gentlemen, shall this yeare be much wronged by their Taylors, for their consciences are now larger than ever they were; for where they were wont to steale but halfe a yard of broad cloath in making up a payre of breeches, now they doe largely nicke their Customers also in the lace and take more than enough for the new fashion sake, besides their olde fees.

This supplies an explanation of this topical allusion. Shakespeare's castigation of the tailor as well as Nixon's was stimulated by some incident of fashion now forgotten but which was just then being talked about at court. Topical matter such as this is ephemeral. Sordido the engrosser was played before James on January 8, 1605. Garnet was hanged May 3, 1606. Nixon's version of the thieving-tailor joke was entered on the Stationers' Register on May 9, 1606. From these pointers an inference can be drawn by anyone as to about when Shakespeare interpolated the porter's business into the play he was writing.

THE HURRICANE OF 1606

In a play about witches one would expect to find much thunder, lightning, rain, and wind, for that the control of these was one of the powers of sorcery was the common belief. King James as a young man had investigated this subject. Tempests raised by witches had delayed the return of his bride from Denmark in the year 1590; accordingly, a few years later he wrote in his *Daemonologie* (p. 46), "They [witches] can rayse stormes and tempestes in the aire, either upon Sea or land, *though not universally.*" * The cautious reservation reappears in the play (I, iii, 24). Reginald Scot, ridiculing this popular superstition in his *Discovery of Witchcraft,* had been more bold. He stated (on the second page of his book) that people who believe in witches

are persuaded that neither haile, nor snowe, thunder nor lightening, raine nor tempestuous winds come from the heavens at the commandement of God: but are raised by the cunning and power of witches and conjurors; insomuch as a clap of thunder, or a gale of wind is no sooner heard, but either they run to ring bels or crie out to burne witches.

At the beginning of the play the witches meet "in thunder, lightning or in rain" and soon reconvene in the same foul weather to meet Macbeth. The witches' revenge upon the shipmaster's fat wife is to be visited upon the master of the *Tiger* by means of their control of the winds. "Though his bark cannot be lost, yet it shall be tempest toss'd" (for, as James explained, their power is *not universal*). Macbeth exclaims, "Time and the hour runs through the roughest day"

* The reason for this limitation of the power of witches over the winds is that they must carry them in bags which when untied release their contents (I, iii, 11–17; IV, i, 52).

(I, iii, 147). The night of Duncan's murder was "unruly," "our chimneys were blown down" (II, iii, 60). "The heavens, as troubled with man's act, threaten his bloody stage" (II, iv, 5). A clap of thunder accompanies each apparition. The malevolent practices of witches as the Elizabethans understood them justify all this.

But when we come to Macbeth's conjuration (IV, i, 50–60), we find a description of a more violent tempest accompanied with details which exactly picture certain notable events which happened while the play was being written, and which were the result of a hurricane of unusual violence which in the popular mind was a direct result of the vengeful powers of evil spirits.

William Camden made notes for a history of the reign of James which he never completed; but these notes (called "Apparatus") were published in 1691 together with his correspondence. Under date of March 30, 1606, he has entered, "Magna Naufragia et Inundationes."

These shipwrecks and floods were caused by a westerly gale of hurricane intensity which swept over the British Isles and the North Sea on March 29 and 30, 1606, expending its fury on the coasts of the Low Countries and Picardy. There is no reason to doubt the contemporary estimates of this storm as the most severe for an entire generation. An account of it occurs in a letter written from Flushing, April 2, 1606, by N. de Blocq to Viscount Lisle.

You will have heard already of the disasters here and chiefly in Flanders, Tergoes, and elsewhere and similarly in Brabant where the whole country is inundated as if by a deluge; the damage is incredible. This town was in danger of being overwhelmed if the storm had continued longer than that day, which was the Monday after Easter 27 March. A breach in the bulwork near the Hospital was serious. The vessels lying at anchor before Rammekins was drowned or driven high ashore. One of the East India Company ships was driven on to a shoal where it threatened to break up. A French ship with 18 men was sunk with all on board. It is a punishment by God. There has been nothing like it for 36 years. The water rose 7 feet above the ordinary. We do not as yet know what happened at Texel in Holland where the road stead is more dangerous than that before Rammekins, in a north wester such as was then blowing. It was impossible to walk the streets and birds were blown into the water, trees damaged, houses blown in and unroofed, The Temple de Marie at Antwerp was half blown away.*

Other letters published in this volume and dated shortly afterward contain many more references to the same catastrophe. An independent contemporary account of this storm is that written by Robert Johnston (see supra page 125). On page 420 of his History he records under the year 1606:

Spring was very stormy this year, with violent winds and great tempests. At the end of March a frightful hurricane, which had broken out with fierce wind and much hail, ravaged our ocean, destroyed the shipping and produced great and dreadful shipwrecks, the tops of churches being torn away from the roofs. In Belgium, and France, and also in Germany many places were struck by thunderbolts. In Antwerp four towers, the greatest and highest of all in the city were thrown down. Amongst us there occurred immense destruction of houses, roofs and trees. Men accustomed to daily labor were prevented from working by the force of the tempest and of the whirlwind, almost as though by the will of heaven.

John Stow, the old chronicler, had died in London in 1605, with an alms basin in front of his house that the public might help him to continue his useful work. Thereafter Edmond Howes continued it by jotting down from day to day the current news. In this *Continuation*, as printed in 1615, is an account, beginning at page 874, of the "Practise of Blowing up the Parliament House," and of the succeeding turmoils; of the arraignment of the plotters on January 27, 1606, and of their trial, sentence, and execution; followed by

---

* Historical Manuscripts Commission, *Report of the MSS of Lord de Lisle and Dudley*, Part III, p. 256.

an account of the trial and conviction of Father Henry Garnet on Friday, March 28, 1606. Then we read (p. 883) what happened *the next day:*

The nine and twentieth, and thirtieth of March, the winde was so extraordinary great and violent, that it caused great shipwrack in England, Scotland, France, and the Low countries, it blew downe part of the Hugonet church, at Diope, and divers other churches in the lower Belgia, and in Germany, in every of which said places, and some others it blew down villages, Trees, and windmills; it also caused the Sea, and divers Rivers to overflow their boundes, and drowned many people, and much cattell."

[Margin] Great windes, floodes and ship
wrack, the wind west and by South

With these accounts of this storm in mind, read the conjuration of Macbeth to the witches (IV, i, 52–60):

Though you untie the winds and let them fight
Against the churches; though the yesty waves
Confound and swallow navigation up;
Though bladed corn be lodged and trees blown down;
Though castles topple on their warders' heads;
Though palaces and pyramids do slope
Their heads to their foundations; though the treasure
Of nature's germens tumble all together,
Even till destruction sicken.

What we should most like to know is the exact wording in which the news of this storm's ravages reached London and was set down by Howes, for it is this news which reproduced itself not many days later in the language of Shakespeare's play. Unfortunately we have not all of Howes's original account but only two differing condensations or paraphrases of it. In the edition of 1615 the paraphrase reads as above. In the "Abridgement" of Stowe as printed in 1611 it reads as follows:

The twenty nine and thirtieth of March the wind was extreame violent, so as it caused much shipwrack upon the coasts of Eng-

land, France and the Low countries; it brought in the sea and
drowned much cattell; and in Picardie neare Dyope, it blew down
a steeple which slew four score persons in the fall thereof; in
Flanders and up towardes Germany there were many Churches,
Towns, Wind-milles and trees blowne downe [p. 461].

In Elizabethan English a steeple was called a pyramid
(*O.E.D.*, B.3). The steeple which fell killing eighty people
has produced lines 56 to 58.

The cartoons evoked by the discovery of the Gunpowder
Plot picture the devil giving instructions to the plotters and
particularly to Father Garnet. In the popular mind the evil
spirits were much dismayed when Garnet was sentenced to
death. The day after his sentence there broke over England
the most severe storm which had occurred in many years,
characterized by widespread destruction, by the wreckage of
churches, and the killing of people by falling spires. To
what could this be attributed but to the chagrin of the witches
that their champion had been overthrown? This was a
triumphant vindication of the current demonology which
assigned such powers to witches. In the play Macbeth's conjuration (IV, i, 52) ascribes these very powers of destruction
to the witches. The old northern English word for utter
destruction is "wracke." At the end of the play (V, v, 51)
Macbeth, rushing forth to his certain death, calls out, "Blow
wind! Come wrack!" thus summarizing these powers and
the penalty which results from his compact with, and conjuration of, the devil. This conjuration was written while
the March hurricane was in vivid remembrance and while
details of the destruction of the Gallic and Flemish churches
were reaching London from day to day, that is, during the
early days of April, 1606.

Nature conspired to keep this in people's minds. When
spring should have come in 1606 England was visited with
storms and inundations, the result of continued westerly
gales.

In Anthony Nixon's *The Black Year,* published in May

or June, 1606 (Stationers' Register, May 9), there are references to these storms. He jocosely prognosticates "a good fire in midsomer" and "a frost of three weeks continuance in July." "This year shall be . . . great trouble by the heavens impressions." There shall be "such various wonders, such strange inundations." And Howes thus tells of destructive floods in June 1606:

the 8. of June following it rained 24. houres, and the next day there rose strange landwaters which carried away milles, trees and houses, made new currents where never any was seene before, it brake down the heads of pooles and trenches, and carried quite away great quantities of cattell, timber, and other thinges from off uppeland groundes. [Howes's Abridgment of Stow, 1611 ed., p. 461].

And as late as August, Blocq wrote to Viscount Lisle (*Penshurst Papers*, Vol. III, p. 305), "The weather bad beyond anything in human memory."

When Arthur Hopton published his *Concordancie of Years* six years later (1612), he put in it "brief Notes of the best Chronicles against every year." On page 228, opposite the year 1606, we read:

The King of Denmark cometh to England. Great inundations in England. The Oath of Aleagance ministered.

This is the first note of memorable weather conditions recorded by Hopton since 1582. All three of Hopton's items have affected the play.

These tempests had a like effect upon the other play which Shakespeare was writing at this time. The storm which runs through the mid-scenes of *King Lear* is the same storm which has affected *Macbeth*. In *Lear* we hear the king say to the storm, "all germins spill at once," and in *Macbeth* the storm is to tumble "nature's germins" all together (IV, i, 59). Both expressions result from the fact that while the plays were being written rivers were overflowing their bounds, causing disastrous upland floods which lodged and destroyed the corn.

The belated spring of 1606 explains the following simile:

> As whence the sun 'gins his reflection
> Shipwracking storms and direful thunders break,
> So from that spring, whence comfort seem'd to come,
> Discomfort swells.

[I, ii, 25–28]

According to the *O.E.D.*, "reflection" in this passage means "turning back." Does the sun begin to turn back at the vernal equinox or at the sunrise? The former is the more natural usage and the word "spring" seems to confirm this, for it designates the spring equinox better than it does the sunrise. Elwin so argued in 1853, and Singer in his edition of 1856 discussed it more fully; but the question is still unsettled. The passage as interpreted by Singer may be paraphrased:

After the sun begins its return on March 21, gales and thunderstorms arrive so that instead of the expected comfort of the spring season, discomfort increases.

After the vernal equinox of 1606, people had longed for an early spring to follow the very dismal winter, but they were disappointed by the hurricane of the end of March, with its "shipwracking storms," and later by continuing floods with "direful thunders." This late spring accompanied by westerly gales delayed King Christian's visit until the middle of July.

Thus has current meteorology affected the play of *Macbeth*.

THE DEMONOLOGY IN MACBETH

Of all the changes made by Shakespeare in dramatizing Holinshed's history of King Macbeth, none was more far reaching than his transformation of the weird sisters into Scotch witches. This was not only a courteous recognition of the intense personal interest of King James in Scotch witchcraft, but it changed the center of gravity of the story. A different situation was created when a Macbeth tempted by devil-taught witches, but free to choose between evil and good, took the place of a Macbeth driven to his doom by a decree of the "goddesses of destiny." Time will not be wasted if we inquire how and why this change was brought about, and what sources were used by the dramatist to familiarize himself with the dismal mysteries of sorcerers and necromancers and their devils, a novel and uncongenial subject to a Warwickshire boy. The miserable creatures who were called witches by the people of Stratford, and who could injure persons or cattle with their evil eye, had little in common with the dreaded Scotch witches with their attending devils who as "instruments of darkness" (I, iii, 124) could plot the fall of kings and meddle with high affairs of state.*

James, while in Scotland, was a high Calvinist and followed the Presbyterian doctrine of that country, which taught that the evil spirits who master witches are permitted by God to do evil in this world as part of the divine decree, according to which such means are used to punish evildoers or to try the patience of the faithful. English Calvinism did

---

* John Hill Burton in his *History of Scotland* (Vol. I, p. 344) has pointed out the difference between Scotch witches and English witches. He speaks of the "grand contrast" between the "wilder crews frequenting such witchland as Scotland" and the "vulgar grovelling parochial witch of England."

not emphasize this difficult point in theology and accordingly English witches were not thought of as instruments of Divine Providence. But Shakespeare had read the king's *Daemonologie* and had studied its prefatory address to the reader, in which James, with a nicety of theological statement remarkable for so young a man, had written:

But one thing I will pray thee to obserue in all these places, where I reason upon the deuils power, which is the different ends & scopes that God as the first cause, and the Devill as his instrument and second cause shootes at in all these actiones of the Deuil, (as Gods hang-man:) For where the deuilles intention in them is euer to perish, either the soule or the body, or both of them, that he is so permitted to deale with: God by the contrarie, drawes euer out of that euill glorie to himselfe, either by the wracke of the wicked in his justice, or by the tryall of the patient, and amendment of the faithfull, being wakened vp with that rod of correction [p. A4].

The dramatist used this diabolism of the Scottish religious philosophy to give meaning to the willful choice by Macbeth of evil as his good. Scotch witches could thus be used by Providence in the "wracke of the wicked" Macbeth, who was determined by the worst means (that is, by contracting with devils) to know the worst, and who called out "come wracke!" as he issued from his castle to certain death. To this end "the powers above put on [that is, spur on] their instruments" (IV, iii, 238). English witches were not capable of any such exalted function. Therefore the dramatist did not make use of the English books about witches, with their stupid and vulgar tales.* Instead, to find out about Scotch witches the

---

* The earliest treatise about sorcery in the English language appears to be *A Dialogue of Witches* by Lambert Daneau, first published in French at Geneva in 1574, but translated into English and published in London in 1575 by "R. W." This is a learned discourse concerning biblical and classical sorcery and it may have been read by King James before he wrote his treatise, although he does not mention it among his authorities; but I see no reason to suppose that William Shakespeare had ever read it.

Scot's *Discovery of Witchcraft* (1587) had been read by Shakespeare,

dramatist went to two purely Scottish sources: Holinshed's lengthy account of the *Witches of Forres,* which was taken from the Scot Hector Boece, and the Scottish king's book on demonology.   How he used these is now to be pointed out.

The most famous witch story in all Scotland was the flamboyant tale of how the witches of Forres vexed King Duffe with their wasting image and their enchantments.   It was first told by Hector Boece, but it may also be read on pages 149 to 151 of Holinshed's *History of Scotland,* where it begins with an account of the visit made by King Duffe to the Western Isles to purge those isles of "barrettors and idle persons as sought to live only on other men's goods."   This provoked a rebellion of the Islesmen in aid of which the witches in Forres, who sympathized with the rebels, undertook to make away with the king by their sorcery and enchantment. Soon after this, King Duffe became ill and the doctors could not help him.   There was a murmuring among the people "how the King was vexed with no natural sickness but by sorcery and magical art practised by a sort of witches dwelling in a town of Murrey land called Fores."   (At this point in the book is a marginal note reading "Witches in Fores," which may have caught Shakespeare's eye when he was reading a few pages later about Macbeth and Banquo journeying to Forres.)   The king had a lieutenant named Donwald who kept his castle of Forres.   A daughter of one of the witches told this lieutenant "in what house in the town it was where they wrought their mischievous mystery."   Immediately the lieutenant "sent forth soldiers about the midst of the night who breaking into the house found one of the witches roasting upon a wooden broach an image of wax at the fire resem-

---

but it did not give him the picture of Scotch witchcraft for which he was seeking.

There was published in London in 1593 *A Dialogue Concerning Witches* by a learned Puritan minister, George Gifford, who tells a great deal about the silly knavery of English witches, garnishing it with a great deal of learned theology and distorted use of scriptural texts, but the book is almost unreadable.   Anyone who plods through it will find that Shakespeare made no use of it.

bling in each feature the king's person, made and devised (as is to be thought) by craft and art of the divill; another of them sat reciting certain words of enchantment and still basted the image with a certain liquor very busily." The witches were apprehended and when examined confessed that they went about such a manner of enchantment to the end to make away with the king, "for as the image did waste afore the fire so did the body of the King breake forth in sweat," and "as for the words of the enchantment they served to keep him still waking from sleep; so were they taught by evil spirits." * This is followed by the story of how Donwald and his wife treacherously murdered King Duffe, which story Shakespeare used as the pattern for his account of the murder of King Duncan in the play.

These witches of Forres, plotting the death of a king in revenge for the wrongs of the Islesmen, are the witches of Shakespeare's play.

In the play the revengeful witch who wishes to destroy the master of the *Tiger* plans to practice wasting:

> I will drain him dry as hay:
> Sleep shall neither night nor day
> Hang upon his pent-house lid;
> He shall live a man forbid:
> Weary se'nnights nine times nine
> Shall he dwindle, peak and pine:
>
> [I, iii, 18–23]

James in his book about witches also refers to this practice of the witches of Forres:

* Outside the town of Forres still stands the "Witches' Stone," a wonderful piece of very ancient carved stonework. In Ben Jonson's *Masque of Queens*, written in 1610, there is a reference to these wasting images. And when Prince Henry asked the author to publish it with notes as to his sources, he attributed this reference to "the well known story of King Duffe out of Hector Boecius." Further proof of the notoriety of this story is afforded by the crude frontispiece of the *News from Scotland* (1591). The artist, wishing to picture the practices of Scotch witches, shows them preparing a liquor in a caldron to baste an image of the king, and in another house is seen the king himself wasting away.

To some others . . . hee teacheth, how to make Pictures of waxe or clay: That by the rosting thereof, the persones that they beare the name of, may be continuallie melted or dryed awaie by continuall sicknesse [*Daemonologie,* p. 44].

But he does not join sleeplessness with drying away as the cause of the wasting of the patient. Holinshed does mention both, and both are spoken of in Shakespeare's lines. It is therefore to be inferred that the account of the wasting of the shipmaster by the witches of Forres had its origin in the similar practice of the witches of Forres upon King Duffe, and came from Hector Boece by way of Holinshed.

But in the play Macbeth is not destroyed by wasting, but by the more efficient method of deceitful prophecies pronounced by witches instructed by devils who have some knowledge of things to come; and by the even more subtle method of oracles having a double sense pronounced by devils according to the forms of necromancy. These methods are characteristic of the witches of Scotland. To learn more of them the dramatist found it necessary to go to the king's treatise which deals with these subjects.

This book, the Preface to which is signed "IAMES R̂," was first published in Edinburgh in quarto with the following title page:

DAEMONOLO-
GIE, IN FORME
of a Dialogue,
Diuided into three Bookes.

[Royal Arms of Scotland]

Edinbvrgh
Printed by Robert Walde-graue,
Printer to the Kings Majestie. An. 1597.
Cum Privilegio Regio.*

* On March 17, 1597/8, this work was entered on the Stationers'

At the beginning of the book is a discussion of Chapter 28 of I Samuel which tells how King Saul sought out the Witch of Endor to tell him his fate in the coming battle. The wise woman of Endor, although called a "witch," was more properly "a pythonisse," that is, a skilled female magician. King James insists upon this (*Daemonologie,* p. 29). When King Saul in his fright asks her to produce before him the dead prophet Samuel to tell him of the future, the marginal note of the Geneva version of the Bible states that it was not really the dead prophet who appeared, but "the devil who took upon him the form of Samuel." Therefore the so-called "Witch of Endor" was a female *necromancer* summoning the devil to tell King Saul by the lips of the dead prophet what to do. This interpretation of the Bible story differentiates the Protestant necromancy of Scotland as propounded by King James from the older necromancy. According to the Hebrew, pagan, and Roman Catholic philosophies, the spirits of the departed in Hades or in Purgatory can sometimes appear and tell their secrets to mortals. To summon them is necromancy. But this was heresy to the Scots. Their Calvinistic theology denied that there is a Purgatory. Such appearances are not departed spirits but devils taking the shapes of dead bodies. This is the Protestant necromancy of the king's book: "This word *Necromancie* is a Greek word . . . which is to say, the Prophecie by the dead . . . because it is a principal part of that art, to serve themselves with dead carcages in their divinations" (*Daemonologie,* p. 9). To the necromancer the devil "will oblish himselfe, to enter in a dead bodie, and there out of to give such answers of the

Register in London by John Legatt; but this entry does not appear to have been followed by publication in England. Another Edinburgh edition appeared in 1600. Later it was twice reprinted in London in 1603 (once by William Aspley and W. Cotton, and once by Arnold Hatfield for Robert Waldegrave). One of the latter two reprints was probably the book which Shakespeare read. It appeared in the folio collection of the king's writings published in 1616–1620. There is a convenient reprint of the first edition printed in London by John Lane in 1924; where it is accompanied by a reprint of the *News from Scotland* (1591).

event of battels, of maters concerning the estate of common-welths, and such like other great questions" (*ibid.,* p. 20).

Because his king was interested in this variety of necro-mancy, the dramatist caused his royal play to show its prac-tice by Scotch witches. English witchcraft did not concern itself with this. Following the king's *Daemonologie,* the play exhibits a king of Scotland seeking by necromancy to learn his fate from Scotch witches, for in the play Macbeth becomes a necromancer summoning devils who appear in "dead car-cages" to pronounce their oracles. King James was sure that the devil can by this method foretell some things to come (*ibid.,* pp. 4, 5). As a ruling monarch he had felt that a knowledge of future events would be very helpful to him, and confessed as much to Sir John Harington (*Nugae Antiquae,* Vol. 1, p. 369), and told him that "he had sought out of cer-tain books a sure way to attain knowledge of future chances." He must have been very young when he did this, for when he came to write his *Daemonologie* in 1597 he warns (p. 10) against this "slipperie and uncertain scale of curiositie" as making men "become in verie deede bond-slaves to their mortall enemie." In his *Basilicon Doron* (ed. 1603, p. 57) he warns his son, "Consult therefore with no Necromancier nor false Prophet, upon the success of your wars: remembering on King *Saules* miserable end."

It has often been asserted that William Shakespeare took his demonology from Reginald Scot, whose *Discovery of Witchcraft* he had assuredly read; but Scot's book deals chiefly with either English witchcraft or with the continental ideas found in the *Malleus Maleficarum* and in Jean Bodin's *Daemonomanie.* Scot's views no doubt influenced Shake-speare's thought that the imagination is a prime factor sup-porting the belief in witchcraft,* but I cannot find that the

---

* Porter and Clarke in their first folio edition of this play have thus summed up Scot's influence upon it: "The scepticism of Scot has found in the poet's mind some deep accord which caused him to breathe into the whole a rationalism and psychology transcending that approached by Scot" (p. xxii).

play of *Macbeth* took much, if any, of its picture of witchcraft and necromancy from Scot's book. Had Shakespeare used that book as his guide, we might have seen Macbeth conjuring with geometrical figures and Latin formulae and a Mephistopheles produced in person as in the Faust legend. Because the dramatist used instead the king's book, we see Macbeth listening to doubtsome oracles proceeding from the lips of dead "carcages" produced by devils. This sort of necromancy was first erected into a technical science by the king in his book, and this book we must read if we are to fathom the demonology of the play.

William Shakespeare had seen that lurid pamphlet entitled *News from Scotland* which had been printed in London in 1591. It tells of the habit of Scotch witches to ride over the sea in sieves, and of the virtue of the toad's venom, and these appear in the play. But he did not make use of the other gruesome tales of Agnis Tompson and the rest of the coven of witches that worshiped the devil in North Berwick church.

Certain classical ideas found in Ovid cannot be ignored. The *Metamorphoses* (vii. 215–293) gives an account of that extraordinary instance of transfusion of blood into old Aeson's veins by the witch Medea whereby he was restored to youth. This called for the preparation of a compound of gruesome ingredients somewhat like those made use of by the witches in the play for the concoction of their charm in the caldron.

This classical influence is, however, small. Anyone who reads the king's book about the demons of Scotland will find that the demonology of the play is that of the book, and I do not think that there is any other book on the subject which enables one to properly understand the part played by the witches under the tutelege of their demons whereby they destroy Macbeth. From Banquo's exclamation, "What, can the devil speak true?" to Macbeth's last words, "Damned be he who first cries hold, enough," the "instruments of darkness" are a controlling influence which the dramatist

never lets his audience forget. This influence is felt by anyone who hath ears to hear. To a sensitive auditor it is the
most characteristic note of the play. It is directly due to the
infusion of King James's *Daemonologie* into Holinshed's
strange tale.

According to this science, a witch is a woman who has sold
her soul to a devil who thereafter attends her as her "master,"
carries her about in the air, and incites her to evil designs.
Every witch has her imp or familiar spirit. James pictures
the world as inhabited by an innumerable number of these
evil spirits "wandering through the world as God's hang-
men" (*Daemonologie,* p. 20), that is, God's instruments to
punish the wicked for their evil deeds.

Except as these evil women are helped by or informed by
their devils, they have no supernatural powers. They cannot
hover through the air except as their devils carry them. They
cannot vanish in the air, but the devils who carry them can
"thicken & obscure so the aire, that is next about them, by
contracting it straite together, that the beames of any other
mans eyes can not pearce thorow the same, to see them" (*ibid.,*
p. 39). They do not know the future, but the devil does, although "he knowes not all thinges future, but yet he knowes
parte" (*ibid.,* p. 4); and this special knowledge of things to
come these devils sometimes communicate to the witches who
are their slaves.

Critics and editors who find "a curious majesty and even
sublimity about the wayward creatures who meet Macbeth"
(Curry's *Shakespeare's Philosophical Patterns,* p. 54) have not
sufficiently studied the king's *Daemonologie* or they would
know that there is no majesty or sublimity whatever imparted
to these hags by the imps who master them. They are simply
and solely hateful, malicious, ugly old hags used by their
devils to do evil deeds.

True it is that William Shakespeare might have changed
the witches described by the king into supernatural beings.

But the truth is he did not do so. Everything the witches do and say in the play is in strict accord with the book of the king which begins by telling the reader that witches are "detestable slaves of the devil."

In the scientific French and German treatises upon the subject, these devils were classified as a hierarchy; and of this scheme James speaks in his book: "There are so manie Princes, Dukes, and Kinges amongst them, everie one commanding fewer or mo Legions, and impyring in divers artes, and quarters of the earth" (*ibid.*, p. 21). So in the play, we find:

> Not in the legions
> Of horrid hell can come a devil more damn'd.
> [IV, iii, 55]

In Scotland witches are grouped in covens and have an infernal ritual used at their conventions or sabbaths when they meet to worship the devil and report upon their evil deeds. Accordingly, in Act I of *Macbeth* we are shown a coven of witches who have convened to learn how to work their mischief, and who after having planned Macbeth's destruction adjourn as commanded by their devils and agree to meet again and give "account of their horrible and detestable proceedings passed" (*Daemonologie,* p. 36). Each of these witches has near her one of these devils acting as her private evil spirit, inducing her to do evil and teaching her how and when to do it and transporting her invisibly through the air for this purpose. And when they reconvene in Scene III, each witch makes her report, whereupon they proceed to the adoration of their three little devils by a triple encirclement with obeisances rendered to each as part of a charm round (I, iii, 32). This is as far as William Shakespeare saw fit to go in describing the devil worship which the king has attributed to witches. To learn more of the unpleasant details of this habit of Scotch witches, one may go to page 37 of the *Daemonologie,* after reading which he will agree that the dramatist exercised a wise restraint in his meager showing of devil worship.

James tells that when the compact between the witch and her master is made, the devil shows unto the witch *"a proper name"* by which he must be called (*ibid.,* p. 19). Only when so called will he appear "in likeness of a dog, a cat, an ape, or such like other beast." So we find that throughout the play the three witches are attended by their three devils whose "proper" names are Graymalkin, Paddock, and Harpier, as is clear upon comparing I, i, 8–10, with IV, i, 1–3. And in the last of these we come upon a character neither mute nor unimportant, but not yet set down among the dramatis personae of the play.

Graymalkin, who attends witch number one, is a devil in likeness to a brinded (brindled) cat.

Paddock, who belongs to witch number two, is an urchin or hedgehog. True, the name is usually a nickname for a toad; but this seems not to have been Shakespeare's understanding, for the words "Paddock calls" (I, i, 9) must be equated with the words "the hedge-pig whines" (IV, i, 2). The people of Warwickshire were well acquainted with the dismal night whine of the urchins under their hedges.

Harpier is the leader, the master of the third witch, who delivers the important prophecies. He is a large owl and has a notable part in the play. Examination of this part uncovers a piece of stage business long since lost but which must have been a striking incident of the original performance at Hampton Court. It was intended, like the frequent use of thunder and tempest in the play, to keep the audience conscious of the presence of the evil spirits who are working Macbeth's destruction through the agency of their witches.

Shakespeare was familiar with the seventh book of Ovid's *Metamorphoses,* which tells of Medea's enchantments. In Arthur Golding's translation of this book (ed. of 1593, p. M3v.) he had read of

> . . . a Witch, a cursed odious wight,
> Which in the likeness of an Owl abroad a nights did flie.

Such an owl it is whom Shakespeare calls Harpier, perhaps considering the word as the masculine gender of the name of those evil female birds of prey called Harpies and which are spoken of in the same book of Ovid.* The stage direction, "a shriek like an owl," which marks the first hoot of Harpier has dropped out of the folio text, but it appears at I, i, 8, in Davenant's version of the play written in 1666, and again in the edited text of Shakespeare's play as published by T. J. at the Hague in 1720.†

* In De Loier's *Treatise of Specters* (p. 16v), a book Shakespeare had recently been reading, there is a longer account of this owl followed immediately by an account of the Harpies.

† Folio text:

>   1.   I come Gray-Malkin.
>   All.   Paddock calls anon: faire is foule, and foule is fair.

Hunter's correction followed in modern texts:

>   First Witch.   I come, Graymalkin!
>   Second "   Paddock calls.
>   Third "   Anon.
>   All.   Fair is foul, and foul is fair.

Davenant, 1674:

>   1.   I come gray Malkin. (A Shriek like an Owl.)
>   All.   Paddock calls! To us fair weather's foul,
>   and foul is fair.

T. J., 1720:

>   1 Witch.   I come Gray-Malkin. (A shriek like an owl.)
>   All.   Paddock calls—anon—Fair is foul, and foul is fair.

Hunter's correction assigning "Anon" to the third witch is generally accepted and is obviously right, but it requires a direction giving a call to which "Anon" is the reply. The last two texts supply this call from stage tradition. For considerably more than 100 years this strigine music accompanied the third witch at Drury Lane Theater; and this notwithstanding the radical change in the play when Garrick in 1744 substituted much of Shakespeare's text for Davenant's. In the 1773 edition of the text of *Macbeth* as then played at Drury Lane (in Bell's

When Macbeth, after his soliloquy about the bloody dagger, leaves the hall to go to Duncan's chamber to kill him, there is silence. Suddenly should be again heard the hooting of this owl with the same modulation as when he first called the witches to practice their diabolical art upon Macbeth, thus suggesting that the same witches who were yesterday at Forres are now hovering about the battlements of the fatal castle of Inverness. This is why Lady Macbeth, awaiting her husband's return, says: "Hark! Peace! It was *the owl that shrieked*" (II, ii, 3). And Macbeth too heard it, for as he stumbles in after the murder he says, "Did'st thou not hear a noise?" to which his wife answers, "I heard *the owl scream*."

When Lennox enters the courtyard the morning after the murder, he tells (II, iii, 41) that the obscure bird, meaning the owl, "clamour'd the livelong night," thus implanting in the minds of the audience at Hampton Court a consciousness of the omnipresence of the malign influence which urged Macbeth on to the murder of Duncan.

In order that the dullest of such an audience might not fail to understand the real significance of Harpier's part in the play, the dramatist caused the Old Man in the scene immediately following the murder night to tell Ross:

> On Tuesday last
> A falcon towering in her pride of place
> Was by a mousing owl hawk'd at and kill'd.
> [II, iv, 12]

In Holinshed (*Hist. of Scotland*, p. 152) it was only "a

Shakespeare) there is a plate dated March 1, 1773, showing the caldron scene. The bloody child has risen and Harpier as an owl may be seen hovering over Macbeth and the witches. In the Folger Shakespeare Library are two prompt copies of *Macbeth* as given toward the end of the eighteenth century. One is a prompt book of Drury Lane (ca. 1785) in which the prompter before the third witch's "Anon" has written "owl within"; the other, of later date, shows in the same place "Owl p[rompt] s[ide]." Harpier's shrieks were banished the stage by John Philip Kemble.

sparhawk strangled by an owl." By changing the sparhawk to a "towering falcon," a splendid piece of symbolism was created intended to make it clear that an evil spirit in likeness of an owl with whose hoot they are now familiar, although usually content with lowly prey, had in fact hawked at and killed King Duncan. The hoot of this owl is again appropriately heard at III, ii, 54, just as Banquo is about to be struck down, and finally at IV, ii, 11, when the family of the Thane of Fife are seen in dire jeopardy. The mere recollection of this noise made Macbeth's blood run cold; and he could never forget it, for on the day of his death he says to himself:

> The time has been, my senses would have cool'd
> To hear a night-shriek.
>
> [V, v, 10]

This business of the hooting of the owl has long been lost to our stage, perhaps because although safe enough before a well behaved court audience, it was found risky in a large public theater where, if the audience is unruly, the scene may be ruined by mimicry. But in the Hampton Court performance it no doubt played a notable part. Blackness and blood are the colors of the play. Thunder and the owl's hoot are its music.

A revelation of the demonic philosophy which underlies the play is found in the ferocious soliloquy of Lady Macbeth. As rendered by the modern actress and heard by the modern audience, this gives the impression of a very powerful invocation of evil to nerve the Lady to her murderous purpose, but the precise meaning of the words is blurred and vague and the speech often only a torrent of terrible and wicked words. But for William Shakespeare and the king who was to hear it every word was full of meaning.

The entire soliloquy I, v, 14–53, is a single chain of thought notwithstanding the interruption of the messenger. Her invocation of the powers of evil is consequent upon her husband's lack of the evil qualities which are necessary for the accomplishment of their purposes. His lack of cruelty, due to his milk of human kindness, leads her to fill herself with cruelty and to have her milk taken for gall. His lack of illness (wickedness) must be overcome by her fell purpose. He would act "holily," but she would not allow the spirits of heaven any knowledge of her evil acts. His "nature" would not play false, but she must have "no compunctious visitings of nature." The word "compunctious" (line 44) is of special interest. It seems to have been coined by Shakespeare for this line (see *O.E.D.*) and to have been framed to inform us pointedly that the Lady, as well as her husband, has a sensitive conscience upon which she will make war (note the word "peace") to prevent it from interfering with her plan.

Three different powers are successively invoked and must be distinguished.

a) In lines 39–46 the devils or "spirits" of evil who provoke murderous thoughts are called upon to enter her breast, unsex her, fill her with cruelty, and thicken her blood so that remorse (which here denotes "pity"—see *O.E.D.* 5) shall not shake her fell purpose and prevent her from murdering Duncan, for she then expects to do it herself.

b) In lines 46–49 the "murdering ministers" or slaves of these devils are invoked. These are witches (for they have "substance," which spirits do not have). But this substance is sightless or invisible, because the spirits who carry these witches can make it so. They are called upon to take her evil milk, which will serve as "gall," that is, rancour (*O.E.D.* 3), and so will incite them to "nature's mischief" (the meaning of which is told us in IV, i, 52–60).

c) In I, v, 51, the Spirit of the Night is personified and invoked to hide the deed from the good Spirits of heaven. This is the "Seeling Night" of III, ii, 46. More often in this play such Night spirits are pluralized. They are "Night's black Agents" (III, ii, 53) and are described in II, i, 49–56, and II, iii, 61–65.

The dramatist pictures all of these as accessory to the murder of Duncan. The audience should be acutely conscious of the presence of all.

At the outset of his book the king systematized his subject by making a sharp distinction (p. 7) between "Magie or Necromancie" and "Sorcerie or Witch-craft," devoting his first book to necromancy and his second to sorcery. Philomathes asks the difference between these arts, and Epistemon, from whose mouth we receive the wisdom of the king, replies (p. 9):

Surelie, the difference vulgare put betwixt them, is verrie merrie, and in a manner true; for they say, that the Witches ar servants onelie, and slaves to the Devil; but the Necromanciers are his maisters and commanders.

Shakespeare meticulously observes the king's distinction. All that happens in the witch scenes of Act I is sorcery, and throughout these scenes the witches as servants respond to the calls of the devils who are their masters, and make their obeisances to them; but in Act IV, Scene I, everything is technical necromancy in which the devils, and also the witches, answer the conjuration and obey the commands of the necromancer Macbeth, who, having given his soul to the devil (III, i, 67), is their master.

Quoting again from the dialogue (pp. 7–8):

PHILOMATHES. What I pray you? and how manie are the meanes, whereby the Devill allures persons in anie of these snares?
EPISTEMON. Even by these three passiones that are within our selves: Curiositie in great ingines: thrist of revenge, for some tortes deeply apprehended: or greedie appetite of geare, caused

through great povertie. As to the first of these, Curiositie, it is onelie the inticement of *Magiciens,* or *Necromanciers:* and the other two are the allureres of the *Sorcerers,* or *Witches* . . .

Shakespeare observes this distinction as to motive. Macbeth, who is a "great ingine," is filled with curiosity. His "heart throbs to know one thing" (IV, i, 100) and hence the necromantic feats and the "sight" of the procession of the kings. But the motive of the witches throughout the play is "thrist of revenge, for some tortes deeply apprehended." A minor instance of this is the grudge of the first witch against the chestnut muncher who withheld her chestnuts and drove the witch away notwithstanding her "greedy appetite for gear." The reason for the witches' "thrist of revenge" against Macbeth is so important that it must be more fully examined in another chapter (see p. 292).

In calling the demonology of the play Jacobean, it is not meant to imply that William Shakespeare made no use of current English notions on this subject with which he was perfectly familiar.

As an example of this, in all ages the superstition of sorcery and magic has been accompanied by a predilection for odd numbers ("Numero deus impare gaudet," Virgil, Eclogue VIII, line 75) especially for the number three, or for three times three, and this has produced a demoniacal numeration not to be found in the ordinary arithmetics. The witch always uses some circumlocution to avoid the naming of an even number. I do not know that this superstition has ever been traced to its origin, which is probably lost in the mists of antiquity. It is not much dwelt upon by the writers on demonology. It is not developed in the king's book, for it is what King James contemptuously called a "freit," being classified by him among the "rudiments" of the devil's teachings or "such kind of charms as commonly dafte wives use"; but William Shakespeare was keenly conscious of these foolish notions. He no doubt learned them in his Warwickshire childhood. The witches' method of counting plays a considerable part in the play of *Macbeth.*

There are three witches and correspondingly three devils. The lines abound with triplets: the witches meet "In thunder, lightning or in rain"; the sailor's wife "munch'd, and munch'd, and munch'd"; the first witch warns, "I'll do, I'll do, and I'll do." When the first witch threatens the master of the *Tiger,* she predicts:

> Weary sen'nightes nine times nine
> Shall he dwindle peak and pine.

The sisters' charm to induce their imps to help them destroy Macbeth involves a ceremony of obeisance to their three devils which causes them to use a triple triplet; for the sisters

> Thus do go, about, about,
> Thrice to thine, and thrice to mine,
> And thrice again, to make up nine.
> [I, iii, 34–36]

Which means that the trio thrice encircle and thrice bow to each of the three imps.

In the necromantical scene (IV, i, 1) Graymalkin mews thrice. Paddock breaks the rule by whining four times, but this bad omen is overcome by the witch by announcing that the "Hedge-pigge" has whined "thrice, and once." Notice the way in which the comma of the folio text splits the count into odd numbers. Our modern texts by discarding the comma have lost this important implication.

The toad has slept under his cold stone for thirty-one days and nights (IV, i, 6). The witches' sow has eaten her nine farrow (IV, i, 64). There are three apparitions, the first and second of which each hail Macbeth three times and the necromancer accordingly wishes he had three ears (IV, i, 78).

The commentators give apposite references to parallel this magical numeration, but I doubt that it is connected with

them. Of course, the adoption by the dramatist of this common superstition is not accidental, but neither is it calculated. It seems rather to be instinctive and the result of
some boyhood association with these numerical tricks.
Neither Scot nor King James enlarges upon this. If we are
to search for a source, the most probable is in Ovid's *Metamorphoses* where Medea, in preparation for the rejuvenation
of Aeson's father, adjures the stars:

> Ter se convertit; ter sumptis flumine crinem
> Irroravit aquis; Ternis ululatibus ora solvit.
>   [VII, 189]

Golding thus translates:

She lifting up her hands did thrice her selfe incline,
And thrice with water of the brooke hir hair besprinkled shee:
And gaping thrice she opte her mouth.

Immediately follows her invocation of the spirits of nature
which is found quoted in *The Tempest*. As Shakespeare
knew these lines, we may be warranted in classing Ovid as one
of the sources of the necromantic scene.

In another respect the dramatist in writing *Macbeth* pictured English witches rather than Scotch. Always in England
witches have been lean, foul, bearded old women, and no
doubt William Shakespeare in Warwickshire had seen such
creatures who were reputed to be witches. But according to
King James, Scotch witches were not so. The king had sent
for and personally examined a large number of Scotch
women accused of witchcraft and had found them comely
and well conditioned. In his *Daemonologie* (p. 30) he states:

. . . a great number of them that ever have bene convict or
confessors of Witchcraft . . . are, by the contrarie I say, some
of them rich and worldly-wise, some of them fatte or corpulent in
their bodies, and most part of them altogether given over to the

pleasures of the flesh, continual haunting of companie, and all kind of merrines, both lawfull and unlawfull.

The dramatist felt that his play would be more effective if he held to the English view. Consequently, in Act I his witches are withered, with chappy fingers, skinny lips, and beards, and in Act IV they are "secret, black, and midnight hags," and again, "filthy hags."

Notwithstanding instances where such influences are traceable, it nevertheless remains true that the ideas about devils, witches, and necromancers which Shakespeare has put into his play of *Macbeth* are those set forth by King James in his *Daemonologie*.

THE NECROMANTIC SCENE

The scene of necromancy is the first scene of the fourth act. I believe that it was written before the scenes of sorcery in the first act. The play then probably began at I, iii, 39. This scene will be examined first, and the initial step must be definition of the text of the scene when the king saw it.

The play contains 48 lines which have been subsequently added to it, and not by Shakespeare. They are the Hecate scene (III, v) containing 36 lines; and of the necromantic scene (IV, i) lines 39 to 43, and 125 (from "But why") to and including 132, with the accompanying stage directions.

None of these lines were written by Shakespeare. When the king saw the play performed, there was no Hecate, no "other three witches," and no songs and no music; for these incongruous things were put into the play five or six years later, probably by Thomas Middleton, and therefore are here called "Middletonian" lines. The scene was far more impressive without them, for Shakespeare's wicked old hags had neither voices nor joints that could sing or dance; and Hecate's words are utterly inconsistent with, and ruinous to, the main motive of the play. Adams's remarks about these lines in his edition cannot be improved upon. He omits them from his text of the play. Chambers, in his Warwick Shakespeare, marks them off from the rest of the text by brackets. This has already been referred to on pages 71 and 72, where part of the Shakespearean text has been printed with excision of the Middletonian lines.

These added lines are written in an iambic meter and not in the trochaic tetrameter of the rest of the witch verses. The rhythms do not mix well and jar. Also, the subject matter of the Middletonian lines conflicts with Shakespeare's lines and with King James's book. Shakespeare's old hags could not "sing like elves and fairies in a ring." That they should wish to cheer up the spirits of their enemy Macbeth by an "antic round" is an absurdity. These lines were written so that the play might include the songs and dances which Middleton had previously written for his discarded play of *The Witch*. As many recent authorities agree in substance to this, it is not here further discussed. It is sufficient to refer to Dr. Bradley's pronouncement (Note Z, p. 466, in his *Shakespearean Tragedy*) and the discussions in the editions of the play edited by M. H. Liddell, J. Q. Adams, E. K. Chambers, T. M. Parrott, and C. H. Herford. The lines should be banished from our texts, and would be but that chronic illnesses are hard to cure.

The interpolation of the Hecate scene (III, v) by Thomas Middleton required that there should be a contrasting scene between it and the scene of necromancy. Consequently, the interpolator took the short scene which is now III, vi, from its rightful place following the necromantic scene and put it in front of it, with very confusing results. Sufficient attention has not been given to this transposition. Dr. H. H. Furness, Jr., adverts to it in the New Variorum (1903 ed. of *Macbeth*, p. 236) but hesitates to accept it because of the interrogation in III, vi, 23–24. But the interrogation is purely ironical, as is all the rest of the speech. Lennox knows that Macduff has fled to England but is cautiously trying to find out whether the other lord knows this, and what he thinks about it, for Lennox is already engaged in the task of inducing the revolt of the thanes.

That the scene III, vi, must have been written to follow IV, i, is clear. After the guests leave the banquet, Macbeth, knowing that his thanes are now sure of his guilt, says he will visit the sisters early the following day (III, iv, 133). He has not yet summoned Macduff but will do so (III, iv, 130). In III, vi, Macduff has received his summons, rejected it, has fled to the English court, and word of his reception there has come back to Scotland. There is no time for all this before Macbeth's visit to the witches' house. At the end of IV, i, word is dramatically brought that "Macduff is fled to England." This is wholly out of place if occurring after "another Lord" in Scotland knows both of the flight and its results. As this scene is now placed, the talk between Lennox and another lord must occur on the day following the banquet, at which time Macbeth has been guilty of no other murders than those of Duncan and Banquo; but lines 34–35 of this scene imply the bloody tyranny of the last two acts of the play. This was all clearly seen by P. A. Daniel years ago, and in his "Time Analysis" he reached the conclusion that the scene "is an impossibility in any scheme of time"; consequently, although it plays well, the scene is omitted from the stage versions; and Adams rejects it from his recent text. These difficulties are eliminated by the transposition,* and a very interesting scene, showing how the defection of Macbeth's thanes was brought about, is recaptured. Lennox was shocked by what had occurred at the banquet and skillfully plants seeds of revolt among the Scottish lords by his veiled ironical speeches, thus leading up to V, ii, where we next find him directing the march of the revolting thanes toward Birnam.

After retrieving the original text, the next question is: Where is the scene laid? Because no scene heading is given in the folio, there is misapprehension about its locality, due to the influence of the Middletonian lines. In Davenant's version of the play (1674) the scene is in "a cave," undoubtedly an inference from Hecate's reference to "the pit of Acheron" (III, v, 15); but as Hecate's words were not written by William Shakespeare, they should have no weight in determining his intent. Nevertheless the cave has become a

---

* The use in III, vi, 19, of "heaven" instead of "God" also indicates that the scene was written after IV, i (see infra p. 313).

fixed tradition. The picture of the caldron scene in Rowe's Shakespeare of 1709 shows this cave, and the scene heading added by Rowe calls it "a dark cave." This is followed in the T. J. edition of 1711, and by Pope and Theobald, and has produced the "cavern" of our modern texts.

But this does not accord with the Shakespearean text in which, as Macbeth approaches, the second witch calls out, "Open locks, whoever knocks," implying a locked door. Later, Macbeth calls to Lennox, "Come in, without there." What follows sounds like the passage of horsemen and their recall to the door of a house outside which Lennox had been keeping watch. That this was Shakespeare's intent is the more probable because the deviltry of the Forres witches of whom Holinshed tells occurs in "a house in Fores." Shakespeare's scene of enchantment then should be laid in a ruinous but securely locked old house somewhere in the town of Forres.

To understand this scene the first step is to know who are the "masters" referred to in line 63. G. L. Kittredge (*Macbeth*, p. 188) says they are the "great powers of fate whom the sisters serve." I know of no demonology which recognizes any such mastery. Certainly Jacobean demonology does not. According to the king's book, witches are slaves of "the devil their master." In his Address to the Reader the king tells that "witches can, by the power of their master," perform certain things (p. xiii), which he explains it is "verie possible to the Devil their master to do" (p. 47).

In the demonology taught in the book of King James, a first principle is that both learned and unlearned persons may sell their souls to the devil. The learned who are magicians or necromancers ("the most curious sort") by their compact are given power to command the devil for a term of years, at the end of which they must pay the forfeit. The unlearned (or "baser sort" as James calls them) are witches or wizards, and these by their compact agree to serve the devil as their master who in return agrees to attend them, but only to perform certain minor services. In the end they too forfeit their souls. As to all this, King James is very explicit. He says (p. 9) "the Witches ar servantes onelie, and slaues to the Devils; but the Necromanciers are his maisters and commanders." This distinction Shakespeare has carefully followed. Consequently, throughout the play the devils are the masters of the ignorant witches; but the learned conjurer and necromancer is the master of the devils and has power to command them.

This is fundamental and is the key to the meaning of this scene.

Macbeth is a conjurer. The word "conjure" in line 50 carries an accent on the first syllable. He pronounces his conjuration and commands the witches to answer "howe'er you come to know it," that is, even though you obtain your information from your devils. He has given his eternal jewel "to the common enemy of man" (III, i, 69). That is, he has sold his soul to the devil (V, viii, 14, 19) and in return he is master and the devil must serve him for a time. The witches' "charms," on the contrary, are only persuasive or enticing with their masters the devils, and not compelling, as are the commands of the conjurer.

If the witches are mastered by fate, the scene is insipid and meaningless; but if one understands that it is a scene of demonology and that the law of mastery as above laid down rules, the entire scene is found to be luminous and highly dramatic.

Macbeth and the witches are at cross-purposes. Macbeth as a conjurer and master of devils has power to demand from them knowledge of the future that he may overcome his enemy Macduff; and if his question be properly propounded the devil must answer it. The witches acknowledge this power and promise to answer him after he has made his demand (IV, i, 61). But the demand must come first, and the witches intend if possible to thwart this. They have prepared "a powerful charm" to persuade their devils to destroy Macbeth and not to give him helpful information as he will conjure them to do; for even though slaves, yet they may so "charm" their devils as to obtain their aid. Macbeth, intending to command the devils to answer him, enters, treats the witches scornfully, and asks what they are doing. They evade by answering "a deed without a name." Macbeth thereupon pronounces his conjuration. The first apparition rises, but before he can propound his demand (see line 69), the first witch checks his question by calling out, "He knows thy thought: Hear his speech, but say thou naught." Three times is interrogation thus checked, the last time only by the combined efforts of all three witches (see line 89). As a result, no demand having been propounded by the conjurer, the devils are not bound to tell Macbeth the truth but are free to respond to the witches' charm and deceive him. Speaking through the mouths of the three apparitions, they gain his confidence, flatter him, and mislead him, so that he believes himself to be invulnerable. He went to the witches "to know the worst" about Macduff's disloyalty. His question has not been asked. But the devils, charmed by the witches, have shown themselves and their office (line 68) and have uttered "things part true, part false" (*Daemonologie*, p. 22), which will destroy him. The charm has served its purpose and the conjurer has been thwarted; and it has been done "deftly" (IV, i, 68), a word which has troubled some of the commentators. The word is Shakespeare's synonym for "with agility," a phrase several times used by James in his book to describe how devils carry out their operations. (See, for example, its use in the sentence quoted below.) Unless the devils had worked deftly, the conjurer would have been able to propound his question and the charm of the witches would have been in vain. This is what the demonology of the scene means, and so understood, much that is otherwise enigmatic or meaningless (for necromancy is a totally forgotten science) becomes full of meaning and the scene is found to be in complete harmony with the main dramatic theme of the play.

I doubt that this can be understood by a modern audience; but I do not doubt that the King's Company could and did make it all perfectly clear to James, conversant as he was with the mysteries of this recondite science of demonology. For the dramatist has been at pains to closely follow the technicalities laid down in the king's book concerning "Magie and Necromancie"; how closely may be understood by comparing what the king says in Chapter VI of Book I of his *Daemonologie* with lines 62 to 68 of this scene. In this short chapter, after reference to those "whether learned or unlearned" who practice this black art, we read (pp. 19–22):

From time that they once plainelie begin to contract with him [the devil]: The effect of their contract consistes in two thinges; in formes and effectes, . . . by formes, I meane in what shape or fashion he shall come unto them, when they call upon him. And by effectes, I understand, in what special sorts of services he bindes himselfe to be subject unto them. The qualitie of these formes and effectes, is lesse or greater, according to the skil and art of the *Magician*. For as to the formes, to some of the baser sorte of them he oblishes himselfe to appeare at their calling upon him, by such a proper name which he shewes unto them, either in likenes of a dog, a Catte, an Ape, or such-like other beast; or else to answere by a voyce onlie. The effects are to answere to such demands, as concernes curing of disseases, their own particular menagery: or such other base things as they require of him. But to the most curious sorte, in the formes he will oblish himselfe, to enter in a dead bodie, and there out of to give such answers, of the event of battels, of maters concerning the estate of commonwelths, and such like other great questions: . . . they abuse the simplicitie of these wretches, that becomes their schollers, that they make them beleeve, that at the fall of *Lucifer,* some Spirites fell in the aire, some in the fire, some in the water, some in the lande: In which Elementes they still remaine. Whereupon they build, that such as fell in the fire, or in the aire, are truer then they, who fell in the water or in the land, which is

al but meare trattles, & forged be the author of al deceit. . . .
But to return to the purpose, as these formes, wherein Sathan
oblishes himselfe to the greatest of the *Magicians,* are wounder-
full curious; so are the effectes correspondent unto the same: For
he will oblish himselfe to teach them artes and sciences, which
he may easelie doe, being so learned a knave as he is: To carrie
them newes from anie parte of the worlde which the agilitie of a
Spirite may easelie performe: to reveale to them the secretes of
anie persons. . . . Yea, he will make his schollers to creepe in
credite with Princes, by fore-telling them manie great thinges;
parte true, parte false: For if all were false, he would tyne credite
at all handes; but alwaies doubtsome, as his Oracles were.

Shakespeare has built directly upon this formal Jacobean
demonology. The witches being "of the baser sort," the
scene begins with the cries of the devils, and the leader is
called by his "proper name." By Harpier's cry the witches
know that it is time to make of their hell broth a "charm of
powerful trouble" to induce the devils to deceive Macbeth,
instead of answering questions "of the event of battles and the
estate of commonwealths" which they expect him to ask.
When Macbeth appears and pronounces his conjuration, their
first question is, "Say if thou'dst rather hear it from our
mouths, or from our masters?" using the technical term to
express the relation of devil to witch. If he will be satisfied
with the witches' answers, deception will be easy. But Macbeth, sensing this, calls for the devils. His answer is cast in
a contemptuous tone, "Call 'em: Let me see 'em," for the
conjurer despises ignorant witches and the base imps of
sorcery. There had been going on when the play was written, for well nigh a hundred years, a controversy among
theologians as to whether King Saul actually saw the spirit
of the dead prophet Samuel or whether the Witch of Endor
only told him what she had seen and what the prophet said.
James in his book considers this (pp. 3–4) and gives reasons
for his belief that Saul had really seen the spirit. To avoid
any such uncertainty, Macbeth demands sight of them.

Thereupon the witches solemnly chant: "Come, high or low; Thyself and office deftly show!"   According to James the high spirits in air or fire were considered truer than the low spirits in water or earth.   James calls this "mere trattles," but, high or low, they are summoned.   James tells repeatedly that the witches' contract consists in *"formes* and *effectes,"* that is, as he explains, the *"shape"* in which the spirit shall come and the *"service"* he must render.   This is why the devils must show *"self* and *office"* (shape and service, forms and effects).   Macbeth being a conjurer of the "most curious sort," necromancy is in order.   Each devil must "enter in a dead body" and thereout give answers to the "great questions" he wishes to ask.   Thus the scene becomes one of necromancy or "prophecy by the dead . . . because it is a principal part of that art to serve themselves with dead carcages in their divinations" (*Daemonologie,* p. 9).   So there successively appear the dissevered head, the bloody child, and the crowned child, from the mouths of which Macbeth was entitled to know of the progress of Macduff's conspiracy and how to thwart it, but by the witches' guile he hears only "doubtsome oracles" which put him off his guard and result in his destruction.

This scene was written, as I think, after the subsidence of the fervor which produced the first three acts of the play, for it is more studiously and artfully constructed.   Therefore it may be profitable to examine it in further detail.

a) *The Witches' Charm.*   This occupies lines 1 to 38.   At the beginning of the scene all three witches are present, each accompanied by her little devil in the form of cat, urchin, and owl which mew, whine, or hoot the requisite number of times to satisfy the requirements of the opening lines.   The imps remain watching the huge three-legged bronze caldron and gloat increasingly over the mixture it contains as the witches stir the caldron with their sticks and fetch their filthy treasures from a cupboard in the rear of the room.   The charm is

the secret of whatever influence the witch has over her master
imp.   James in his Preface said that he would pretermit to
tell "the secrets of these unlawful arts"; therefore Shakespeare was compelled to go elsewhere for suggestions—so far
as he needed them—concerning the "poisoned entrails"
which make the bubbling charm "firm and good."   The first
thing the witches put into their caldron was a

> Toad, that under cold stone,
> Days and nights, has thirty-one:
> Sweltered venom sleeping got.

This was of particular interest to King James, for in 1590
Agnis Tompson, one of the Scotch witches, confessed in the
king's presence that by the devil's persuasion she had tried to
bewitch him to death, and for this purpose "she took a blacke
Toade, and did hang the same up by the heeles, three daies,
and collected and gathered the venome as it dropped" (*News
from Scotland*, p. 16 of the reprint).

For further suggestion the dramatist went to Ovid, where
he found lists of the ingredients which Tisiphone, the avenging Fury, had cooked in her caldron (*Metamorphoses* iv. 504),
and also of those which Medea, the witch, gathered to renew
old Aeson (*Ibid.* vii. 262).   Ovid's "validum posito medica-
men aheno fervet et exultat" may be translated: "a powerful
drug boils and bubbles in the caldron."

This was first noticed by Upton (*Critical Observations on
Shakespeare*, 1746, p. 51).   His note 14 is well worth reading.
Ovid's lines above referred to are near to other lines which
appear in *The Tempest* (IV, i, 128).   Ovid has put into
Medea's caldron the fillet of the fenny snake and the owl's
wing; but the resemblance is not so much in the names of the
ingredients, for Shakespeare invented most of these, as in the
ghoulish descriptions.   A satisfactory comment on Shakespeare's charm lines is found in Upton's work above cited,
even though now two hundred years old:

There is such a cast of antiquity, and something so horridly solemn in this infernal ceremony of the witches, that I never consider it without admiring our poet's improvement of every hint he received from the ancients or moderns.

If we more modern moderns cannot bring ourselves into sympathy with this (and many cannot), it is our misfortune.

At the end of line 38, in which is the announcement of the second witch that "the charm is firm and good," she continues (omitting the interruption by the Middletonian intrusion):

> By the Pricking of my thumbs
> Something wicked this way comes.
> Open locks, whoever knocks!

No printed source for this has been discovered. It does not come from Reginald Scot nor from the king's book. But Joseph Glanvil, one of the last of the defenders of sorcery, had in his possession an original transcript of the proceedings in the Scottish Trials of 1590 which passed to the hands of Glanvil's editor, Henry More. It contained an account of the devil's "opening locks by sorcery, as one by mere blowing into a woman's hand while she sate by the fire" (*Sadducismus Triumphatus*, 1726 ed., p. 397). Evidently the connection of pricking thumbs with opening locks was veritable Scotch sorcery.* These four doggerel lines are sometimes attributed to Middleton; but they are not in Middleton's verse. They are Shakespearean verse and serve well to show the anxiety of the witch that Macbeth may come while the charm is in full force and, as she hopes, thus put himself in the witches' power that they may work their revenge.

b) The conjuration occupies lines 50 to 68. In interpreting it, we will go astray if we follow popular ideas concerning

---

* See Spalding's *Elizabethan Demonology* p. 113, n. 3. Blowing into a woman's hand suggests the pricking thumbs of the witch. Scot's charm for opening locks (Bk. XII, Chap. XIV) is quite unsuggestive of Shakespeare's idea.

conjuration instead of the teachings of the *Daemonologie*. We are apt to think of a conjurer as summoning the devil by the use of circles, ceremonies, and magical formulae (see, for example, *Henry VI, Part 2*, I, iv, 25). But according to James's book (Chaps. III–V) such things are only used in the "Divil's school," where the learned are first led "to seeke that black and unlawful science of Magie" (p. 10). As soon as they have attained knowledge of this black art, they become "weery of raising of their Maister by confused circles" and "come plainlie to a contract with him." Macbeth has graduated from the "Divil's school," and as the result of "a plain contract" has become a master conjurer who can command the devil without ceremony. No "conjured circles" are necessary. His commands must be obeyed. The devil must serve him for a time, after which Macbeth must yield himself to the devil, who will destroy him body and soul.

The play records the making of this contract (III, i, 68), for Macbeth states that he has given his "eternal jewel to the common enemy of man." And immediately following this, Macbeth proceeds to announce and use the power which it confers upon him. The devil must help him in the use of destruction to the uttermost, if necessary, to attain his ends. Under no circumstances must the seeds of Banquo obtain the imperial power in Scotland, which he covets for himself and his expected issue. Rather than so, must fate (destruction) be his champion.* He has destroyed Duncan. He will de-

---

* This sentence (III, i, 71–72) was misinterpreted for a century and a half under the unfortunate influence of a note by Dr. Johnson. The New Variorum cites this note and paraphrases the sentence, "let fate enter the lists *against* me." The Clarendon editors follow suit, although they state, "This seems to be the only known passage in which the verb [champion] is used in this sense." The fact is that no authority for such an unusual interpretation has ever been found. Matthias Mull (*Macbeth* [London, 1889], p. lxxxv) seems to have been the first bravely to attempt to overthrow this weight of authority.

Liddell in 1903 strongly opposed Dr. Johnson's construction, saying: "The phraseology of this passage and the use of 'me' after 'champion' make it scarcely possible that the modern [i.e., Dr. Johnson's] con-

stroy Banquo and Fleance and all others who stand in his path. "Things bad begun make strong themselves with ill" (III, ii, 55).

The conjurer therefore commands the devil to answer the question he expects to ask even though all manner of destruction follow (IV, i, 50–61), even his own destruction or "wracke," which is the contract price which he expects to pay. When he comes to pay this, he exclaims, "Blow wind, come, wrack."

The witches call upon him to "Speak," "Demand," that is, propound the question; and promise to answer it. The witches' powers being derived solely from their devils, Macbeth requires these devils to be produced to his sight (IV, i, 61–63). Thereupon the apparitions rise; but by the deft strategy of the witches, Macbeth having been restrained from making his demand, the apparitions are free to deceive him and proceed to do so.

c) *The Three Apparitions.* Lines 69 to 100. "Apparition" is the technical name for the spirit which the magician summons, in this case the devils who tend upon the three witches and who are the sources of their foreknowledge; and because Macbeth is a conjurer of the "most curious sort" (*Daemonologie,* p. 20), they appear in dead bodies to pronounce their oracles. There were two schools among the Protestant writers on necromancy. One held that the devil only took the *form* of a dead person, and the other held that the devil exhumed actual dead bodies, entered them, and spoke from the dead lips. King James in his book supported

struction 'fight *against* me to the uttermost' was the one which an Elizabethan audience would put upon Shakespeare's words. . . . There can be little doubt that Macbeth means that fate is to be *his* champion." Parrott in 1904 interprets "Macbeth calls upon fate or death, to enter the lists as *his* champion against Banquo." Cunningham takes the same position. When thus properly interpreted, Macbeth requires destruction to enable him to attain his ends and this is just what the play discloses.

the latter view (pp. 41 and 59). Therefore we must assume
that Shakespeare intended his audience to view the armed
head, bloody child, and crowned child as actual dead bodies
from the mouths of which the devils spoke, the last two being
presumably exhumed bodies of unbaptized infants such as
are graphically described in lines 30–31 of the same scene.

There is a definite dramatic progression in the pronouncements of the devils. To gain Macbeth's confidence, the first
devil, speaking from an armed "rebellious head," bids him
beware Macduff. *Rebellious head* is the proper reading of
line 97. The folio reading is "Rebellious dead," which needs
to have one letter changed. Modern texts generally make
greater changes which are not necessary. *Rebellious head* is
but a description of the armed head of the stage direction
following line 68, in which "head" carries additionally the
Shakespearean sense of "a force raised in insurrection" (see
O.E.D., Head, 30). To overcome the fear created by the
armed head, the second devil assures him that "none of
woman born shall harm Macbeth." To strengthen this com-
forting assurance, the wily witch assures him that the second
devil is "more potent than the first." But this is not enough,
as lines 83 to 86 disclose, and so the third devil caps the pronouncement of the second by the assurance that Macbeth
"shall never vanquished be until Great Birnam wood" shall
come to Dunsinane. As this seems impossible, we find Macbeth now fully assured of his supposed invulnerability, and
neglectful of his enemies because convinced that he will die
a natural death. This confidence leads him to glory in his
newly acquired infernal power and to talk of "our high-
placed Macbeth." The Clarendon editors, echoed by many
later commentators, remark that "our" seems strange in Macbeth's mouth. But read what James says about would-be
conjurers attending the devil's school who

seeke to that black and unlawful science of *Magie.* Where, finding at the first, that such divers formes of circles & conjurations

rightlie joyned thereunto, will raise such divers formes of spirites, to resolve them of their doubts: and attributing the doing thereof, to the power inseparablie tyed, or inherent in the circles: and manie words of God, confusedlie wrapped in; they blindlie glorie of themselves, as if they had by their quicknes of ingine, made a conquest of *Plutoes* dominion, and were become Emperours over the *Stygian* habitacles [*Daemonologie*, pp. 10–11].

Macbeth's royal plural is the language of the infernal emperor addressing his devilish legions, who may well call himself "our high-placed Macbeth"—a strange phrase indeed, except as written by one who had just been reading the book of the king and who therefore adopted the king's strange thought.

d) The Sight of the Kings. Lines 100 to 125. If Macbeth is to die a natural death, who will reign in Scotland after he is dead? Will the issue of Banquo succeed him? This is the dynastic question—the "imperial theme" with which the drama opens. It is never absent from Macbeth's mind. He succeeds in pronouncing this question notwithstanding the protests of all three witches. They must answer if they can tell so much. Hautboys sound and the caldron sinks. Threatened by Macbeth's curse and knowing that their devils cannot produce the issue of Banquo, they resort to a different procedure and show him not apparitions but "a sight." The way in which this is managed is admirable and founded upon a distinction emphasized by King James, and, I believe, in part of the king's own invention. Only a year before the play was written the king had been greatly interested in certain "sights" which had been seen by people in the north of England—armies of horsemen fighting in the air and accompanied by the sounds of battle. This diabolical appearance was disproved by the verdict of the Cambridge doctors who found it due to the overactive imaginations of Frances and Beatrice. (See supra pp. 114–116.)

So in the *Daemonologie* (p. 22) after telling how the devil reveals wonderful secrets and produces strange things "according to the skil and art of the Magician," the king next tells of certain wonderful things which "the greatest of the Magicians" can make visible which are but "impressions in the air."

He will guard his schollers with faire armies of horsemen and foote-men in appearance, castles and fortes: Which all are but impressiones in the aire, easelie gathered by a spirite, drawing so neare to that substance himselfe: . . . And yet are all these thinges but deluding of the senses, and no waies true in substance, . . .

So there were not really any kings in the procession. It was not an apparition, but merely a "show" or "sight," as Macbeth twice calls it—an impression in the air, shown to the eyes, deluding the senses, but nonexistent.

In truth, the subtlety of this part of the king's philosophy leads easily to Shakespeare's more modern view that such phenomena are wholly due to the imagination. For "impressions in the air caused by evil spirits" substitute "impressions in the mind caused by evil thoughts," and you have defined accurately the step which William Shakespeare was asking his king to take.

e) Macbeth's Disillusionment. Lines 133 to 156. His words are: "Let this pernicious hour stand aye accursed in the calendar!" and "damned all those that trust them." And yet he trusts them to the end, for his conscience is "cauterized," burnt out, dead. In his *Daemonologie* (pp. 6–7) the king declares that for a magician to contract with the devil when he knows that he wrongs his conscience is to be deemed the sin against the Holy Ghost. Thus do necromancers "become in verie deed bondslaves to their mortal enemy" (p. 11).

So does this necromantic scene picture with fearful earnestness the tragedy which results from the choice of evil instead of good as the end of human life; and thus has the dramatist converted what might have been a mere spectacle into a scene which interprets the great theme propounded at the opening of the drama where foul is pronounced fair. The result is a scene which has never been matched as a picture of enchantment. To deal seriously with this subject was a some-what dangerous matter. Marlowe was the first to attempt it in his *Doctor Faustus*. In Shakespeare's *Second Part of Henry VI* and in Greene's *Friar Bungay* there are scenes of conjuration, but in both the subject is treated with levity or contempt. In *Macbeth* for the first time on the English stage necromancy was given a full and serious setting. Shakespeare relied upon the interest of the king to protect him against those who might feel that to show such things was either wicked or at least unwise; for the king had given to these things a significance and meaning quite different from the popular view, and this significance is implicit throughout the play of *Macbeth*.

SORCERY IN MACBETH

After writing the scene of necromancy, the dramatist thought it best to add, as prelude to his play, a scene of sorcery. It occupies all of Scene I and the first thirty-seven lines of Scene III of the first act. The chief sources used were the King's *Daemonologie* and Holinshed's *History*. The play therefore opens with the three witches, accompanied by their three little devils, exulting because "fair is foul and foul is fair," and plotting to destroy Macbeth.

Why did the witches wish to destroy Macbeth? The dramatist does not answer this question directly. He assumes that his Scottish audience knows that the evil witches of Forres are always on the side of the rebellious Islesmen, and therefore side with the "merciless Macdonwald" in his fight against the King of Scotland which, when the play opens, has just ended in his slaughter by Macbeth. Obviously, therefore, they may be expected to seek revenge against Macbeth for this. They are to meet again,

> When the hurly burly's done,
> When the battle's lost, and won.

Two fights were involved in the day's hurly burly. From the witches' point of view the first has been *lost* when Macdonwald was slain by Macbeth. The second is the fight against the foreign invaders, and this will be *won* when they are driven into the sea later on the same day. The meaning of these lines has been lost because our texts always remove the emphasizing antithetical comma * which Shakespeare put after the word "lost." Restore the folio text and the meaning becomes sufficiently evident.

* See Percy Simpson's *Shakespearian Pronunciation*, p. 29.

A few lines later (I, ii, 11) the play affords further evidence that the witches of Forres are on the side of the rebel Macdonwald. To get the full force of this one must have a sense of the atmosphere of Scotland as King James pictures it in his *Daemonologie* and as the dramatist has reproduced it in his play.

The opening words of the King's Preface to the Reader are these:

The fearefull aboundinge at this time in this countrie, of these detestable slaues of the Deuill, the Witches or enchaunters, hath moved me (beloued reader) to dispatch in post, this following treatise of mine [p. 2].

These witches, or slaves of the devil, who so fearfully abound in Scotland are according to James transported by the devil invisibly from place to place in the air (*Daemonologie*, pp. 38–39). This is why the air of Scotland is "filthy" (I, ii, 11) or "infected" (IV, i, 138); for this multitude of evil spirits who carry these witches as the "instruments" or "ministers" to work their mischief or villainy, swarm everywhere in the air.

This thought several times emerges in the play. The witches hover through the air (I, i, 11) and are "posters of the sea and land" (I, iii, 54). They vanish into the air "as breath into the wind" (I, iii, 82) and they "make themselves air" (I, v, 4). Lady Macbeth addresses them when she says:

Come to my woman's breasts,
And take my milk for gall, you murdering ministers,
Wherever in your sightless substances *
You wait on nature's mischief!

[I, v, 48–51]

Nature's mischief is defined by Macbeth in his conjuration (IV, i, 50–60) where he enumerates the fearful powers of destruction which the witches profess to possess.

* The "substance" or physical body of the witch, who waits (hovering in the air) on nature's mischief, is "sightless," i.e., invisible.

With this picture of Scotland in mind, consider what the bleeding sergeant means when he says that the merciless Macdonwald was worthy to be a rebel because "the multiplying Villanies of Nature doe swarm upon him." Surely these are the same creatures which Lady Macbeth calls the "murdering ministers" that wait on Nature's mischief and which so abound in the air of Scotland that it is filthy. They are witches transported by their devils, swarming about Macdonwald and inciting him to rebel against his king and quick to avenge his death when he is slain by Macbeth. The play is almost wholly concerned with showing how they accomplish this, and it is important that we should be told at the outset of the origin of this vengeance.

A long succession of editors, who it would seem have not carefully read the *Daemonologie* of King James, tell us that these Villanies of Nature are only the villainies of Macdonwald's nature, thus wholly missing the poet's effort to tell us at the beginning of his play that the witches of Forres with their little devils swarm about the rebel as he fights with Macbeth so that we may know why they wreak their vengeance upon Macbeth after he unseamed the rebel from the nave to the chaps.

In writing these scenes of sorcery, Shakespeare fell naturally into the same characteristic meter which he has used in the charm verses of the necromancy scene. Technically it is trochaic tetrameter catalectic. It is better described as a seven-syllable verse, stressed on the first rather than the second syllable of each foot, and used with the freedom of doggerel in a way characteristic of a child's mind and therefore peculiarly suited to form the speech of ignorant witches. Nothing can be more ill judged than the efforts of versifiers to "rectify" these lines, whereby the wild and primitive effects are lost. It is noticeable that when using this meter Shakespeare confines himself to words of the ancient time. He uses it to express childlike thoughts of ignorance or rusticity or antiquity, as in the fairies' songs in *Midsummer Night's Dream,* or the scroll rhymes in the *Merchant of Venice,* and Orlando's verses in *As You Like It.* His use of it is not studied but intuitive, with much disregard of rule, just as he had used it when a boy with other children. Doggerel admits this irregularity, and Shakespeare claims this privilege with powerful effect. He often lengthens the fourth syllable so as to emphasize a word strongly, or he may omit the fourth syllable altogether, producing a long caesura, as in the seventh line of the first scene, where by this means the full significance of the words "with Macbeth" is brought out. The third witch is forced to pause in uttering them, giving time for a devilish peal of laughter from the trio—the first hint to the audience of their planned murderous revenge. Any one whose ear is tuned to the witchery of Shakespeare's music should listen to the cadences of lines 1 to 37 of Scene III. The verse is as wild as a mock-bird's song and as perfectly achieves the desired effect. The strange appeal of these lines is more dependent upon meter than words. The clumsy vulgarity of the dimetric line 2 and the long-drawn-out malignity of the heavy spondees of line 10 are feats in free versification. This freedom allows the dramatist at will to relapse into his regular pentameter verse in narrative lines such as 4 to 6. The other lines are varied at pleasure to fit the changing mood. Only in *Midsummer Night's Dream* and in *The Tempest,* and perhaps not even there, has such perfect lyric coordination of verse and thought been created.

Commentators and critics have generally failed to give attention to the meter of these verses, which anyone who wishes to catch the full import of the witches' words should do. D. L. Chambers's book is very useful, but M. H. Liddell is, I think, the only one who has adequately handled this subject. His *Tragedy of Macbeth* is hard to get and therefore not often used, but it should be in the hands of anyone who hopes to penetrate to the heart of this tragedy. Among other important things to be learned by a study of the versification of the play is the sharp distinction which marks off the Middletonian lines, for the ear of Thomas Middleton (or whoever it was who inserted these lines) was not attuned to doggerel. He wrote regular iambic tetrameter verse. This affords a simple way of tracing the line of demarcation between Shakespeare's work and that of Middleton, whose lines are usually in rhymed couplets of what is called by hymnologists long meter—a ludicrously inappropriate verse for witches (D. L. Chambers, *The Metre of Macbeth*, pp. 11–13).

Sorcery is a most ancient superstition. The Hebrews and other Eastern nations had their own beliefs on the subject, of which something may be learned from the Hebrew Scriptures. The Greeks and Romans had different notions about sorcerers and closely connected with their own pagan philosophy, although in part derived from Eastern ideas. Medieval Europe clung to these superstitions, developing them into a truly marvelous science of which a picture is given in the *Malleus Maleficarum* and in the even more infamous *Daemonomanie* of Jean Bodin. Mankind never developed a more monstrous and thoroughly bad figment of the imagination than this cruel medieval terror which during the fifteenth and sixteenth centuries hunted down its tens of thousands of victims on the continent of Europe.

The British people, though influenced by it, never took very kindly to this. In Tudor England the ideas about witches were bad enough, but simple, vulgar, and innocent as compared to the outrageous contemporary growth on the continent of Europe. The Englishman chiefly concerned himself about the witches' compact with the devil, their transferring of corn or grass from one place to another, their power to cast diseases on or off, their hurting of children or cattle with the evil eye, and their power to bewitch butter, cheese, and ale.

Not much is heard in England of the coven of witches who meddle in political affairs, their ceremonial sabbaths, their

liturgy in worshiping the devil, or their relations to the imps
or familiars who aid them and who transport them invisibly
through the air, but these things were highly developed by
the Scots and are fully discussed by King James in his book
and have correspondingly affected the play of *Macbeth*. The
Scots were a Celtic people of imaginative faculties and living
in a gloomy climate. They were in close touch with the
thought of continental Europe, especially of France, and
absorbed many of the continental views. But they also developed fictions of their own, so that Scotch witchcraft was
quite different from English witchcraft at the time the play
of *Macbeth* was written.

The scenes of sorcery in the play show a typical coven of
Scotch witches, skulking near a battle, discussing its progress,
and planning their revenge upon Macbeth for his slaughter
of their friend and ally the rebel. They break up their
coven at the call of their devils, to "hover through the fog
and filthy air," until they reconvene to meet Macbeth on the
"blasted heath" near Forres. The interval is spent in doing
evil deeds, upon which each one makes report. Nothing of
this is characteristic of English witchcraft except the short
answer of the second witch (I, ii, 2) telling her sisters that she
has been "killing swine." All the rest is distinctly Scotch—
the grudge and revenge of the first witch against the chestnut-
muncher, the winds tied up in bags which they can release
to toss the ship on whose master they wish to wreak their
vengeance; and the ceremonials whereby they can visit their
enemy with wasting diseases and sleeplessness so that he
peaks and pines away; and finally the first witch's exultation
over the possession of "a pilot's thumb, wrecked as homeward
he did come." Pertinent to this procedure are the following passages, taken from King James's *Daemonologie:*

These witches . . . being intised ether for the desire of revenge,
or of worldly riches, their whole practises are either to hurte
men and their gudes, or what they possess, for satisfying of their
cruell minds in the former, or else by the wrack in quhatsoever

sort, of anie whome God will permitte them to have power of,
to satisfie their greedie desire in the last poynt [p. 35].

As to their consultationes . . . every one of them propones unto
him, what wicked turn they would have done either for obteining
of riches, or for revenging them upon anie whom they have
malice at: who granting their demande as no doubt willinglie
he wil since it is to do evill he teacheth them the means, wherby
they may do the same. As for little trifling turns that women
have ado with, he causeth them to joint dead corpses, & to make
powders thereof, mixing such other things thereamongst, as he
gives unto them [p. 43].

They can rayse stormes and tempestes in the aire, either upon
Sea or land, though not universally, but in such a particular place
and prescribed boundes, as God will permitte them so to trouble
[p. 46].

The cause whie they haunte solitarie places, it is by reason that
they may affraie and brangle the more the faith of suche as them
alone hauntes such places. For our nature is such, as in companies wee are not so soone mooved to anie such kind of feare,
as being solitare, which the Devill knowing well inough [p. 58].

Everywhere witchcraft was associated with the presence of
some sort of an imp or minor devil who helped the witch in
her deviltry, but the powers of the English "puckrel" were
far less than those of the "familiar" in Scotland. Everywhere
witchcraft busied itself with the idea of aerial transportation
of the witch, but how it was accomplished was differently explained. On the Continent the preparation of a suitable
ointment manufactured from the limbs of unbaptized infants
(see *Malleus Maleficarum,* p. 104) was part of the transporting
mechanism. In England a broomstick seems to have suf-
ficed; but in Scotland there was a different exuberant theory
which may be read about in the *News from Scotland,* which
tells (p. 17) of "witches sailing in their riddles or cives" into
the midst of the sea. This language seems to have slipped
into the play at I, iii, 8.

In both the scenes of sorcery of the play the witches have
with them their imps who transport them through the air,

and when they have finished their reports they proclaim themselves "posters of the sea and land" and execute their charm-round about the devils whom they serve.

The lines which accompany this round of the witches as they watch for Macbeth call for examination:

> *All.* The weird sisters, hand in hand,
> Posters of the sea and land,
> Thus do go about, about:
> Thrice to thine and thrice to mine
> And thrice again, to make up nine.
> Peace! the charm's wound up.
>
> [I, iii, 33 to 38]

In his book the king devoted an entire chapter to the subject of the transportation of witches by their devils: They are

carryed by the force of the Spirite which is their conducter, either above the earth or above the Sea swiftlie, to the place where they are to meet: which I am perswaded to be likewaies possible [*Daemonologie*, p. 38].

The verses just quoted speak of the witches as "posters of the sea and land," so we may expect to find the devils as the transportation agents near by, and they are. "Thine" means *thy devil* and "mine" means *my devil*. The three imps who called the witches from their coven in Scene I and carried them away have now brought them to the blasted heath where Macbeth is soon to pass, and are waiting there as the sisters execute their charmrounds, encircling first one of them and then another in an effort to obtain their aid in the destruction of Macbeth. It is important that Graymalkin, Paddock, and Harpier be thus seen by the audience waiting for Macbeth. The devilish inspiration of the prophecies which immediately follow is thus visibly suggested.

The foregoing ideas accord with the teachings of continental writers which James had read. But when we come to the question of why witches are invisible during their aerial transportation, we find the king fascinated by the subject and led into some philosophical theories which are seemingly his own. He says:

And in this transporting they say themselves, that they are invisible to anie other, except amongst themselves; which may also be possible in my opinion. For if the devil may forme what kinde of impressiones he pleases in the aire, as I have said before, speaking of *Magie,* why may he not far easilier thicken & obscure so the air, that is next about them by contracting it strait together, that the beames of any other mans eyes, cannot pearce thorow the same, to see them? [*Ibid.,* p. 39.]

This kingly speculation has affected the language of the play. The sisters are always visible as they stand on earth, but become invisible when transported "by the force of the spirit which is their conducter" through the air. At the end of Act I, Scene I, they are called by their devils, "hover through the fog and filthy air," and vanish. In Scene III, as they vanish, Banquo asks, "Whither are they vanished?" Macbeth answers, "Into the air"; and he immediately writes to his wife that "they made themselves air into which they vanished" (I, v, 5). Again, near the end of IV, i, the witches vanish as they pass out the door. Macbeth asks Lennox, standing without, if he saw them; and finding that he did not, says, "infected be the air whereon they ride." *

Notwithstanding that the language of the play is thus explicit in stating that the witches vanish in air, the stage for many years pushed them down into the earth through a trap, often accompanied by flashes of fire. This involves a total disregard of the dramatist's intent. Scotch witches do not live below the earth but on it, and into the air they vanish

---

* It is in *Macbeth* (I, v, 50 and I, vii, 23) that Shakespeare for the first time uses the word "sightless" in the unusual and then recent sense of *invisible;* but it is a spirit in the air which is "sightless." We can better understand this usage if we remember that King James attributes this invisibility to a thickening of the surrounding air so that the beams of man's eyes "cannot pierce through the same to see them." "Sightless" properly describes that to which our sight cannot reach.

when transported by their devils. The scenes of sorcery were probably played on the rear stage with the curtain drawn back so that they could slip behind it under cover of a puff of smoke.

No one can sense the atmospheric condition which surrounds the play of *Macbeth* unless fully conscious that the air of Scotland is filthy because inhabited by this multitude of villainous spirits. Nowhere is the air more "infected" by them than around Macbeth's castle at Inverness. This it is which so sharpens the irony of the talk between Duncan and Banquo as they approach the castle of Inverness: "The air nimbly and sweetly recommends itself unto our gentle senses"; "Heaven's breath smells wooingly here"; "The air is delicate." This, as their wicked hostess leads the king to his cell of doom, while we can almost hear the exultation of the invisible aerial devils surrounding the castle who are planning the king's destruction! Aiken's long-forgotten ballad entitled *Duncan's Warning* pictures this "loaded sky." As "the royal Duncan" is about to enter "Macbeth's strong towers," a warning voice cries out:

> "Stop, O king, thy destined course,
> Furl thy standard, turn thy horse,
> Death besets the onward track,
> Come no further—quickly back.
>
> "Hear'st thou not the raven's croak?
> See'st thou not the blasted oak?
> Feel'st thou not the loaded sky?
> Read thy danger, king, and fly." *

The play of *Macbeth* should always be read in full consciousness of this omnipresent diabolical influence. The devils are dramatis personae of the play. Only so can we really appreciate the significance of the witches' plan for Macbeth's destruction. The witches would be impotent to accomplish this were it not for the three devils which accom-

* *English Minstrelsy* (Edinburgh, 1810), Vol. I, p. 230.

pany them. To force this upon the attention of the audience we are shown in both scenes in which the witches meet Macbeth that they begin their operations by "charming" these devils, by a "charm" round in I, iii, 32–37 and by a "charmed pot" in IV, i, 4–38, thus insuring their aid. For the witches have no supernatural powers nor foreknowledge, save as they get them from the devil who though "he knows not all things future, but yet he knows parte" (*Daemonologie*, p. 4). The devils know that Macbeth before meeting the witches has entertained a thought "whose murder yet is but fantastical" (I, iii, 139); thus they know his vulnerability and how he may be tempted by the suggestive prophecies on the heath, and by the deceitful prophecies which lead him to certain destruction when he later puts himself in their power by visiting them.

Is there evidence as to when these prefatory scenes of sorcery were added to the play? There are two indications worth considering.

"Aroint," a word unknown to the books until Shakespeare used it twice, must have been derived from the ballad-scrap which is found in the play of *King Lear* (III, iv, 129). He soon used the word again in *Macbeth* (I, iii, 6) because it had a sound which he needed for the alliterative verse he was writing. *Lear* was begun in 1605 and was first performed on December 26, 1606. If the third act of *Lear* was written during the first half of 1606, this warrants us in dating the sorcery scenes of *Macbeth* but little later.

The husband of the chestnut-muncher sailed to Aleppo as "Master o' the Tiger" (I, iii, 7). In the days of King James, the *Tiger* was a ship owned by Sir Edward Michelbourne, an Oxford gentleman well known at court and famous for his Latin verses. This *Tiger* sailed for the East on December 5, 1604, with John Davis as master, and with Sir Edward on board his ship. After a dangerous and unlucky voyage, during which the master of the vessel and many of the crew were killed by pirates, she found her way back to England, arriving at Milford Haven on June 27, 1606, and on July 9, 1606, at "Portsmouth Roade when all our companie was dismissed" (*Purchas His Pilgrims,* 1905 ed., Vol. II, p. 347). That the name "Tiger" was thus suggested to Shakespeare seems highly probable.* This was first pointed out by Mr. G. B. Harrison in his Edition of the play (p. 100). If so, the sorcery scenes were written not long before the king saw the play on August 7, 1606.

* Either this ship, or another of the same name, made a voyage to Aleppo in 1583 (Hakluyt's *Voyages,* 1589 ed.).

THE ACT OF ABUSES

An act of Parliament, commonly called the "Act of Abuses," which forbids the profane use of God's names on the stage, became effective on May 27, 1606. The play of *Macbeth* contains no such profanity, nor so far as can be seen did it ever do so. This cannot be said of the previously written plays by William Shakespeare. Let anyone read over the first act of *Hamlet* in the text of the second quarto (1604) and he will note at least six palpable violations of the "Act to restrain the Abuses of Players" (Chambers's *Elizabethan Stage*, Vol. IV, p. 338), had such enactment then been in existence. *Hamlet* was written about four years before the act was passed, and serves to show why the Puritans, who had a clear majority in the House of Commons, urged the passage of the act and ultimately secured it. The act has had little effect upon Shakespeare's later work, because *King Lear, Antony and Cleopatra, Coriolanus, Timon of Athens, Pericles,* and *Cymbeline,* which follow in immediate succession, are all heathen plays, not admitting of the sort of profanity against which the act is directed. Even *Winter's Tale* must be similarly classed. The oaths name only the pagan gods. The only plays in writing which Shakespeare found his art affected by this act are *Macbeth* and *The Tempest.* They are both royal plays, the latter written with special view to performance before Prince Henry, who was particular all his short life to avoid profanity. Profane use of the divine names is not found in *Macbeth* or *The Tempest.*

This act of James's second Parliament is very precise in its terms. It provides that if any person "shall in any Stage play . . . jestingly or prophanely speake or use the holy Name of God or of Christ Jesus, or of the Holy Ghoste or of the Trinitie, which are not to be spoken but with feare

304

and reverence," he shall forfeit for every such offense £10. It is to be enforced by what lawyers call a *qui tam* action, that is, an information is to be filed by an informer and half the forfeiture goes to the informer. This placed a potent weapon in the hands of the puritans. But offenses under the act are strictly limited to the irreverent use of the four divine names specified, and do not include other kinds of profanity as the puritans had urged should be the case. The act was passed after nearly two years of debate, and was a compromise between the two houses of Parliament, during which time the proper definition of profanity was a very live subject both in and out of Parliament.

After the passage of the Act of Abuses, the players hastily expurgated the books of their current plays. The folio text of many of Shakespeare's plays when compared with the earlier texts bears clear evidence of this, and also shows the haste with which it was carried out; for although some oaths have been excised or modified, others are retained which would seem to be within the purview of the statute. Perhaps the players suppressed oaths on the stage which had not been stricken from the promptbook. A common way in which this hasty expurgation was carried out was to substitute "heaven" for "God," a change very characteristic of the folio text.

When we come to consider how the act has affected the language of the play of *Macbeth,* we find, as might be expected, some reverent use of the name of God throughout the play. We further find that while no substitution of "heaven" for "God" occurs in the first three acts of the play, such substitution does occur as a precautionary measure ten times in the last two acts of the play; indicating with high probability that the first three acts of the play were written before the statute was enacted and the last two acts, after its enactment. Another finding is that there is neither profanity nor any evidence of expurgation in the first three acts. To explain this requires examination of what was going on in Parliament during the months just preceding the enactment.

The journals of the House of Commons and of the House of Lords covering James's first two Parliaments give this information.

James's first Parliament met on March 19 and was prorogued on July 7, 1604. The House of Commons reflected the puritan sentiment of the time, which was opposed to stage plays and to profanity of any sort. On June 27, 1604, there was introduced in the House of Commons a bill "for Reformation of the Common Sin of Swearing and Blasphemy." It passed the Commons by a vote of 105 to 70 after having been disputed in the House on July 3 by four puritans against three nonpuritans. It was then presented to the House of Lords and on July 4, 1604, was referred to a committee of which the Earl of Shrewsbury was chairman. There were two bishops on this committee. The attitude of the bishops of the Church of England as to the proper limit to the use of oaths was very different from that of the puritans, and we may therefore assume that the bishops opposed the passage of this bill; not that they favored profanity but that along with the judges they felt that nothing should be done to lessen respect for the oaths used in judicial and administrative procedures. Accordingly, the bill never came out from this committee and never became a law. We may assume that the dramatists and the players breathed more freely and did nothing about the matter.

James's second Parliament met on November 5, 1605, the fatal day on which they were to be blown up by Guy Fawkes. They adjourned until January 21, 1606, without doing anything, after which date they were in continuous session until prorogued on May 27, 1606. On January 28 the same bill which had failed in the last Parliament was again introduced, but this time in the House of Lords, by whom, on its second reading, it was referred to a large committee of whom the Earl of Southampton (a friend, be it noted, of the players) was the chairman, and upon this committee were ordered to attend several of the judges. As a result of their hearings they reported on February 4, 1606, by the Earl of Southampton, "that they did not hold it sufficiently drawn for reformation of that offense," promising that they would try "to frame a new bill of the same matter." The journals indicate lengthy discussion in the committee. Do not overlook the fact that this was the Parliament which passed the act imposing the Oath of Allegiance to be taken by all to whom it was tendered. On February 22, 1606, the committee reported that the bill was "not meet to be proceeded in"; but a new bill was presented to the House of Lords by the Earl of Northampton. Notice that the liberal Earl of Southampton, to whom the matter had been entrusted, has been displaced by an earl who was the spokesman of James's Privy Council, and the one who was very active in engineering the Oath of Allegiance. The new bill is entitled "An Act for the Punishment of Profane, Blasphemous and Irreligious Swearing," and upon second reading this bill was referred to the same large committee, but with addition to it of the Archbishop of Canterbury and the Lord Bishop of London. Evidently the Church was insisting that there should be no abridgment of the use of oaths such as the Church deemed not profane or irreligious. The bill again rested in committee until April 10, 1606, when it was returned to the House of Lords with amendments, and in this form reached a second reading but never was proceeded with and never became a law. The stumbling block was that no one could say just when swearing became "irreligious."

The puritans having found that they were not likely to get an act such as they had hoped for, but knowing that a bill of more limited scope to prevent certain defined profanity in stage plays would not be opposed by the lords, introduced in the House of Commons on February 17 the Act of Abuses just as we now know it. This bill was rapidly passed, went to the House of Lords on April 17, and passed there on May 19, taking the place of the more far-reaching bills which had been smothered in committee. Thus it was that this act re-

ceived the royal assent on May 27, 1606, while all other efforts to regulate profanity by act of Parliament failed and
were never revived.

The players and, even more carefully, their dramatist
must have narrowly watched these proceedings; and we may
have assurance that during the early months of 1606 William
Shakespeare felt that for precautionary reasons the play which
he was writing should be kept entirely free from profanity
of any sort.   This accounts for the extraordinary restraint in
this regard shown in the first three acts of *Macbeth*.   When
a few weeks later he came to write the rest of the play, the
Act of Abuses had been passed and he knew precisely what
he could do and what he could not do.   In the two final acts
of his play he strictly observed the injunctions of the statute
but allowed himself distinctly more liberty of speech.   It remains to point out how these two feats were accomplished.

Violations of the Third Commandment which we call
"profanity" commonly occur in connection with either cursing or swearing.   As to both, the line of demarcation at which
they become profane is hard to draw, for it often depends less
on the words used than on the mood in which they are
spoken.   The dramatist must have heard numerous echoes
of the debates in Parliament about these distinctions and
must have been thinking much about it himself.   His play
of *Macbeth* shows how acutely he reasoned it out.

Cursing is only a special form of prayer.   One may ask
God to do good.   This is benediction.   We use it when we
say "Good morning."   One may ask God to do evil.   This is
malediction or cursing.   No one objects to the first; all such
benignant precatory expressions are permissible and usually
laudable.   They occur associated with the name of God
throughout the play of *Macbeth*.   But malediction or imprecation usually involves a profane mood.   There is no
cursing whatever in the first three acts of the play notwith-

standing abundant suitable occasion. In the last two acts
cursing is common, although the divine name is never used
in association with it because this irreverent use of God's
name is forbidden by the Act of Abuses. These generalizations must now be made good:

Benediction occurs throughout the play:

> God save the king! I, ii, 48
> Bid God 'ild us for your pains. I, vi, 13
> > ['ild = yield = reward]
>
> God bless us! II, ii, 26, 29
> God's benison go with you. II, iv, 40
> God be with you! III, i, 44
> God help thee. IV, ii, 59
> God above Deal between thee and me! IV, iii, 120
> Good God, betimes remove the means that makes us
> > strangers! IV, iii, 162
>
> Pray God it be, sir. V, i, 64
> God, God forgive us all! V, i, 83
> God's soldier be he. V, viii, 47
> God be with him! V, viii, 53

In all these expressions God's name is freely used but spoken
with reverence as the act requires. Shakespeare's judgment
that such benedictions would not be forbidden was evidently
correct.

Malediction is totally excluded from Acts I–III. But beginning with the caldron scene (IV, i) and on to the end of
the play, Macbeth's speeches contain much cursing.

> An eternal curse fall on you! IV, i, 104
> Let this pernicious hour stand aye accursed. IV, i, 134
> Damned [be] all those that trust them! IV, i, 139
> Under a hand accursed. III, vi, 49 [written after IV, i]
> A devil more damned in evils. IV, iii, 56
> By his own interdiction stands accursed. IV, iii, 107
> Out damned spot. V, i, 39

> The devil damn thee black. V, iii, 11
> Death of thy soul! V, iii, 16
> Accursed be that tongue that tells me so. V, viii, 17
> Damned be him that first cries hold enough! V, viii, 34

In I, ii, 14, the sergeant speaks of the rebel's "damned quarrel"; in III, vi, 10, Lennox ironically exclaims "damned fact!" I do not know if these expressions should be considered profane; but if they are, note that they occur in scenes written after IV, i, was written.* The inference from these quotations is clear. Prior to the writing of IV, i, the dramatist's pen was stayed, to an extent found nowhere else in his plays, by the expectation that the puritans would secure the passage of their act to punish "irreligious swearing." What that phrase might be construed to mean he could not tell, and he kept on the safe side. But by the time he came to write the fourth act of the play, it had become clear that no general prohibition of cursing and swearing would be enacted by the Parliament, but that instead there would be only the limited prohibition of the profane use of the four divine names specified in the act. Accordingly, in the parts of the play written after this, the restraint of the first three acts is lacking and we find an unusually free use of maledictory expressions but accompanied by a strict observance of the act.

Even more restraint has been exercised by the dramatist in the matter of swearing, and this throughout the play. In I, iii, 52, Banquo's mild adjuration is "I' the name of truth."

The drunken porter is the character in whose mouth the dramatist would likely have placed profane oaths, had he not been on his guard. His adjurations are "i' the name of Beelzebub," "i' the other devil's name," "faith" (three times), and "marry." "Marry" (by Mary) is an abbreviated oath, but not offensive to any but Roman Catholics. Surely "faith" is

---

* See p. 276, for the date of writing of III, vi, and p. 30 for that of I, ii.

a watery exclamation for this base-born, foul-minded servi-
tor.* Shakespeare was holding a strong curb on his pen.

In II, i, 7–9, Banquo exclaims:

> merciful powers,
> Restrain in me the cursed thoughts that nature
> Gives way to in repose!

This pious prayer has controlled the dramatist throughout
the play.

I have omitted one expression of the porter in which the
name of God is used. When admitting the equivocator, he
says that he "committed treason enough for God's sake, yet
could not equivocate to heaven." I have heard actors read
these lines as though "for God's sake" were an expletive,
but it is not. The treason was committed for God's sake because a Jesuit might do such things only for the sake of the
glory of God, for that was the end which justified the means,
and James and his court would understand this. The usage
was thoroughly reverent.

Thus has Shakespeare handled the delicate questions, both
of adjuration and imprecation, in this play. But he has gone
further. We find serious and even quasi-religious expression
taking the place of excited expletive.

After the murder has been discovered there is intense excitement, and one might expect strong asseveration. Instead
we find language such as a puritan might use. In II, iii, 74,

---

* When Sir Henry Herbert was Master of the Revels, nearly thirty
years later, he had in hand to censor one of Davenant's plays, and in
doing this he struck out the exclamation "faith," deeming it an oath;
but King Charles I ordered him to restore the word, which he did,
entering in his office book the following protest:

The king is pleased to take "faith" (and others) for asseverations and no
oaths, to which I do humbly submit, as my master's judgment; but under
favour conceive them to be oaths, and enter them here to declare my opinion and submission.

Clearly the king was right, and Herbert merely fussy.

Duncan is "The Lord's annointed temple," a scriptural phrase taken from I Samuel 24:7–11, combined with II Corinthians 6:16. When Banquo announces in emphatic terms his determination to find the perpetrator of the great treason, his adjuration is:

> In the great hand of God I stand; and thence
> Against the undivulged pretence I fight
> Of treasonous malice.

The scriptural thought and language of I Peter 5:5–9, has thus been transferred to the play. Donalbain's parting shaft, "the near in blood, the nearer bloody," seemingly is connected with the saying (Matthew 10:36) that "a man's foes shall be they of his own household." In III, vi, 32, we read: "with Him above to ratify the work," a similar pious circumlocution. The dramatist was on safe ground with the puritans in building his phraseology upon that of holy writ.

Other than as quoted above, the expletives of the play are insignificant. In the murder scene, II, ii, Macbeth and his Lady exclaim "Hark" (thrice), "Ho," and "Ha." After the discovery of the murder, II, iii, there is no profanity, only "O," "O," "Woe," "Alas," "O," "O," "Ho." Ross's exclamation, II, iv, 23, is "Alas the day." When Banquo is struck down he cries, "O treachery" and "O slave." And in the banquet scene the most emphatic exclamations are "O," "O," "Fie for shame." Lennox uses the oath "Marry," III, vi, 4. Malcolm speaks of appeasing "an angry god," but he is referring to a pagan god. The two doctors speak only professionally, the Scotchman saying, "Go to, go to," and "Well, well, well." The only asseveration of Lady Macbeth's waiting woman is (V, i, 20) "Upon my life." No such restraint is to be found in Shakespeare's plays written before this.

A remarkable and significant phenomenon appears when one examines the usage in the play of the word "heaven" (or "heavens"). The *O.E.D.* distinguishes the several significations of this word, and generally speaking they may be classified as:

a) the celestial canopy of the day and the starry sky of the night (*O.E.D.*, 1–4);

b) the abode of saints and angels, that is, heaven as distinguished from hell (*O.E.D.*, 5);

c) a synonym for Providence or God (*O.E.D.*, 6).

If now all the occurrences of the word "heaven" in the play be listed, and their significations noted, the result is as follows:

I, v, 54	Heaven peep through the blanket of the dark	b
II, i, 4	There's husbandry in Heaven; their candles are all out	a
II, i, 64	That summons thee to Heaven or to Hell	b
II, iii, 12	Could not equivocate to Heaven	b
II, iv, 5	The Heavens threaten his bloody stage	a
III, i, 142	thy soul's flight if it find Heaven	b
III, vi, 19	an't please Heaven	c
IV, ii, 72	Heaven preserve you	c
IV, iii, 6	Sorrows strike heaven on the face	a
IV, iii, 144	Such sanctity hath Heaven given his hand	c
IV, iii, 149	How he solicits heaven	c
IV, iii, 207	Merciful heaven!	c
IV, iii, 223	Did heaven look on	c
IV, iii, 231	gentle heavens	c
IV, iii, 235	Heaven forgive him too!	c
V, i, 55	Heaven knows what she has known	c
V, viii, 72	by the grace of Grace	c

III, vi, really belongs to the fourth act of the play and should follow IV, i (see p. 277). Therefore it is found that in the first three acts of the play the word "heaven" was not used as a synonym for God; but in the last two acts it was thus used ten times. The inference to be drawn from this list must be related to the fact that at some date closely coinciding with the passage of the Act of Abuses the members of the King's Company decided that the safest and easiest way to keep themselves clear of the penalties of the Act would be to substitute "Heaven" for "God" whenever there was a possibility that the latter usage might be held to be profane. Consequently they went through the promptbooks of their current repertory and made this substitution. This did not affect the play of *Macbeth,* for it was not yet in their hands. But its author knew what was going on, and consequently in writing Acts IV and V of his play when he was about to write the word "God," he checked himself and wrote "Heaven" in every case where even the most pious puritan might otherwise take offense, allowing the divine name to stand only when spoken with evident reverence, and where any substitution would really have marred his play. Note that in V, viii, 2 he deviated from this practice and used the word "Grace" rather than "Heaven" because he wished the word to rhyme with "place." This warrants a finding, with which many other considerations agree, that the last two acts of the play of *Macbeth* were written after the passage of the Act of Abuses was assured. For had the whole play been written before this time, we would expect to find the same evidence of substitution in Acts I to III as is found in Acts IV and V.

There is another influence which may have helped to create or augment the restraint which the dramatist exhibits in his play of *Macbeth* as to profanity.

As has been sufficiently demonstrated (in the chapter "The Kingly Gift), Shakespeare was careful that his play should accord with the moral system outlined by the king in his book of instructions to his son Henry, in which are found these precepts:

And especiallie, beware to offend your conscience, with use of swearing or lying, suppose but in jest; for oathes are but an use, and a sinne cloathed with no delight nor gaine, and therefore the more inexcusable even in the sight of men [*Basilicon Doron,* p. 17].

and again: "Keepe God more sparingly in your mouth, but aboundantly in your heart" (*ibid.*, p. 20).

That these instructions influenced the dramatist is altogether likely, but they afford no explanation of the sharply differing standards found in the two parts of the play. I see no way to explain this except by the assumption, which has just been made, that the first part was written prior to May 19, 1606, when the House of Lords passed the Act of Abuses but that the rest of the play was written after this had occurred.

Some of the indications thus far enumerated which help to fix the time of the writing of the play may now be fitted together. Shakespeare probably did not return to London in the autumn of 1605 until the theaters were reopening, that is, about the middle of December. His proposed royal play was shaping in his mind but he had written nothing. When he reached London the excitement about the powder plot was intense, and he found his company under requirement from the Master of the Revels to produce at Whitehall an unusually large number of plays (ten), beginning at Christmas and extending to Shrovetide.

Furthermore, two great masques or court spectacles were being staged at Whitehall on January 5 and January 6, 1606. They were written by Ben Jonson. The elaborate scenery was devised by Inigo Jones. They were to honor the ill starred marriage of two young children, the utterly juvenile Earl of Essex and Frances Howard, the featherweight daughter of the Earl of Suffolk. When court masques such as these were given, the King's Company was called upon to supply actors or supernumeraries for the unpopular parts of the masque. They might even make suggestions as to stage business and the proper delivery of lines. But after Shrovetide the dramatist was free to set his mind on his play for the king.

The effect which the powder plot has had on the play, the influence of the Act of Abuses, and the reference in the caldron scene to the destruction by the wind on March 31, 1606, of the Flemish and Gallic churches, all agreeing with other indications which have been mentioned, seem to assign the writing of the first part of the play to the months of February, March, and April of the year 1606.

But when was it finished and performed before the king? To answer this question we start with the information, afforded by the records, that the King's Players performed plays at court that winter until Shrovetide (February 17) but *not thereafter* until the visit of King Christian of Denmark to London during the summer, when *three plays* were performed, and not again until *after Christmas 1606*. This sets a narrow limit within which the required date of performance must be found, for we shall see (pp. 403–407) that the play was known on the public stage before the end of 1606. It is therefore proper at this point to examine the doings at court which accompanied the visit of the Danish king, and this will occupy the ensuing chapter.

KING CHRISTIAN'S VISIT

The visit to England of King Christian of Denmark in the summer of 1606, although of much interest to all Englishmen when it occurred, carried with it no political implications and was followed by no consequences of importance. It is therefore usually passed over by the modern historian with little or no mention unless it be to refer to the often quoted letter of Sir John Harington describing the inebriety of the kings during their visit to Theobalds (*Nugae Antiquae*, 1804 ed., Vol. 1, p. 348). This lively letter was written by a very facetious gentleman who was noted as a raconteur, and it should be read with this in mind. The kings must not be judged as though this highly embroidered document were written as plain matter of fact.

Nevertheless, it is true that there was an overabundant flow of wine during the festivities of this visit and that the usual results followed. And it is equally clear that King Christian, finding that he could not control the excesses of his huge retinue, suddenly determined to shorten his visit greatly, thereby showing a wisdom scarcely to be expected from so young a ruler, for he was only twenty-nine years of age. What we are chiefly to note is that this curtailment of the visit seems to have resulted in a sudden call for the immediate production of Shakespeare's royal play, when it was not quite finished, and for this reason we find signs of hasty writing in the battle scene at the end of the play and an unfinished condition of the second scene of the first act, which was the part of the play last written.

Because the doings of the visit are unfamiliar to most readers, and because they have had some influence upon the play, some account will here be given of the occurrences of these three weeks. Later will follow examination in detail of the

317

parts of the play which are found to be related to events occurring during the visit.

That the Danish king would visit England to see his sister Queen Anna was announced in England in April, 1606.* Edmond Howes in his *Continuation of Stow's Chronicle* states:

All this Sommer [1606] here was great expectation of the comming of Christianus the 4 of that name, king of Denmarke, brother unto our Soveraigne lady the Queene, whose princely purpose was heartie kindnesse, to see his said sister, and royall brother our dread soveraigne King James, with their children the young princes of this Land, but through contrary winds he was five weekes hindered in his expedition, so as it was Thursday the 17. of July, before he came into the River of London [1615 ed., p. 885].

On this latter date William Camden, who was accumulating materials for a projected history of the reign of King James, entered in his *Annals:* "Christianus Rex Daniae venit in Angliam *inexpectatus.*" Two days later the Earl of Salisbury wrote to Winwood telling him of Christian's arrival, adding, "It is thought his abode here will be about forty days" (*Memorials of Affairs of State,* Vol. II, p. 247).

On July 31st Camden wrote:

> Rex cum Rege Daniae transit
> Per urbem pompa magnifica.

And on the same day the Venetian ambassador wrote:

All day today I have enjoyed the Solemn entry of the King of Denmark into the city—The city was not able to mark such preparations as it desired—indeed there was nothing but a

* Under date of April 20, 1606, the Venetian ambassador wrote to the Doge, "The visit of the King of Denmark is announced" (*Cal. of State Papers—Venetian,* Vol. X).

single arch of very happy design, for the date of the entry was anticipated because the King of Denmark had resolved to leave within ten days.

On August 7 the Danish diarist who accompanied his king wrote:

After HRM of Denmark had taken leave of HM of England and of his sister, Queen Anna, HM of Denmark was prevailed upon to stay a day or two longer in order to see the custom and ceremony which is used with the investing of the order of the garter of St. George of England [translated from the Danish original].

In addition to the well known English sources giving accounts of Christian's visit (nearly all of which are referred to by Nichols in his *Progresses of James,* Vol. II, p. 53 *et seq.*), there is an account of the visit printed in the German language at Flensburg in Denmark but published at Hamburg in 1607. For the most part this is a translation into German by Conrad Khunrath of what is told in *The Most Royal and Honorable Entertainment* written by Henry Roberts; but comparison shows that at several points additional material has been added, evidently because of information received from an eyewitness.

And there are in the Royal Library of Copenhagen three copies of a diary kept by an unknown Danish gentleman, apparently of some position or rank, who went with his king to England and wrote down what he observed. Unfortunately his chief interest was in the horns of unicorns and suchlike things, and at times his dates seem to be at fault, but he supplies some new information. I have referred to him as the "Danish diarist."

King Christian was some ten years younger than James and a much more attractive man, expert in manly exercise. He came to England chiefly because he wished to see his older sister the Queen of England, to whom he was much attached.

She had recently (June 22nd) given birth to a little princess who survived but a single day.

The Danish king had sailed from his home with a fleet of eight ships, taking with him six of his Privy Council, others of his nobility, officers, friends, and their retinue to the number of 314 persons, in addition to the mariners.

The Danish fleet entered the Thames on July 17 and sailed up the river to near Gravesend, where it came to anchor and awaited the arrival of the King of England. Word had been sent to him as soon as the ships were sighted, but James was at Oatlands when he heard that Christian had arrived, and it was not until the morning of July 18th that the royal barges carrying the English king with his royal train, including Prince Henry, rowed down the river to the Danish anchorage to greet the Danish king. After ceremonial greetings and a dinner on board the Danish ships, both royal parties were rowed that afternoon up the river in the barges to the palace at Greenwich, which the King of England made his official residence during the visit. Here also the Danes with their king were lodged in the two great towers and galleries within the garden on the tiltyard side of the park.

A noteworthy ceremony on Friday, the 18th, which seems to have suggested the simile of I, ii, 37, was the saluting cannonade of the Danish ships as the monarchs left them, and the answering greetings from the English guns.

The barges falling off from the shippe, after they had rowed some small way, the Admirall discharged such a thundering peale of ordinance, whereof many are cannones of brasse, as the smoake dimmed the skies, and the noyse was heard a farre way off; after her, the Vice and Reere-admiral, and so all the rest; which made a long peale, every shippe taking his turne very orderly in exceeding good sort. By this time they came to the Blocke-houses situat neere Gravesend, who followed in discharging their ordinance in like manner, with such industry and care as was very

KING CHRISTIAN IV OF DENMARK IN THE YEAR 1606

well commended and highly praysed of both Kings and their companies.*

On Saturday, July 19th, the kings spent the morning hunting in Eltham Park and the afternoon at the tennis court, where they watched sets of tennis played "between a French Gentleman and one Webbe an English Gentleman." The anonymous writer who put forth *The King of Denmarkes Welcome* stood on the side of the tennis court opposite to the two kings and had a good look at them. He thus describes Christian's appearance that day:

His haire is of a whitish browne; his beard somewhat whiter then his head: his cheekes he keepeth smooth without haire: his haire uppon his chinne about three-fingers long, cutte of an even cutte: in his cheekes hee hath a pure and fresh blood: his countenance cheerefull and amiable: his fore-heade white and hie: his eyes bright and lively: In all; his face is full, rounde, and enriched with beautie: and to speake without errour, such and so like, that any one that hath behelde her, might chalenge him by the face of the Queenes Maiestie his Sister. Hee is of bodie strongly made, broade, large, and of the best composition, hee appeares bigge under his waste, hath an exceeding cleane made legge, and a delicate fine made foote: to conclude, his proportion shewes him to bee a man of great strength, activitie, and indurance, such as are the markes of the best Conquerours. The apparell which that day he wore, was a Doublet & Hose of a kinde of Bryer-ball coloured Satten, plaine, and onely cut with a byas cutte, the fashion, such as is at this day most of request in this Kingdome: hee wore a paire of white Silke Stockings, and a paire of blacke Spanish leather shoees: about his arme he wore a faire Scarfe, and on his heade he had a gray Beuer Hat, with a Hat band of Pearle, and Diamonds set in Goldsmiths worke, and a Jewell of Diamonds, which held up the right side brimme of his hat: in my conceyte of price not to bee valued [pp. 9, 10].

* *The Most Royal and Honorable Entertainment of the Most Famous and Renowned King Christian the Fourth, King of Denmark,* by Henry Roberts.

On Sunday the 20th, with great ceremony and magnificence, both monarchs attended divine service in the chapel, where a Latin sermon was preached by the Bishop of Rochester. All of the sermons and most of the speeches pronounced before the kings during the visit were in Latin, a concession to His Danish Majesty, who knew little or no English. Latin was the only language common to both kings, and it is evident that social intercourse between the kings was severely limited by the language barrier. But the truth is, Christian came to England to see his sister. His friendship with James was rather ceremonial.

Monday, Tuesday, and Wednesday (July 21–23) were spent riding together through the park at Greenwich, dining at the White Tower on the top of the hill with the Earl of Northampton, hunting the buck in the park during the afternoons, and in the evening at Eltham. Thus the monarchs rode, feasted, hunted, and otherwise enjoyed themselves at Greenwich until Thursday, July 24th, when they went to visit the Earl of Salisbury at Theobalds, where they were most sumptuously entertained for four days. Here they witnessed the entertainment written for this occasion by Ben Jonson and to be found printed in the editions of his *Works*. Hence on July 29th, they returned for a second visit to Greenwich, which lasted until July 31st.

On Wednesday evening, July 30, "the Children of Pauls, played before the two kings a play called *Abuses;* containing both a comedy and a tragedy, at which the kings seemed to take delight." This is stated in the *King of Denmarkes Welcome*. Christian would no doubt enjoy seeing how well children could imitate the acting of their elders, assuming both male and female parts. The play and its author are unknown.

This invites inquiry as to what part the King's Players took in the ceremonials of this visit. They ranked in the royal household as grooms-extraordinary of the king's chamber, and on important state occasions were called to do service there. During the visit to England in 1604 of the Spanish peace embassy, they had been thus summoned to court and were in attendance on the king and his guests; and the King of Denmark's visit was an occasion of even greater dignity and pomp. Christian had brought with him a very large retinue, and James must match this. We may therefore deem it altogether likely that during parts of the visit the King's Players took their turn in the presence chamber at Greenwich and helped to attend the visitors.*

In Howes's *Continuation of Stow's Chronicle* we read that on July 20:

King James understood that his brother by reason of his late comming, as aforesayd, meant not to stay so long, nor to visit so many parts of the Kingdome, as he purposed, when he first prepared to come for England: gave forthwith order to the Lorde Maior of London, to prepare the cittie against Thursday sennight following, and to make such Trophies, and devices, as the time would permit, and that the grave citizens should sit in their accustomed state, and order, in their liveries, as is used at coronations of Princes, which they very dutifully performed.

Thursday, July 31, was the date which had been thus set ten days ahead for the great procession when the kings were to pass in state through the City of London. Anticipating this, a committee of the Common Council of London had made a written suggestion concerning the entertainment of the kings which is preserved among the *Salisbury Papers* (Vol. XVIII, p. 227) and endorsed "1606, Shows in London

---

* Ernest Law expresses a contrary opinion (*Shakespeare as a Groom of the Chamber,* p. 57) but he gives no reason except the failure to find an entry of payment for their service in the accounts. But it may well be that their share of the "30,000 dollars to the King's household" given by King Christian (the Danish diarist notes a further gift, "to the servants of the royal household of England 200 rose nobles"), when added to the £30 received as fees for their three plays, was thought to afford full compensation. Being midsummer, when the court and the visitors spent most of their time out of doors, their duties at the presence chamber would have been light.

for the King of Denmark." It begins, "The manner of receiving the Kings' Majesties through the City of London in their passage from the Tower Hill to Whitehall." It outlines a proposed pageant at the upper end of Cheap, but one which differs not a little from the one actually given as described in the contemporary accounts. The latter seems to have been a hasty makeshift in which materials which had been used in connection with the Lord Mayor's pageant of October 29, 1605, were repainted and used over again. We may be reasonably sure that about the time when order was given to the City of London to make the city ready for the passage of the kings, the King's Players were also notified by the Master of the Revels to have ready for performance the three plays which the record shows that they did get ready and perform, "two at Greenwich and one at Hampton Court," before the two kings.

When King Christian arrived, William Shakespeare was probably taking his usual summer rest with his family at New Place in Stratford on Avon. If so, he would at once have been notified by his company to return to the city and finish the play of *Macbeth* in time for performance before the kings. We must allow a week or ten days for him to reach London, and so we can realize under what pressure and with what haste he may have been compelled to complete his play.

Here is an appropriate place to list the London dramatists who made their contributions toward the entertainment of King Christian. John Ford wrote a poem called "The Monarchs' Meeting," with an "Applause Song" intended to be recited or sung as the kings greeted each other on July 18. Ben Jonson wrote the entertainment which was given at Theobalds on July 24. John Lyly wrote a song given at Theobalds, and the "Pastoral Dialogue" recited at Fleet Conduit on July 31. John Marston wrote the verses for the Cheapside pageant of July 31. John Ford wrote *Honor Triumphant* to accompany the tiltings of August 3 to 6 at Green-

wich. William Shakespeare wrote *Macbeth,* played August
7 at Hampton Court, of which more hereafter.

The best account of the "most pompous passage" of the
kings through London on July 31st is to be found in an
anonymous pamphlet of twenty-eight pages entitled *The
King of Denmarkes Welcome: Containing his arivall, abode,
and entertainement, both in the Citie and other places. London. Printed by Edward Allde. 1606.* It has not since been
reprinted except for certain parts relegated by Nichols to his
Appendix (Vol. IV, p. 1074), and a few short extracts given
by Bond in his *Works of John Lyly* (Vol. I, pp. 505 f.). But a
part of this account which has not been reprinted is of the
greatest interest to all Shakespeareans. The fact that *all* of
King James's grooms of the chamber rode in this procession
would not otherwise be known to us. We may now picture
them in their scarlet liveries embroidered with the king's
arms and riding somewhat ahead of the two kings and observant of all that went on. The sight of the King of Denmark's chief "Drum" on his horse with two kettledrums
hanging one on each side, "which he beat with two red sticks
made like morter pestles," would have been likely to catch
the fancy of the dramatist who wrote, "A drum, a drum!
Macbeth doth come."

This portion of the account (p. 17) is therefore quoted at
length.

First road some xx & odde of the Knight Marshals men for
clearing the way, in white Hats, with greene & white bandes,
white Fustian Doublets, and greene Cloath-hose. After them
roade all our Kings Trumpeters sounding their trumpets, behinde
whom roade our Sergeant Trumpeter with his Mace: After him
rode one of the King of *Denmarkes* Drums, having on each side
his horse hanging a Kettle Drum, which hee beate with two red
sticks, made like two morter pestles, after him roade al the King
of *Denmarks* Trumpeters, sounding their Trumpets: then roade
all our Kinges Groomes and Messengers of the Chamber: after

whome followed one of our Purseuants at Armes; then roade
mounted on great Horses ritchly furnished and themselves
adorned in most costly and rich suites, by two and two, all the
Knights and Gentlemen Pensioners, and Knights & Gentlemen,
our kings sworne Servants. After them roade likewise by two
and two mounted also upon great Horses, ritchly trimde and
themselves verie rich (after the English fashion) all the king of
Denmarkes Gallants and ordinarie Servants: After them roade
another Purseuant at Armes: then roade al the Knights and Gentlemen of our kings Privie Chamber, Bed-chamber, and places of
especiall regard: then the king of *Denmarks* of like place and
degree: then a Herrald at armes: after him all our Barrons and
Vicountes: then the Lord Bishops in their Rochets, then the
Maisters of Request: then all our Earles, according to their
places, not being of the Counsaile: then the Lords of our kinges
Privie-counsell, and them of the king of *Denmarkes* Counsell:
then our Lord Treasurer with his white staffe, & the Lord
Chauncelor with the Pursse, and the Lord Mayor of the Cittie:
then the Duke of *Lynox* all alone: then the Sergeants at armes
with their Maces, then *Garter* king at armes, and all the Gentlemen Ushers: then the Lord Admirall, bearing the sworde, and
the Lord Chamberlaine with his white staffe: after whome roade
the yong Prince, mounted upon a most delicate Courser: after
him on the right hand road the king of *Denmarke,* and on the
left hand our King, about whome went all our Kinges footemen,
in rich coates of Crimson Velvet, yellow Satten Doublets, yellow
Satten Hose, and yellow Stockings. Close behinde the Kings
road the Earle of Worcester, master of the horse: after whom followed almost an hundred or more Gentlemen, the Kings servants,
and on each side went on foote the King of *Denmarkes* Guard of
Harquebushes, being about an hundred or more:

This ceremonial procession through the city occupied the
afternoon of July 31st. As to where the kings spent that
night, the records are contradictory. Apparently some secrecy
was attempted, for there is evidence that Christian spent the
evening quietly at Somerset House, with his sister, and there
remained until the next day. King James and the Danish
nobles went on to Whitehall and were there entertained that

night with fireworks on the river. And James remained at
Whitehall until the afternoon of August 1st, when he was
rowed down the river and met Christian at the Tower of
London.

On the morning of August 1, King Christian proceeded
incognito, together with Prince Henry and several English
and Danish nobles, to Westminster Abbey, which the Danish
diarist describes as "a very fine church of hewn stone, exceedingly well built with sculptures of divers *goddesses* within
and *plaster of Paris* without."

The Danes were much interested in the coronation chair,
which the diarist thus describes:

There was also a fine ornamented chair of alabaster, which,
some hundreds of years ago, was brought from Scotland from a
monastery called Scone. In that same chair all Scottish kings
were crowned before they came to reside in Scotland and in
England. And on that chair was inscribed in Latin verse as follows, "Ni fallet fatum schotti quocomq: Locatum Invenient Lapi-
dem regnum tenentur Jbidem", which means in the Danish language, unless the prophecy fail, wherever the Scots find this chair,
there shall they also rule. There is also under the chair a stone
on which, according to the old English tradition, the patriarch
Jacob rested, when the angel came down the ladder to the
patriarch Jacob. According to the prophecy it had now come to
pass that King Jacobus himself was crowned in that same chair.*

After dinner Christian, together with the Lord Admiral
and the Lord Chamberlain, passed by coach privately to the
City of London, where for a time he was unnoticed until the
citizens found that he was standing on the roof of St. Paul's
Cathedral, there making the print of his foot in the lead.
Thence he went to the Royal Exchange and thence to the
Tower, where James joined him and showed him his armory,
his menagerie, and his mint. Further reference to this visit

---

* The coronation of a King of Scotland at Scone is twice referred to
in the play of *Macbeth:* II, iv, 31 and V, viii, 75.

328 The Royal Play of Macbeth

to the mint will be found in the chapter on the Royal Touch.

The night of August 1 was spent by both kings at White-hall, and the Danish diarist says that a play was acted that night. Assuming that the Admiral's Company, attached to Prince Henry, had some part in these performances, this would seem to have been their opportunity. On Saturday, August 2, the kings were again at Greenwich. During this third Greenwich interval the chief pastime was running at the ring in the tiltyard, at which sport the Dane much excelled the English king. Sunday the 3rd was set for the churching of the queen. On Monday and Tuesday (4th and 5th) running at the ring was supplemented by "bull baiting, bear baiting," and other sports (V, vii, 1, 2). It is recorded by Khunrath that on August 5th they spent the night with plays, dancing, and the like. This play must have been one of the two plays given at Greenwich by the King's Company before the two kings. When the other Greenwich play was given by that company is not recorded, but it was no doubt earlier, for the lines in *Macbeth* attacking Concord, Peace, and Unity (see pp. 359–365) compel us to date the performance of the play of *Macbeth* subsequent to the Greenwich plays. Evidently the order in which payment for the plays is recorded in the *Accounts* (see p. 41) corresponds to the order in which they were actually performed; that is, first there were two at Greenwich and then one at Hampton Court. *Hamlet, Prince of Denmark,* then at the height of its popularity and with Burbage in the title role, was probably one of the plays thus given by the King's Players at Greenwich. Even if the Danes could not understand the English verse, they would have enjoyed seeing the ghost of the Danish king on the platform at Elsinore and the pictures of the Danish kings in the gallery.

The doings of the week of August 4th are further described by Howes:

From this tyme the King of Denmarke during his abode in England in his dailie exercises, used either to hunt, hawke, play

King Christian's Visit 329

at tenis, see wrestling, or the manly play of the English fencers, 6. of the best being selected, and played three against three with foyls, at sundry weapons, according to the manner of fight: there was also the like play between a skilful Scot, and a Germaine: or running at Ring, or Tilt, he ranne at Tilt against the Duke of Lenox, the Earls of Arondell, and Southampton, and the Lord Compton: or else in ryding to see the king's pleasant parkes, and stately houses within twenty myle of London: and upon thurs-daie the 7. of August, he was enstalled knight of the Garter at Windsore, and in his robes of order he did his beisance at the Altar, and the next day, all his privie Counsellers were very solemnly and honorably feasted by the Earle of Rutland at Detford, where both Kinges were expected, but it was late before they returned from Windsore [1615 ed., p. 886].

Howes's account of the doings of the last week of this visit, being meager, needs to be supplemented from other sources. Evidently the program was dislocated by the sudden deter-mination of the King of Denmark to return home, followed by his yielding to persuasion to stay long enough to visit Windsor and there receive his installation as a Knight of the Garter. From Roberts's account we learn that they all left Greenwich on August 6th and went to Richmond, "where they rested that night." The next day (August 7) they dined at Hampton Court and in the afternoon went on to Windsor for the installation; "long did they not stay at Windsor" but returned to Hampton Court, where, the Danish diarist tells us, "in the evening after supper a play was performed." This is all he tells about the first performance of the play of *Macbeth* by the King's Company.

The royal party returned to Greenwich on Friday (August 8) and on the next day went to Rochester, where they spent Sunday, and the following day King Christian boarded his ship and departed for home. The events of the last days of the visit are not here described; for the play of *Macbeth* hav-ing been performed, the occasion loses its interest for us. How easily the unknown Dane might have obtained lasting fame had he described the play which was given at Hampton Court after supper on August 7, 1606!

In observing how the play has been accommodated to conditions arising out of King Christian's visit, we should know how Englishmen felt toward their royal visitor. Arthur Wilson wrote, during the reign of King James, a *History of Great Britain* which was published in London in 1653. Wilson was a boy eleven years old at the time Christian's visit occurred. His recollection supplies the needed picture.

In *July* this year the King of *Danemark* (brother to the *Queen*) came in person as a *visitor,* where he found their shakings somewhat setled, their Terrors abated, and met with not onely all those varieties that Riches Power, and Plenty are capable to produce for *satisfaction,* where *will* and *affection* are the *dispensers,* but he beheld with admiration the *stately Theatre,* whereon the *Danes* for many hundred of yeares had acted their bloody parts: But how he resented their *Exit,* or the last *Act* of that black *Tragedy,* wherein his Country lost her interest, some *Divine Power,* that searches the capacious hearts of *Princes* can onely discover. The *short Moneth* of his stay carryed with it as pleasing a countenance on every side, and their *Recreations* and *Pastimes,* flew as high a flight, as *Love* mounted upon the wings of *art* and *fancie,* the suitable *nature* of the *season* or Times swift foot could possibly arrive at. The Court, City, and some parts of the Country, with Banquettings, Masks, Dancings, Tiltings, Barriers, and other Galantry (besides the manly Sports of Wreastling, and the brutish Sports of bayting Wild-beasts) swelled to such a greatness, as if there were an intention in every particular man, this way to have blown up himself.

The "shakings" and "terrors" are those aroused by the powder plot, and the passage suggests that the gloom of this treason had not wholly passed; but the significance of the quotation is the disclosure of the consciousness of the Englishman of the time of James that the Danes had once been the mortal enemies of the English. The present-day Englishman knows this as a matter of history, but no longer as a racial antagonism. It was felt that a special effort must be made to prevent any discourtesy to Christian, and this has affected those parts of the play of *Macbeth* which were written with knowledge that both kings were to see the play.

THE BLEEDING-SERGEANT SCENE

This scene is no doubt the most difficult problem presented by the play. But if it can be solved, it may tell us more about the writing of the play than can any other source of information.

The solution which is here proposed is that the sudden departure of King Christian is responsible for the unfinished condition of the text of Act I, Scene ii, usually called the "bleeding-sergeant scene." This solution has in substance been advanced by G. B. Harrison in his edition of *Macbeth* published in 1937 (p. 15). To his further proposition that a collaborator took part in the writing of this or any other scene, I cannot agree. The whole play seems to me to be Shakespearean except for the Middletonian lines which have been above specified (p. 275).

This scene is located in a camp near Forres and not far from a battlefield, as is indicated by the stage direction "Alarum within." As produced by Charles Kean and by Henry Irving, and their imitators, King Duncan and his two young sons, the elder of whom has his hand bound up, for he has taken some part in the fight, were surrounded by much bustle and many evidences of proximity to the battle: reinforcements going forward and wounded men coming back to have their wounds dressed by the surgeons in the light of the camp fires, for it is a dark day. The sergeant is brought in on a litter carried by two men less severely wounded than he is. The king and the elder prince question him as to the progress of the fight. He feels honored by this royal attention, raises himself up on one arm and, gesturing with the other, delivers his reply in the formal pompous way in which the old soldier deemed it proper to address his king, punctuated, however, by pauses compelled by pain or short-

332

ness of breath. When because of faintness he can speak no longer, he falls back on his litter, and the young Thane of Ross, who has just entered and who has come in haste from the fight to tell of the victory, completes the account which the sergeant left unfinished. King Duncan at once sentences the traitor Cawdor to death and orders Ross to inform Macbeth that he is now Thane of Cawdor. Thus played, the scene is a very spirited one and has genuine dramatic progress and power.

But the scene has been subject to searching criticism for many years. The Clarendon Press editors rejected it as a spurious addition by an inferior hand, writing in their preface to the play:

We believe that the second scene of the first act was not written by Shakespeare. Making all allowance for corruption of text, the slovenly metre is not like Shakespeare's work, even when he is most careless. The bombastic phraseology of the sergeant is not like Shakespeare's language even when he is most bombastic. What is said of the thane of Cawdor, lines 52, 53, is inconsistent with what follows in scene 3, lines 72, 73, and 112 sqq. We may add that Shakespeare's good sense would hardly have tolerated the absurdity of sending a severely wounded soldier to carry the news of a victory [1869 ed., p. ix].

This judgment has often been controverted. The reason for the metric faults is not difficult to trace, for the troubles all result in the same diagnosis and all yield readily to the same remedy. To hypothesize another hand does not help to explain them. The sergeant's so-called "bombast" is a part of the dramatist's characterization of the man who uses it; and quite clearly this wounded soldier was not sent to carry news and knew nothing of the victory.* All must agree that the

* It is obvious that in writing the concluding sentence of his judgment the writer thereof confused the speeches of Ross with those of the sergeant, and this could only result from hasty writing. This leads me to suspect that the entire judgment of the Clarendon editor was hastily conceived and that it should not be taken as seriously as it has been. It has had an unfortunate effect upon the criticism of the play.

scene plays well on the stage and is quite Shakespearean in its exposition of character, serving excellently to introduce Duncan to the audience and to show how brave a warrior was Macbeth before he met the witches. For these reasons the conclusion of the Clarendon editors has been generally rejected; but reexamination of the whole question is in order, the more so because Professor Dover Wilson in his recent edition of *Macbeth* announces (p. xxiv) that "the sorry state of the second scene, the only blot, but a real blot, upon the play's perfection, is demonstrably the work of an alien hand." Sorry state is strong language to use in reference to a scene possessing such dramatic excellence and acting quality. Whoever wrote it was most assuredly a skilled playwright. The scene is exceedingly effective when the sergeant is in the hands of a competent actor, as was the case when given by the Lyceum Company of Henry Irving, which performance I personally saw several times. The long pauses * during which he struggles for breath enable him to quiet his audience and to give his lines their full effect as he tells of the feats of "brave Macbeth," thus paving the way for Macbeth's sudden entrance in the next scene. To the conclusion that it is the work of another hand than William Shakespeare, I must enter a strong dissent.

The distribution of the "faults" among the characters must first be noted. The king's lines in this scene are smooth,

* I assume the essential correctness of the proposition that as Shakespeare wrote his plays he punctuated them in such a way as to aid the actor in the proper rendition of the lines rather than to aid a reader to understand them when printed. And to a considerable extent this method of punctuation has been perpetuated by the printer in those plays which were printed from the author's manuscript. Consequently, in these plays—and *Macbeth* is one of them—we find dramatic rather than grammatical punctuation. The colon is the point used in this play to tell the actor to make a dramatic pause. This scene in the Cambridge text counts 67 lines of which 33 are assigned to the sergeant. Of 13 colons found in the text as printed in the folio, 9 occur in the sergeant's lines. This disproportionate use of the colon is to give the gasping soldier time to catch his breath.

clear, and concise, as are his lines throughout the play. The lines of the wounded sergeant are inflated, involved, and in three places, badly versified. He was in pain, and his rhetorical style was a conscious affectation of the old soldier, intended to contrast with Duncan's simple and direct style. Ross's lines are written in the same rapid narrative style in which he speaks throughout the play. He is apt to indulge in the exaggeration of a messenger. At two points in the scene his verse breaks down for reasons which are easily discoverable. The scene contains two informative anachronisms both of which evidence consciousness of the recent courtesies of the Danish king in saluting the English king with a grand cannonade and distributing large gratuities to his court. Though hastily written, the dramatist succeeded in making a really good scene of it. Instead of assuming another hand, such failure of versification as occurs in lines 20, 26, 38, 51, and 58 is better accounted for by assuming that the scene was hurriedly written by the author just before its performance, and that it has come down to us without the benefit of that final revision which it would have received had it not been for King Christian's sudden departure for Denmark.

The consequences of this conclusion are sufficiently important to warrant analysis of the inferences on which it is based; for if sound, it not only tells much about how and why the play of *Macbeth* was written, but it may supply an instrument of value for the investigation and understanding of similar difficulties in several other Shakespearean plays.

Reasons have already been given (p. 29) for holding that Shakespeare began writing the play of *Macbeth* with Banquo's question, "How far is it called to Forres?" If this be true, this Scene ii was written later than Scene iii. To make sure of this, compare this scene with lines 89–116 of Scene iii. Both tell of the rebellion and its putting down by Macbeth; both tell of an immediately succeeding attack of Norwegians successfully opposed by Macbeth: and both tell of Cawdor's treachery and condemnation and the bestowal of his title upon Macbeth. The account of these events in this scene is lively and detailed and worked up with a free hand and with wide variances from the source in Holinshed, all of which are calculated to magnify Macbeth's bravery. But the summary of these events in Scene iii is meager and written without reference to things told in Scene ii but with Holinshed's account open before the writer. If scene ii was written first, lines 90–97 of Scene iii are quite superfluous, for the audience already knows what is there told, and Macbeth needs not to be told of what he himself had been doing that day. But if scene ii had not been written, then the lines of Scene iii are needed to explain the account of Cawdor's treachery found in lines 111 to 114 and his sudden and unexpected condemnation.

So then if William Shakespeare wrote this play beginning at Act I, Scene i, and thence went on from scene to scene as we now read the play (which is something I think few dramatists ever do), we find a lively account of Macbeth's notable services to his king immediately followed by a tame and redundant condensation of it. But if the more condensed account of Scene iii was written first, it accomplished a useful dramatic purpose in that scene, and yet there is an adequate reason for the more elaborate account found in the later-written scene.

All things considered, it seems fairly clear that Scene iii was written first, and on a day when Holinshed's account of Macbeth was fresh in the author's mind and while its words lay in his ear; and that at a later date and after a more full development of Macbeth's character had grown in his mind, Scene ii was written; and because the drama was by that time complete he no longer felt tied to what the chronicler had said but gave to his imagination liberty so to mold the traditional account of Duncan's wars as to magnify Macbeth's prodigious accomplishments on the day of battle, thus contrasting sharply his original bravery and loyalty with the cowardice which he later exhibited after superstition took hold of him and his criminal career was under way.

Accordingly, from here on the examination of the scene proceeds upon this hypothesis, and will concern itself with: (*a*) the two accounts of Cawdor, (*b*) the sergeant's "bombast," (*c*) the metric faults, (*d*) the two anachronisms.

a) This conclusion as to the order of writing these scenes affords a new starting point for examination of the problem presented by the differing accounts of Cawdor's treachery, probably the most troublesome contradiction in the plays of William Shakespeare. One must approach this ancient problem with diffidence, but it will not do to say "it is insoluble."

One who reads the play of *Macbeth* for the first time learns in the second scene of the play that when the invading King of Norway assaulted the Scots he was "assisted by that most disloyal traitor the thane of Cawdor," and that Macbeth personally

> Confronted him with self-comparisons,
> Point against point, rebellious arm 'gainst arm,

and won a victory. These lines tell us that the point of Macbeth's sword opposed the point of Norway's sword. This is one *self*-comparison. And that the arm of Macbeth opposed the rebellious arm of Cawdor (for surely Norway was in no sense a rebel). This is the other *self*-comparison.* Macbeth is thus credited with a double victory over two redoubtable warriors opposing him in personal combat at the same time, both of whom are forced to surrender and tribute. King Duncan immediately orders the summary execution of Cawdor and directs Ross to greet Macbeth with the title of Thane of Cawdor.

But this reader passing on to the next scene (iii) is startled

---

* See *Henry IV, Part 1*, IV, i, 122, for a like construction.

to learn that later that same evening, as Macbeth returned from his victory, to the witch who hailed him as Thane of Cawdor he exclaims in surprise "How of Cawdor? The Thane of Cawdor lives a prosperous gentleman." There is no blinking this contradiction. As Dr. Johnson said, "It cannot be palliated." * But if Scene ii was written later than Scene iii, an explanation presents itself. Nothing at all is gained by conjecturing that a second hand wrote it. In fact the difficulty is increased, for although William Shakespeare might have written Scene ii in sole reliance upon his memory concerning what he had written some months before, this other hand would have had no such excuse, for he must first have read what Shakespeare had written before he could start his work.

But it is not hard to see how the text took its present shape if Scene ii was not only written last but was written in a hurried effort to finish the play quickly. When the dramatist began to write his play, the dramatic interest was being built upon the startling effect upon Macbeth of the sudden fulfillment of the second prophecy, and therefore pains were then taken to keep Macbeth ignorant of what Cawdor had been doing that day. In this the *Chronicle* helped, for it knows nothing of the nature of Cawdor's treason. But when, nearly six months later, the same dramatist in great haste wrote Scene ii, his interest had shifted to the development of character. Macbeth as the worthy and brave warrior is to be built up by magnifying his personal valor and accomplishment. And Duncan becomes a king who, though kind and courteous, can be swift and severe in the condemnation of treason against his realm. This shift in dramatic purpose required Cawdor to play a role in this scene different from

* Those who try to explain this are driven to suppose either that Macbeth did not know whom he had been opposing in his fight, or (A. W. Verity) that he feigns ignorance in calling Cawdor "a prosperous gentleman" only to draw forth further information. I cannot take either supposition very seriously.

that assigned to him in Scene iii, and this was accomplished by the addition of a few lines near the end of the scene.

And now we must make choice between two hypotheses. Either the dramatist in doing this had forgotten what he had written about Cawdor in Scene iii; or he was conscious of the contradiction thus created and intended to make an appropriate change in Scene iii, but the play was called for before any change was made.

I prefer the latter alternative. It better accords with other phenomena in Scene ii. In any event I ask the reader to choose one or other of these explanations, or a better; but not to say "insoluble," and not to assume "another hand" whose carelessness would be more incomprehensible than the unfortunate results of Shakespeare's haste.

b) The next matter calling for examination in this scene is the so-called "bombast" and other "faults" in the sergeant's lines.

The heading of this scene calls for the entrance of "a bleeding captaine," and accordingly three speech headings read "Cap." But when he wrote line 34, Shakespeare caused King Duncan to designate Macbeth and Banquo as "our captaines." It seemed incongruous to allow this soldier to rank with Macbeth and Banquo; therefore he went back and changed "captaine" in line 3 to "serieant," but failed to change the headings similarly. "Capitaine" was trisyllabic through the seventeenth century and was so used in lines 3 and 34. The substitute "serieant" was not so, and does not fit well metrically.

Note particularly that all three of the sergeant's speeches begin with a formal simile introduced by the word "as." *

---

* The sergeant's 33 lines contain five similes introduced by "as." Two of them (in line 35) are skeletonized and Aesopian. For the other three the hurried mind of the dramatist turned to current events. These three are (1) the spent swimmers, (2) the equinoctial storms, and (3) the overcharged cannons. The timeliness of the second and third

Shakespeare wished to make it clear that when this old soldier spoke to his king he thought it proper to use rhetorical language and stilted speech; and he would not forego this propriety even though suffering severely. When Hamlet forged a letter from the King of Denmark to the King of England, he filled it with "As'es of great charge" (V, ii, 43). This sergeant did just the same thing in addressing his king. If there are too many of these figures in the sergeant's lines, there are likewise too many in "Aeneas' tale to Dido" in the play of *Hamlet*. But in both cases this style is intentionally used to mark old-fashioned formal speech.

In the first of the sergeant's speeches there are three clauses set off by parentheses. There are only a few such throughout this play. To find three in one short speech is a sign of haste. Careful revision often remolds such clauses so that they fit better into the sentence structure. But there was no time for this, and thus the enclosure of "Like valour's minion" lets us into a secret as to the writing of these lines, which is the next matter for consideration.

It was the dramatist's habit when writing a rapidly developing scene to plunge ahead, notwithstanding verbal or

---

has already been shown. The first has occasioned much debate, and the proper interpretation remains to be found. Were the spent swimmers in a contest? Or was it a rescue? The former is usually assumed, but a race in which one swimmer chokes the other's art is a singular performance. If the latter, were both, or either, or neither saved, and how can this be likened to the doubtfulness of a battle? Some day the answer to these questions may turn up in a news item of the summer of 1606, for the way the incident is told points to topical reference which the expected audience would understand even though we do not.

This excessive use of formal simile confirms the conclusion of Mr. Nosworthy (*Review of English Studies*, April, 1946) that in writing the sergeant's lines the author was more or less consciously reverting to the so-called "Senecan style" which he had used in writing "Aeneas' tale to Dido," and which he thought "smacked of honour," as did King Duncan (I, ii, 45). I wholly agree with Mr. Nosworthy in this, and in his conclusion that there seems to be no reason "for suspecting collaboration or interpolation" in this scene.

metrical difficulty, sometimes leaving marginal suggestions to help him to smooth out the lines on revision. *Timon of Athens,* which he never finished, is full of this sort of thing. Some of it is found in the *Merry Wives.* This particular scene well exhibits this process, for there was no revision and the printer has worked four marginal notes into the text, sometimes in the wrong place and with poor results. To this extent, and only to this extent, was this scene the work of "another hand." *

Lines 16 to 22 of this speech, as printed in the folio, exhibit trouble of this sort:

16   For braue Macbeth (well hee deferues that Name)
17   Difdayning Fortune with his brandifht Steele,
18   Which fmoak'd with bloody execution
19   (like Valours Minion) caru'd out his paffage,
20   Till hee fac'd the Slaue:
21   Which neu'r fhooke hands, nor bad farwell to him,
22   Till he vnfeam'd him from the Naue toth' Chops.

Line 19 requires that three syllables and two unpleasant stresses be given to "minion." Line 20 is a half line, and begins with two unstressed syllables, which latter imperfection Shakespeare does not allow to begin a line if he can help it. Line 21 has caused much discussion as to the intended antecedent of "which." Line 20 and line 22 both begin with "Till"—an unpleasing repetition. There is therefore reason to think that the lines are not printed as Shakespeare intended. The best explanation of this trouble is that soon after writing line 17 the dramatist came to feel that Fortune (the rebel's favorite: see lines 14–15) should not merely be disdained but should be opposed by some antithetical personage, and as he wrote line 29 "Valour" came to mind as the

---

* A "clean copy" written by a scrivener may have intervened between the author's MS and the printer. If so, the scrivener may have been the "other hand." But I think it more likely that because of haste the clean copy was never used, and that the play remained in Shakespeare's MS until printed in the folio.

proper opponent; so he went back and wrote in the margin "like Valour's minion," to take the place of "Disdayning Fortune," but unfortunately without erasing the latter. Consequently the compositor put the marginal gloss in parenthesis and in the wrong place, thus creating the difficulties.* By making the intended substitution in line 17, not only do the metrical defects disappear, but the structure of the entire sentence is bettered, and its true meaning becomes much more clear.

In the sergeant's second speech as printed in the folio there is no verb at the end of line 26, although obviously one is needed. Editors have by common consent supplied "break," as first printed by T. J. 1 † and followed by Pope, and so our modern texts read. It is likely that Shakespeare originally wrote "come," but also wrote the same word again at the end of the next line; and noticing the disagreeable repetition, struck out the first occurrence, expecting to find a good substitution on a revision which never took place.

The sergeant's third speech as printed in the folio evidences transposition. Lines 36 to 38 read:

36   If I say sooth, I must report they were
37   As cannons ouer-charged with double Cracks,
38   So they doubly redoubled stroakes upon the foe:

The last line is unbearable verse.
I think that Shakespeare had first written:

a   If I say sooth, I must report that they
b   Doubly redoubled stroakes upon the foe.

* This solution of the difficulty with these lines was first proposed by John Mitford. It has been occasionally discussed since, is repeated in Furness's New Variorum (rev. ed., p. 19) and by Liddell and by Parrott, but has never had the full attention it deserves nor has it been properly followed up. It is simple and points the way to solve other defects in this scene.

† The Tragedy of Macbeth written by Mr. W. Shakespear; London, printed in the year 1711. [Really at the Hague by Thomas Johnson.]

After writing this, the dramatist determined to make some reference to King Christian's recent courtesies. One of these was the well timed cannonade fired by the Danish ships as the kings rowed up the Thames. Accordingly, he wrote in the margin, opposite the line telling of the "redoubled stroakes," the words: "As cannons over-charged with double Cracks," intending them to be inserted after line *b*, where they fit nicely. But the printer (or scrivener) mistakenly worked them in ahead of that line, and to do so resorted to the poor patching found in our texts.

c) The metric faults in *Ross's lines*. Ross has 14 lines in this scene, and 120 lines in other scenes. By reading all consecutively, one becomes conscious that this Scottish thane possesses a characteristic style of speech. He is commonly a messenger bringing news from a distance in the telling of which he resorts to hyperbole. His lines in this scene are quite in the same style and at the same level as his other lines throughout this play; but in two places *the versification fails*. It is not merely poor verse but a breakdown due to mechanical dislocation. The first such is in line 51, and it disappears if the unmetrical words "with terrible numbers" are removed. The second is in lines 58–59, and it disappears if the words "That Sweno now" are removed. How did these offending and unnecessary words find their way into the text?

It cannot be too much emphasized that in Holinshed's account the invaders were Danes and that there were two different invasions. The first was by a band of Danes commanded by Sweno of Norway, the Danish king's brother. This invasion was repelled, but by a mean trick; so that Shakespeare passed it over. The second invasion (which the play calls "a fresh assault," I, ii, 33) is thus described by Holinshed:

word was brought that a new fleet of Danes was arrived at Kingcorne, sent thither by Canute king of England, in revenge of his brother Suenos overthrow. To resist these enimies, which were alreadie landed, and busie in spoiling the countrie; Macbeth and Banquo were sent with the king's authoritie, who having with them a convenient power, incountered the enimies, slue part of them, and chased the other to their ships. They that escaped and got over to their ships, obtained of Makbeth for a great summe of gold, that such of their friends as were slaine at this last bickering, might be buried in Saint Colmes Inch [170b].

This account Shakespeare followed. I believe he wrote Scene iii before he knew that the King of Denmark was to see the play, and called the invaders Danes as did Holinshed. But before he came to write Scene ii, Christian of Denmark had arrived in England, and it would have been most ungracious to exhibit before the King of Denmark the defeat of Danes by a king of Scotland. Therefore in iii, 95, he erased the words "the invading Danish ranks" (or whatever similar phrase he had written) and substituted "the stout Norweyan ranks," and in line 112 he changed "Denmark" to "Norway," and thereafter in writing Scene ii he used only "Norweyan" and "Norway." No King of Denmark had been named, for Holinshed supplied no such name; but after Norway had taken the place of Denmark it became possible to name the king, for in a previous passage in Holinshed it is stated that "word came that *Sweno, King of Norway,* was arrived in Fife with *a puissant armie to subdue the whole realm of Scotland.*" This sentence not only gave him a name for Norway's king, but suggested that Macbeth's victory over this "puissant" army should be emphasized. So he wrote "with terrible numbers" * opposite the words "Norway himself" as a memorandum that the size of the Norwegian army should be mentioned, but the line which was to embody this suggestion was never written. Also he wrote "That now Sweno" in the margin opposite "Great happiness" (line 59),

* These words resist versification and were not intended to be put into the text without change. Even an "unskillful collaborator" would have made them metrical by writing "with numbers terrible."

so that it might take the place of Duncan's unnecessary ex-clamation, which was to have been deleted. The printer's misuse of these marginalia caused the two metrical break-downs. Steevens recognized this and said, "The irregularity of the meter induces me to believe that *Sweno* was only a marginal reference injudiciously thrust into the text." This is true, and the same is true of the words "with terrible num-bers."

To regain the text of this scene as originally intended, make an intelligent use of these four marginal notes and there emerges a text of which the lines are "absolute in their numbers" and the expression of the thought wholly Shake-spearean. It is by all standards a less violent and more rea-sonable solution than to attribute the scene or any part of it to the lack of skill of some unknown collaborating drama-tist.

d) The two anachronisms are now to be considered. The Elizabethan stage condoned such things; but the two in this scene are so obtrusive and glaring, and so reminiscent of what the Danes had just been doing, that they call for ex-amination. This indicates that they were put into the play just before it was performed, in order to gratify the Danish king and his court.

During Christian's visit the English court suddenly be-came dollar-conscious. On August 12, 1606, John Pory wrote to Sir Robert Cotton:

The King of Denmark in the gifts hath not been inferior, for he hath given in court 30,000 dollars, viz to the household be-neath the stairs 15,000 dollars, to the officers above the stairs 10,000 dollars, and to Querry or Stabler 5,000 dollars.

William Shakespeare as a groom of the outer chamber was an "officer above the stairs" and entitled to a share of the "10,000 dollars" given to them by Christian as largess. Eng-lishmen knew little about the "dollar." But Shakespeare now knew just how much a dollar was worth in English currency. Therefore it was that in place of Holinshed's statement that the ancient Danes had obtained a right of sepulture in Saint Colme's Inch *"for a great summe of gold,"* the dramatist, to show consciousness of the 10,000 Danish dollars, some of which were in the pockets of himself and his fellow actors, altered Holinshed (for dollars were first coined in 1518 and they are silver coins, not gold) and wrote that these Danes (now called Norweyans) had purchased a right of burial at Saint Colme's Inch, by disbursing *"Ten thousand dollars to our general use"* (I, ii, 64).

The other anachronism, "As cannons overcharged with double cracks," is found in line 36. How this superfluous line crept into the text from a marginal note has already been suggested. It has always been considered an intruder. Cunningham in his edition of the play says, "This is indeed 'an awkward phrase' as the Clar. Edd. remark, and we may be quite certain that Shakespeare is not the author of it." Why so? The phrase is poor English but good Scottish; and the play was for Scots, who had long called the shots of cannon "crakkis." (See *O.E.D.*, Crack sb. I-1-b. Note the citations from Barbour's *Bruce*.)

During the days of Christian's visit, people talked much of the magnificence of the cannonade delivered by the Danish ships. Roberts's account of this has been quoted (p. 320). Howes (1615 ed., p. 885) tells that "the Danish ships proclaimed their joy by the cannon's mouth." Khunrath says that the Danish ships fired many shots from heavy cannon, "mostly metal ones," one after another and because every ship kept its precise time a long chain of firing was made; and Pory's letter (see the next footnote) tells of "three or four skorr of great shott discharged" from the ships of Denmark. On August 1, 1606, the kings visited the Tower of London and beheld "ordinance of all Sorts, even from the double canon to the hand pystoll" (*King of Denmarkes Welcome*, p. 26). After seeing the ordinance, King Christian ascended the

White Tower and himself discharged a piece (Stow, *Chronicle*, p. 886b).

Evidently these heavy cannons were of special interest to the kings, and a Scot might well call their loud discharges "double cracks." Therefore we should not be surprised to find the words "as cannons overcharged with double cracks" put in the margin of the draft of the play with intent that at the first performance they should be spoken following the line ending "foe" (I, ii, 38), and perhaps thereafter be discarded. But a perverse fate has perpetuated them in the text, squeezed into the wrong place. This occasioned an unfortunate anachronism, for the word "cannon" as a piece of ordnance first appears in *O.E.D.* in 1525: "5 gret gounes of brasse called cannons."

"Cannons" and "dollars" in the days of Edward the Confessor, and in both cases pointedly and gratuitously thrust in, are the two anachronisms in the play. The salutes and gifts of the King of Denmark were the things which people were talking about during the first ten days of August, 1606.* The play thus exhibits consciousness of these royal courtesies.

After examining the defects which have caused some to reject this scene as non-Shakespearean, certain things should

* There has survived a letter of John Pory to Sir Robert Cotton dated August 12, 1606 (Cotton Library, Julius, C. III. 45). Pory was a member of Parliament and Sir Robert's correspondent, sending him the city news when he was in the country. This letter was written the day after Christian left and tells what had happened in London during the last few days. Interestingly enough, it tells about the King of Denmark's gifts of dollars (this has just been quoted), the salutes of the cannons, and notes that "Sir Edward Michelbourne hath cleared himself with great honour." Sir Edward was the owner of the *Tiger* just returned from the East (see supra p. 302). Thus do we find in the gossip of this contemporary letter reference to three different things which are referred to in the late-written prelude of the first act of *Macbeth*. Part of the letter is printed in Nichols's *Progresses of James*, Vol. II, p. 91. It is also incorrectly printed in *Court and Time of James I* (London, 1848), Vol. I, p. 65. Only in the latter will be found the reference to Sir Edward Michelbourne.

here be noted which point to William Shakespeare as author of the scene.

The eight speeches of Duncan in this scene are marked by singular brevity and clarity of thought, as indeed are Duncan's speeches in other scenes in this play. He does not use unnecessary words. He uses a clear and direct style, and has a habit of passing with characteristic abruptness from one thought to another. In his longest speech (I, iv, 33–43) there are two sudden changes of thought so abrupt that some have suggested the loss of some lines. But this was Duncan's manner of thought. In sharp contrast with this is the ornate and involved style of speech of the sergeant. Why did the dramatist create this contrast?

The statement of John Davies of Hereford, written shortly after *Macbeth* was produced, to the effect that William Shakespeare played kingly parts in his plays, has been quoted on page 9. Baldwin and others have thus been led to conjecture that Shakespeare wrote Duncan's part for himself; and this conjecture is well supported by stage tradition.* It was but natural that the author of lines which he expected himself to recite before a King of Scotland should take care to observe what that king had said about how a King of Scotland should speak, for it so happens that in his *Basilicon Doron* the king had given precise instructions to his son as to the language which a King of Scotland should use:

In both your speaking and your gesture, use a naturall and plaine forme, not fairded with artifice: for (as the Frenchmen say) *Rien contre-faict fin:* but eschewe all affectate formes in both.

In your language bee plaine, honest, naturall, comely, cleane, short, and sentencious: eschewing both the extremities, as well in not using any rusticall corrupt leide, † as booke-language, and

* John Litchfield (whose wife played Lady Macbeth in G. F. Cooke's performances) in his edition of the play (London, Mathews and Leigh, 1807), p. 13, stated that "Shakespeare is the supposed original performer" of the part of Duncan.

† Leide: lead, or other base metal.

penne and inke-horne tearmes: and least of al mignarde and effoeminate tearmes. But let the greatest part of your eloquence consist in a naturall, cleare, and sensible forme of the deliverie of your mind, builded ever upon certaine and good groundes; tempering it with gravitie, quicknes, or merines, according to the subject, and occasion of the time [pp. 114–115].

This thought was again expressed by the king when on March 19, 1603/4, he addressed his first Parliament, and told them that "it becommeth a King, in my opinion, to use no other eloquence than plainnesse and sincerity."

The easy grace and the clear manner with which a king should speak was attractive to Shakespeare, and we may think that he could assume this air of royal dignity and use this simple diction on the stage with good effect. But this kingly style could be made even more striking by interspersing Duncan's words with those of an interlocutor who speaks just as James says a king should not speak. The pompous old soldier therefore speaks to his king in what James calls "penne and inke-horne tearmes," overloaded with simile and figures of speech. When the sergeant's part is played in this spirit, it proves exceedingly effective on the stage, well setting off Duncan's simple, gracious, and kindly deliverance.

This distinction between "speech that savoureth of the affectation of art and precepts" and the royal gift of clear speech had just been pressed upon the attention of the people of England in the address to the king with which Bacon's *Proficience and Advancement of Learning* is prefaced. This book issued from the press early in November, 1605. Bacon contrasts labored speech, which he defines as above, with "Your Majesty's manner of speech [which] is indeed prince-like, flowing as from a fountain." It was a very happy thought to exemplify what the king had said in his *Basilicon Doron,* and what Francis Bacon had thus emphasized, by causing the labored speech of the sergeant to be contrasted in the play with the clear speech of Duncan, King of Scotland. This is why, as the sergeant ends his third speech quite exhausted by the effort, the kindly Duncan commends the soldier's honorable style: "So well thy *words* become thee as thy wounds; they smack of honour both." It would seem that the dramatist wrote these words so that the actor of Duncan could at the same time call attention to his own simple words and obtain the pardon of the audience for the labored speeches of the sergeant.

There is in this scene another distinctly Shakespearean touch. Many Sophoclean ironies, so characteristic of this play, have been pointed out by Bradley (see p. 6). There is a remarkable one in this scene which I think could have been evolved by no other mind than that of the author of this play.

Duncan, hearing of Cawdor's treason, exclaims,

> No more that thane of Cawdor shall deceive
> Our bosom interest: go pronounce his present death,
> And with his former title greet Macbeth.

In the first of these lines how innocently the demonstrative slips in! No more *that* Thane of Cawdor shall deceive; and it is spoken in the same breath in which Duncan creates *another* Thane of Cawdor, who so soon will thrust his dagger in Duncan's bosom! This is the sign manual of William Shakespeare with which the scene closes.*

---

* Since the above chapter was written there has come into my hands Dr. Richard Flatter's recent book entitled *Shakespeare's Producing Hand*. This contains a chapter on the bleeding-sergeant scene which, although approaching the subject from a different standpoint, arrives at the same conclusion that I have reached independently, and has expressed it in language which I take the liberty to quote because it so well expresses what I believe to be the truth about this scene:

Summing up, I find it impossible to imagine any "interpolator" or "assistant" who would have been able to write this episode of the "Bleeding Sergeant." The gaps and pauses found there are unmistakable hall-marks of the master's forge, and the craftsmanship with which the Captain's exhaustion is characterized by his manner of speaking is unsurpassed by anything we can find even in Shakespeare's best plays. And yet during three centuries the editors were bewildered by what they should have admired as an apex and marvel of dramatic expressiveness [p. 101].

TOPICAL INTERJECTIONS IN
MACBETH IV, ii AND iii

The swift rush of events, which helps to make *Macbeth* such a truly great play, slows down after the caldron scene; and a relaxation of the dramatic tension is perceptible in the last two scenes of Act IV, the original pace not being regained until near the end of IV, iii.

It is during this lull before the stormy ending of the play that one would expect to find inserted topical matter such as might attract the special personal interest of the two kings before whom it was to be given. The following lines are distinctly of occasional rather than dramatic value. They were put into the play, I think, by Shakespeare himself, but after the drama was otherwise written, and with a view to the expected audience.

a)	IV, ii, 38–41, and 59–64	(The hasty widow)
b)	IV, ii, 44–58	(Swearing and lying)
c)	IV, iii, 91–99	(Concord, Peace, and Unity)
d)	IV, iii, 140–158	(The royal touch)

I have said that these additions were by Shakespeare. The last three of them were surely written by him, although suggestion from the Master of the Revels as to subject matter is not excluded. The first addition is so harsh an intrusion that I would be glad to think that under its power to "perfect" any royal play the Revels office, without reference to Shakespeare's desires, put nine or ten lines into this play to be spoken by a little boy in the King's Company whom someone at court wished to show off. And yet Shakespeare may have written them even though unwillingly.

There are reasonable grounds for holding that George

Buck, as Acting Master of the Revels, had some part in initiating and promoting the production of the play of *Macbeth*. He had recently acquired responsibility for the king's Revels. He had previous knowledge of the Banquo story (see supra p. 21). It would have been natural for him to suggest to Dr. Gwinn the theme for the Oxford playlet, and noting the cordial reception of this by the king to suggest to the dramatist of the King's Company that he expand this theme in a play for the king. When the decision was made to have the play finished in time to be shown before King Christian, the Master of the Revels would be responsible for the accomplishment of this. He was required to attend the rehearsal of a court play. He had the right to make suggestions for what he considered its betterment, and we may see signs of this in the rather awkward way in which some things have been thrust into the text of a drama which in other respects is a model of the best type of dramatic structure.

These four topical insertions will be examined seriatim, *a* and *b* in this chapter, *c* and *d* in the next two chapters.

a) IV, ii, 38–41, and 59–64. These lines jarringly interrupt a scene in which the more to enrage the audience against Macbeth's cruelty, they are compelled to witness the murder by his order of Macduff's wife and little boy. To make the scene more heart-rending, Shakespeare wrote a pathetic dialogue between the boy and his mother as to the safety of little birds, all spoken in childish sincerity. Lady Macduff having told her boy that his father is "dead," he has wit enough to say (line 37), "My father is not dead, for all your saying"; to which, as the scene was written, the mother rejoins (line 42), "Thou speak'st with all thy wit; and yet, i' faith, With wit enough for thee," meaning that his boyish wit has been able to divine that his father has not really deserted his family, but has gone abroad for high and controlling reasons. All this is in good verse and in characteristic Shakespearean diction. But we are disturbed, some are even shocked, to find in this pleasing dialogue some prose lines interjected which are quite out of keeping with the pathos of the scene, transforming the boy for the moment into a pert juvenile. Liddell has very forcible and apt remarks on the subject.

> *L. Macd.* Yes he is dead; how wilt thou do for a father?
> *Son.* Nay, how will you do for a husband?
> *L. Macd.* Why, I can buy me twenty at any market.
> *Son.* Then you'll buy 'em to sell again.

("Sell" here means to "cheat," *O.E.D.*, I, 9. See Argument to Jonson's *Volpone*.)

Lines 60 to 64 are a similar prose interjection:

> *L. Macd.* But how wilt thou do for a father?
> *Son.* If he were dead, you'ld weep for him:

if you would not, it were a good sign that I should quickly have a new father.

> *L. Macd.* Poor prattler, how thou talk'st!

These lines are wholly at variance with all that has gone before. So far from blackening the murderer, they seem designed to lessen our esteem for both mother and child. Shakespeare was not above this sort of thing on occasion, but did not resort to it in plain violation of his dramatic art. We can only confess that if there was some temporary pertinency of the idea of the widow buying twenty husbands at market to deceive them again, which made the lines bearable at the time of the play's performance, the pertinency has passed and the lines jar. That our diagnosis of after-insertion is correct is proved by what immediately follows.

b) IV, ii, 44–58. These lines are also a *prose* insertion in the midst of *verse*. They continue, although less objectionably, the "smart boy" dialogue. They are without dramatic significance, but not so wholly inapt as the lines previously inserted; and in this case the topical reason for the insertion is quite obvious.

No doubt Shakespeare's company had a little boy with a peculiar talent for sophisticated talk. They wished to exhibit his feats before the two kings. They gave him the "hasty widow" lines, and also added further lines, telling that all who "swear and lie" are traitors and must be hung.

To understand the pertinency of this otherwise tedious chatter, we must recall that after the Gunpowder Plot Parliament held a long session which did not end until May 27, 1606, on which day went into effect the statutes which had been passed during the session, including, as we have seen, the Profanity Statute. The fourth chapter of the *Acts* of this Parliament, passed at James's request to sift his Catholic subjects, required them to take an Oath of Allegiance, which must be read before we can understand the significance of this talk. The oath:

I, A. B. doe truely and sincerely acknowledge, professe, testifie and declare in my conscience before God and the world, That our Soveraigne Lord King James, is lawfull King of this Realme, and of all other his Majesties Dominions and Countreyes: And that the Pope neither of himselfe, nor by any authoritie of the Church or Sea of Rome, or by any other meanes with any other, hath any power or authoritie to depose the King, or to dispose of any of his Majesties Kingdomes or Dominions, or to authorize any forraigne Prince, to invade or annoy him or his Countreys, or to discharge any of his Subjectes of their Allegiance and obedience to his Majestie, or to give Licence or leave to any of them to beare Armes, raise tumults, or to offer any violence or hurt to his Majesties Royal person, State or Government, or to any of his Majesties Subjectes within his Majesties Dominions. Also I doe sweare from my heart, that, notwithstanding any declaration or sentence of Excommunication, or deprivation made or granted, or to be made or granted, by the Pope or his Successors, or by any Authoritie derived, or pretended to be derived from him or his Sea, against the said King, his Heires or Successors, or any Absolution of the said subjects from their Obedience; I will beare faith and true Allegiance to his Majestie, his Heires and Successors, and him and them will defend to the uttermost of my power, against all Conspiracies and Attempts whatsoever, which shal be made against his or their Persons, their Crowne and dignitie, by reason or colour of any such Sentence, or declaration, or otherwise, and will doe my best endevour to disclose and make knowen unto his Majestie, his Heires and Successors, all Treasons, and traiterous Conspiracies, which I shall know or heare of, to be against him or any of them. And I doe further sweare, That I doe from my heart abhorre, detest and abjure as impious and Hereticall, this demnable doctrine and Position, That Princes which be excommunicated or deprived by the Pope, may be deposed or murthered by their Subjects, or any other whatsoever. And I doe beleeve, and in conscience am resolved, that neither the Pope nor any person whatsoever, hath power to absolve mee of this Oath, or any part thereof; which I acknowledge by good and full Authoritie to be lawfully ministred unto me, and doe renounce all pardons and dispensations to the contrary. And all these things I doe plainely and sincerely acknowledge and sweare, according to these expresse wordes by me spoken, and according to the plaine and common sense and understanding of the same words, without any Equivocation, or mentall evasion, or secret reservation whatsoever. And I doe make this Recognition and acknowledgement heartily, willingly and truely, upon the true Faith of a Christian. So helpe me God.

As originally introduced in the Parliament, the bill was still more stringent and required every affiant to swear that the Pope possessed no power to excommunicate the King of England, as he had once excommunicated Queen Elizabeth. During this stage of the debate Zorzi Giustinian, the Venetian ambassador, wrote under date of February 24, 1606, to his seignory:

I am informed that in Parliament they will enforce an oath, to be taken without exception by all, that they do not believe the pope has authority to depose or excommunicate a Sovereign. If any refuse he will be held for a Catholic forthwith, and they will proceed against him not for the eighty crowns a month that recusants have to pay, but for the entire two thirds of his income.

This will render the position of the Catholics intolerable. These and other provisions will have one or other of two results, either the Catholic religion will disappear entirely, or the Catholics, driven to desparation, will attempt something similar to the recent plot [*Cal. of State Papers—Venetian*, Vol. X, p. 321].

But James saw that this would not accomplish his purpose, and he had the oath changed so that it only denied that his excommunication by the Pope would release any of his subjects from their allegiance or give them the right to take his life, as the powder plotters had tried to do.* Consequently, as soon as this Statute went into effect, there broke out a violent difference of opinion among the English Catholics as to the lawfulness of taking this oath.

The Archpriest Blackwell and many of the secular priests exhorted the English Catholics to take the oath (*Mr. George Blackwell, his Answer &c.* [London, 1607], pp. 9, 13, 21 to 25). The Jesuits were against the oath because in violation of their most cherished principles. James expected in this way to harry them out of England. But equivocation would enable many Catholic subjects to take the oath. *Only a few days before the play of* Macbeth *was first performed*, the Venetian ambassador Giustinian wrote again to the Doge and Senate:

It seems that almost all these Catholics are resolved to take the Oath, and although many clerics who are here do all they can to prevent it, as too great an injury to the Apostolic See, still as loss of property and ruin overhangs those who refuse, and as there are to be found some clerics who hold that in such dire stress the oath may be taken without jeopardizing the soul, it is thought that the greater number will submit to the necessity [*Cal. of State Papers—Venetian*, Vol. X, p. 391].

While the latter part of the play of *Macbeth* was being

---

* See King James's *Apology for the Oath of Allegiance* (London, 1609), p. 9; Article on George Blackwell in *D.N.B.*, Vol. II, p. 607; and Dodd's *Church History*, Vol. II, p. 366.

written, there was no subject more universally discussed and debated in England than the questions resulting from the Oath of Allegiance, which was to be tendered by the magistrates to all Englishmen suspected of Catholicity, and this was true of about 25 per cent of the population of England.

In Harris's *Account of James the First* (London, 1753, p. 95), it is stated that the Catholics, for the most part, complied with this oath until the Pope in October, 1606, issued the first of his breves forbidding them to do so.   Thus we know that at this moment most of the Catholics did "swear and lie," that is, take the oath, although they thereby swore to that which they did not believe to be the truth.   The phrase was current with this meaning.   John Lyly in his *Love's Metamorphosis,* as revived in 1599 or 1600, wrote: "If men *swear and lie,* how will you trie their loves?"   It is quite possible that John Lyly, who was still a sort of supernumerary in the Revels Office, wrote these lines for the little boy.   There was also in use the equivalent phrase "swear and forswear" with which equivocating Catholics were charged.*

Lady Macduff's loneliness makes her petulant.   She suggests that her husband has left her because his fears had made him a traitor.   A little later the dialogue proceeds:

Son.   What is a traitor?
L. Macd.   Why, one that swears and lies.
Son.   And be all traitors that do so?
L. Macd.   Every one that does so is a traitor, and must be hanged.
Son.   And must they all be hanged that swear and lie?
L. Macd.   Every one.
Son.   Who must hang them?
L. Macd.   Why, honest men.

* See, e.g., *The Arraignment and Execution of the Late Traitors* (London, 1606); reprinted in *Harleian Miscellany,* 1809, Vol. III, p. 50.
See also the *Examination of John Tucker:* "Jesuits and priests are now allowed by the Pope to deny their profession, or to swear and forswear anything to heretics for their own preservation."   And note its use by Shakespeare in 1599 in *As You Like It,* V, iv, 57.

Son. Then the liars and swearers are fools, for there are liars and swearers enow to beat the honest men and hang up them.

A good commentary upon these lines is the declaration of the militant Jesuit Robert Parsons in his *Judgment of a Catholic Gentlemen* (St. Omers, 1608), where he says:

This oath . . . drives men into David's dilemma of streights, to fall either into the hands of God or men; of God, if the oath be taken, because they swear against their conscience; of men in that their goods, life and liberty are liable to law.

This was the dilemma in which King James wished to place the Catholics, and the little Macduff boy is telling the king how well his plan is working out. Those who refused to take the oath were subject to heavy penalties, but Lady Macduff, tracing the other horn of the Catholics' dilemma, says that the larger number who take the oath are traitors and should be hung because they "swear and lie."

All of the prose portions of this pert-boy dialogue appear to be late additions to the play made probably just prior to its performance and while final rehearsals were proceeding, likely in some suitable apartment in or near the palace at Greenwich. The opportunities for knowledge of, and interest in, what was going on were great, and suggestions from members of the court or the Master of the Revels as to the forthcoming play were to be expected. By good fortune the topical insertions thus added under external influence are confined to the latter part of the fourth act or to the late-written bleeding-sergeant scene, and are of such a nature as to interfere little or not at all with the progress of the play.

CONCORD, PEACE, AND UNITY

After the flight of Macduff it only remained to bring the play of *Macbeth* to an end by exhibiting the reduction of Great Dunsinane and the overthrow of the tyrant. This scarcely afforded enough material to fill the last two acts of the play. Therefore to maintain suspense the dramatist, following his source in Holinshed, interposed an unexpected obstacle to the revolt of the thanes. Its success depended upon Malcolm's willingness to take his father's throne; but Malcolm tells Macduff that he is unfit for kingship because of imaginary vices and therefore unwilling to lead a revolt. The recitation by him of these supposed vices ends in lines the true significance of which has been entirely lost.

> Nay, had I powre, I should
> Poure the sweet Milke of Concord, into Hell,
> Uprore the universall peace, confound
> All unity on earth.
>
> [IV, iii, 97–100]

These singular lines are a ranting attack upon Concord, Peace, and Unity, the three national virtues most dear to the heart of King James. Why were such lines put into the play?

It is first to be noted that the lines are an after-insertion taking the place of other lines which have been removed.*

The scene in which the lines occur follows its source in Holinshed very closely and transmits to us the most ancient and fixed tradition concerning the Macbeth story, derived from John of Fordun (1385), who was enough of an artist to see that his tale would gain in interest if this obstacle were

---

* Mr. Dover Wilson in his recent edition of *Macbeth* asserts, and I think rightly, that Shakespeare's rewriting of the original dialogue at this point cannot be denied (p. xxxi).

thrown in Macduff's way. Fordun filled no less than six chapters of his *Chronicle* with fictitious conversations between Macduff and Malcolm disclosing Malcolm's initial distrust of Macduff and his efforts to test his honesty. This fiction was found so pleasing that, although it now seems tedious, it reappears in Andrew of Wyntoun, Boece, Bellenden, Holinshed, and Buchanan. In these accounts, after accusing himself of other faults, the final and most intolerable vice with which Malcolm charges himself is always that of deceitfulness and lying, which Macduff deems a fault not to be endured in a king; so that he gives up the struggle, whereupon Malcolm retracts his words and explains that he has falsely accused himself of vices which he has never practiced and that he will immediately head the proposed revolt.

That Shakespeare, too, threw these obstacles in Macduff's way and that the final vice of lying, as well as the other two, was originally designated in the text of the play are evident from lines 125 to 131, where an accusation of lying is specifically retracted by Malcolm. And yet the charge thus retracted is no longer to be found in the play, and in the place where it ought to be we find the lines which have been quoted above.

The immediate inquiry, therefore, is: Why did the dramatist thus desert his source in Holinshed, excise from his play the charge of lying, and substitute this new subject matter? It was because of an occurrence in the City of London on July 31, 1606, when King James and King Christian of Denmark made their "most pompous progress" through the city.

The three abstract virtues attacked in Malcolm's inserted speech are Concord, Peace, and Unity.

As King James of Scotland made his slow progress in the spring of 1603 from Edinburgh to London, he let it be known that Peace and Unity were his cardinal political ideals; for he wished to bring about peace with Spain and the union of his kingdoms. The welcoming speeches with which he was greeted and the panegyrical poems written to honor the new king reflect these ideals. In his speech to his first Parliament he told them: "I bring you two gifts, one peace with foreign nations, the other union with Scotland" (Green's *History*, Vol. V, p. 154). As a result, the phrase "Peace and Unity" soon attained wide currency throughout England.

But there was strong opposition. The profiteers of the war party were bitterly opposed to peace with Spain. And the London mob foolishly feared that the Scots would descend upon the southern kingdom and exercise too much power. They therefore seized every opportunity to attack the proposed peace and the union of the kingdoms. In the year 1606, to blunt this opposition, the kingly phrase was enlarged and became a triplet proclaiming Love, Peace, and Unity as the royal ideals. In the early summer of that year appeared (S. R., May 9) Anthony Nixon's little serio-comic tract entitled *The Black Year*. Here (p. D²v) we read: "Many think well of themselves in making the Doctrine of love, peace, and unity, the occasion of strife, contention and heresie."

This accurately sets forth the situation as it existed when the Danish king arrived in the Thames on July 17, 1606, and was invited to make his ceremonial progress, together with his brother-in-law, through the City of London on July 31. For this occasion the dramatist John Marston was commissioned to write the Latin speech (for King Christian understood little English) to be spoken to the two kings as they beheld the pageant of the day erected in Cheapside. This address was designed to glorify Love, Peace, and Unity. The original holograph MS of the address, signed by John Marston, is preserved in the British Museum. It has been printed in Bullen's edition of Marston's *Works* (Vol. III, p. 407). But the Latin tongue possessing no word accurately denoting Love as a political virtue, Marston chose *Concordia* as the best Latin substitute for Love. Thus it came about that for this single occasion the triplet became Concord, Peace, and Unity. The address, as the reader will find, contains a glorification by Concordia of Heavenly Peace and Britons' Unity.

There are several accounts of the events of this day reprinted by Nichols in his *Progresses;* but the most interesting is the one entitled *The King of Denmarkes Welcome.* Here is to be found the description of the composition of the royal procession as it passed from the Tower to Whitehall. It has already been quoted (pp. 325–6). Thus we learn that near the front of the procession, following the King of Denmark's trumpeters, "roade all our Kinges Groomes and Messengers of the Chamber" (p. 18). William Shakespeare was a "Groom of the Chamber," and we may therefore feel assured that he rode in person in his king's procession, and saw the unfortunate disturbance which occurred when they reached the pageant in Cheapside which is now to be described.

This so-called "pegme" was a huge arched wooden structure, some forty feet in height and erected overthwart Cheapside where it reaches Paul's Churchyard, and abounding with allegorical and mythological figures. Near the top were the arms of Great Britain and Denmark joined together; and on a turret above this was the hatchment of Great Britain within which "sate enthroned the genius of Concorde," who at the proper moment was let down as the *deus ex machina* to deliver her address to the kings in praise of Peace and Unity.

The accounts published during the days of Christian's visit tactfully omit reference to the disgraceful tumult of the mob which accompanied this pageant. To learn the truth about it the account of the annalist Howes, in his *Continuation of Stow's Chronicle* (1615 ed., p. 886a), must be read:

Then the pageant after it had ceased her melodious harmonie, began to expresse the purpose thereof, viz. Divine *Concord* as sent from Heaven, descended in a cloud from the toppe unto the middle stage, and with a loud voyce, spake an excellent speech in Latine, purporting their heartie welcome, with the heavenly happines of *peace* and *unitie* amongst Christian Princes, &c but through the distemperature of the unrulie multitude, the Kings could not well hear it, although they inclined their ears very seriously thereunto.*

John Davies of Hereford was so sensitive to this insult to his king that when he wrote a poem of welcome to the Danes called *Bien Venu* (reprinted in Grosart's edition of Davies, Vol. I) he inserted an apology for what had happened. One stanza of this is here quoted:

> And, let thy Muses so in Pageants speake,
> That they may make the Clamorous Crowde attend:
> Although their voice, through wants, become so weake
> That they may seeme to speake to little end:
> Sith the rude Multitude will silence breake,
> Though speake there may an Angell, or a Feind:
> Yet what they speake, in Print, in Print may be
> Convai'd aloft, downe to Posteritie.

Thus we learn that the "clamorous crowd" created an uproar which spoiled the pageant and prevented the kings from hearing the words addressed to them.† John Davies could

---

* The noteworthy words are here italicized.

† Evidently trouble of this sort had been expected, for in the parallel account by Henry Roberts of *The Most Royal and Honorable Entertainment &c.* we read that during the procession the marshals of the city "with such regard did they apply themselves in placing and governing them that thereby much harm was prevented, which might otherwise have happened by the unruly multitude." The interruption of the pageant was evidently premeditated.

There is a picture of this "unruly multitude" who created this disturbance in *The History of Great Britain, Being the Life and Reign of King James the First,* published in 1653 and written by Arthur Wilson who had witnessed the times of which we are speaking. In this work, after describing King James's negotiations for peace and union, there is the following description of the condition of the Londoners in 1604–1605 (p. 28):

The Sword and Buckler trade being now out of date, one *corruption* producing another (the City of *London* being allwaies a fit *Receptacle* for such, whose *prodigalities* and *wasts* made them Instruments of *Debaucheries*) divers *Sects* of *vitious Persons*, going under the Title of *Roring Boyes*, *Bravadoes, Roysters*, &c. commit many insolencies; the Streets swarm night

only express the hope that people, though they could not hear the words of Concord, would yet read what she had said as soon as it appeared in print. But this was not soon; for Bullen's edition of Marston was not published until 1887. There one may now read what Concord said in praise of peace and unity in forty-three lines of Latin iambics.

All that the kings and their retinues could do as the crowd drowned the voice of Concord was to pass quietly on their way, thinking their own thoughts. And William Shakespeare personally witnessed this.

Now we are in a position to understand why he changed Malcolm's speech by taking out lines already written which proclaimed lying or deceitfulness as the most offensive vice and substituting this insulting treatment of Concord, Peace, and Unity as a still greater vice, thus making clear to the kings just what the King's Company thought of the conduct of this mob. The lines now seem mere rant, but Shakespeare wrote them glowing with indignation at what he had witnessed. There was no such verb as "uproar"!* He coined it as the only word fitting such a scene.

Christian's visit came to an end when he left Greenwich for Rochester on August 9 and the next day went aboard his ship. Reference has already been made (p. 41) to the facts which concur in pointing to the play performed by the King's Players before the two kings at Hampton Court on the eve-

---

and day with bloody quarrels, private *Duels* fomented, specially betwixt the *English* and *Scots*.

The Roaring Boys no doubt included sons of the men who returned ten years earlier from the sack of Cadiz swaggering with Sword and Buckler and proudly displaying their "Cades beards." They were in favor of Sir Walter Raleigh's expansive schemes. The peace of King James was odious to them. Equally so was union with Scotland.

* Many emendations have consequently been proposed. The text should stand, the reason for the special coinage being understood. The verb "uproar" was a natural one for Shakespeare to coin and use when describing the tumults raised by the "Roaring Boys." In *The Tempest*, I, i, 18, he wrote, "what care these roarers for the name of King?"

ning of August 7, 1606, as the first performance of the play
of *Macbeth*. Sufficient time had then elapsed after the disturbance in Cheapside for the author to insert these lines in
his play, obtain their allowance by the Master of the Revels,
and try them out in rehearsal. An earlier date of performance at Greenwich after July 31 but before August 9
seems improbable, although of course not impossible. All
things considered, I think we make no mistake in assigning
the performance to August 7, 1606. Therefore let the en-
thusiastic Shakespearean picture in his mind's eye the first
performance of *Macbeth* in the great hall of Hampton Court
as it was fitted up on the evening of August 7th, with a stage
and two royal chairs immediately in front of it, in which sat
the two kings, with accommodation on either side for the
English, Scottish, and Danish courtiers. Keeping this picture in mind, he may watch the face of the Scottish king as
he sees his royal ancestors descended in line from Banquo,
personated by actors of the King's Company slowly passing
one after the other over the stage as the procession of the
kings. And as the last one passes he may hear Macbeth en-
viously say, "some I see that two-fold balls and treble sceptres
carry"—fit words to warm the heart of the king. He may
also hear Malcolm, another of James's ancestors, describe as
the most outrageous possible vice for one to

> Poure the sweet Milk of Concord into Hell,
> Uprore the universal peace, confound
> All unity on earth.

Strange words these: in the mouth of Malcolm they were
mere rant, extravagant and insincere; as written by William
Shakespeare, glorious rant expressing his just indignation;
as heard by King James, a soothing salve to his wounded
pride. Since then, for a long period of years, the words have
seemed empty and without significance. But it now comes
about that again the same words have real meaning in the
play; and what is more startling, they now describe with ter-

rible distinctness a stark reality with which the world is faced and which causes them to give forth a most ominous sound today.

TOUCHING FOR THE KING'S EVIL

as described in Macbeth IV, iii

The scene is in England at the Court of Edward the Confessor.

Enter a Doctor.

Mal. Well; more anon.—Comes the king forth,
                    I pray you?
Doct. Ay, sir; there are a crew of wretched souls
That stay his cure: their malady convinces
The great assay of art; but at his touch—
Such sanctity hath heaven given his hand—
They presently amend.
    Mal.   I thank you, doctor.   (*Exit* Doctor.
    Macd. What's the disease he means?
    Mal.   'Tis call'd the evil:
A most miraculous work in this good king;
Which often, since my here-remain in England,
I have seen him do. How he solicits heaven,
Himself best knows: but strangely-visited people,
All swoln and ulcerous, pitiful to the eye,
The mere despair of surgery, he cures,
Hanging a golden stamp about their necks,
Put on with holy prayers: and 'tis spoken,
To the succeeding royalty he leaves
The healing benediction. With this strange virtue,
He hath a heavenly gift of prophecy,
And sundry blessings hang about his throne,
That speak him full of grace.

It would be hard to point to any passage in the plays of Shakespeare more irrelevant to the drama, and more obviously inserted to serve some topical interest, than these lines. In the acting versions they are always omitted, for

367

they interrupt the action rather distressingly. Cut them out and there are left two half-lines, both assigned to Macduff, which coalesce as a complete verse to take the place of the excision.* Obviously they were put in as an afterthought for some special purpose. The puzzle before us is to discover this purpose. There are suggestions in plenty.

In Bell's edition of Shakespeare published in 1773 there is the following note by Francis Gentleman, who was a playwright and actor of the time of David Garrick, and who consequently reflected the theatrical point of view:

The author has here lugged in, by neck and heels, a doctor for the strange purpose of paying a gross compliment to that royal line, which ridiculously arrogated a power of curing the evil, by a touch. But that scene is properly left out in the representation [Vol. I, p. 55].

A few years later, in his notes on *Macbeth,* Edward Capell expressed a somewhat similar thought, viewing the matter from a literary rather than a stage standpoint:

This engrafted particular, of the *virtue* of Kingly *touches,* serv'd the purpose of incense to him [King James], as well as it's witchery and the fortunes of his ancestor Banquo: *Touching* for the "evil" was revived by this king in his reign's beginning, and practiced with great ceremony, a ritual being established for it: the mention of it's source, when a novelty, had some grace on the stage, and in the ear of it's reviver; and to that period, the king's third or fourth year, reason bids us assign the speech in question [*Notes,* Vol. II, p. 26].

But these statements are very inaccurate. When James

---

* These half-lines were never meant to be separated. There is characteristic Shakespearean presentiment in the words *"unwelcome things"* if, by omitting the topical lines, we read:

> Macd. Such welcome and unwelcome things at once
> 'Tis hard to reconcile. See, who comes here?
>
> *Enter* Ross.

for Ross's news is indeed to be unwelcome to Macduff.

came to his English throne, touching for the evil possessed no novelty, Queen Elizabeth having practiced it throughout her long reign; and King James when he came to England, so far from arrogating miraculous healing power, expressly disclaimed any such power and avoided as long as he could the use of the ceremony of touching for the evil. Therefore it is proper to inquire what manner of touching, if any, was practiced by James during the early years of his reign, and what interest in this ceremony caused these lines to be put into the play in 1606. There was, in fact, an evident purpose, but it was very different from the suggestions of Gentleman or Capell.

The king's evil, or scrofula, must have been distressingly prevalent in the olden times. It is now known to be a tubercular infection of the glands and bones of the neck contracted by drinking milk from infected cattle. Better dairy conditions have made the disease rare.

The kings of France had since ancient times claimed a miraculous power to heal the king's evil by touching. The claim was not made in England during the Norman period, but when Henry II came to the throne he took to himself this power and frequently touched his scrofulous subjects. This was natural, for his French empire was larger than that of the King of France. Touching was continued by the succeeding Plantagenet kings, but fell into disuse during the troublous reigns which followed.

Under the Tudors the royal touch flourished again, practiced with an elaborate ritual. The sufferers from scrofula were examined by surgeons to make sure that they were proper cases for treatment by the king. Their sores were washed and if infected were covered up with plasters. The king sat in a chair of state as the patients were successively brought to him. A chaplain read the service which is found in some ancient prayer books. Each patient was first touched by the king's bare hand, and then the sign of the Cross was made by the king with an angel over the sore, and the angel was given to the patient to be worn as an amulet until the cure was complete.

For use in touching for the evil, the Tudor sovereigns coined the angel, a gold coin worth about ten shillings. The stamp on the obverse showed the Archangel Michael slaying the dragon, and on the reverse a ship charged with the royal arms and carrying a huge cross at the masthead. The angel slaying the dragon was emblematic of the king's power over the evil, and the legend on the reverse was an appropriate text from the Vulgate, "A Domino Factum est Istud et est Mirabile" (Mark 12:11). The ordinary gold ten-shilling piece lacked the angel and the cross-bearing ship, and was not used as a touchpiece.

Queen Elizabeth frequently touched for the evil and in doing so used a ritual calling for prayers, responses, and readings from the Gospels. The first Gospel was from Mark 16, opposite which, at the fourteenth verse, a rubric directed: "While these words are repeated her Most Serene Majesty lays her hands on each side of them that are sick and diseased with the evil, on the jaws, or the throat, or the affected part, and touches the sore places with her bare hands, and forthwith heals them." Tooker informs us that he often saw the queen "knead" the neck of the patient with both her bare hands and then cross the sores with the angel. The second Gospel was from John 1, and opposite the ninth verse the rubric directs:

At which words Her Majesty rises, and as each person is summoned and led back singly, and receives a golden coin of the value of ten shillings, bored and strung on a ribband, she makes the sign of the cross on the part diseased: so with a prayer for the health and happiness of each and with a blessing, they are bidden to retire a while till the rest of the Gospel is finished.

This ritual calls for two essential acts of the sovereign: the *touching* with the royal hand and the *crossing* of the diseased part with the coin. We have many accounts of the success with which Queen Elizabeth thus used this office.*

To appreciate the importance of this royal power in the eyes of her subjects, it must be understood that not only were her curative powers devoutly trusted and the royal donation thankfully received, but this miraculous power was deemed a most essential proof that the sovereign was the truly descended legitimate sovereign of Great Britain, otherwise no success would attend the ceremony.†

But while Elizabeth, following her grandfather's usage, had retained in her ritual the requirement for the sign of the Cross made with the coin on the sore of the sick, this practice was offensive to the Scottish reformers, who looked upon it as a remnant of popish superstition.

The great queen died March 24, 1603, and her cousin James of Scotland, who had never been in England, was invited by the Council to come to Westminster to be crowned King of England. Whatever may have been his own views as to its efficacy, Shakespeare knew how much his countrymen venerated this custom. We can therefore understand that he and the people of England generally were much disappointed when it was learned that James, journeying to England, had made three requests of the English ministry:

* The authorities which underlie these statements have been most satisfactorily collected by Dr. Raymond Crawfurd in his book *The King's Evil.*

† In 1597 Dr. William Tooker published *Charisma: Sive Donum Sanationis,* a historical vindication of the power inherent in the English sovereign of curing the king's evil. This won him special regard from Elizabeth because her possession of the power proved the validity of her succession (*D.N.B.,* Vol. XIX, p. 978). Such proof was even more sought for when King James succeeded to the throne. In 1605 William Camden published his famous little book entitled *Remaines Concerning Britaine* in which he states: "As for that admirable gift hereditary to the annointed princes of this realm in curing the king's evil, I refer you to the learned discourse thereof lately written." (He means Dr. Tooker's book.)

1. Not to be served on bended knee (as was done to the deceased queen) seeing that such reverence was more due to God than to man.

2. *Not to touch for scrofula,* not wishing to arrogate to himself such virtue and divinity, as to be able to cure diseases by *touch* alone.

3. That the title of head of the Church, which belongs to Christ alone, should not be attributed to himself.*

These scruples had been bred in him by the air of Scotland. Notwithstanding them, James was proclaimed head of the Church soon after he breathed the air of England, and an oath was taken by his officials recognizing him as such. So much for his third request. His first request, too, was often disregarded. In Sully's *Memoirs* is an account of a dinner at which Sully was a guest with King James at Greenwich, on June 19, 1603. Sully notes with surprise that the king "was served on the knee" (Nichols's *Progresses of James,* Vol. I, p. 162, note 7). But the second scruple as to "touching" was more difficult to overcome, and time and patience were required; for the Scotch clergy who accompanied him insisted that touching for the evil was very superstitious, and he was inclined to agree with them.

During the month of April, 1603, which James spent journeying to London, he learned many things. He found out how agreeable was life as lived in England; and he found the English attached to many old practices which, although highly offensive to the Scotch Presbyterian, had not been rejected by the Protestantism of Elizabeth. The task of the English Council headed by Cecil was to coax the new king to accommodate himself to the English ways of thinking, and it was not an easy one. The question of the royal touch was one point at issue.

The ambassadors of the Catholic countries were watching what he would do about this and like questions. On June 4, 1603, the Venetian representative wrote to the Doge and

* *Archives of the Vatican: Roman Transcripts,* Gen. Ser. Vol. 88, p. 9.

Senate: "King James says that neither he nor any other King can have any power to heal scrofula, for the age of miracles is past, and God alone can work them" (*Cal. of State Papers —Venetian,* Vol. X, p. 44).

But his English councilors wanted him to touch for the evil. To show this virtue would strengthen his title to his throne. Plainly it would be prudent for James to give way on this second point also; but he was cautious about it and told his Council that if he did so he would be condemned by many of his Scottish advisers for countenancing such a ceremony. The Venetian concludes his letter with the prediction, "However he will have the full ceremony so as not to lose this prerogative which belongs to the Kings of England as Kings of France." But in saying this he was merely echoing the wishes of the court and was mistaken. King James never used the ritual of Elizabeth. He was, before long, persuaded to touch the patient but not on the sore spot. He refused to cross the patient with a coin as required by the queen's ritual, for he considered this superstitious thaumaturgy. By way of compromise he consented to use a much abbreviated ritual which only required him to hang an angel around the patient's neck.

We are now to examine the evidences showing how and when the king was induced to accept this compromise.

Under date of October 8, 1603, a letter sent from London to Rome contains the following information, which shows that six months of English air have wrought a change in the king:

At this time the King began to take interest in the practice pertaining to certain ancient customs of the Kings of England respecting the cure of persons suffering from the King's Evil. So when some of these patients were presented to him in his antechamber, he first had a prayer offered by a Calvinist minister, and then remarked that he was puzzled how to act. From one point of view he did not see how the patient could be cured without a miracle, and nowadays miracles had ceased and no longer happened: so he was afraid of committing a superstitious act. From another point of view however inasmuch as it was an ancient usage and for the good of his subjects, he resolved to give it a trial, but only by way of prayer, in which he begged all present to join him and then he touched the sick folk. It was observed that when the King made this speech, he several times turned his eyes toward the Scotch ministers around him, as tho he expected their approval of what he was saying, having first conferred with them [*Roman Transcripts,* Vol. 87].

We may here read between the lines that the Scotch ministers did not approve; and also that in accordance with his and their scruples he used no angel, for the healing was *"only by way of prayer."* Doubtless the patients were disappointed by their failure to receive the customary coin; and because no crossing was made by the king, it was doubted there would be any cure. For this reason accounts of these abbreviated touchings during the early years of his reign in England are rare and meager and carry with them a note of uncertainty. Such information as we have concerning them comes from dispatches of the Venetian representative to the Doge.

In his dispatch of November 17, 1604, the Venetian says:

Yesterday after the sermon which the King attends every Tuesday, besides feast days, his Majesty touched a number of sufferers from scrofula. It remains to be seen with what success [*Cal. of State Papers—Venetian,* Vol. X, p. 193].

No record of any touchings by King James during the year 1605 has been found; but the following occurs in a letter dated May 4, 1606, from the same Venetian:

These last few days the King has been attending to his devotions, which according to the custom of the country occupy Holy Week. He has touched many for scrofula, they say with hopes of good effects remembering the earlier cases of healing conferred by his hand [*ibid.,* p. 343].

As these dispatches indicate no change in procedure, pre-sumably the touch was still accompanied only by prayer. In expressing "hopes" of success, the court suggest a doubt in their minds as to whether prayer with no angel and no cross-ing can effect a cure. Had the old ritual been used, there would have been no doubt concerning this proof of the king's title to his throne.

The next news on this subject sent to the Doge is very brief, only telling that on April 3, 1608, the King of Eng-land "touched for scrofula" (*ibid.*, Vol. XI, p. 116). But on April 15, 1610, the word is: "All this week the king, as bear-ing the title of King of France, has touched for the scrofula" (*ibid.*, Vol. XI, p. 465). This implies not only that touch-ings were now more numerous, but that they were more formal, for the King of France performed his similar office with great ceremony; and from this time on the evidence is clear that a formal ritual was in use and that the king hung an angel around the neck of the patient; for about 1610 a certain James Maxwell wrote a poem with the following in-formative title:

A Poeme shewing the Excellencie of our Soueraigne King James his Hand, that giueth both health & wealth, instanced in his Curing of the Kings evill by touching the same, in hanging an Angell of Gold about the neck of the diseased and in giuing the poorer sort money towards the charges of their iournie.

This is found in Maxwell's book entitled *The Laudable Life,* published in 1612. It shows that a formal ceremony had come into use, for the verses picture the king in his "seat of majesty," surrounded "by God's priests," touching the patient, and hanging an angel on his neck. A broadside copy of the ritual used for this ceremony is preserved in the Library of the London Society of Antiquaries. It was later printed in prayer books of the time of Charles I, who retained his father's ritual. Crawfurd has reprinted this ritual in his book on the king's evil at page 85. It preserves parts of

Elizabeth's usage. The Gospels are unchanged. But the prayers and responses have been shortened and the rubrics changed. Accompanying Mark's Gospel the rubric reads, "Repeate the same as often as the King toucheth the sicke person"; and for John's Gospel it reads, "Repeate the same as often as the King putteth the Angel about their neckes." The requirement to make "the sign of the cross on the part diseased" has been omitted, as also the requirement to touch the sore places "with the bare hands."

The first eyewitness account of the king's usage after the adoption of this ritual seems to be that of Prince Otto of Hesse who visited England during July, 1611. The prince attended the ceremony of " 'touching' several scrofulous patients, two bishops being also present; during the benediction the King laid two fingers upon them, and hung around the neck of each an angel with a white silk ribbon." (W. B. Rye's *England,* p. 144). This "two-finger" touch by James is to be contrasted with Elizabeth's practice of touching the sore places with both her bare hands. It is characteristic of James's constitutional repugnance to the sight of disease.

An account of another of James's touchings occurs in the Journal of the visit of John Ernest, Duke of Saxe-Weimar, to King James at Theobalds on September 19, 1613.

. . . . his Majesty stood up, his chair was removed to the table, and he seated himself in it. Then immediately the Royal Physician brought a little girl, two boys, and a tall strapping youth, who were afflicted with incurable diseases (*unheilbare Schaden, i.e.,* the Evil), and bade them kneel down before his Majesty; and as the Physician had already examined the disease (which he is always obliged to do, in order that no deception may be practiced), he then pointed out the affected part in the neck of the first child to his Majesty, who thereupon touched it, pronouncing these words: *Le Roy vous touche, Dieu vous guery* (The King touches, may God heal thee!) and then hung a rosenoble round the neck of the little girl with a white silk ribbon. He did likewise with the other three. During the performance

of this ceremony, the above-mentioned Bishop, who stood close
to the King read from the Gospel of St. John, and lastly a prayer,
whilst another clergyman knelt before him and made occasional
responses during the prayer. Now when this was concluded,
three lords—among whom were the Earl of Montgomery and his
brother—came forward at the same time, one bearing a golden
ewer, another a basin, and the third a towel. They fell on their
knees thrice before the King, who washed himself. . . . [*ibid.*,
p. 151]

As these accounts expressly relate, he hung the coin on the
patient's neck; *but he would not make the sign of the cross*
as required by the ritual of Elizabeth. He never did. Thus
we read in Hamon L'Estrange's *Alliance of Divine Office*
(London, 1659), page 147:

which [crossing with the coin] raising cause of Jealousies, as if
some mysterious operation were imputed to it, that wise and
learned King [James] not only, with his son the late king, practically discontinued it, but ordered it to be expunged out of the
prayers relating to that cure, which has proceeded as effectually,
that omission notwithstanding, as it did before.

And again, in Peter Heylin's *Examen Historicum etc.* (London, 1659), page 144:

As to the sign of the cross made by the royal hands on the place
infected, there is no such crossing used in that sacred ceremony,
the King only gently drawing both his hands over the sore at
the reading of the Gospel.

Comparison of these accounts discloses the gradual disap-
pearance of some of the king's scruples as to touching, but
still leaves uncertainty as to precisely when the coin was first
used by him. Seemingly, it was not used earlier than 1606.
By 1610 its use seems to have become habitual.

Therefore we pass to another source of information. The
angel, although a current coin, was not one of the standard

coins of the realm. As a rule it was coined only for use in touching. We must find when James's coiner first struck angels for him and what sort of angels they were. No angels were coined by Elizabeth after 1600; and her angels exhibit only a small pierced hole through which she passed a very fine silk string. But James was clumsy and needed a very large hole to permit him to pass through it the wide white ribbon on which he strung his angels. The angels of Elizabeth are not found pierced with this large hole, whereby we know that Elizabeth's angels were exhausted when James first began to use the coin in touching, and therefore he was compelled to coin new ones. Elizabeth's angels showed on both sides a large cross appropriate when used with a ritual which required the signature of the Cross with the angel upon the patient. But James would not use such angels. Something therefore may be learned by examining the differences between Elizabeth's angels and those coined for James after his accession.

The gold coins of England for this period are not dated, but their approximate dates may be determined from their inscriptions and mint marks. The latter were changed usually once a year, after the trial of the pyx,* whereby the coiner obtained his discharge upon settlement of his accounts. On James's first coinage he was designated JACOBUS D. G. ANG. SCO. FRAN. ET HIB. REX. (James by the Grace of

---

* The pyx was a brass-bound chest with a slot in the lid and three keys for three separate padlocks, one key being in the keeping of the king or his Lord Treasurer, one in the keeping of a warden of the Goldsmith's Company, and one in the keeping of the coiner of the mint. The pyx was kept at the Royal Mint in the Tower of London and of every 15 pounds of gold coin struck one coin was placed in the pyx. At stated intervals there was a trial of the pyx by opening it in the presence of the holders of the three keys. The coins found therein were weighed and assayed, and the accounts of the coiner were passed after balancing the value of the gold and of the seniorage against the value of the coinage passed into circulation. After each trial of the pyx a new mint mark was put upon all new coins.

God King of England, Scotland, France, and Ireland.) No
angels of this coinage are known. On October 24, 1604,
James was officially proclaimed King of Great Britain.
Thereafter he was designated on his coins JACOBUS D. G.
MAG. BRIT. FRAN. ET HIB. REX. (James by the Grace
of God King of Great Britain, France, and Ireland.) On this
second (so-called mag. brit.) coinage the early mint marks
and their dates run thus:

Thistle	1604
Lis	1604–1605
Rose	1605–1606
Escallop	1606–1607
Grapes	1607

*The earliest known Jacobean angel is of the mag. brit.
coinage and bears the rose mint mark.* The date when it
was struck can be fixed still more closely. The standard gold
pieces of this, as of the previous coinage, were the sovereign,
half-sovereign, crown, and half-crown, all of *"crown* gold."
In addition to these a warrant dated April 16, 1605, gave order to the chief graver of His Majesty's mint to grave "yrons
for the striking of 3 sorts of moneys of *fyne* gold viz. pieces of
30^s called Rose Ryalls, pieces of 15^s called Spur Ryalls, and
pieces of 10^s called Angells"; but use of these new dies for
coinage was not authorized until July 16, 1605, under which
date a recorded indenture directs the minting of a limited
number of these three *fine* gold pieces. There is still preserved in the Royal Mint a trial plate prepared as the standard for fixing the fineness of the new angels. This bears an
impression of the angel and is inscribed, "This standard
comixed of XXIII Karrects III grains and halfe of fine gold
and half a grain of alloy in the pownd waight Troy of England made the 20th daye of August 1605." Therefore James's
new angels cannot have been struck until after the latter
date. Of these three new fine gold coins there was only a
scanty issue. They are rare coins and probably minted, as

Sir Charles Oman concludes, only for royal gifts and for distribution at ceremonies. These three coins collectively are sometimes called James's third coinage.

On the opposite page is an illustration showing an angel coined for Elizabeth in the year 1600, and below it the earliest known angel coined for James. The latter coin could not have been struck earlier than August 20, 1605, nor later than the date in 1606 when the rose mint mark was changed to the escallop. Note that from the coin both crosses have been removed, as also the phrase ET EST MIRABILE, in order to make it more acceptable to the king.

In his book the *Coinage of England* (p. 289) Oman remarks that "King James was a man of an inquisitive and ingenious mind, much given to numismatic experiments." Confirming this, we read in Stow's *Annals* (p. 835) that he took Queen Anna to his mint on March 13, 1603-1604, "where both the King and Queen coyned money and gave to divers persons there present." And again on August 1, 1606, as we learn from Henry Roberts *(Englands Farewell)*, the English and the Danish kings visited the mint in the Tower. Conrad Khunrath, who was present in the train of King Christian *(Relatio oder Erzehlung,* Hamburg, 1607), adds the further detail that much money in gold and silver was then minted while they looked on. Ryalls and Angels, authorized by the indenture of July 16, 1605, would have been among this gold coinage. These coins were of a higher gold content than the ordinary "crown" gold coinage, and presented a very handsome appearance. Some of them were distributed, and James could not fail to note the removal of the crosses from his angels. During this visit James presented to his royal guests £1,235 in money (Pory to Cotton, Aug. 12, 1606), no doubt in this "fyne gold" coinage.

After the king had thus handled his new angels, would additional persuasion be needed to induce him to use them when touching for the evil?

Just six days later, on August 7, 1606, James took his

A LATE ELIZABETHAN ANGEL—*Double Natural Size*

On the obverse the archangel Michael with cross on his corselet, thrusts his spear through the head of the prone dragon. The inscription reads: ELIZABETH·D(ei):G(ratia): ANG(liae):FR(anciae):ET·HIB(erniae):REGINA· = Elizabeth by the grace of God Queen of England, France and Ireland.

On the reverse is the Royal Ship headed right bearing the arms of England, and the large cross at the masthead, between E(lizabeth) and the Tudor rose. The inscription reads: A:D(omi)NO·FACTUM·EST·ISTUD·ET:EST·MIRABI(le: = This is done by the Lord and it is marvelous. The mintmark O precedes each inscription, and indicates that the specimen above drawn was minted about 1600.

THE EARLIEST KNOWN JACOBEAN ANGEL—*Double Natural Size*

On the obverse is the archangel without the cross on his corselet. The inscription reads: JACOBUS·D(ei):G(ratia).MAG(nae):BRIT(aniae):FRA(nciae):ET·HI(berniae)·REX:=James by the grace of God King of Great Britain, France and Ireland.

On the reverse is the Royal Ship headed right bearing the arms of England quartered with Ireland and Scotland. The large cross has been removed. The mast is between I(acobus) and the Tudor rose. The inscription reads: A.D(omi)NO:FACTUM·EST·ISTUD: The rose mintmark indicates that the coin was minted 1605-6.

brother-in-law to Hampton Court, where Shakespeare's play of *Macbeth* was given by the King's Company before the two kings. As James watched the play, he must have been first surprised, then interested, and then pleased as he heard Shakespeare's carefully chosen and beautifully phrased lines, already quoted. They fit this juncture exactly. The healing benediction was the work of a good king. He bequeathed it to the succeeding royalty. The king prays for the patients: "How he solicits heaven, himself best knows." At his touch they presently amend. He does not cross the patient with the coin, but hangs the golden stamp about their necks, put on with holy prayers. This was the compromise desired by his Council. And the king agreed to it. His inconsistency is understandable. Quotation has been made from a letter telling of the king's touchings at Theobalds on Sunday, September 19, 1613. This writer at the end of his account states, "This ceremony of healing is understood to be very distasteful to the King, and it is said he would willingly abolish it."

Explanation of this distaste is afforded by the statement of Arthur Wilson in his *History of Great Britain, being the Life and Reign of King James the First* (London, 1655, p. 289):

He was a King in understanding, and was content to have his Subjects ignorant in many things, as in curing the *King's Evil,* which he knew a *Device* to ingrandize the *Vertue* of Kings, when *Miracles* were in fashion; but he let the World believe it, though he smiled at it in his own *Reason,* finding the strength of the *Imagination* a more powerfull *Agent* in the Cure, than the *Plaisters* his *Chirurgions* prescribed for the *Sore.*

This skeptical tendency explains many of the king's inconsistencies. A good example is found in the following incident. The Turks had sent a Chiaus (or special agent) to negotiate with the London Turkey merchants. He was accorded an audience with King James on November 3, 1618. At the end of the interview the Chiaus told the king that his son, who was with him, was afflicted with the king's evil and he begged the king to touch him. This is told us by Sir John Finett, who was present as assistant master of ceremonies and afterward recorded it in his *Finetti Philoxenis* (p. 57). He says that His Majesty touched the youth, "signing the place infected with the cross, but no prayers before or after." This is somewhat startling in view of the assurance we have from other sources that James never did make the sign of the Cross in his ceremony of touching. But the apparent contradiction is explained in a letter dated November 7, 1618, from Pory to Sir Dudley Carleton, in which the interview is thus described:

In fine, after his majesty had asked him many questions, the Turke said his sonne was troubled with a disease in his throat, whereof he understood his majesty had the guifte of healing; whereat his majesty laughed heartily, and as the young fellowe came neare him he stroked him, with his hande, first on the one side and then on the other: marry without Pistle or Gospell.

This makes it clear that to this king, who had written a poem (the "Lepanto") celebrating the victory of the Cross over the Crescent, it was a huge joke that this Moslem should ask for this Christian ceremony. Such a chance for a Christian to sign the Cross on a Moslem's cheek was too good to be missed, and the king could not refrain from merrily and perhaps profanely carrying out this unusual gesture, but in such a jocose way as to make sure that no one could ever accuse him of being guilty of superstition by reason of what he did.

Indeed, one may suspect that this learned king sometimes resorted to not a little duplicity in such matters. In the account which has been quoted of his touchings on September 19, 1613, the king's formula as he touched is said to have been, "Le Roy vous touche, Dieu vous guery." This was the French king's formula, and it implies that although the king touches the patient only God can heal him. Thus the king absolved himself of an act of superstition; and by speaking the words in a foreign tongue he prevented the patients from knowing that he in fact disclaimed the miraculous power of his hand upon which they put such reliance.

The king's reluctance to practice touching must therefore be attributed in part to his fear of being thought superstitious, in part to his well known constitutional repugnance to the sight of disease, and in part to his skepticism concerning the efficacy of the royal touch. We may therefore sympathize with his difficulties, and if possible pardon his inconsistencies, and at all events we should admire the way in which William Shakespeare tried to help him over one of the rough places in his path.

Thus we come back to the original question: How did these lines get into the play? The scene in the midst of which they occur is a crescendo scene leading up to the highly dramatic outburst of the final ten lines by which the fate of Macbeth is sealed. Why interrupt such a scene with these irrelevant lines? The natural inference is that the king's councilors wished help in their effort to bring the king to their way of thinking concerning the royal touch. The scene at Edward's court afforded a most opportune place to introduce the subject. The dramatist of the King's Company knew of their wishes and respected them. This must be the answer to the question.

How this desire was communicated to Shakespeare can only be matter of conjecture. The following is a good working hypothesis.

Court plays were at this time under the jurisdiction of Sir George Buck, Acting Master of the Revels. He attended a performance or rehearsal of a play prior to its presentation before the king. This is recorded by Thomas Heywood in his *Apology for Actors,* printed in 1612 but written four or five years previously, where he says, speaking of the Office of the Revels, that it is the place "where the court plays have been in late days yearly rehearsed, perfected and corrected before they come to the public view of the Prince and the nobility." Therefore in *Macbeth* (and the same is true of *The Tempest*, which was also a court play) we may expect to find matters which had Shakespeare alone been in control of his play would not have been written, but which have found their way into the play by way of perfection and correction for the court.

Buck was a well read man with a good knowledge of history. Being a cousin of the Lord Chamberlain, he knew the desire of the Council to break down the king's scruples against using the angel when he touched for the evil. Angels had been coined but the king hesitated. So we may think that when Buck saw *Macbeth* rehearsed, and noted that there was a scene in the play occurring at the Court of Edward the Confessor, his memory brought to his mind the reputed origin of the royal touch, and he told the author of the play of the king's disinclination to use the coin, and asked him if he could help to overcome these scruples.

Both Buck and Shakespeare knew that Holinshed in his account of Edward the Confessor had stated: "He used to help those that were vexed with the disease, commonly called the King's evil, and left that virtue as it were a portion of inheritance unto his successors the Kings of this realm" (Vol. I, Bk. 1, p. 754).

Nothing is said by Holinshed about the use of any coin. But in the play it would be possible for the dramatist to add to what Holinshed told about the practice of the Confessor further lines which would cause his reputed practice to correspond with what it was thought James as his successor might be willing to do. Accordingly the dramatist wrote the lines here under consideration, including in them a statement that a "golden stamp" was hung by King Edward about the patient's neck, and thus tactfully created as a persuasive for the king an exact precedent in the Confessor's practice. It was a skillful "perfecting" of the play at the request of the court.

Thus may be explained the after-insertion of these "engrafted" lines which have puzzled so many. Perhaps they eased, even if they did not wholly set at rest, the king's scruples. He certainly used healing angels from this time on and hung this coin on the patient's neck, although he did not make the sign of the Cross, and never ceased to have qualms of conscience when called upon to perform the ceremony.

And these fine lines, irrelevant though they be, have remained in our text of this play to this day, a sort of enigma for posterity to enjoy. If the enigma be not solved by what has been said, the joys of future Shakespeareans will therefore be increased.*

* Let me further suggest that such Shakespeareans should read the following works on the subject: William Tooker, *Charisma: Sive Donum Sanationis* (London, 1597); T. J. Pettigrew, *On Superstitions . . . of Medicine* (London, 1844); Raymond Crawfurd, *The King's Evil* (Oxford, Clarendon Press: 1911); Cornelius Nicholls, "Touching for the King's Evil," *Home Counties Magazine,* June, 1912; Helen Farquhar, "Angels as Healing Pieces," *Royal Charities* (London, 1919), Part I.

From these books I have gathered many of the facts which have been stated.

SPECIAL INTERESTS OF THE KING

Sir Sidney Lee's observation that this play discloses the dramatist's effort "to conciliate the Scottish King's idiosyncrasies" has already been quoted (p. 140). Enough examples have, I feel sure, been cited in this book to convince the reader of its truth. Three more are added in order to illustrate the way in which William Shakespeare adapted his imagery to the thoughts of the king without interfering with the dramatic development of his theme; for it is perfectly evident that at no point has he allowed his drama to suffer harm from such adaptation. Often it only takes the form of selection of sympathetic subject matter such as a polite person always strives to accomplish when addressing a person of whose mind he knows enough to do so.

The first such example takes us back again to Oxford. The Latin disputations which occurred there in August, 1605, were conducted with great formality. The question was twice read by the moderator, "loudly and distinctly," together with four Latin verses in elucidation of the point. On August 29, in the presence of the king, the question was thus propounded:

An mores nutricum a puerulis cum lacte imbibantur?

> Mores vix mater, nutrix minus inserit; indit
> Mos mores; corpus lac alit, haud animam.
> Capra Jovi nutrix, Cyro canis, et lupa proli
> Martigenae, ex illis num lupa, capra, canis? *

The nurse's influence upon the baby's character has been discussed by old wives from very early days. This is indi-

---

* Are morals of nurses imbibed by babies with their milk?
  Scarce does the mother, much less the nurse, implant morals. Usage makes morals; milk nourishes the body, not the mind.
  A goat was nurse to Jove, a dog to Cyrus, and a wolf to the Martian progeny; from these came there a wolf, goat, or dog?

cated by the numerous myths, dating back to the infancy of
our race, which tell of heroes who were suckled by kindly
animals.

This question was chosen for debate because the king had
a peculiar personal interest in this subject. He had never
known his Roman Catholic mother. By direction of the
Countess of Mar, he was nursed by Mistress Helen Litell, a
stout Protestant who was given a daily allowance of "six
loaves of bread, 1 pint of wine, and 1 gallon of ale." To her
nursing James attributed his strong Protestantism. While
yet in Scotland, his curt message to the Pope who had asked
him to change his religion was, "I suckte Protestante's
milke." When he came to England, this phrase was taken
up by his councilors and became current, as will be seen by
reading pages 189 to 191 of Baildon's edition of Hawarde's
Reports of Cases in the Star Chamber. In his opening speech
to his first English Parliament, on March 19, 1603/4, he made
the same statement: "I thank God I sucked the milk of God's
truth with the milk of my nurse." Still later, in his *Apologia
pro juramento fidelitatis* (London, Norton, 1609), he said (p.
93): "Ego Christianus sum, nec unquam eam quam propemo-
dum cum lacte imbibi, religionem deserui."

Bad qualities too may be thus imbibed. Mistress Litell
turned out to be a drunkard. To this was attributed James's
awkward gait, for he did not walk until he was five years old.
Also, this was held to be accountable for his inebriety. In
the *Basilicon Doron* (p. 45), when scolding the Scottish nobility, he told his son that the nobility are "subject to . . . a
fectless arrogant conceit of their greatnes and power: drinking in with their verie *nouris-milke* that their honor stood in
committing three points of iniquitie."

It was most fit that one of the Oxford disputations should
propound this question. Its interest for the king was thus
brought to Shakespeare's attention, and it emerged in three
notable metaphors in the play he soon wrote.

Macbeth, I, v, 18, though now a commonplace, must have

been very striking when first heard. Lady Macbeth deems that her husband's nature "is too full o' the milk of human kindness to catch the nearest way." Shakespeare thus speaks of kindness as though it were a virtue resulting from milk of the proper sort.* I can think of no phrase coined by William Shakespeare which has obtained wider currency than "the milk of human kindness." We use it without thinking of its origin. When first spoken in 1606, it must have struck the mind as a new idea. Its immediate acceptance shows the forcefulness of the metaphor.

Shakespeare in the same scene more fully shapes the thought and tells that vices may be similarly acquired. When Lady Macbeth hears that Duncan will spend the night at her castle, her murderous desires break forth in that ferocious soliloquy the rendition of which made Mrs. Siddons immortal. Lady Macbeth is evil, and she calls upon the murderous witches who are invisibly carried to her by their devils to imbibe her evil milk so that their rancor against mankind may become more bitter. She says in I, v, 48–51:

> Come to my woman's breasts,
> And take my milk for gall, you murdering ministers,
> Wherever in your sightless substances
> You wait on nature's mischief!

Again, in IV, iii, 98, we find Malcolm, when falsely maligning himself, expressing his desire to "pour the sweet Milk of Concord into Hell." Concord is personified as a woman who with her sweet milk nourishes Peace and Unity, the two lifelong political ideals of James. His enemies desire to see such milk poured into hell.

These metaphors concerned with moral qualities as imparted by milk rarely occur in Shakespeare's other plays.

* Some have thought that the word "kindness" here denotes human nature rather than the specific virtue of kindliness (see Moulton's *Shakespeare as a Dramatic Artist,* p. 149), but the *O.E.D.* supports the view that Shakespeare here is referring to *kindliness* and endowing Macbeth with this trait.

When writing *Romeo and Juliet* ten years earlier, somewhat the same idea had been in his mind (I, iii, 67, and III, iii, 54). Wisdom and philosophy are there associated with milk. The idea disappeared thereafter until called back by the Oxford debate. It does not occur in his other plays, except in *King Lear* (I, iv, 364), which he was writing at the same time he was writing *Macbeth*.

Another example of the way in which the presence of the king has affected the play is the use of similes likening a king to the physician who must purge his commonwealth of its diseases. When James was a small boy, his tutor George Buchanan wrote his treatise *De Jure Regni apud Scotos,* in which occurs an elaborate comparison between the art of the physician in curing his patient and the work of a king in restoring health to his body politic.* This work was most obnoxious to the young king. He did not like to be lectured by his aged schoolmaster about the limits of the power of a king. But it was dedicated by its author, "Jacobo VI Scotorum Regi, S.P.D.," and he read it, and never forgot that he was there called the physician of his commonwealth. Twenty-five years later, when he wrote his *Counter-Blaste to Tobacco,* published in 1604, he prefaced it by an "Address to the Reader" in which we find this language:

We are of all Nations the people most loving. . . . Our peace hath bred wealth: And peace and wealth hath brought forth a general sluggishness . . . and generally all sorts of poeple more careful for their privat ends, than for their mother the Common- wealth. For remedie whereof, it is the Kings part (as the proper Phisician of his Politicke-bodie) to purge it of all those diseases, by Medicines meete for the same.

William Shakespeare had read these words, and this homely

* "An incorporation seemeth to be very like our body, civil com-motions like to diseases, and a king to a physician" (p. 10 of the English translation published in 1680). The comparison is continued for several pages.

thought of the purgation of a commonwealth by the king as its proper physician emerges in *Macbeth* no less than four times.

In III, iv, 76, we find the phrase, "Ere human statute purged the gentle weal." That is to say, before statute law purged the state of its original barbarity.

Next, in V, ii, 27–29, the Scottish thanes on their way to meet Malcolm say:

> Meet we the medicine of the sickly weal,
> And with him pour we in our country's purge
> Each drop of us.

In V, iii, 50, Macbeth says to his doctor:

> If thou couldst, doctor, cast
> The water of my land, find her disease,
> And purge it to a sound and pristine health,
> I would applaud thee to the very echo.

And again, line 55:

> What rhubarb, cyme, or what purgative drug,
> Would scour these English hence?

The insistent repetition of this rude but powerful simile is to be attributed to its forceful employment by the king in his book which people had been reading the year before.

A third example is the elaborate similitude distinguishing a mere "bill" of dogs which "writes them all alike," from a "valued file" which designates them according to their "gifts" (III, i, 90–102). Shakespeare's admiration was for the horse and not for the hound. His sensitive nature took no pleasure in the hounds' cruelty, for the hound is a professional murderer. The most offensive epithet he could hurl at the doomed Macbeth was "hell-hound" (V, viii, 3). How then explain the rather overworked simile in this play which points out the useful gifts which nature has bestowed upon the hound?

It seems to have resulted from the special personal interest which the "gifts" of hounds had for King James at this particular time. All his life the king was devoted to the chase, giving more of his time to it than to affairs of state. Under the recent Tudor sovereigns the royal hunt had been little more than an honored ceremony; but when James came to England it became a serious business. The royal parks, stables, and kennels were enlarged and restocked and the machinery of the hunt entirely reorganized. The king created an unimaginably large establishment for the care of his hounds. There was a Master of the Hart Hounds, a Master of the Buckhounds, a Master of the Harriers, a Master of the Otter Hounds, and a Master of the Crossbows and Lyam Hounds. (A lyam, or lyme, or lym, is a bloodhound held in leash to pick up the scent which the buckhounds have lost.) Subordinate to these were Sergeants of the Buckhounds, a greater number of Yeomen Prickers of the Privy Buckhounds (the mounted huntsmen), Grooms of the Buckhounds, the Keepers of the Buckhounds, and the Yeomen Waggoners of the Privy Buckhounds. Then there were Yeomen Prickers of the Privy Harriers, Keepers of the Privy Harriers, Keepers of the Dogs for the Otter Hunt, and finally the Lymiers. This list is by no means complete. The documents in the Public Record Office show grants of these offices, often for life, and the warrants show large sums paid to them, and also the considerable grants for their liveries.* At the end of a hunting trip the king was apt to order special recompense to the prickers or keepers for whom he had taken a liking, particularly if he admired the performance of the hounds they had in charge.

To operate this great establishment, the royal kennels must be well supplied, and to this end James exercised a

* In *Truth Brought to Light or the History of the First 14 Years of King James I* (London, 1651, pp. 58–59), there will be found transcripts of the Exchequer Accounts showing the annual payments to gamekeepers and huntsmen. They are worth examining.

right of purveyance by issuing special commissions for the "taking up" of suitable dogs. On January 30, 1604, Patrick Hume, Keeper of the Privy Harriers, received a commission "for the taking up of such hounds and grey hounds as his office shall require." On June 15, 1604, Silvester Dodsworth, Sergeant of the Buckhounds, received a commission "to take up hounds in the North parts for the King's hunting and to hunt with them in the king's parks *or those of any of his subjects.*" On November 10, John Parry, Master of the Otter Hounds, was granted a commission "to take up dogs for the King's diversion."

But naturally there was remonstrance by the owners when their favorite hounds were taken in the name of the king. Purveyance was under attack at this time (Hawarde's *Cases in the Star Chamber,* Baildon ed., p. 248). People felt that their sovereign spent too much time in the chase and too little upon the public business. On December 4, 1604, Lascelles wrote to the Earl of Shrewsbury telling of a "reasonable pretty jest" which had recently happened at Royston:

There was one of the King's special hounds, called Jowler, missing one day. The King was much displeased that he was wanted; notwithstanding [he] went a hunting. The next day, when they were on the field, Jowler came in amongst the rest of the hounds; the King was told of him, and was very glad; and, looking on him, spied a paper about his neck, and in the paper was written; "Good Mr. Jowler, we pray you speak to the King (for he hears you every day, and so doth he not us) that it will please his Majesty to go back to London, for else the country will be undone; all our provision is spent already, and we are not able to entertain him longer." It was taken for a jest, and so passed over [Lodge's *Illustrations,* 1838 ed., Vol. III, p. 108].

On December 18, 1604, Matthew Hutton, the venerable Archbishop of York, wrote to Robert Cecil boldly warning the government that the king's hunting was a great burden to his subjects:

As one that honoreth and loveth his most excellent Majesty with all my heart, I wish less wastening of the treasure of the realm, and more moderation in the lawful exercise of hunting, both that poor men's corn may be less spoiled, and other his Majesty's subjects more spared. [*id.,* p. 116].

This letter was circulated by the archbishop throughout his northern diocese. In a letter dated February 1, 1604/5, Cecil took the archbishop to task for doing this (*id.,* pp. 129–130). This correspondence was sent to the king and in reply the Earl of Worcester wrote to Cecil from Royston, February 25, 1604/5, telling him of the king's petulant reaction to the archbishop's criticism and of his great enjoyment of Cecil's answer to it (*id.,* pp. 130–131); but the archbishop's brave letter had its effect, for although complaints about the enlargements of the king's parks continued, the "taking up of hounds" was abandoned by the king as gracefully as possible by the issuance of the following royal proclamation:

A PROCLAMATION FOR THE ANNIHILATING OF
COMMISSIONS FORMERLY GRANTED FOR
TAKING UP OF HOUNDS, &c.

Where upon our first comming to the succession of this kingdome, at the sute of divers persons, who had or pretended to have from the Queene of famous memory our sister deceased, Commissions as annexed of course to several Offices which they held, for the taking up of Hounds, Greyhounds, Spaniels, and dogges of other sorts accustomed for venery, faulconry or other sports of Princes, wee did renew unto them their said Commissions, and grant the like to some others who had no offices, upon divers suggestions made unto us, which commissions we have since bene informed from divers parts of our Relame, that inferior officers who have bene trusted with them, have abused and do dayly abuse, contrary to the meaning of the same, which was to be executed no further foorth then the necessity of our Service should require: And forasmuch also as we have had good proofe that gentlemen and others, who delight in the like pastime of hunting and hauking have and will be ready at all times of their owne good will and respect to our recreations, to furnish us of sufficient number of dogges of all sorts which we shall have cause to use, when they shall be informed that we have need of them: We have therefore found it unnecessary to continue the execution of any our Commissions heretofore given for that purpose, And do hereby notifie the same to all our Subjects, and especially charge and command all those, who have any such Commissions or Warrrants from us under our great Seale, or any other our Seales, that they doe not onely forbeare to put the same in execution from henceforth, but also do bring in and deliver up the said Commissions and Warrants into our Chancery or any other office where they have been sealed, within the space of 20 days after the publishing hereof as they will answere the contrary at their perill. Willing also and command-ing our Attourney generall and all other of our Counsell learned, that whensoever they shall receive information, that any person, who hath had such Commission from us, shall after the time above limitted execute the same, that they do prosecute their offence therein as in case of contempt by all such ways and means as in like case as usual.

Given at our Honour of Hampton Court the 27 day of September in the third yeere of our Reigne of Great Britaine, France and Ireland.

Anno Dom. 1605

This deliverance, judiciously penned by Robert Cecil, is a polite invitation to country gentlemen to *present* a suffi-cient number of dogs of all sorts to the king. During the following months (and therefore while *Macbeth* was being written) the Master of the Buckhounds must have received letters from many of the king's loving subjects expressing their readiness to supply His Majesty with dogs. But it was not merely dogs that the king wanted. He was concerned with getting the right kind of dogs. He well knew the traits of his hounds as well as their names.* No doubt some of

---

* A year or so after the writing of *Macbeth*, a Scotch minister, Thomas Ross, when attempting in his book to paint a picture in the terms of antiquity of King James's fondness for hunting, wrote:

these letters gave a description and listed the excellencies of
each dog offered, while others merely stated how many dogs
the donor would supply. But the king wished to know about
the "gifts" of the hounds, for with dogs as with men,

> the valued file
> Distinguishes the swift, the slow, the subtle,
> The housekeeper, the hunter, every one
> According to the gift which bounteous nature
> Hath in him closed; whereby he does receive
> Particular addition, from the bill
> That writes them all alike.
>   [III, i, 96–101]

All this was the small talk of the court; and the king's players were on the fringe of the court, and when they came to
play at court their contacts were with people who talked
chiefly about the king's tastes and foibles. Thus it here becomes possible to trace the workings of Shakespeare's mind.
Macbeth had just asked if *"those* men" were in attendance
(III, i, 44), a designation giving no information. What he
really wanted to know was whether they were men who
would commit a murder for him. In Shakespeare's mind
the hound was a murderer, and by likening *"those* men" to
hounds he was led to the distinction between the "dog" and
the "hound." In answer to questioning, *those* men said
merely, "We are men, my liege" (III, i, 90), so that Macbeth
was again faced with the same difficulty which Shakespeare
knew to be in the king's mind when an offer of "dogs" was
received. Thus the king's thought filled out the thought in
Shakespeare's own mind, and he caused Macbeth to exclaim:

Venatione delectatur, salusque indagine sepit, et lustra ferarum, Indicis,
Caspiis, Albanicisque canibus, atque Molassis, et Lycissis scrutatur et obsidet:
et illud Amasis Regis secum voluit [*Idaea, sive de Jacobi &c.* (London, 1608)
p. 262].

Thus he told of the king's pleasure in obtaining choice breeds of
hounds like those of the famous hunters of old.

Ay, in the catalogue ye go for men;
As hounds and greyhounds, mongrels, spaniels, curs,
Shoughs, water-rugs and demi-wolves, are clept
All by the name of dogs.

[III, i, 92–95]

It is significant that there are only two lists of dogs in Shakespeare's plays and both occur in plays written in 1606. The *Macbeth* list has just been quoted. The other is found in *King Lear:*

Mastiff, greyhound, mongrel grim,
Hound or spaniel, brach or lym
Or bobtail tike or trundle tail.
[III, vi, 71–73]

These two plays both contain much of this sort of Jacobean furniture. It is different with Shakespeare's later plays. There is found in them very little reflection of matters of interest to the king and his court. *The Tempest* was written to be played at court; but it reflects, not the king's taste, but matters of interest to Prince Henry and the Princess Elizabeth. This is only one of many signs that Shakespeare's attitude and that of the people of England toward their king had changed. It is saddening to take note of this change. The king's plans, except the peace with Spain, all failed. The Parliament and the people did not believe in the divine right of their king. They doubted the divine right of the bishops. They did not want the union of the kingdoms; nor did they care for James's elaborate theological arguments concerning antichrist. They wanted a useful king and not a learned theorizer. Consequently, adulation yielded to distaste which ultimately turned to contempt as the day drew nearer when the Parliament and not the king was to be all-powerful in Britain, and when James was dubbed "the wisest fool in Christendom"—most unfairly of course, for although an egregious misfit as a king of England and guilty of many foolish acts, he was never a fool.

WHEN AND WHY THE PLAY
WAS WRITTEN

A point has now been reached where we may gather up and differentiate some of the urges, sources, and influences which helped to mold the great drama of *Macbeth* into the play which we find in the folio.

The delight which the king experienced from hearing Dr. Gwinn's *Tres Sibyllae* recited by the boys of St. John's was the genesis of the determination of the dramatist to see whether the prophecy to Banquo could be worked into a play founded on the story of Macbeth and Banquo as told by Holinshed; and after some considerable reading of Holinshed's *Description of Scotland* it had become evident that by combining selected portions of the history of Scotland there set down a highly dramatic play could be constructed. Along with this came the realization that by a careful use of the king's description of the conscience as found in his *Basilicon Doron,* and of Scotch witchcraft as described in his *Daemonologie,* the story of Macbeth could be embellished and made peculiarly attractive to the author of these two books. Therefore they, together with Holinshed's *Chronicle,* should be set down as the primary sources of the play.

But these three primary sources were supplemented by other knowledge, obtained often from books with which a connection can be definitely traced, but not so extensively that the books can be classed as sources.

For example, the main historical foundation provided by Holinshed has been added to, and in a few cases modified by, what he learned of the history of Scotland, as then understood, from other current historical works which are pointed

399

out in the chapter "Shakespeare's Knowledge of Scottish History." (P. 204.) His use of the *Basilicon Doron* as an analysis of the working of the conscience of a criminal has been illuminated and expanded by the dramatist's intimate knowledge of the Bible. The picture of Scotch witchcraft which he found in the king's *Daemonologie* has been most interestingly metamorphosed by his knowledge of the current speculations as to the part which the human imagination plays in creating the delusions of sorcery and necromancy. Here Montaigne's book is a clearly recognizable influence, but the personal investigations of the king himself in this field are chiefly responsible for the notable dualism of the play in its showing of the subjectivity which underlies the doings of witches and magicians.

These influences which have thus supplemented the dramatist's use of his primary sources are often found to be indirect and not entirely conscious. William Shakespeare had an extraordinarily retentive memory. He read books and stowed away the thought and even the language of what he read, and as occasion arose, drew upon this reservoir—not always it would seem with full consciousness of the original source, often, indeed, without any consciousness of dependence; and yet dependence exists, and the tracing of it is possible and instructive. Therefore in what is said as to writings which have influenced this play, let it be understood once and for all that Shakespeare's borrowings were not often made with anybody's book open before him, or even clearly in mind. He did thus use his Holinshed as copy. But other important influences belong to a different category. He knew his Bible well, and constantly its thoughts and words creep into the plays, often without any conscious borrowing. So with Ovid's *Metamorphoses*. The language of the Bible and of Ovid so permeates all Renaissance literature that it is not possible to know when their influence upon Shakespeare is direct and when secondary. The writings of Montaigne stimulated Shakespeare's natural gift for looking into the minds of the men and women he was creating. Probably John Florio led him in this direction. We find in the great plays of his mature years a deeper interest in observing the operations of a human mind than in the working out of the plot of the drama. In no play is this more notable than in *Macbeth*. And yet it is to be doubted that he felt that this great excursion into the workings of the human imagination was attributable to Montaigne. Montaigne was an influence but not a source.

In addition to these influences which are due to books, there are many others which are often loosely classed as "topical" and which always seem to creep into every drama and make it the image of its time.

Macbeth was written in the midst of stirring events. One could hardly expect to find that a play written in 1606 had not been influenced by the Gunpowder Plot and the train of events following it. And this indeed we do find. Garnet's trial and execution and the Oath of Allegiance were absorbing topics of the day, and the play has reacted to this. Christian's visit, although to a lesser degree, has left most clearly its stamp upon the play. And, finally, the fact that King James was to see the play was always in the writer's mind and influenced him in many ways, sometimes in a very large way, but more often in a multitude of minor touches which resulted from the fact that as the dramatist sat at his desk and wrote, he was conscious of the face of the king looking straight at him, so that his words formed themselves to fit this expected audience.

This, I trust, is a sufficient justification for calling *Macbeth* a royal play.

It is often conjectured, sometimes even assumed, that the intensely tragic note struck in *Macbeth* and *Lear,* the two great plays written in 1605 and 1606, must have been due to some tragic personal experience through which the dramatist passed at this time. It may be so; but as we have no way of knowing about this it does not fall within the scope of this book.

The evolution of the royal play of Macbeth having been traced from the first suggestions emanating from Oxford in August, 1605, it is the proper time to set down as definitely as possible the dates of the writing of the several parts of the play. It has been found that the first three acts (except for the prelude) were written before the end of March, 1606. Macbeth's conjuration in the first scene of the fourth act must have been written after the news had reached London of the destruction of the Gallic and Flemish churches by the storm of March 30–31, thus compelling us to assign this more slowly written necromantic scene to April or May. The lines about the equivocator were an after-insertion in the drunken-porter's part made after Garnet's conviction. Or if his execution is implied by his arrival at hell-gate, then this date must be set after May 3. The free use of cursing throughout Acts IV and V and the references in Act IV to the Oath of Allegiance advance the date of writing the ending of the play to June and July; and there is good evidence that short additions were made to the text during Christian's visit (July 18–August 10, 1606), and that part, at least, of the prelude was then written. Finally, there is satisfactory evidence that August 7 was the date of the first performance of the play at Hampton Court Palace. No other play of Shakespeare, except it be the *Merry Wives of Windsor,* affords such exact indications as to date of composition.

MACBETH AT THE GLOBE THEATER

Plays which had been performed at court were the more sure of an audience when given in a public theater. Therefore it is likely that *Macbeth,* having been performed at court before two kings in August, 1606, by the King's Company, was shown by the company to the public at the Globe Theater soon after it opened in the following autumn. If we can find when the public first attained knowledge of this play, we can fix a date before which the play must have been performed at the Globe.

There has been suggestion that the play of *Sophonisba* by John Marston reveals knowledge of Shakespeare's play. *Sophonisba* was entered S.R. on March 17, 1606/7, and was published shortly afterward "as it hath been sundry times acted at Blackfriars." Bradley in his *Shakespearean Tragedy* (Note BB, p. 471) points out "for what they are worth," three possible parallels in this play to lines in *Macbeth.* The two plays were evidently written at about the same time, but the parallels are not impressive; nor if there be dependence can we tell which dramatist took a hint from the other, and therefore it is best not to base any inferences upon Marston's play.

William Warner was a considerably older man than William Shakespeare. He was an attorney of the Common Pleas and was deemed by some to be a poet worthy of comparison with Homer. But truly his old-fashioned, alliterative, seven-footed rimed verse is much more fit for the crowd than for the court. For years Warner had been bringing out piecemeal a versified heroical history in thirteen books called *Albion's England.* After King James came to his English throne, Warner thought it appropriate to add three new books to this history in celebration of England's new king. Of this *Continuance* the title page reads as follows:

A Continuance of Albions England: By the first Author. W. W. [Ornament] London, Imprinted by Felix Kyngston for George Potter, and are to be sold at his shop in Pauls Church-yard, at the signe of the Bible. 1606.

Being only a "continuance," it was not entered on the Stationers' Register; but a more exact date for the book is gained from the dedication to "The Right Honourable Sir Edward Coke, Knight, Lord Chief-Justice of his Majesties Court of Common-Pleas, &c." Coke did not become Chief Justice of the Common Pleas until June 30, 1606, and as the imprint bears the date of that year it is clear that this work appeared after June 30 and prior to March 25, 1606/7.

The early chapters of this *Continuance* (80–92) treat of the ancient wars of the Picts and Scots. Chapter 93 passes to the ancient history of Wales and ends:

Yet, though against the *Welsh*-Kings will, our royall Surname now
(If Historie therein we may authenticall allow)
It Seedster from that kingly Streene derives,* ensueth how.

Thereupon Chapter 94 begins:

One *Makebeth*, who had traitrously his sometimes Sovereigne
    slaine,
And like a Monster not a Man usurpt in *Scotland* raigne,
Whose guiltie Conscience did itselfe so feelingly accuse,
As nothing not applide by him against himselfe he vewes,
No whispring but of him, gainst him all weapons feares he borne,
All Beings jointly to revenge his Murthres thinks he sworne,
Wherefore (for such are ever such in selfe-tormenting mind)
But to proceed in bloud he thought no safetie to find.

· · · · · · · · · · · · · ·

One *Banquho,* powrefulst of the Peers, in popular affection
And Prowesse great, was murthred by his tyrannous direction.
Fleance therefore this *Banquhos* sonne fled thence to *Wales* for
    feare,

* i.e., derives its disseminator from that kingly strain.

Dr. Gwinn had told of the descent of the Stuart family from Banquo without making reference to Macbeth, for until Shakespeare took hold of it there had been in England little knowledge of the history of Macbeth.* But Warner, turning from Wales to Scotland, plunged abruptly into an account of Shakespeare's Macbeth, evidencing recent interest in the story as told in the play. The intense hatred of Macbeth's crime and the references to Macbeth's "guilty conscience" and "self-tormenting mind" are Shakespearean. "Monster," "usurper," and "in blood" are terms not found in Holinshed but applied by Shakespeare to Macbeth. Warner had evidently seen the play on the stage and under its influence wrote the lines in question.

After this account of Macbeth there follows a rather neat account of Fleance and Nest and the flight of their son Walter to Scotland. Warner then proceeds:

He was Lord *Steward* of the Land: which Sur-name all inherit
Of him descended to this day: which Surname, and which
    Streene [strain]
Hath blest the *Scots* with Princes eight, Ours also numbers
    neene [nine]:
Great Monarke of great *Britaine* now, so amply never any:
Long may he live an happie King, of him may Kings be many.

The count of the kings as eight plus one is Shakespearean— very judicious in the play but clumsy here, for the Scots had been blessed (?) with nine Stuart princes, not eight.

The next chapter of the book, after vituperation of the Pope and the Jesuits, leads to an attack upon the doctrine of equivocation, which is referred to as "that divlish Doctrine whence they now equivocate."

Tongues-othes, Harts-thoughts, Distinctives, by a *mental* re-
    servation,

* There is no good reason to suppose that the *Ballad of Macdobeth* referred to in an entry in the Stationers' Register dated Aug. 27, 1596, concerned Macbeth, King of Scotland.

What Lawes, whose life or State secure, should such not be
  Nugation? *

This is the argument of Coke as attorney general during the
Garnet trial, and it is the argument of Macbeth:

> be these juggling fiends no more believed
> That palter with us in a double sense.
>   [V, viii, 19–20]

From all this we may properly conclude that when the
theaters opened in London in the autumn of 1606, *Macbeth*
was played at the Globe Theater and that William Warner
saw it and at once put the story into Chapter 94 of the book
he was then writing, which appeared in London before
March 24, 1606/7.

Dr. Farmer found a reference to *Macbeth* in the play of
The Puritan which was entered S. R. on August 6, 1607, and
was probably brought out not long before that date. But
the connection of this play with *Macbeth* is really more than
doubtful, as J. M. Manly has convincingly shown in his Introduction to *Macbeth,* pp. x and xi, in Longmans' English
Classics. So also Liddell (p. xvii, note 2).

That lines in Beaumont and Fletcher's *Knight of the Burning Pestle* (V, i, 19–29) are a sort of burlesque upon the
banquet scene of *Macbeth* is probable, but there is no cer-
tainty as to when that play appeared. It has been assigned
to dates from 1607 to 1611.

William Camden's famous *Britannia* had gone through
successive editions since its first appearance in 1584, in none
of which had there been any reference to either Macbeth or
to Banquo. But there was printed in London in 1607 an
edition with "revisions and additions by the author," in
which the new interest of people in the tale of Macbeth and

---

* Put into understandable English, this means: If one may by a
mental reservation distinguish the oaths of the tongue from the
thoughts of the heart, what laws, or whose life or state, will be secure,
unless this be treated as mere trifling?

Banquo is evidenced by the following addition, the tone of which is distinctly Shakespearean:

Comites, quos legi, habuit Loquhabria nullos, sed circa an. Salut ML Thanum nominatissimum Banqhuonem, quem Macbethus nothus cum caede & sanguine regnum occupasset, timidus & suspiciosus e medio tollendum curavit, quod e quarundam Magarum vaticinio comperisset fore ut ejus posteritas extincta Macbethi sobole aliquando regno potiretur, & longa serie regnaret. Quod sane side non caruit.

Which may be translated:

Lochabria, as I have read, has had no earls, except for a most noted Thane named Banquo whom about the year A.D. 1050 Macbeth the usurper, after he had seized the kingdom by murder and bloodshed, being full of fears and suspicions, took care to put out of the way, because he had learned from the prophecy of certain witches that it would come to pass that Banquo's posterity, upon the extinction of the issue of Macbeth, would someday acquire the realm and rule in a long line; which did not fail to occur.

The references to Shakespeare's *Macbeth* in Warner's *Continuance,* and in Camden's revised *Britannia,* constitute convincing evidence that *Macbeth* appeared upon the stage of the Globe Theater during the winter of 1606/7.

Were changes made in the play when it went to the Globe in order to better fit it for the crowd in the public theater? I find clear evidence of only one. King James did not like to see a king murdered on the stage, and consequently neither the killing of King Duncan nor that of King Macbeth had been shown to him. When Macduff and Macbeth are engaged in their mortal combat, the stage direction reads, "Exeunt fighting. Alarums," and then a few lines later we read, "Enter Macduff with Macbeth's head." But in the folio text, immediately after the first of these directions, is another inconsistent direction reading, "Enter fighting, and

Macbeth slain." The disintegrators of the text rely heavily upon this as evidence of "another hand." This does not follow. It is more likely that before his play was taken to the Globe the author, knowing that the audience there would want to see the death of Macbeth with their own eyes, inserted this inconsistent direction but failed to erase the second.

Whether other changes were made at the same time is highly conjectural. It is entirely probable that the scenic arrangements available at Hampton Court were more adequate than those obtainable on the stage of the Globe Theater. Certainly they must have been different. Consequently, it may be that before the play was put on the stage of that theater the actors asked for more exit lines emphasized by rimed couplets in order to accord with the conventions and usages then ruling at the Globe.* Anyone may, if he pleases, imagine that Burbage and others sat down with the author of the play in conference, and that about a dozen rather commonplace terminal couplets (some very flat) were inserted, chiefly in Act V. But until we know more than we now do about the scenic usages in court plays of this time as compared with the usages of the Globe, we have no sufficient basis on which to reach such a conclusion; and I will therefore rest upon the presumption that the play as shown at the Globe was the same as that which the kings saw at Hampton Court.

Somewhat of the subsequent history of the play may be gathered from the following:

On February 2, 1609, there was performed at Whitehall a sumptuous masque by Ben Jonson called *The Masque of Queens*. Interest in the play of *Macbeth* seems to have produced a desire on the part of the court, and particularly of Prince Henry, to see more witches; consequently the author introduced an antimasque presenting an "ugly Hell" with

---

* There seems to have been at this time a claque at the theaters (*The Isle of Gulls,* 1606, Sig. A2). These couplets have the appearance of being signals to the claque to begin their applause.

twelve dancing witches. Prince Henry was so much attracted by this display of sorcery that, as the author tells in
his Dedication, he asked Ben "to retrieve the particular authorities" for his delineation of these witches, a task which
the author of the masque was at some pains to perform.
Jonson immediately published the text of this masque (1609),
with copious reference to the vast necromantic literature,
both classic and medieval, concerning these evil spirits. Apparently this inspired the unfortunate experiment, made two
or three years later—I suspect at the request of Prince Henry
—of putting into Shakespeare's *Macbeth* a Hecate and a
second trio of witches provided with songs and dances taken
from Middleton's unsuccessful play called *The Witch* (supra
pp. 275 and 276).

Simon Forman saw the play of *Macbeth* at the Globe
Theater on April 20, 1611, before it was thus maltreated, and
wrote an account of what he had seen which has been preserved in the Bodleian Library.* He entitled this a *Book
of Plays* "for Common Pollicie," meaning that his notes
were business hints. His description should be read with
this in mind. He did not remember what had happened
near the beginning of the play (perhaps he was a little late
getting to the Globe that afternoon), and therefore took
down his Holinshed to help him to piece out his account; but
what he records after the first scenes is what he saw on the
stage, except for one or two unimportant slips. Certain
things in the play were vividly remembered by the wily and
disreputable quack doctor and astrologer. He was struck
by the horror exhibited by Macbeth when he saw the blood
on his hands. The portents which accompanied the murder

* The genuineness of Simon Forman's *Booke of Plaies* was questioned
in 1931 by J. Q. Adams, who suspected a Collier forgery. Shortly
afterward Tannenbaum (*Shakespearean Scraps*) pronounced it a forgery.
The evidences and inferences on which these judgments rest are not
at all convincing, and they are, I think, effectually refuted by Dover
Wilson and Hunt in their articles in the *Review of English Studies*
for July, 1947.

impressed him.   But the most terrifying thing was the appearance of Banquo's ghost at the supper table and the involuntary revelation of the murderer's guilt which followed.

Forman did not like to be reminded by this, and by Lady Macbeth's sleepwalking scene, that murder will out.   He had himself concocted many philters and poisonous potions, the uses of which he hoped would never be known.   His notes should be studied by actors who wish to play the part of Macbeth with as powerful effect as did Richard Burbage. The important thing revealed by Forman is that as given at the Globe Theater the play was not a melodrama.   He does not even mention the wood that came to Dunsinane nor the man not born of woman, things apt to be better remembered by the modern audience than other parts of the play.   What Forman saw and remembered was a play powerfully portraying the workings of a guilty conscience and showing how easily they may betray the murderer.   Three months later he was found drowned in the Thames after telling his wife that he would die that day.

After 1612 the influence of *Macbeth* as a stage play disappears, and such few references to it as occur are evidently due to the publication of the text of the play in the folio of 1623.

Slatyer's *Palaealbion* was published in 1621 but written two years earlier.   It contains an account of Macbeth's reign seemingly compiled from Holinshed without knowledge of Shakespeare's play.

Peter Heylin as a young man gave lectures on history at Oxford in 1617.   In 1621 he printed these lectures as:

Microcosmos / or / A Little De- / scription of—
the great world. / A treatise Historicall, Geographical /
Politicall, Theologicall. / P. H.

The chapter on Scotland in this work makes no mention of Macbeth; but in 1625 the author issued an "augmented and revised" edition of the same work in which is to be found the condensation of the story of Macbeth which was afterward used by Sir William Davenant as the Argument prefixed to his version of the play. Heylin, it seems, had not seen Shakespeare's play on the stage but had read it as soon as the Folio edition of Shakespeare's plays was printed in 1623, consequently his story is found to be derived from both Boece and Shakespeare.

In the year 1621 appeared Robert Burton's *Anatomy of Melancholy* in which reference is made (London, 1826, page 67) to a narration by "Hector Boecius of Macbeth and Banco, two Scottish lords, that as they were wandering in woods, had their fortunes told them by three strange women." The author appears to be unconscious of Shakespeare's play.

Heywood's *Hierarchie of the Blessed Angels,* printed in 1635, has an account of Macbeth but it was taken directly from Boece.

Henry Adamson published his *Muses Threnody* in Edinburgh in 1638. This contains an account of Macbeth taken from Bellenden.

The other supposed allusions to Shakespeare's play prior to the civil wars and collected in the *Shakespeare Allusion-Book* are either very dubious or are clearly nonexistent, except for Sir Thomas Browne's quotation of V, v, 49, in his *Religio Medici*. This he no doubt obtained from reading the play in the folio.

From these and other indications it is to be inferred that the play of *Macbeth* was known on the London stage until about 1612, when it was "enriched" by putting into it Middleton's songs and dances.* This compelled insertion of the extra lines to which reference has previously been made (p. 275), and in this shape the play again appeared at court. But thereafter the absence of references showing familiarity with the play (which, of course, had never yet been printed) con-

* W. J. Lawrence assigns this change to 1610 (*Shakespeare's Workshop,* p. 35). I think it was made late in 1611 or early in 1612, for it was after Forman saw the play.

trasts sharply with the frequency of such references to *Hamlet, Othello,* and the Falstaff plays. It therefore would appear that after Prince Henry died in November, 1612, *Macbeth* was soon laid aside. To permit a large number of boys dressed as women witches to dance around the stage was poor business in a play with such a high purpose. The prince's death put an end to this sort of thing because this shifting of the interest from the dramatic to the spectacular ruined it.

In 1658 Edward Phillips in his *Mysteries of Love and Eloquence* quotes from *Macbeth* V, v, 24 to 28, but he no doubt took it from the folio. No more is heard of the play of *Macbeth* until after the restoration of Charles II, when after a few performances it was taken in hand by Sir William Davenant and so thoroughly changed as to make it a very different play. Shakespeare's *Macbeth* was not restored to the stage until about the middle of the eighteenth century. This gap it is which explains why in certain respects the true significance of the play has been forgotten. It has no continuous stage tradition such as attaches to the plays of *Hamlet* and *Othello.* As a result the play is now given according to stage traditions, most of which run back no farther than Garrick and Mrs. Pritchard, and which were created at a time when the terror of Scotch witches had passed away and when the Stuart dynasty was in disgrace. For these and other reasons modern audiences no longer see the "tyrant Macbeth with unwashed bloody hands" which Burbage showed to King James. This Macbeth is yet to be recreated.

Did the play please the king?

The answer to this question is as tantalizing as that to many other queries propounded in this book. In 1709, immediately after Nicholas Rowe published his six-volume edition of the plays of Shakespeare (accompanied by the first Life of Shakespeare), there appeared a small volume printed in London by the very reputable bookseller, Bernard Lintot,

containing the poems of Shakespeare and obviously intended
to supplement the plays as printed in Rowe's edition. At
this time little was known about Shakespeare's poems, and
it appears that Lintot was induced to print them by the aged
dramatist William Congreve, who supplied him with his own
early copies of these poems. Bernard Lintot prefaced his
little book by an Advertisement, at the end of which the following interesting information is given:

I cannot omit inserting a Passage of Mr. Shakespeare's Life, very
much to his Honour, and very remarkable, which was either
unknown, or forgotten by the Writer of it.*

That most learn'd Prince, and great Patron of Learning, King
James the First, was pleased with his own Hand to write an
amicable letter to Mr. Shakespeare; which Letter, tho now lost,
remain'd long in the Hands of Sir William D'avenant, as a
credible Person now living can testify.

It further appears that the "credible person" was John Shef-
field, the Duke of Buckingham. This we have on the authority of William Oldys the antiquary. The particulars are
set down by Sir Edmund Chambers in his *William Shakespeare,* Volume II, pages 280 and 281.

Undoubtedly the Duke of Buckingham is good authority.
He was the friend and munificent patron of John Dryden, the
repository of the Shakespeare tradition after Davenant's
death; and the only question is whether Sir William Davenant told the truth. There is no reason to doubt this.
William Shakespeare had stayed so much of his time at the
house of John Davenant as to render it likely that some of his
papers were left there and thus might ultimately have fallen
into Sir William's hands. Therefore we may take it as
highly probable that the king did write an amicable letter
to Mr. Shakespeare in his own hand. What did the king
say? The letter, of course, has never turned up, and therefore conjecture has been busy. It has often been suggested

---

* He is referring to Rowe's Life of Shakespeare.

that the king may have written this letter to show his pleasure on seeing the Scottish play of Macbeth. The proofs now adduced to show when and where the play was first performed before the king tend to render the existence of such letter of acknowledgment from the king much more probable, and to make it not at all unlikely that it may have been the expression of the king's satisfaction with a play which magnified the antiquity of the royal line from which he was descended, helped him to account for the strange phenomena of witchcraft which had long been troubling his brain, pointed out a compromise which would satisfy the qualms of his conscience as to practicing the royal touch, and best of all, disclosed the workings of the conscience of the wrongdoer in a way which so well accorded with his own thoughts.

Ben Jonson in his verses "To the memory of my beloved The Author Mr. William Shakespeare" makes reference to "those flights upon the banks of Thames which so did take Eliza and our James." He was not here thinking of performances at the Globe Theater, for neither Queen Elizabeth nor King James ever went there. Nor do I think Whitehall was in his mind, for it is not so closely associated with the bank of the river.

It was at Windsor that the *Merry Wives* was performed for Elizabeth, and at Hampton Court that *Macbeth* was performed for James. Both of these places are so near to the river that I think they are the places which Ben Jonson had in mind. At both places Shakespeare's flights "did take" the monarchs. Elizabeth had commissioned him to write the *Merry Wives*. James personally wrote him a letter of thanks for *Macbeth?*

EPILOGUE

The play of *Macbeth* is above all an actor's play. It is no play for a reciter; nor for one who merely acts himself, which is the vice of most modern acting. The sentences are usually short, pregnant, often compressed even to obscurity. The utmost skill of the actor is needed to bring forth the full meaning of the lines. It is his glances, facial expressions, shrugs, pauses, hesitations, and inflections on which Shakespeare relied for the finer effects which reside in the lines of this drama. Anyone reading the play, as distinguished from an auditor in the theater, must supply these himself. Therefore more imagination is called for in reading this play than is the case with any other play of Shakespeare.

The last lines of Act III, Scene iv, when properly acted are among the most suggestive and pitiful in the whole play. Not much is said. The effect is attained by what is not said. The ill fated banquet has been disrupted by Macbeth's behavior. The guests have retired with ostentatious solicitude for His Majesty's health but with dangerous, almost outspoken, whisperings among themselves. It is very late. The murderer and his wife, now alone, seat themselves some distance apart, facing each other, and for quite a time in painful silence. She does not reproach him, nor does she try to cheer him up. Guilt has suddenly separated them. She wants no more bloodshed. He must have more, for he is ruled by fear and knows his danger, as he mutters, "Blood will have blood." She recognizes this murderous mood of his and wonders where the next blow will fall. His next words reveal this. Macduff has kept himself in sullen retirement ever since Duncan's murder. What does she think about this? Now she knows on what his bloody mind is brooding; and she is fond of Macduff's wife. Her quick wit at once throws out a suggestion to protect her friend from her imminent danger. "Did you send to him, sir?" This formal address is different from her usual affectionate tone when alone with her husband. If the king sends a summons to Macduff, perhaps time will be gained so that she may warn her friend. Macbeth at once sends a messenger to summon Macduff to come to the palace at Forres, but the answer is "an absolute 'Sir, not I,' " whereupon

> The cloudy messenger turns me his back,
> And hums, as who should say "You'll rue the time
> That clogs me with this answer."
>
> [III, vi, 40–43]

The messenger returns the same day and tells what has happened. This increases Macbeth's fear, and early next morning he hurries to the witches to ask them how to meet this insubordination. He had noted the ugly looks on the faces of his thanes as they left the banquet with their suspicions fully confirmed. The first witch's devil, harping his fear aright, tells him to "beware Macduff." This fear is allayed by the "sweet bodements" of the other two devils. But assurance is quickly checked; for as he goes out from the witches, horsemen galloping in haste bring him word that Macduff has fled *to England,* where the rightful heir to the Scottish throne is protected by the English king. His instant resolve is:

> The castle of Macduff I will surprise;
> Seize upon Fife; give to the edge o' the sword
> His wife, his babes, and all unfortunate souls
> That trace him in his line. No, boasting like a fool;
> This deed I'll do before this purpose cool. [IV, i, 150–154]

Lady Macbeth is thus placed in a fearful dilemma. She has not before thwarted her husband in anything. Dare she now send a note of warning to her friend? Hesitating between opposing impulses, she unlocks her closet and taking forth a sheet of paper folds it and writes upon it a note, which

she reads and then seals, but hesitates to send it. This conflict with her husband affects her so deeply that she repeats
this action in her sleep, and her waiting-gentlewoman tells it
to the doctor [V, i, 3–8].

Thus much, but no more, we gather directly from the
play. Did Lady Macbeth send or try to send the note to
her friend? Why is it that in IV, ii, 63–72, an unknown
messenger hurries in—whence we are not told—warns Lady
Macduff of impending danger, and runs away, we are not
told whither? This episode has no dramatic value, for the
audience is already fully aware of the Lady's imminent peril.
It would seem that the answer was to have been embodied
in a missing scene. But what the scene would have told us
is now left to the imagination of each reader, for the scene
never was written. It would, we may think, have been a
powerful scene, adding poignancy to Lady Macbeth's ago-
nized cry, as she passes from our sight, "The thane of Fife had
a wife: where is she now?" [V, i, 47].

Reasons have already been given for a belief that an interval occurred after the writing of the caldron scene and
before the final scenes of the play were written.* When
Shakespeare resumed work at IV, ii, the strong urge under
which he produced the first three acts was exhausted. For
a time the drama marches heavily. He was compelled to
write the first part of IV, iii, describing Macduff's interview
with Malcolm, laboriously and with his Holinshed open on
the table in front of him. Not until the arrival of Ross with
news from Scotland is a new start really made. Then the
big folio is closed and put away as the fire burns again.
Thereafter the play proceeds with rapidity and vigor through
scenes of resolution and daring, horror, dismay, desperation,

---

* By the time the author again came to his work on this play, he
had forgotten that in IV, i, 93, he had pronounced Dunsinane with
an accent on the penult, according to the Scottish usage; and in the
fifth act he consistently pronounced it eight times as an English word
accented on the antepenult.

combat, and destruction. "The powers above put on their instruments." Nemesis is achieved. And these scenes occur in the daytime: "The night is long that never finds the day."

Sometime during the writing of these closing scenes, word came to the dramatist that his play must be quickly made ready for production before King Christian left England for home. Consequently, the last scene gives a reader the impression that the play is being hastily brought to an end. Malcolm's closing address [V, vii, 59–75] is very brief and begins with an apology for this brevity. The creation of a large number of earls, en masse, in a speech of seven words is a most summary proceeding. But the dramatist was working against time under extreme pressure. For the same reason the bleeding-sergeant scene never reached a finished form; and the projected scene between Macbeth and his wife, which would have told us what her letter said and whether it was sent, was never written at all.

The brevity of speech which is found throughout this play may also have been in part induced by the fact that King Christian could not understand English. It was hard for King James to sit through a long play, and still harder would it be for his brother-in-law. Furthermore, the author of this play had read in the king's *Basilicon Doron* the following advice to his son: "If your engine spurr you to write any works, either in verse or in prose—take no longsome workes in hand."

There were therefore several circumstances concurring to urge the author of this play to make it short. As a result, it is next to the shortest play he ever wrote. Yet this did not prevent it from attaining the highest reach of his dramatic genius!

INDEX

Quoted passages are indicated by "q."

419

424 Index